A History of Crossroads in Early Modern Culture

A History of Crossroads in Early Modern Culture

Bill Angus

EDINBURGH
University Press

Edinburgh University Press is one of the leading university presses in the UK. We publish academic books and journals in our selected subject areas across the humanities and social sciences, combining cutting-edge scholarship with high editorial and production values to produce academic works of lasting importance. For more information visit our website: edinburghuniversitypress.com

© Bill Angus, 2022

Edinburgh University Press Ltd
The Tun – Holyrood Road
12(2f) Jackson's Entry
Edinburgh EH8 8PJ

Typeset in 11/13 Adobe Sabon by
IDSUK (DataConnection) Ltd

A CIP record for this book is available from the British Library

ISBN 978 1 4744 9982 8 (hardback)
ISBN 978 1 4744 9984 2 (webready PDF)
ISBN 978 1 4744 9985 9 (epub)

The right of Bill Angus to be identified as the author of this work has been asserted in accordance with the Copyright, Designs and Patents Act 1988, and the Copyright and Related Rights Regulations 2003 (SI No. 2498).

Contents

List of Illustrations	vi
Acknowledgements	vii
Introduction: The Ways – Transformation, Binding and Presence	1
1. Axes: Ecstatic Heights and Nightmare Depths	25
2. Magic: Transformation and Self-determination	39
3. Music: Going Down to the Crossroads	57
4. Gods: Appointments with the Divine	84
5. Terminus: The Night, the Crossroads and the Stake	106
6. Literature: Liminal Ground in Early Modern Drama	129
7. Hallowed Roads: Routes to the Crossroads	154
8. Wanderers: The Predicament of a Stranger	168
9. Monsters: 'Spirits of another sort'	194
10. Protection: The X in the Landscape	205
Conclusion: The Parting – Intersections	221
Notes	228
Index	294

Illustrations

I.1	Crossroads dance, Knockmonlea, roads between Youghal and Killeagh, Cork, Ireland (Photo: Horgan Brothers, Youghal, Co. Cork, Ireland, c. 1910)	7
I.2	Woodcut – gravedigger and staked bodies, c. sixteenth century	17
1.1	Roman coins. (Roma Numismatics Ltd <www.romanumismatics.com>)	35
1.2	Volute krater, Hades abducts Persephone, Hecate holds up cross-form Eleusinian torch; the Iliupersis Painter, c. 350 BCE (London: © The Trustees of the British Museum)	37
3.1	Eshu Elegbara statue	60
4.1	Dosojin shrine (Photo: © Michael Ashkenazi, 2002)	85
4.2	Woodcut – Mercury cairn (Andrea Alciato, Emblematum liber, Augsberg, 1531)	89
5.1	Gallows outside Tower of London, Postern Gate, c. 1562 (Janelle Jenstad, ed. The Agas Map, image © London Metropolitan Archives, City of London)	107
5.2	Tyburn execution, c. seventeenth century	112
5.3	The execution of the idle apprentice at Tyburn (Engraving by T. Cook, 1795, after W. Hogarth, 1747; Creative Commons)	113
5.4	John Williams burial, London, 1811	120
5.5	Kitty Jay's Grave, Dartmoor, at the crossing of the road from Batworthy to Widecombe in the Moor and the track from Manaton to Grimspound (Image Capture: April 2009, Map data ©2021 Google)	127
10.1	1664 witch post *in situ*, Postgate Farm, Glaisdale, North Yorkshire (Photo: © Bill Angus, 2016)	217
10.2	Witch post from Stang End Farm, Danby, North Yorkshire; now in Ryedale Folk Museum	218

Acknowledgements

Many thanks to Michelle Houston and all at Edinburgh University Press for their enthusiasm and professionalism; to Pete and Jess Gilgan for timeless friendship and kindness and for directing me to the crossroads in the first place; to Andrew Elliott for unwavering cameraderie and essential clues; to Associate Professor Gina Salapata for pointing to the X in the sky; to Professor Lisa Hopkins and Dr Robert Redmond for valued readings; to Lina, Amy, Mark, Joseph, Lily, Stephen, Sonny, Georgie, Aidan, Elin, Melody, Ciara, Nova and Wilfred for their continuing love, patience and good will; and to all the beloved who understand the true cost and value of pursuing knowledge and writing on this path.

Introduction: The Ways – Transformation, Binding and Presence

> I know there is no straight road
> No straight road in this world
> Only a giant labyrinth
> Of intersecting crossroads.
> Federico García Lorca, 'Floating Bridges' (1923, pub. 1983)[1]

In early modern Europe, as in many other places and times, the physical crossroads has been regarded as a site of the highest significance. It is a singular phenomenon that something as commonplace as a road junction should have exercised and excited the human imagination to the extent that it has throughout recorded history. As a reification of the hopes and dreams of a species whose existence is predicated on movement, however, the appeal of the crossroads which has persisted in our cultural sympathies for thousands of years might be obvious. Throughout literary and religious history, from the earliest of recorded times, human life has been imagined and memorialised as a journey, on both the level of the individual and the community. Perhaps because of this, the significance of the parting of roads seems to be similarly venerable. Crossroads may have been revered initially as both a literal place of momentous choice of direction and as a simple motif for other significant moments of decision taken along the way. The choice of the right road, both literally and metaphorically, has been an obvious concern of the traveller throughout time, as has been most notably expressed for the modern age in Robert Frost's poem 'The Road not Taken' (1916), that describes the experience memorably, just as it expresses some ambiguity over the outcomes of that fateful choice: 'Two roads diverged in a wood, and I – / I took the one less traveled by'. Although this particular Y-shaped crossroads offered the speaker a choice whose significance was not directly obvious, it nevertheless 'made all the difference'.[2]

The persistence of the crossroads experience in human societies seems to be connected with the perseverance of the life-narrative metaphor of the road. For the last few thousand years, from the earliest narrative writing onwards in the West at least, this has taken on an epic dimension in its memorialisation and metaphorisation of human experience. Whether it is Homer's *Odyssey*, Beowulf's 'whale-road' or the Oregon Trail, this is most often rooted in a traditional quest narrative, developing around the Homeric or Hebraic desire for homeland or promised land, then to an extent overlaid by a humanist idea of progress, and perhaps of late seen obliquely in the idea of the 'career' path, now largely waning. But the long-standing metaphor seems still to stand strong. The great humanist educator Erasmus included this overarching metaphor in his *Adages* under the title 'In trivio sum', or 'I am at the crossroads', which he applies to those who are 'hesitating as to which alternative to choose, like travellers who come to a place where three roads meet, and are doubtful about which way to take'.[3] Erasmus notes that the metaphor of the 'way' or the 'path' is often used by Greek authors to mean a choice of strategy or plan and cites Plato's *Laws*, where the writer advises the person confronted with an unusual decision to pause and first to investigate where each road leads, simply as Plato puts it, 'like a man at a crossroads'.[4] Another of the early modern period's best-loved stories, found in Xenophon's *Memorabilia* (c. 371 BCE), tells of Heracles as a youth at a metaphorical crossroads, being tempted by the female personification of Vice he sees there saying 'mark you how hard and long is that road to joy . . . I will lead you by a short and easy road to happiness', and his finally choosing the path of Virtue over Vice.[5] These figurative usages stand alongside a Christian exegetical tradition which sees the path as a metaphor for moral probity, as the unpopular prophet Jeremiah commands the people of Israel: 'Stand ye in the ways, and see, and ask for the old paths, where is the good way, and walk therein, and ye shall find rest for your souls' (Jeremiah 6: 16). Later versions translate the word rendered here as 'the ways' as 'crossroads', with the Hebrew for 'at the crossroads', *yal-darakeem*, coming from the root *derek*, which means 'trodden path or way', working also as a metaphor for life.[6] Another prominent ancient crossroads encounter of classical literature sees the illustrious Oedipus kill his own natural father in a road rage incident, a fatal meeting which was prophesied at another crossroads: the shrine of Apollo and the oracle at Delphi. Sigmund Freud of course attempted to use this example as an approach to understanding the roots of human desires and actions, and much of his still-influential thinking on this is foreshadowed in the original dramatic *Oedipus* cycle of Sophocles.[7] These are some of the foundational tropes not only of Western literature but also of the Western psyche.

To research the historical significance of the place where two or more roads cross is to discover the metaphorical currency and weight of the idea of the crossroads in our literary thought-languages and cultures. Besides the documentary history, there are very many crossroads elements in the fiction of significant authors from the classical era onwards.[8] To traverse the nodes of what was once called the 'information super-highway', Google Books lists no fewer than 769,000 hits for books with the word 'crossroads' in the title. One turns out things like 'Writers at the Crossroads of Culture' or 'Ethos at the Crossroads of Disciplines', and may witness any of 'Latin America', 'Jola Architecture', 'Conservation', 'Pest Management', or 'The P.L.O.', all seemingly pausing to reflect 'at the Crossroads'. The metaphor that these titles are employing is not quite as straightforward as it may seem. It is not merely that each of these entities is 'looking for the best path forward', but it also implicitly includes the history of the thing itself, and, perhaps most importantly, its present moment of reflexive deliberation, in all its richness and complexity. Its imagined projection into the future then forms an integral part of these deliberations. The dominant cultural idea of the crossroads therefore may be said to map a temporal intersection, of past, present and future, upon a geography which describes these concepts in literal terms: where the boot leather has hit, now hits, and will hit the road. The crossroads it seems is a physical manifestation of the hermeneutic principle.

It is possible, however, that the use of the metaphor of the crossroads in the progressions of human lives, concepts, organisations or countries, reveals more than simply cultural conceptions of a choice between different paths on the same temporal plane, but further points to something which ultimately defines such a body's very existence in some way and therefore makes 'all the difference' on a more existential level. Also, aside from its purely metaphorical use, in many cultures the physical crossroads has been invested with a metaphysical significance beyond itself and has long been a stage upon which both the desires of human aspiration and the fears of mortality may be enacted. Its literary representation, myths, superstitions, histories, traditions and ritual praxis, in early modern and other societies, are the subject of this book.

Geographically speaking, a parting of ways is always simultaneously a confluence of ways and so the crossroads also conveys within itself a central paradox. Its seemingly divergent discourses merge and concatenate and it is for this reason perhaps that the crossroads lends itself to other seemingly opposed binaries or paradoxes of this kind, both conceptual and in terms of their spatial and physical symbolism. It was perhaps a short superstitious step from appreciating the paradoxes of the place for human societies to have come to regard the crossroads as simultaneously a potent location for conventions of binding and spiritual restraint and a point of origination for the loosing of fresh beginnings and transformational possibilities. So, a crossroads's perceived multivalency may be related to its inherent multiplicity. Crossroads have thus been regarded as places of spatiotemporal duality where one may be bound into a past or transformed into a futurity and in a sense into another kind of being; to remain the same at such a place is not a third option, but is simply to opt for the first of these. Its binding quality implies an enforced absence from the wider community while its transformational quality is dependent upon the idea of immanent presence. This is another paradox which energises the network of cultural meanings, the narrative manifestations of ancient desires and fears and the intersection of temporal and spatial paradigms that are imagined at these highly significant in-between places.[9] The physical crossroads of this study are in many traditions peripheral to human settlements, registering almost as a cultural non-space. Nearly always marginal, they instance both an intersection and overdetermination of liminalities. Conversely, however, the crossroads has also long been perceived as a kind of central axis, a capital node to which all roads ultimately lead, and has therefore thus enjoyed a symbolic value as a place of connection between worlds, and ultimately as a nexus for the living and the dead.[10] When early in the fifteenth century the English language develops the word 'trivia' from Latin to designate the place where three roads meet (from *tri-* 'three' and *via* 'road') another contradiction emerges. The term 'trivial' initially means simply 'of or belonging to the crossroads', but from this time the meaning 'commonplace' or 'vulgar' develops alongside it, and the senses 'ordinary' and 'insignificant' follow in the decades after 1580.[11] In this way, a place seen as possessing great significance is simultaneously designated as inconsequential.[12] The ambiguity, liminality and duality of the crossroads in popular perception are consonant with its status as a site where the fabric of cultural and religious metaphors of mortality and divinity may wear thin and where categories of authority, and even of normality, are disordered. These multiple contradictions are expressed through a polyphony of cultural expressions and interconnected experiences, some even claiming to transcend both life and death, as we will see. Seeing how the crossroads draws on these discourses, it is difficult not to be struck by the enduring if tremulous centrality of this remarkable liminal common-place to many cultural forms, expressions and understandings.

In many cultures, the crossroads has long been seen as a place of communion, where the past, present and future are somehow made manifest, but also where forces human, demonic and divine have been felt to converge. Its very geography seems to somehow render the walls between these concepts slight, their boundaries negotiable, subject to propitious timing, religious sacrament or magical artifice. It is imaginable that this other-wordly significance dates back as far as hunter-gatherer communities pausing at certain crossways on the migrational tracks of the ancient plains to camp and make animist offerings before deliberating and making communal decisions for the next phase of hunting.[13] When one is at a physical crossroads, any decision about the immediate future direction may result in profound and far-reaching consequences. It may also be a time for leaving previous paths or associations behind. The gravity of these crucial decision times might cause a social group to conceive a desire for either a significant encounter of presence, or a shedding of one, at the parting of ways. It may be no surprise therefore that the transformational or liminal gods of many cultures are imagined to inhabit crossroads, or that there are many traditions worldwide aimed at contacting, propitiating or binding the spirits of the dead, or even demons there. Throughout history the numinous character of the crossroads has allowed the brave or the desperate access to imagined power through its privileged connection with the gods of transit, transition and transformation.

In cultures spanning much of the planet, from Swanage to Sweden, from Kerry to Korea, and from Marlborough to Massachusetts, crossroads have also been regarded more generally as uncanny places where strange or disturbing things are likely to happen. In the ancient Greek tradition, a poltergeist was said to trouble the crossways.[14] In Russia, crossroads were the haunt of the *ustrechnyi*, a goblin who liked nothing better than to lead travellers astray.[15] The mischievous djinn of Arabic mythology were also said to frequent the crossroads.[16] When Samuel Harsnett's *A Declaration of Egregious Popish Impostures* (1603) laments the fear he perceives as stalking England at that time, attributing it to Catholic influence, the most telling example he can muster is that of people afraid of various monsters and fairies they might meet at what he calls a 'three-way leet' – the Y-shaped crossroads most commonly associated with the goddess Hecate.[17] Communication with devils at crossroads was common to many sixteenth-century Portuguese descriptions of sorcerers, who were supposed to draw 'circles or *sigma Salomonis* there in order to control the forces that had been invoked'.[18] In one European witchcraft case the defendant confessed that she 'and the other women would go to certain crossroads to talk with the devils', simply in order to schedule further meetings.[19] Especially in Wales and Italy, it was believed that some of these crossroads-haunting spirits might be seen in riotous assembly, including Welsh traditions of hideous spirit hounds that troubled crossroads, leading hosts of the 'restless spirits' of sinners there.[20] These traditional apparitions, suggesting perhaps older European resonances around Odin's Wild Hunt, were particularly vigorous on the nights or the eves of various liturgical festivals, of St John, St David, All Saints, Christmas and Good Friday, when they were seen in packs or processions on some occasions, and singly at other times.[21] In both Wales and Germany it was thought that witches danced with the Devil at crossroads at midnight on May Day's eve.[22] In Germany, Estonia, Finland, Czech Republic and Sweden this was, and still is, celebrated as 'walpurgisnacht': St Walpurga's Night, or 'hexennacht': 'Witches' Night'.

These associations of crossroads with encounters of supernatural presences die hard, and the belief in monstrous and spiritual meetings at crossroads is by no means coterminous with the ancient and early modern periods but has been surprisingly persistent in many places through to modern times. Writing in 1754, William Borlase could still report that what he calls the 'common people' of Cornwall are convinced that there is something 'more than ordinary at such places', declaring that their stories of apparitions 'gain greater credit, if the Spirit, Demon, or Hobgoblin is said to have appear'd where four Lanes meet; there they think apparitions are most frequent, and at such places it is common for these people travelling in the dark to be most afraid'.[23] In a Swedish tradition of the nineteenth century, Horace Marryat describes how because a bridegroom on his wedding day is greatly afraid of elves, 'he gathers strong-scented herbs, as garlic, chive, and rosemary, a sure protection against sprites, and sews them in his wedding-clothes', as he says 'on no account would he on that day tarry … where the cross-roads meet'.[24] In Russia also, crossroads were simply at all costs to be avoided as spiritually dangerous by wedding processions.[25] One writer reported in 1882 of the highly superstitious parishioners in Pembrokeshire, Wales who fervently believed in spectre funerals, witches and fairies; noting that here crossroads were very superstitiously regarded especially at night.[26] Night, however, was not a prerequisite to the operation of the crossroads, and an account given in Kerry, Ireland, in 1941 describes two farmers who encounter apparitions of long-dead neighbours at an intersection in broad daylight.[27]

Many examples also attest to other conceptions of the cultural significance of crossroads. In rural Ireland in the nineteenth and early twentieth centuries, crossroads dancing was common on summer Sunday evenings, though the origins of the practice may be lost (see Figure I.1).[28] In the islands of Vanuatu in Oceania crossroads also function as dancing places but there they also both determine one's cultural identity and represent 'a relay node in the chain of relations of alliance'.[29] In some places, even thoughts entertained at a crossroads might be more likely to come true.[30]

Besides the more folkloric and popular accounts of its uses, established religions that involved crossroads mythology and conjuration practices are many and varied, and it may even be the

Figure I.1 Crossroads dance, Knockmonlea, roads between Youghal and Killeagh, Cork, Ireland. (Photo: Horgan Brothers, Youghal, Co. Cork, Ireland, c. 1910)

case that these spring from the veneration of the place itself. The ancient Persian scripture of the Parsis, the Zend Avesta, describes their ancient sacrifices 'to the forkings of the highways, and to the meetings of the roads' themselves.[31] There is also an ancient Hindu tradition of veneration of the crossroads as a locality.[32] Meanwhile in the classical tradition, the Greek thinker Theophrastus describes the character of the superstitious man as anointing and venerating a stone herm that he finds at a crossroads, while the Roman poet Tibullus also 'promises to venerate the ancient stone, wreathed with flowers', that he finds there.[33] Alongside this sense that the crossroads is venerable in itself comes the idea that strange and powerful things dwell there, and so the gods themselves proliferate at the revered parting of ways. Divine dwellers at the crossroads include, from the Western classical traditions, Puck's 'triple Hecate', Diana, Proserpine, Hermes/Mercury, Bacchus, Ceres, Hercules, Apollo and the Lares; in the Norse and Germanic mythoi, Odin/Woden; in the African traditions, the Yoruba of Nigeria and Benin have Eshu Elegba while Malawi has the god Mulungu; in Japan, the crossroads god is Dosōjin; in India, the gods Rudra and Bhairava are found there; and in Guatemala, it is the abode of the Lord Maam.[34] Christian involvement with crossroads is surprisingly sparse, but in medieval and early modern London, supervisory Christian hermits were stationed at crossroads.[35] There is also at least one Christian saint who is revered at the parting of the ways: St Theodore of Cyprus.[36] In modern-day Poland, one may commonly find still statues of the Virgin Mary and Catholic crosses set up and venerated at crossroads of all kinds.[37]

Despite these later appropriations of the space, what might have been an ideal early opportunity for the cultural assimilation of the crossroads with the Christian cross, the kind of incorporation of paganism at which the church was always so adept, was ultimately lost or abandoned.[38] The crossroads continued throughout the period of Christendom as a site of significance in European witchcraft and for other superstitious practices, and rituals performed there were thus the subject of bans from church authorities from early times onwards.[39] An association of the crossroads with the Christian idea of the cross as a healing concept might especially have been expected but this may have been precluded by its earlier associations with healing and beneficial transformations.[40] Since at least the early classical era, crossroads had been viewed as places of magical or divine transaction, able to give supplicants access to transformative powers beyond the earthly, through the performance of specific rituals. Christian writers may simply have struggled with the presences already *in situ* there. In his *Seaven books of the Attick antiquities* (1654), Francis Rous notes this classical history and geography, describing how Hecate was worshipped by the Athenians, 'where three wayes met'.[41] In *Dido and Aeneas*, Virgil calls her 'Hecate howl'd-for in crosse wayes!'[42] In this vein, S. I. Johnston describes how 'suppers were taken to the images of Hekate found at crossroads' at the new moon and that magic was performed there.[43] Edmund Spenser's *Faerie Queene* (1590) takes up the narratives of church writers to connect Hecate obliquely with Christian ideas of Hell, and this resonance seems to stick through later times.[44] With Hell in mind, the horizontal intersection of the crossroads seems to suggest a further projection, into a vertical axis, inhabited by divinities like Hecate, whose tripleness refers both to the three horizontal ways of her Y-shaped crossroads and her vertically triune nature which incorporates Luna of the Moon and Diana of the Earth, she herself representing the underworld.[45] This narrative of celestial gods above the crossroads and cthonic ones below it suggests perhaps a three-dimensional dream of the middle earth-bound which may have been difficult to overlay without it being obvious. The dream might include the ecstasy of rising to the spiritual realms or the nightmare of falling into the hellish depths, or worse, being dragged there like Faustus, unwillingly, by the unhappy dwellers at this crux of matter and the immaterial.[46]

It should be apparent from the above examples that the crossroads has been considered an unruly, subversive and otherwise dangerous space for at least two thousand years, in many cultural traditions and in various parts of the world. Despite persistent opposition from church authorities, crossroads mythology and praxis remained relatively dominant through the early modern era, and although its influence slowly waned over the intervening four hundred years, its presence continues as a residual current in Western and other cultures. So we might ask why this should be: what exactly is the crossroads offering? Johnston notes that the uncanny nature of the crossroads makes them 'uneasy places [that] necessitated ... protective rituals', which she divides these into two categories: 'those in which an individual sought help and protection at an uncertain liminal point', and 'those in which the detachment of the liminal point was exploited'.[47] The first calls the appellant to the uncertain place to ask protection of the uncertainty; the second often pertains to some kind of banishment, or binding qualities of extra-authority places, and both of these offer transformational possibilities. A third experience here involves the avoidance of the place altogether for one of the above reasons, or to do with an unwanted encounter. The various historians, folklorists and anthropologists who have recorded accounts of these practices up to modern times describe rituals in terms of what may be effected by them, or otherwise avoided at all costs by their performance. Abilities gained at the crossroads might include musical chops, skill at churning, invisibility, invincibility, finding lost property, luck in hunting or protection from wolves (Latvian farmers sacrificed there for this last purpose at least as late as the seventeenth century).[48] In Polish mythology the crossroads were a sacred place of divination and magical invocation, where 'talismans and amulets were hung or buried . . .[and] spell work was conducted'.[49]

The potentially lethal freighting of such magical practices is apparent in Martin Puhvel's recounting of a witch trial in Steiermark, Austria, where one unfortunate minister of religion was executed 'on conviction of having been the organizer of witches' crossroads revelry'; this took place as late as 1689.[50] These supposed ritual practices at crossroads did not by any means die out with the passing of the witch-scare or the onward march of Protestantism into Europe and beyond. James Waylen describes how, at Marlborough in 1831, effigies of two debaters on the Great Reform Bill were burnt at the crossroads.[51] Alice Morse Earle describes an altogether different early nineteenth-century American crossroads ritual in which 'the widow who wished to renounce her husband's debts was married in her shift, often at the cross-roads, at midnight'.[52] Morse Earle suggests that these 'shift-marriages' were taking place in Massachusetts 'as late as 1836' and, in order to verify this, claims to have 'a copy of a court record of that date'.[53] Llewellyn Lloyd records a Swedish crossroads tradition in 1870 in which 'great fires are . . . made at the cross-roads' which may be thought to both attract and repel wandering monsters.[54] In England meanwhile, Charles Herbert Octavius Curtis in *Bright's Illustrated Guide to Bournemouth* for 1891 advises 'to all who really care for primitive old world customs and queer ways, we say go to Swanage before the railway demon engulphs it, where the women still believe that a ride on a donkey's back to four cross-roads . . . is an infallible cure for whooping cough'.[55] Of interest in this connection is the fact that Curtis images the technology of rail travel itself as exhibiting demonic power. The railway is also shorthand for a modernity that many folklorists of the time felt was poised to snuff out the last vestiges of British folk memory and culture, like this crossroads cure. The fear that new tech would help to do away with such traditional practices was probably well founded.

Isabella Lucy Bird's famous 1898 account of her travels in Korea describes what she calls a 'singular form of exorcism . . . repeated daily by the Shamans throughout Korea' in which a demon's name is inscribed upon paper next to an empty bottle prepared for the process, and then 'the paper being touched with the magic wand jumps into the bottle, which is hastily corked and buried on the hillside or at the cross-roads'.[56] Such legerdemain can only have added to the crossroads reputation, on which it in turn depends. Those in pursuit of a transformational experience were not entirely limited to occult practices however, since there were also some liminal sites of Christian pilgrimage which might also be repaired to in extremity. One such was in the Ripplingate area of Lincolnshire where 'a certain statue' popularly known as 'Jurdon Cros . . . stood out in the fields . . . within the parish bounds near the high road' and was claimed to have performed miracles.[57] One might assume by its title that this stood not only near a boundary road, but also near the crossing of roads. Puhvel also recounts a Welsh and Irish Christian tradition reported in Carlow as late as 1940 in which 'during funeral processions the coffin was placed on the ground at every crossroads and "de Profundis" [Psalm 130] was recited by four venerable laymen', testifying again to the crossroads's significance in traditions which made their presence felt within an otherwise Christian religious environment.[58]

The precise reason that the crossroads began to be perceived as effective for these many and varied purposes is, and will likely always remain, unknown. Although the origins of the functional aspects of the crossroads have escaped being much of a subject for debate, from the evidence of recorded history and literature we may, however, infer something of the derivation of its significance. In this space, Johnston outlines the debate over the origins of Hecate's presence at crossroads, a discussion which may be exemplary. This matter rests on mutually exclusive ontological positions amounting to a chicken-and-egg problem in which the chicken is Hecate and the egg is the 'uncanny', or the domain of ghosts. The first position in this debate proposes that Hecate was associated with crossroads because she was 'a goddess of uncanny things, which were, in turn, by nature associated with the crossroads' while the second argues that 'crossroads only became uncanny places because Hekate – an uncanny goddess – dwelt there'.[59] While the first position gets us no closer to the origins of the crossroads's power, in the second case this logic would only follow if it were also the same for a significant number of the other crossroads gods. Johnston also points out the further paradox in the fact that, since Hecate offered protection against ghosts and 'ghosts were imagined to gather at liminal points', then she became 'associated ever more closely with the ghosts themselves'.[60] This reciprocality offers the most reasonable explanation for the phenomenon, and Hecate's instance may serve as a model for what has drawn other divine presences to the powerful parting of the ways. Even the gods themselves, it seems, may undergo transformations at the crossroads.

There may also have been more practical reasons for them being drawn there. The Romans saw much significance in what they called *compita*, or crossroads, the intersections of their 'streets', which extended far beyond their cities. In both Rome itself and in their conquered territories, crossroads gods called Lares Compitales were revered in shrines or chapels at crossroads in which might be found one of the Lares Compitales for each road intersecting.[61] These shrines were maintained by official bodies whose sole purpose was their maintenance and their cult was observed especially by the poor, by freedmen and by slaves.[62] This suggests a perception of the efficacy of crossroads for self-improvement or aspiration. The Lares may initially have been protective household gods which progressed to being the spiritual guardians of field boundaries and thereafter came to be associated with crossroads since boundaries and roads often coincided, carrying their mystical quality with them in that posting. They were probably not, however, the first deities to be revered at crossroads (Hecate and Mercury at least are gods whose antiquity may predate them) but their geographical origin may tell us something of the significance that was accorded the locale.

Further, in as much as a road is liminal or ambiguous, a crossroads is doubly so: a boundary of boundaries. As Johnston points out, crossroads have typically been understood as 'transitional gaps between defined, bounded areas, that is, between roads or between the areas of land that roads define'.[63] The chief quality of these interstices is indeterminacy, of a kind which invites interpretation; like a frontier, the crossroads is a sort of void. It is a 'middle place, composed of interactions and inter-views' as Michel de Certeau says of such a boundary.[64] To take this a stage further, the crossroads also acts as 'a narrative symbol of exchanges and encounters'.[65] Its ambiguous status between jurisdictions may allow it to be a sanctuary for any presence unauthorised by local orthodoxies: a geographical information gap which invites a heterodox or dissenting imagination. Rome itself may have been conceived of as 'a multiplicity of nodes', as Richard Jenkyns argues.[66] If such liminal places have 'structured the world, preventing it from becoming an unintelligible chaos', as Johnston says, then it is another paradox of the crossroads that its numinous essence may be energised by exactly the kind of generative and unruly chaos that structured religious practices are designed to harness.[67]

The outward-bound progress of the Roman Lares towards the crossroads may be mirrored by the spiritual consequences of an ancient ritual practised in England until recent times: the annual Rogation Week perambulation of boundaries. In this ritual, the parish boundaries were prayerfully circumnavigated and evil spirits were thereby cast into outlying areas. By one tradition this practice may be traced to the fifth century in France, where it superseded the Roman festival of Robigalia which had the same purpose.[68] By 1559 in England, Royal Injunctions had put a stop to most religious processions in the name of encouraging the church away from its naturally Catholic proclivities and towards the safer territory of Protestantism, but this one was a notable survivor of that historical process.[69] The ritual involved a prayer procession around the margins of a locality, latterly a parish, to bless the crops and rid the area of evil spiritual influences.[70] Rogation prayers recommended in a medieval sermon from Lincoln include asking that God might 'withestonde the batell of owre enmyes bothe bodyly and gostly, ffor in that tyme of the yere the devylls and other wickyd spyritis are moste besy a bowte for to drawe a man in to synnes and wrechednes'.[71] The sermon suggests that bells be rung and crosses and banners be carried, so that 'the spyritis that flye above in the eyer as thyke as motis in the sonne scholde flee away from us'.[72] Despite the suggestion that after the sixteenth century few people believed the ceremony had any efficacy, this practice was in fact mandated by Elizabeth I in 1599, along with some detailed instructions about precisely how to perform the ritual.[73] Clearly this was not because the practice was thought ineffective, and evil spirits would continue to require ousting not only from positions at the borders of authorised space, which were often the roadways, but towards the most liminal of liminal spaces somehow between them. These spirits seemed at least to some to then be pushed to undemarcated places which, in a country not fully Christianised even perhaps as late as 1350, might still be found to echo with persistent older beliefs around the nature and place of spiritual experience.[74] There, full of potential for ritual magic, where boundaries between the natural and unnatural spheres were perceived to wear thin, refugee spirits might preside over a place which would come to be overdetermined with conceptual echoes: a palimpsest of the ages' expectations of spiritual encounter, transition and transformation.

The supernatural quality of crossroads may also be rooted in the ancient traditions of the qualities of paths and roads themselves, including the imagined pathways of spiritual traffic between sites of interest to the restless walking dead. Routes imagined would be between barrows and other burial sites of ancient peoples, between more recent cemeteries, or between home and the place of burial on rural funeral routes by which a corpse or 'lich' might need to be carried from a remote parish to one which had rights of interment. Such 'lich-ways', 'funeral paths', or 'church-way paths' were regarded with some level of superstitious reverence and fear, as one might imagine, and it is not a huge conceptual leap for such a path to develop the reputation for being a route along which an unquiet spectre might return. The roots of these lich-ways in Britain may well reach back into human prehistory and such spiritual roads may possibly relate directly or indirectly to the Neolithic earthen 'cursuses' which archaeologists have found to run for substantial distances between ancient burial or ceremonial sites. Whatever connection there might be in this respect, there seems to be ample evidence that at least some of these ancient roads were afforded a spiritual significance, either sacred or malevolent.

It is clear then that in many cultures the crossroads has acted as a psychologically facilitative space, one that is believed to give either access to, or protection from, dangerous spiritual forces and that allows a fantasy of privileged connection with transformative gods. Such an imagined crossroads space offers metamorphic experiences through specific rituals, and resounds with an inherent power to either enhance or inhibit human potential. Since the traditions which encompass these amenities and impediments are both highly pervasive and widespread, we might ask whether or not there is any intrinsic connection between these seemingly opposed powers of binding and of transformation: whether they are in some manner connected by a central attribute which energises both reciprocally at the place of their meeting. Although this is certainly a paradox, I would argue that the power to transform comes from a perceived access of supernatural power which in a sense seems to be stored there by implication of its ability to bind powerful evils. Both the binding and the transformative modes have a certain ultimate otherness: an ultraliminality which derives from sitting not only at boundaries but between them, and in this case even perhaps between separate domains of experience or thought. That is, between 'worlds'. Such an ideological non-place then may suggest an anti-episteme where even the doxa of God's righteous disposal of the spirits of the dead may be confounded, but where nevertheless the gods themselves are easily accessed: a small domain of control where the living may be unusually empowered and the dead egregiously mortified. Therefore, the binding facilitated by the interlacing lines of the crossroads is the natural counterpart of the transformative function and in fact the two work as necessary corollaries.

Another possible connection between binding and transformation may be found in the Platonic conception of ideal forms and the related Christian notion of a nature that is immutable by any but God, as is developed in Augustine's *The City of God*.[75] In this formulation, to bind a spirit or person is to fix them in their past created form; it is to delineate and define their mode of being such that further transformation is denied them (for instance into revenants or free-wandering spirits), except by illusions perpetrated by devils (or the hallucinogenic drugs Augustine describes) to deceive them.[76] This comes to form part of the argument of early modern commentators on the possibility of magical transformations. The central point of this logic is that to admit a binding need occur at all is to acknowledge that a transformation is at least possible. In the same way, the attempted binding of identity into essential, inevitable, god-given attributes testifies to the propensity for humans to change, and of their facility to do so. As a social species, humans may not like change, but we are nevertheless most spectacularly evolved to adapt to it. In that sense then, crossroads may offer a historical access-point for the self-construction and transmission of identities, whether or not any dominant contemporary epistemological discourse supports that notion.

Perhaps also it is the cumulative effect of both common and uncommon practical usage and the accretion of cultural discourses about its transformative nature that causes the boundaries between categories found at crossroads to wear ever thinner. In terms of the rituals such use involves, a crossroads transformation is usually made possible through the extrinsic power of a god manifested intrinsically through a physical sacrifice of some kind or almost as commonly, the supposed gifting of the supplicant's soul. The subsequent metamorphosis takes place either directly, as in some European and Vodou/Vodun traditions, or through the mediation of divination and prophecy, as in Oedipus' example. In this most infamous instance, Oedipus finds not only prophecy at the crossroads but its fulfilment, and destiny and death into the bargain. The hope of the more direct type of transformative experience has historically been not only the territory of the ambitious manipulator of a community, or that of the spurned lover, but also of the itinerant musician. This has spawned a Faustian mythology which has been appropriated by many artists, from Paganini to Lil Naz X.[77] This has been encouraged in particular by the teachings and traditions of Christian church authorities around the status of secular music which have often perpetuated an image of the musician as an iniquitous and restless wanderer, and have fed and augmented a mythology of the 'demons' haunting the authentic artist that has survived to the present day. Musicians themselves have not necessarily been at pains to deny these allegations but rather have often welcomed the associated whiff of sulphur and been happy to appropriate cultural resonances around the crossroads as a transformative place. This transformative aspect of the crossroads has thus produced a history that lingers within some of our modern artistic forms.

Beyond allowing access to powers of spiritual encounter and metamorphosis, the crossroads has possessed other abilities too. It was considered to be where very worldly problems might be contained in its well-trodden earth. Many archaeological examples attest to the fact that the corpses of suicide victims and those hanged were often buried at crossroads. It was a common place where many feet might step symbolically on the head of a criminal spirit, and one effective for the binding of their unquiet and wandering revenants.[78] In England, this form of outcast burial occurred from pre-medieval times onwards, and legally so up until the early nineteenth century.[79] A practice clearly ancient even in the time of the Anglo-Saxons, this was probably being driven by still older strata of belief and superstition.[80] The crossroads may have performed a similarly apotropaic role in ancient Greece, where the corpses of people whose crimes were thought to create contamination were unceremoniously dumped and stoned or burned at the parting of the ways.[81] In the Russian tradition, not only were crossroads both 'magic and unclean places' where suicides and unidentified corpses were buried, but they were also where unwanted religious icons were taken to be burned.[82] When Shakespeare's Puck warns Oberon of 'damned spirits' at the approach of day, that 'in crossways and floods have burial', who have already gone to 'their wormy beds . . . / For fear lest day should look their shames upon' (*A Midsummer Night's Dream*, III, ii, 381–4), he is referencing exactly this long history of outcast burial. This practice involved a ceremony which was intended to exorcise the disquieted soul from the bosom of the community via a ritual of dishonourable interment and was meant to protect the populace by preventing the return of the spirit and so guard against their evil deeds somehow polluting the generality by association.

Although it is notoriously difficult to identify suicide as a cause of death in an ancient burial, it is easier to conclude through other indications of the undesirable nature of the interree: in the body's cramping or orientation, or via the presence of a stake of some kind (see Figure I.2). Of this type of burial there are many examples found at crossroads. The original motivation of the siting of outcast burials at crossroads has remained somewhat opaque, but if we consider that in various places the straightness of roads was thought to somehow ease the movement of spirits, for instance between burial sites, then by the same logic, the tangled routes of crossroads may have been thought able to arrest them, or at least to hinder their wandering.[83] The manifold possibilities represented by its intersecting roads have a binding effect and prevent the passing of spirits or other evil influences. Many other examples of attested apotropaic semiotics accord with this idea: signs used on buildings for protection against evil, which are also made up of intersecting lines, with the X-shaped 'saltire' cross being a dominant form that is echoed still in many modern signs indicating a ban of some kind. This book explores these functions using some unique examples of apotropaic

Figure I.2 Woodcut – gravedigger and staked bodies, c. sixteenth century

sign carving which instance the binding of evil spirits associated most likely with the witch-crazes of the seventeenth century. Sited by the fireplace, these X-carrying domestic 'witch posts' were believed to arrest the ingress of a witch's spirit through the house and its egress up the chimney. The idea that a malevolent spirit of some kind might be halted in its course by transverse marks accords with similar folk beliefs found around the world and evidence from English literary traditions, especially of the early modern period. Taken together, these suggest a firm historical basis for the apotropaic significance of these symbols which I argue also function on a geographical scale in the binding attributes of the crossroads.

Given the antiquity, and the generally mystical nature, of many of the historical examples and testimonies upon which this book draws, it is not possible or desirable to approach this subject with the kind of quantitative methodology that a purely anthropological text might require. My approach here is therefore resolutely literary and historical in its focus, but establishing the necessary contexts has resulted in a kind of material anthropology that renders the research to an extent cross-cultural, or what is increasingly termed 'holocultural'. This more literary approach allows stories to be stories and thereby to reveal cultural formations and imperatives through readings attentive to the detailed nuances of cultural expression. Nevertheless, its main methodological tool for understanding the field is still a comparative morphology which looks for similarities in the ideations, cultural practices or social structures around crossroads through history, with a focus on the European context and the early modern period. The essential hypothesis of this kind of research is that meaningful comparisons are possible simply because 'patterns (kinds of phenomena that occur repeatedly) can be identified', as cultural anthropologists Carol R. Ember and Melvin Ember affirm.[84] Where these patterns are found, the intention is not to make assumptions about the derivations or motives of such practices, or to assume similar contexts, but to discern their common elements and to comprehend the nature of their appearances in historical texts. One element of this isomorphic method is its synchronic comparison of instances of crossroads practices within an early modern time frame; another is to contextualise this within a diachronic dimension which aims to place the period of Shakespeare and his contemporaries within a topos with global scope and application.

The research method also draws on the kind of cultural geography established by the influential ideas of de Certeau, Henri Lefebvre, Janette Dillon and others. The book's basic premise accords with

Dillon's dictum that space is 'both topographical and conceptual'.[85] It is, as Lefebvre says, not only 'molded from historical and natural elements', but is 'literally filled with ideologies'.[86] Andrew McRae's reading of the road experience as communal knowledge has also been useful, as has Dillon's and Julie Sanders's reading of the experience of roads within early modern city, court and dramatic contexts. In assimilating and utilising these theories, it has been necessary to transcend them in some respects. Lefebvre conceives of an understanding of spatial practice that sees the actions and signs of 'the trivialised spaces of everyday life' in opposition to those of spaces 'made special by symbolic means as desirable or undesirable, benevolent or malevolent, sanctioned or forbidden to particular groups'.[87] Crossroads cut across this distinction by existing in both categories simultaneously. They partake of the qualitative grading of ground from the utterly trivial and commonplace to the sacred or cursed: localities that accrue power which may be accessed by arcane or occult knowledge. In this 'turn towards movement', cultural geographers have also produced theoretical modes that aim to understand how people move through various terrains and landscapes. These theories suggest that the very mobility itself helps to shape those cultural spaces, as Peter Merriman and John Urry have outlined in differing ways.[88] Tim Cresswell meanwhile has noted that culture itself is more 'about routes than roots', and that the word 'place' applies to these as 'meaningful segments of space – locations imbued with meaning and power'.[89] Here mobility is something that is practised, experienced and embodied, as Cresswell shows.[90] These ideas in turn build upon the work of earlier theorists like Maurice Merleau-Ponty who argued that movement is not simply the act of 'submitting passively to space and time' but rather it consumes them and 'takes them up in their basic significance'.[91] In this respect, as this book will show, the crossroads is not to be understood simply as something to be moved across, or danced upon, but rather is itself a dynamic medium, 'always in movement, always in making'.[92]

In his still-influential *The Dialogic Imagination*, Mikhail Bakhtin's language reaches out towards the crossroads when he speaks of the 'intersection of axes and fusion of [spatial and temporal] indicators' which is the artistic 'chronotope', Bakhtin's literary conception of space-time.[93] Bakhtin's chronotope is a useful tool here in its acknowledgement of the primacy of history to the attenuation of transcendental interpretations of the aesthetic, and in the emphasis it gives to the body in interpretations of material reality. Like crossroads, chronotopes are 'points in the geography of a community where time and space intersect and fuse'.[94] Just as time is made observable in this narrative model, so 'space becomes charged and responsive to the movements of time and history and the enduring character of a people'.[95] This present study deals with conceptions of the intersection of time and space at crossroads and hopes to give insight into communities for whom such a geographical element comes to be so significant. Bakhtin's focus on the effect of responsive space on a people's character is reminiscent of Keith Basso's seminal study of the moral consequences of a sense of place on the Western Apache in which 'features of the landscape' were understood to represent not only 'the symbols of a culture' but also 'the enduring moral character of its people'.[96] Such a manifest interaction of geography and human communities suggests Joël Bonnemaison's concept of the 'geosymbol', a term which refers to 'any place, site, space . . . or human construction that gives meaning to landscape and thereby expresses and nurtures the identity of populations' and in many cultures the crossroads has certainly had this function.[97] In Bakhtin's view, literary chronotopes do a similar job of standing 'as monuments to the community itself, as symbols of it, as forces operating to shape its members' images of themselves'.[98] Bonnemaison asserts simply that 'no identity exists without a space that sustains it, or without a territory marked by geosymbols'.[99] Alongside other world views and myths, he argues, geosymbols 'give strength to belief systems. They underlie all cultures. They structure and sustain the order of the mind.'[100] In many historical cultures, the crossroads functions in this way.

The active interaction between human cultures and geography is not merely an abstraction of the fact that people are mobile in a landscape and have always striven to describe that process of movement. Rather it affects the very forms of description and imagination that make up the networks of discourse that form a culture, or for that matter the cognitive world of an individual human personality. As de Certeau notes, 'every story is a travel story – a spatial practice'.[101] But more than this, narrative structures themselves have 'the status of spatial syntaxes': journeys map onto them and possess their own grammar 'linked together more or less tightly or easily by "modalities" that specify the kind of passage leading from the one to the other', and thus our stories of all kinds 'serve us as means of mass transportation'.[102] For de Certeau, a *place*, or *lieu*, denotes 'the order . . . in accord with which elements are distributed in relationships of coexistence', whereas a *space* includes 'vectors of direction, velocities, and time variables' and is thus 'composed of intersections of mobile elements' and is 'actuated by the ensemble of movements deployed within it'.¹⁰³ His conception of *space* is, like the spoken word, 'modified by the transformations caused by successive contexts', lacking the inherent stability of the *place*.¹⁰⁴ These notions both map onto the idea of the crossroads as *place*, which slips the binding stability of ownership, the 'proper' of which de Certeau speaks, and speak of its status as a conjured *space*, one subject to the transformative vagaries and vicissitudes of the spoken word.¹⁰⁵ This perhaps explains the compelling default of the crossroads metaphor in narratives which are 'actuated by a contradiction that is represented in them by the relationship between the frontier and the bridge, that is, between a (legitimate) space and its (alien) exteriority'.¹⁰⁶ In as much as 'space is a practiced place', the crossroads may not be surpassed in its capacity to exemplify the exotic symbiosis of these two aspects of geographical perception.¹⁰⁷ All of these theories depend on the interaction of the real human being with the geographical phenomenon. This book agrees with Bonnemaison's dictum that, 'no identity exists without a space that sustains it' and deals with the various mutually sustaining interactions between the physical environment of the crossroads and the experiencing human subject.

Our first chapter begins by exploring the traditions of spiritual encounters both above and below the crossroads. Taking into account the cosmological and the archaeological, it deals with gendered intersections and shows how the axes of the crossroads suggest a duality that holds in creative tension inescapable aspects of the human subject and its perceptions of the divine. It also touches upon the creation of the universe and the crossroads in the sky. The second chapter demonstrates the ways in which crossroads have been revered as sites of magical interest and have hosted rituals of everyday religion and superstition. Focusing on the early modern as the era of greatest flourishing for accounts of these magical rites, it places newly discovered crossroads spells alongside a variety of other early modern crossroads practices. It takes an isomorphic approach to the unrelenting significance of the crossroads as a site of ritual potency that combines indefinable mystical content with attractive transformative agency. Chapter 3 examines the place of music in this story and considers crossroads' soul-selling, Faustian transformations and other metamorphoses. Finding resonance between musicians across time, one a collaborator with Shakespeare and the other the epitome of the blues legend, it connects early narratives of crossroads metamorphosis with more recent versions of the myth and registers both the potency of music as a catalyst for transformation and the ultimate futility of the Faustian pact. Chapter 4 discusses crossroads gods as the gatekeepers to otherworlds of experience: the miraculous, the sublime, or the conversion from one state to another. It proposes that one paradox of the crossroads, its seemingly opposed functions of binding and transformation, might be reconciled in the relationship between the spirits bound there and the gods encountered there. It recognises that crossroads are spaces for figures who disrupt the bases of cultures, so externalising transformative chaos which may then be forbidden but still accessible. The fifth chapter discusses the nature, historical popularity and cultural resonances of outcast burial at crossroads. It compares examples over time and suggests that the process is not as straightforward a rejection as it might seem. In fact, such interment may become almost auspicious to the culture that orders it, a deeply ironic result of such historical outcasting of the undesirable dead. The fact that Shakespeare knew at least five people so disposed of, yet rarely even mentions the process is considered in Chapter 6 alongside the contrasting approach in George Peele's *The Old Wives Tale*, where treatment of the subject is comedically light. This chapter argues that to place a body at a boundary like a crossroads is to write it into the margins of a story as a part of the defining frame. Denying this interment may be to refuse this influence of the marginal, but on the dramatic stage such things have a way of returning despite their exclusion from the script. Chapter 7 discovers the status of the crossroads in the early modern imagination to be bound up with ideas of the road itself, and certain types of roads in particular. This chapter explores sacred and cursed paths, including ancient countryside funeral routes which lent some of their presence to the places where roads crossed and so inform the understanding of the crossroads. Their liminality and relationship to boundaries and borders is found to compound their ambiguous and slippery nature, along with their ineluctable relation to the language of human movement. Chapter 8 then reflects on the crossroads in relation to the ambiguity of the wanderer of roads whose appearance may be an alarming sign that the status quo is out of joint. It discusses the nature of the crossroads as a locus for demonic restlessness and submits that the wanderer shares a duality with the nature of crossroads which includes both attraction and repulsion. These narratives then are found to be related in their threatening unboundedness and their centrality to some of the cultural myths of modernity. Chapter 9 explores the crossroads as a meeting place for traditions of the dangerous and disturbing creatures one might encounter at night in the liminal places of the world. It goes on to suggest that the perception of the crossroads includes its potential for alleviating the common human feeling of powerlessness at the hands of such capricious forces, perhaps even affording protection from the gods themselves. The tenth chapter then makes a case that the very shape of the crossroads accords with the symbolism of intersecting lines used for the binding or banning of evil forces. It considers the concept and practice of spiritual binding through a variety of early modern examples of apotropaic devices and suggests that the reason the crossroads has been thought a locality of access to power for binding is that it is also in itself an apotropaic sign in the landscape. Lastly a brief concluding chapter draws together the themes and functions around the crossroads which are explored in the book and places them within modern frameworks of similarity or equivalence. It speculates on the nature of such places in the present and on the possible meaningful futures of crossroads.

The geographical scope of the research for this book was essentially global and its temporal range was anything within recorded history. However, the nature of the research material and the author's own academic specialism draws these towards the West (more particularly the British Isles) and the early modern period, and together these constitute the chief focus of this book. Also, since the early modern period is when the potency of the crossroads is most keenly felt and experienced in Western Europe, the literary texts analysed here from that time may serve as fair exemplars for wider cultural perceptions of crossroads. But in this unapologetically forthright account of the phenomenon of the crossroads in history, a note of caution might be appropriate. Just as there are spiritual sceptics about in Shakespeare's world, as Harsnett's critique of the fear of 'three-way leets' might suggest, or as James I's somewhat forced response to scepticism of witchcraft text attests, it may be a mistake to make too strong a claim for the place of the crossroads in the general cultural awareness of any period in question. As Hayden White has pointed out, any given culture is 'only as strong as its power to convince its least dedicated member that its fictions are truths. When myths are revealed for the fictions they are, then, as Hegel says, they become "a shape of life grown old."'[108] Tracking a 'hidden' history of this kind runs the danger of suggesting that its subject is somehow key to understanding a whole period, or a people. I hope to avoid this and instead to provide a balanced account of the importance of crossroads to the cultures addressed in this text. If there is a difficulty in researching this kind of material, it is that that one may be classified as somehow 'Fortean' – at best not quite in tune with the cold rational critique expected of a discipline whose natural romantic drift might require us to protest too much our innocence in these tendencies, at worst, simply credulous. I would ask the reader to understand, as I describe the beliefs of communities at various times, that these beliefs may represent dominant forms, or be either the residual echoes of earlier times or the effects of unrefined contemporaneous thinking. Unless otherwise specified, at no point do I assert my own beliefs in relation to these narratives, aside from, of course, in the act of interpretation, and quite possibly, of omission. This material occupies the place where history shades into legend, and legend shades into myth, and it may be for this reason that it can find itself beset by those who use mystery to hide their own inadequacy to factual and credible research. With the intent of avoiding such Fortean mysticism, I have approached this subject from many angles: with drama, poetry, history, classical mythology, folklore, the original manuscripts of occult magic, material anthropology, archeology and a little etymology. In this last respect the possibility that the crossroads lurks in commonplace and trivial words, in the very idea of the trivial, might offer a model for its residual status in Western culture. For other cultures, however, the physical place of the crossroads is still a vibrant element in a world view that expresses the fullness of human fear, desire and the possibility of unusual transformative empowerment.

Chapter 1

Axes: Ecstatic Heights and Nightmare Depths

> Invoking Hecate hither to repair:
> A pow'rful name in hell and upper air.
> Virgil, *Aeneid* (c. 19 BCE)[1]

> 'You who live under the cross . . .'
> Of Legba, bidden during dismissal of loa, Vodun ritual (1946)[2]

To an ancient or early modern mind suffused in the potentialities of religious myth and sympathetic magic, the apparent symmetries between the starry cosmos, the 'middle' earth and the deep underworld must have seemed fitting and obvious. Although to a modern mentality the supposed similarities are obviously artificially contrived, the false positives of pattern recognition, the narrative of continuity in these matters has had a profound influence on the mythologies, religions and literatures of human cultures across the globe.

On the ground, roads have often operated historically as boundaries between private land, parishes, or even kingdoms, and so they are often in themselves liminal places. The crossroads, as a nodal instance of where such lines intersect, is therefore a multiply liminal space merely along its horizontal axes, inviting ritual and meaning into its space. But to take this one dimension further, the evidence of crossroads practice associated with gods and spirits both above and below the surface of the road also suggests a tradition of another axis, this one vertical. Both above and below the crossroads are dimensions to which the place itself is thought to give access. These may be conceptual, experiential or 'spiritual'; they are the underworld or the heavens, the realms of the divine and the dead. Just as the crossroads exerts a metaphorical effect on the horizontal plane, it also implies a metaphysical element on the vertical. The crossroads goddess Hecate's triple form expresses this precisely as it embraces both the underworld and the Moon with her co-divinities Proserpine and Diana.[3] Among many other examples, Mercury's go-between status from Earth to the realm of the gods also relies on this vertical axis in the nodal complexity of the crossroads. Since this is essentially an intersection of synchronic and diachronic axes with both spatial and temporal elements, it seems a physical manifestation of Bakhtin's concept of the narrative 'chronotope', while in geographic theory, de Certeau's concept of *space* as 'a practiced place' also includes just these vectors of direction and variables of time.[4] To begin with a geographical and temporal narrative seems appropriate then, leading us below and above the surface of the crossroads.

In Cambridgeshire, England, at the crossing point of the Roman and older roads of Ermine Street and the Icknield Way, is the ancient market town of Royston. In 1742, the floor of the butter market at the town crossroads was undergoing renovation when a buried millstone was discovered, beneath which was what looked like a steep, roughly hewn entrance shaft leading downwards into darkness.[5] The workers who found it paid a young boy a shilling to descend into the tunnel tied onto a rope and upon further investigation discovered what P. T. Houldcroft described as 'a man-made beehive shaped cave cut in the chalk substratum'.[6] When fully excavated, this long-hidden grotto beneath the crossroads was found to be covered from floor to ceiling with crude carvings of a religious, cultic, or possibly Freemasonic nature. In describing this discovery in 1866, Joseph Beldam's report of the area mentions 'a hermitage at the cross, beneath which lay the long concealed but since celebrated cave or oratory'.[7] As of 2021, evidence of this hermitage is still lacking, although in Beldam's time it may still have been in the town's folk memory. Nevertheless, the cave below remains as an anomalous and strangely indefinable presence adjacent to the modern crossroads.

In 1603, over a century before its discovery under the butter market, the new King James I had passed through Royston on his way from Scotland to his coronation in London and found the place strangely appealing. Just a few months later James returned to Royston and did so on a number of occasions while 'superintending the building and preparation of a residence of his own', as Beldam notes.[8] James subsequently purchased a considerable amount of housing in the town, where he habitually lodged his court for the purpose of hunting in the game-rich lands thereabouts.[9] The cave found under the crossroads was situated within yards of much of the property that was owned and frequented by the King and his hunting parties. The precise antiquity of the cave is unknown, but it is thought to date to Roman times or earlier, and may have been dedicated as a crossroads shrine to Diana, though direct evidence for this also is lacking.[10] Due to the chemically delicate nature of the walls of the cave, its carvings have proven difficult to date and may be fourteenth century or possibly later additions to a pre-existing construction.[11] Other similar structures exist, with possible indications of Masonic activity, at Newark and Warwick castles, both also near the junctions of ancient roads.[12] Also, further along the Icknield Way, on Therfield Heath, there are a series of Neolithic barrows and burial mounds, suggesting that the road's ancient use as a thoroughfare may have doubled with a ceremonial function of some kind.[13] Whatever its age and origin, the cave's position beneath an ancient crossroads, and its probable function as some kind of underground religious site makes it compelling as a possible site of ritual usage related to crossroads myth.[14]

Its proximity to the chosen stomping ground of such a notable reputed early Freemason as James adds another early modern link, and on this count it is interesting that the area's history suggests longer connections with crusading. After the Norman invasion of 1066, the lands around Royston had been handed over to Eudo Dapifer, William's Steward, and thereafter passed through the hands of landlords more or less associated with pilgrimage to the Holy Land.[15] Aspects of the cave's layout have been read as having Templar aspects, including its orientation in relation to the feast of John the Baptist, their patron, and in terms of its floor plan.[16] Freemasonry has long fantasised about Templar origins and, although the two are not connected, early Freemasons may well have scrawled roughly Templar-looking motifs on the walls of this cave provocatively sited at a place with known ritual associations such as the crossroads.[17] One of these carvings is a supine figure with characteristically crossed legs, as may be found in some crusader burials.[18] Another is of the skull and crossbones, a motif which appears still on some Masonic regalia, and seems to echo the *chi-rho* of Constantine, to which we will come back shortly.[19] The fact that a skull and bones were apparently discovered in 1742 when the cave was opened is of interest here, though these were of uncertain order due to the haphazard circumstances of the early exploration, and were afterwards lost.[20] Whatever was going on in the Royston cave, somebody clearly spent a long time carving images meaningful to them in a subterranean space proximally sited beneath the crossing of two ancient highways, and on route to ancient burial sites.

Like the space beneath the theatrical stage, the underground projection of a crossroads, the lower half of its vertical axis, was often associated with the idea of Hell. This was partly through the Christianising of a version of Hecate as both the goddess of the crossroads and of the underworld. Long before her Christian consignment to hellfire, Hesiod's *Theogony* (c. 700 BCE) describes Hecate as a maternal figure that from the beginning was celebrated as 'a nurse of the young', and whatever her underworld connections these are coloured to an extent by an association with womb-like nurture.[21] In Ovid's *Metamorphoses*, the witch Medea raises an altar of grassy turf that bears Hecate's name in a passage that speaks of what lies beneath:

> Then delves a double trench in lower ground,
> And sticks a black-fleec'd ram, that ready stood,
> And drench'd the ditches with devoted blood:
> New wine she pours, and milk from th' udder warm,
> With mystic murmurs to complete the charm,
> And subterranean deities alarm.[22]

Other gods also have the reputation of dwelling underneath the crossroads, as this chapter's epigraph to the Yoruba god Legba suggests. The burial at the crossroads of the corpses of suicides and other social undesirables also helps to associate it with a malevolent underground as well as constructing it as a place where extraordinary power might manifest. The subterranean aspect of the crossroads's vertical axis functions to contain the dead as much as it may receive seeding in its depths for the transformation of the living. Much transformative magic appears to depend on this uncanny connection for its credibility. At least one healing spell, for the seemingly trifling complaint of a sore throat, actively depended on its being performed upon the ground of a crossroads 'where nine dead persons are lying'.[23] For a mere sore throat this may seem to be overkill, or otherwise might be an indication of the commonplace nature of such rituals. We may recall Isabella Bird's Korean exorcism ritual involving a bottle buried at the crossroads.[24] Many spells and rituals require the burial of objects such as catskins at crossroads, or even that of living cats themselves, while a healing spell might require other animals to be buried for protection against disease.[25] The incubation of offerings for healing or other magic in the fecund earth of a crossroads is, to the convinced believer, like planting seeds of transformation in a richly generative soil, whose very dust may be a catalyst for various protective or magical rituals. In 1323 in France a Cistercian abbot engaged a local sorcerer to recover some lost property and in the proceedings a cat was buried alive in a box at a crossroads. In one anonymous early modern manuscript, an experiment named 'To have thy desire of all things carried and brought to thy hands' is recorded which requires 'a parchment of a black cattes skin' inscribed with magical and sacred-sounding words and commands the user 'going Bare foote Put it in ye earth'.[26] Of the magical-pharmaceutical efficacy of the dust of the ground, Pliny advises the 'burying of frogs at crossroads as a precaution against fever'.[27] And it is not unusual that mere dirt may energise or be energised in this way. Reading Pliny, Heinrich Cornelius Agrippa von Nettesheim (1486–1535) describes various recipes and uses for significant dust: 'of a Cuckow, in what place any one doth first hear him, if his right foot be marked about, and that foot-step be digged up, there will no Fleas be bred in that place where it is scattered'; the dust of 'the track of a Snake . . . scattered amongst Bees, makes them return to their hives'; also dust 'in which a Mule hath rolled himself, being cast upon the Body, doth mitigate the heats of love'.[28] Pliny further advocates also that 'women in labour wear an amulet filled with plants that have grown up inside a sieve thrown onto the crossroads'.[29] An old Hindu tradition determines that in the fourth month of pregnancy a woman wears a bracelet to protect her from the evil eye on which is fixed 'a packet of dark coloured cloth, containing scrapings from the image of Hallooman and dust from the cross-roads'.[30] In Fernando de Rojas's dramatic dialogue *La Celestina* (1500), Pármeno's mother is accused of being a witch 'because she was discovered by night at a crossroads, carrying candles and digging up handfuls of earth'.[31] In its fundament, the crossroads speaks of both tomb and womb, a combination which is not quite a dichotomy since the generative power of its womblike aspect may actually depend on its containing capacity as a tomb.

On its horizontal axis too, the crossroads has long been seen in terms of the imagery of motherhood. This is not merely in its traditionally proper containment of transformative desires or dangerous souls in its depths, but also in its extension outwards from a central generative point. In its Christianised version, however, this is most often depicted in negative terms. The Christian Bible gives an admonitory account of the King of Babylon who 'stood at the parting of the ways, at the head of the two ways, to use divination' (Ezek. 21: 21). Here, the 1611 version glosses 'parting of the ways' as the 'mother of the ways', taking its etymology for this from the original Hebrew *em* that signals motherhood. In his 1722 account of the Greek Church,

John Covel notes this female crossroads imagery when he observes that many of the oldest monumental crosses at crossroads, such as 'Charing, Geddington, Northampton, Coventry, and several others in England, as well as elsewhere, are placed in what we call, a three way Leet, that is where only three ways meet like, Y'.[32] In what might be called its othography on the landscape, the Y-shaped crossroads is related to the image of female sexuality and fecundity. Harsnett's account may be rooted in the most obvious kind of misogyny of his time, but when he also cites the pagan-Catholic dangers of the three-way leet, his main concern besides the effect on children is that it will primarily affect 'old women and maides', presumably by means of sympathetic magic.[33]

In this context it is not surprising that the leet's generative action is to bring forth monsters. The vaginal symbolism of the three-way crossroads may also have a basis in Greek etymology, as Jeffrey Rusten suggests in his reading of the Oedipus myth, where it also causes trouble.[34] Expanding on Heracles' example of the choice of two paths, early church writers like Lactantius (c. 250 – c. 325 CE) had used the Y metaphorically in the same way, to distinguish the two destinies of life, virtue leading to Heaven and vice leading to Hell.[35] But this form could pose ideological danger: crosses set at actual Y-shaped crossroads might somehow lead to the heterodox suggestion that Christ's cross was Y-shaped, and therefore emblematic of the feminine. As Covel points out, 'an Anathema was once formerly pronounced (as against Hereticks) . . . against all those who call the Honorable Cross, a Fork, or Crotched Stake'.[36] The symbol of the Y also has a generative resonance in representing the tree of life, an interpretation that may possibly be traced to pre-Pythagorian times.[37] Tracing these issues back into the Bible, there is another tree of life in Eden of course, Adam and Eve's site of transformation and a place where humans walk together with the divine. This tree occupies a place in the story besides the tree of knowledge of good and evil, whose low-hanging fruit Eve tastes and originates thereby the deviation from the one true path of God's intention. In the ultimate depiction of a female bifurcation, Eve, in her biblical depiction, is the originator of the very idea that there could be two moral paths and is certainly the first human in that story tradition to choose between them (preceded only by Lucifer). It is hard to imagine that both Western and Near Eastern cultures have not been affected by these ontological models of metaphorical paths to be chosen. As the mythic site of this fundamental moral parting of ways, and humankind's subsequent transformation, Eden is itself situated at a supposed quadrifurcation of one mythological headwater into four great rivers: the Pison, the Gihon, the Hiddekel and the Euphrates (Gen. 2: 10–14). Since great headwaters do not tend to split into other rivers but rather the opposite, we might regard this as a metaphor more apt to apply to the concept of division of roads, these rivers of course operating in that capacity for ancient peoples might signify in this case the universal dispersal of the efficacious magic of God's curse from its origin in this leaky garden and the dissemination of its transformative poison throughout the world with which its narrative is concerned.

One is led to wonder whether the church's aversion to the symbolism of the Y indicates a mere clash of symbologies, or whether it is something more akin to a rivalry over the once-sacred, sexualised and often feminised space of the crossroads which the church never successfully overlaid in its usual palimpsestic manner. Such objections may explain the historic reluctance of the Christian church to engage with the crossroads as a religious site.[38] Church history suggests that wherever a material expression of spirituality cannot be assimilated it must surely be erased. In St John Chrysostom's prayer of 'Exorcism' (c. 390 CE) he commands spirits of all kinds to 'shudder, tremble, be afraid, depart, be utterly destroyed, be banished!' In this he is going after not only 'a day and nocturnal spirit' and 'an imaginative spirit', but also the very pagan-sounding 'encountering spirit' and this, he says, is to be found in 'in a forest, or among the reeds, or in trenches, or in a road or a crossroad'.[39] Christian preachments of this kind not to worship or make offerings of any kind at crossroads are common in Europe between the seventh and eleventh centuries CE.[40] The seventh-century St Audoneus commanded that 'devilish amulets shall be employed neither at springs, nor at trees, not yet by forks in the road'.[41] On similar lines of command and control, Burchard of Worms's early twelfth-century penitential text *Corrector, or the Physician* (c. 1008–12) anathematises the practice of 'suspending objects, including human limbs and herbs with magical properties, at crossroads'.[42] One of his recommended questions that a confessor should ask a penitent was extremely specific on this:

> Have you made knots, and incantations, and those various enchantments which evil men, swineherds, ploughmen, and sometimes hunters make, while they say diabolical formulae over bread or grass and over certain nefarious bandages, and . . . throw them where two roads, or three roads, meet, that they may set free their animals or dogs from pestilence or destruction and destroy those of another?

Obviously this had been an issue in the area, and the penalty for having performed such crossroads rites was that one must 'do penance for two years on the appointed days'.[43] In England, years as late as 1542, 1563 and 1604 witnessed legislation aimed at stamping out such activities and imposing various penalties not excluding death.[44] Legislative assertions of this kind are only ever enacted in response to a perceived threat to power, but I would suggest that there is no real threat here to anything but a dominant social narrative. Rather than being properly subversive, the kind of witchcraft that goes on at crossroads surely evidences a certain desperation; it is the voice of the voiceless versus the cold indifference of fate or God, life or death.

Although church opposition was thorough and long-lasting, one exception to this is a Greek Orthodox Christian tradition in which the crossroads still acts as a fecund recipient of seed in what seems to be a residual manifestation of an ancient fertility rite. Marianthi Kaplanoglou describes the modern folk cult of St Phanourios with its divinatory 'bread-based confection or pie, the phanouropita' which is afforded predictive powers: 'for unmarried girls . . . the revelation of a good "fortune"; that is, a good bridegroom – and, respectively, a good bride for the unmarried men'.[45] Kaplanoglou relates this to devotions to St Theodore in which 'unmarried girls (or boys) would collect or steal . . . wheat, rye or broad beans' from women who had been 'married only once'. They would then 'throw or "sow" it over one (or three) crossroads'.[46] There they would sometimes also leave other sacrificial objects: 'a sickle . . . a jug, or a mirror', although the significance of these is not noted and may not indeed necessarily be known to the participants.[47] This is accompanied by 'a magical invocation' to the saint 'to mediate with the young person's Fate' and reveal the person she or he will marry: 'Good St Theodore, both good and humble, there in the desert where you go and greet the Fates, greet my Fate too and tell.'[48] The linguistic element here is combined with the sacrificial burial of seed at the parting of the ways in the hope of the transformation of one's prospects in love and marriage. The imperatives of human desire somehow manage to aspire at the crossroads still through the silted layers of centuries of religious accretion.

Unsurprisingly perhaps, given its dual nature, besides its womb-like aspects the crossroads also exhibits characteristics which have been perceived as a generatively masculine. In ancient Greece, crossroads were literally a space of phallic aspiration and various 'herms' venerating Hermes in his priapic form were situated there. One of these still extant is 'a stone pillar with a bust of the god above', on one side of which it displays the entwined serpents of Hermes' symbolic rod, the caduceus, and on the other 'an erect phallus', as Joseph L. Henderson reports.[49] These were also to be found on the street corners in ancient London.[50] Henderson's suggestion that this phallus 'penetrates from the known into the unknown world, seeking a spiritual message of deliverance and healing' may be a poetic account of a bare fact, but it seems in accordance with a god whose function is to connect the earthy world with the upper realms of the divine along the vertical axis.[51] His snakes then may be seen as emblems of 'cthonic transcendence', as Henderson suggests: two more earthbound aspirants.[52] In Haitian Vodou, Papa Legba, the pre-eminent crossroads god of destiny and Master of Crossroads, is represented by 'a wooden or iron phallus mounted in a little mound of earth in front of every house'.[53] In Japan meanwhile, wooden and stone phalluses are left at crossroads for the fertility deity Chimata-no-kami, the tutelary kami of forking paths. To the present day, in some well-known hot-spring spas, at his shrine, 'men with sexual problems, as well as women wishing for children, will come to stroke the phallus and ameliorate their condition', as Michael Ashkenazi recounts.[54] Chimata-no-kami is an aspect of the god Dosōjin, who is another crossroads god and one associated with knowledge and prosperity, two things which Ashkenazi regards as being 'clearly related in Japanese thinking (as elsewhere, for example, in Greek mythology) by the association with crossroads'.[55] In India also, stone phalluses are erected to the Hindu god Bhairava who guards the crossroads and other boundaries.[56] Healing, knowledge, prosperity, protection and transcendence are some of the qualities of the aspirational transformation of the self that traditional societies have chosen to pursue at the crossroads, alongside this emblem of masculine fertility and generation.

Through all the functions of both the underground and overground manifestations of the crossroads, the aspiration acted out there aims to connect somehow with the powers above. Below the crossroads may be a graveyard of corruption and a secretive generative space; ascending above the intersection, however, the upper part of the crossroads's vertical axis points skywards to an array of shining divinities: gods whose attractions might draw one on still further towards a higher crossroads, one with a cosmological dimension. Like its earthy equivalent, this celestial crossroads was also to prove the scene of some rivalry between pagan and Christian world views.

In the ancient world, the sky was the limit of transformational possibilities and astrology was its best attempt to understand how this worked. The erroneous proposition that the planets, as seen in the night sky, were crucial to the correct alignment of activities on earth animated intellectuals like the alchemist and magician John Dee, Elizabeth I's chief astrologer who was consulted accordingly on many of her major decisions. The planets were classically associated with the gods after whom they were named and the place where the track of their orbits crossed the visible path of the Milky Way was imaged by early philosophers to form a crossroads. This X sign in the night sky was regarded as the gate to the higher celestial realm. Outlining this path to the divine dimension, Plato's *Timaeus* (36 BCE) describes the planets' movement in crossing this perceptible line as tracing a heavenly X mark and he consequently identifies this as the signature of a demiurge creator, whom he names the World Soul.[57] This creator, Plato believed, had split the heavens 'lengthwise into two halves; and making the two cross one another at their centres in the form of the letter X, he bent each round into a circle and joined it up'.[58] In this way of thinking, the humble earthly crossroads mirrors the created form of the universe itself. In the Platonist thinker Manilius' *Astronomica* (c. 20 CE), he also identifies 'two circles' in the night sky which 'lie athwart and trace lines that cross each other', the first being that containing the Sun, Moon and the five known planets of his day, and the second, comprising the Milky Way, he describes as being 'placed crosswise to it'.[59] As George Beke Latura has persuasively argued, this interpretation of the solar system forms a 'crossroads in the sky' that played a crucial role in not only the cosmology but also the soteriology of the classical world, functioning as a pagan symbol of a heavenly afterlife.[60]

Latura's research in this area includes numismatic evidence, demonstrating that this cosmological X appears on successive Roman coins across the centuries, from the republic to the end of the empire until it is consciously Christianised as Constantine's *chi-rho* symbol, a sign of papal authority, interpreted as a 'christogram'.[61] Roman coinage also depicts the standards of Roman legions carrying the symbolism of the planets 'stacked along the ecliptic' (see Figure 1.1). Latura attributes this to the teachings of neo-Pythagoreans and neo-Platonists that the planetary spheres might provide the departed soul with the necessary steps to a heavenly existence in the stars after death.[62] This accords with teachings of various religious persuasions, of the Mithraic cult, of the esoteric Hermes Trismegistus, of the early Christian writer Origen, and of the opponent of early Christianity, Celsus.[63] The latter's 'diagram for the passage of the soul' was depicted as a ladder consisting of seven gates, with the eighth gate at the top being Plato's heavenly X, the crossing place into the very meaning of creation.[64] The

Figure 1.1 Roman coins. (Roma Numismatics Ltd <www.romanumismatics.com>)

fact that this cosmological theory involved the measurable movement of the planets in a superstitious age, no doubt fed into the conception of the earthly crossroads as a particularly potent space for rituals in sympathy with astrological movements and conjunctions happening at auspicious times of the year.

To venture a little further on this path, amongst the notoriously astrological Chaldeans, it was thought that the human soul was modelled on Plato's world soul, as the logic of natural sympathies might suggest in a pre-scientific age. Since this crossroads in the sky is a mark of the act of original creation, this would obviously find itself reflected in the composition of the creatures themselves, in this case manifesting as a kind of crossroads in the soul.[65] Hence the soul itself was believed to take an X shape, the shape of a Greek *chi*.[66]

Given its supposed relation to both the original act of creation and the composition of the human soul, it is not surprising that Christian commentators would wish to co-opt this discourse around the X to fit with their own ideological imperatives, especially in relation to the soteriological doctrine of the Cross. Space after all is, as Lefebvre says, 'literally filled with ideologies'.⁶⁷ Any connection here with an actual cross of the 'Jesus' type though is of course spurious, since the cross of Roman crucifixion would almost certainly have been a capital T shape, evolving towards the more recognisable lower-case variety † with the addition of an upper spur to make structural sense of the proposed mocking notice of the 'King of the Jews'.⁶⁸ The X-shaped saltire cross of Plato's description has never been associated with Christ, and in the Christian tradition is supposed to have been requested by St Andrew specifically to contrast with that of Christ.⁶⁹ Andrew, however, has about as much connection to the original act of *ex nihilo* creation as he does with Scotland. Nevertheless, in spite of there being no real justification for the connection, Justin Martyr's *Apology on Behalf of Christians* (c. 155 CE) refers to what he calls Plato's 'scientific discussion of the Son of God', disingenuously claiming that 'when he says: "He arranged him as an X in the cosmos" – Plato took from Moses, and spoke in similar terms'.⁷⁰ David T. Runia identifies this as 'the first step in the re-branding of Plato's ancient symbol' and doubts the accuracy of Justin's claim that 'Plato was discussing the Son of God 350 years before Jesus was born, and . . . had somehow purloined the shape of the cross from Moses'.⁷¹ John Kleiner also notes Dante Alighieri's later adoption of this idea in *Divine Comedy* that having found 'a Christian function for Plato's "chi in the sky"', he invites us to gaze up into the heavens and see it for ourselves'.⁷² Whether accurate or not, Dante presents this of course, as a poet might, in Canto X.

The Christian hagiographers of the Emperor Constantine have also associated Plato's cosmic X with the *chi-rho* of Constantine's supposed divine vision of the Cross in 312 CE, but here his biographers mirror those of Robert Johnson in distorting or inventing a crossroads encounter for their own narrative purposes, in order to attempt to explain the subsequent destiny of their subject.⁷³ In fact, Constantine's only barely attestable 'vision' was indeed at a crossroads, where he specifically claimed to have encountered the god Apollo. When the Emperor was on the way either to or from Marseille, he was given news of the defeat of a barbarian uprising on the Rhine, facts which were conveyed 'at the precise point of the journey at which there was a road leading to a sanctuary of Apollo'; it was supposedly at this parting of ways that 'the god himself appeared to the Emperor, accompanied by Victory'.⁷⁴ This is considered by Samuel N. C. Lieu and Dominic Monserrat to be 'the only authentic vision of Constantine' with the legend of his Damascene 312 CE vision of a cross of light in the sky being 'nothing but a Christian distortion' of what was in fact a purely pagan religious experience at the crossroads.⁷⁵ All of this cultural appropriation testifies to the currency of the original idea.

Bringing this imagery back down to earth again, it is certain as mentioned previously that the cosmic crossroads was perceived to exhibit astrological connections to the business of its terrestrial equivalent. At certain times of the year the zodiacal light is more visible as it crosses the Milky Way, and in the ancient Greek context this was particularly so at the time the annual initiations into the cult of Persephone and Demeter, the 'Eleusinian mysteries', were performed. Latura notes that neophytes arriving on their torchlit parade towards Eleusis via the sacred road from Athens would have seen this light.⁷⁶ One of these rites recalled the crossroads deity Ceres' search through all the earth for the kidnapped Proserpina as she 'called her with shouts where three or four roads meet'.⁷⁷ It was believed also that Eleusis was where the gates of Hades could be found.⁷⁸ On a vase dating to c. 350 BCE in the British Museum, London, Hades is depicted abducting Persephone, and Ceres or Hecate is found holding up the specifically cross-form Eleusinian torch (see Figure 1.2).

Figure 1.2 Volute krater, Hades abducts Persephone, Hecate holds up cross-form Eleusinian torch; the Iliupersis Painter, c. 350 BCE. (London: © The Trustees of the British Museum)

Hecate was reputed to be present 'whenever souls crossed over the boundaries between life and death' and as goddess of the crossroads her influence over passage through liminal places also included the authority to open and close the gates of Hades.[79] It is a highly appropriate alignment then that the gate to the heavens should manifest in the night sky at this time and in a place where the gate to the underworld is also found. As an example of Bakhtin's chronotope, this forms a point in 'the geography of a community where time and space intersect and fuse'.[80] Here, the mythology of the terrestrial crossroads seems very much to stand at the foundation of this stairway to its higher manifestation, with Hecate's heavenly equivalent Cynthia as the Moon, and then Mercury offering the next step in the soul's upwards journey towards transformation or release at the X-gate to paradise.[81] Equally the gates of Hades could provide access to the lowest depths.

Despite their rivalries, ultimately the opposing camps of pagan and Christian interpretation of the sky-crossroads or heaven-gate had something in common. Stuart Clark argues that both the cosmology of the early Greeks and of medieval Christianity were preoccupied with an inescapable dualism. The church, with the exception of Purgatory, was especially addicted to this world view.[82] Clark suggests that these 'habitual magnetic poles' to which Renaissance thought was captive shifted only when the eighteenth century offered new models of consciousness.[83] Perhaps then the crossroads is enduringly attractive precisely because it manages to carry its ambiguities without the need to oppose, reconcile or integrate them. Because it is a between-place, where the contraries and binaries of centre and periphery, binding and transition, womb and phallus, X and Y, even Hell and Heaven are encountered in creative and transformative tension, at least as metaphor, and more so perhaps as the enactment in ancient ritual of creative and transformative possibilities.

Chapter 2

Magic: Transformation and Self-determination

> Burye this plate in a crosse waye wher 2. wayes meete.
> Anonymous Spellbook (c. 1600)[1]

The desire for an encounter with magic at the junction of roads testifies to a need for a form of self-determination in which one's knowledge, nous or ability counts for something in the equations of destiny. Scholars have noted a rise in scepticism over Christian religious rituals such as exorcism and consecration in sixteenth- and seventeenth-century England, but it seems that this did little to weaken people's recourse to the peripheries of orthodoxy and alternative belief in times of trouble, and thus to transformative options at other 'locations imbued with meaning and power'.[2] In 1590, the experience of rituals outside the Christian norm was familiar enough to people that the preacher Henry Holland could complain credibly of 'the continual traffic and market which the rude people have with witches'.[3] Something of both credulity and scepticism on these matters may be seen in Shakespeare's *Henry IV, Part 1* (c. 1597), where without irony Glendower claims that he can 'call spirits from the vasty deep', and with equal plausibility Hotspur can reply, 'Why, so can I, or so can any man; / But will they come when you do call for them?' (III, i, 51–3). William Vaughan's *The Golden-Grove* (1600) meanwhile asserts that a man 'is not adjudged any scholar at all, unless he can tell men's horoscopes, cast out devils, or hath some skill in soothsaying', and in *Hamlet*, Marcellus's request of Horatio to speak to the ghost of old Hamlet because he is a 'scholar' (I, i, 41) accords with this assumed familiarity with the ins and outs of communication with spirits.[4] In this period, it is likely that those figures known as 'wizards' numbered around the same as the parochial clergy so that in early modern Essex, as Keith Thomas tells us, 'no one lived more than ten miles from a known cunning man'.[5] Seen in this light, *Macbeth*'s witches seem to be presented in such an egregious manner that they must bear little relation to common social experience (although they may still speak to the elemental concerns of some learned contemporaries). It would be wrong to assume that the vast majority of people were pathetically credulous about witches, fairies and monsters and on this there is some contemporary debate, and understanding that witches may be wrongly accused or be merely delusional individuals.[6] But either way, these opinions were largely kept separate from discussions about either the existence of spirits and devils or the transformative principle itself. Notwithstanding the various theatrical caricatures, the existence of spiritual beings was settled fact to all but a very few atheists. And the possibility of actual metamorphosis, despite its waning theological centrality to religious services, seemed to be well attested not only by leading writers and intellectuals but also by many examples from nature.

As much as any wanderer is mystified, transfigured into something incommensurable, by the dust of the road, so events enacted in the dirt of a crossroads seem to take on multiple valencies, its horizonal axis suggesting a further vertical axis, proposing both ecstatic heights of metamorphosis and nightmare depths. Each gives access to spiritual entities. Belief in the existence of demons and devil-spirits is consistent with the doctrines of the major religions in the early modern world and throughout the period. To the embarrassment of modernity these ideas still persist. Both sacrifices to demons and performances of exorcism and magical conjuring at crossroads are not only widespread but also display a remarkable continuity over time and across cultures.[7] There may be a thousand years of syncretism separating European pagan religion and early modern Christian practice, but the ritual magic and study of the occult that were by then entrenched in both élite and popular culture in Europe, though often thoroughly Christianised, appear to have retained certain echoes of earlier beliefs and practices.[8] The perception of these practices varied by the social rank of the perpetrator, and even by the sixteenth century the term 'witchcraft' tended to refer mainly to the activities of peasants while, with few exceptions, élite practitioners largely eluded censure, especially if male.[9] In seventeenth-century England, religious authorities were concerned with maintaining a distinction between mainstream religious belief and popular folkloric traditions. On their side was the shift in the late Middle Ages to seeing demotic witchcraft as equivalent to devil-worship (a reaction to the Manichean tendencies of Cathar heretics).[10] In this respect, the activity of the liturgical Devil was at least comprehensible within a biblical framework, whereas popular magic on the other hand implied a Manichean world view essentially outside their narrative control.[11] Suffering under the bonds of this emergent construction were those accused of witchcraft and, although it was not until the seventeenth century that the 'diabolical compact' featured heavily in witch trials, the biblical Devil was almost always present in the 'confession' narratives of the accused. The beneficiaries of this distinction were clearly the élite practitioners, whose esoteric conjurings could be couched in the gnostic terminology of angelic communication and heavenly strata. But the Devil often appeared also as an element in the ritual mix of crossroads charms, alongside oblique evocations of Christian liturgy.[12]

Whether high rank or popular, 'an act of witchcraft is a psychic act', as E. E. Evans-Pritchard says and somehow, across the spectrum of conjuring, the crossroads draws the ritual psyche in search of significant space. The fourteenth century grimoire *The Key of Solomon the King* teaches the practitioner that for magic to work one must seek out the most desolate places, but, it recommends, 'best of all are crossroads'.[13] Bonnemaison's conception of geosymbols is that they not only strengthen belief systems and underlie cultures, but they 'structure and sustain the order of the mind'.[14] As such a geosymbol, the crossroads' node of intersecting lines attracts ritual practitioners with centripetal force, not only offering efficacy and an access of power over otherwise unruly spiritual forces but also feeding these ideas back into the culture.[15] The crossroads outlives all its devotees. In antiquity Plato mocks the superstitious who are anxious about the magical wax dolls used at crossroads, but since he finds himself unable to refute their effectiveness he criminalises the practice in any case.[16] In his *Characters* (c. 300 BCE), Theophrastus derides such a 'Superstitious Man' who has various fearful dealings with the parting of the ways, and who is apt to 'pour oil from his flask on the smooth stones at the cross-roads, as he goes by, and . . . fall on his knees and worship them before he departs'.[17] The Superstitious Man also frequently purifies his house, alleging that 'Hecate has been brought into it by spells', and whenever he sees someone feasting on garlic left at crossroads, he will 'pour water over his head, and, summoning the priestesses, bid them carry a squill or a puppy around him for purification'.[18] The Latin poet Tibullus (d. 19 BCE) recommends that we 'devoutly revere the old stones at the crossroads that bear garlands of flowers'.[19] In pre-Christian Europe, Druidic rituals may also have been performed at the crossing of two ways.[20] In India, Brahman rituals were enacted at crossroads in which they might be purified of the taint of any mortal sin or minor transgression.[21] Elsewhere in the world these traditions also persist into the recent past and even to the present day. In the American South, until recently, it was considered very bad luck to turn back at a crossroads. In this case, one might rid oneself of the bad luck by turning around three times, spitting or marking the ground in a particular way.[22] Returning to the house and incanting some charm might lift the curse, while the device of returning and entering by another door is noted among the European traditions of Pennsylvania Germans as effective in lifting the hex.[23] The writer Kehinde Adeola Ayeni describes coming across certain crossroads in Nigeria in the late twentieth century, where she might find 'pieces of broken clay pots . . . palm oil, a coin, dead rat, chicken skull, some large feather belonging to some bigger bird like a hawk . . . the head of a dog . . . the eye of a big animal . . . precious beads like corals and other weird and bizarre combinations of things'.[24] The African diasporic religions of Umbanda and Quimbanda enact ceremonies at crossroads in present day Brazil to conjure Exus and Pomba Gira spirits.[25]

Alongside the performance of rituals for purification and cursing and charms for fertility or for the riddance of disease, the crossroads has also been seen as an auspicious location for rituals of divination, a place where one might overhear the conversation of spirits speaking about the future.[26] Its power may even be felt by accident, as if its potential energy is simply stored there, waiting to emerge. In a passage from Diogenes Laertius, a man wanting advice about his forthcoming marriage is directed to the crossroads by a temple priest where he finds boys playing with spinning tops who quite unwittingly give him prophetic guidance.[27] As much as it spans Europe, this facility extends also to Persian crossroads traditions of divination at auspicious times, Christmas Eve or New year's Eve for instance, when spirits may whisper the secrets of the coming year, including who might die that year. In some cases, one might actually witness a procession of those who would die.[28] The Bulgarian version of the biblical Lot story has him go down to the crossroads to discover whether God has forgiven him.[29] In Russia meanwhile, practising divination at crossroads might send the would-be diviner insane.[30] Heinrich Kramer and Jacob Sprenger, the writers of the *Malleus Maleficarum* (1487), take this further to suggest a link between the activities of divination and more malodorous practices, alleging that 'just as soothsayers obtain their results by curious means, so do witches look for and obtain from the devil the injuries which they do to creatures'; they conclude therefore that both are guilty of idolatry.[31] The basis for their interpretation of such activity is biblical: the passage in the book of the prophet Ezekiel which says that 'the King of Babylon stood at the cross-roads, shuffling his arrows and interrogating idols'.[32] In the 1611 Bible authorised by James I, the translation reads, 'the king of Babylon stood at the parting of the ways, at the head of the two ways, to use divination: he made his arrows bright, he consulted with images, he looked in the liver' (Ezek. 21: 21). For Christian believers throughout the ages, this biblical example verifies the continued existence of a world in which real divination is possible, and where those prepared to use magic charms and incantations at crossroads rituals might access real spiritual power, and quite possibly that of the Devil himself.

Some magical charms still in use in Britain in the sixteenth and seventeenth centuries appear to display a continuous line of descent from the Anglo-Saxon era and at the same time are almost indistinguishable from those used on the European continent.[33] Since witchcraft manuals like Johann Nider's *Formicarius* (c. 1436–8) were amongst the earliest books to be printed, these connections were sealed in literature from the beginning of the printing revolution.[34] Thomas notes the significance of Scot's *Discoverie of Witchcraft* (1584) and Robert Turner's translation of the *Fourth Book of Agrippa* (1655), in this continuing process. Typical of the genre is the *Notary Art of Solomon* (1656) which described procedures ranging from fasting and prayer to the drawing of chalk circles and specific incantations, and prescribed such necessary equipment as 'holy water, candles, sceptres, swords, wands and metal lamina'.[35] As we have seen, the transformational and aspirational narratives that led and lead people to practise such magic rituals have also led inexorably to the crossroads. This seems very much to be linked with burial practices around the disposal of the outcast dead, and the two activities seem to possess values which are reciprocal. From ancient times, spells may have been performed at crossroads simply because 'the restless souls who carried them out gathered there', while the fact that 'some Greek crossroads rituals were performed with the eyes averted' does indeed seem to suggest a protection measure against any 'uncanny creatures' that might be feared likely to materialise, as Johnston says.[36] The late tenth- or early eleventh-century Anglo-Saxon writer Ælfric attests to this connection, describing how 'witches resort to crossroads, and to heathen burial sites with their evil rites, and call upon the devil, and he arises in the form of the person who lies buried there as if he had risen from death'.[37] Agrippa's *Of Occult Philosophy* (1651) also suggests that the souls of the unquiet dead are vulnerable to being raised and used by witches, who then could 'easily abuse them for the effecting of their witchcrafts', in order to 'kindle unlawfull lusts, cause dreams, diseases, hatred and such like passions'.[38]

Whatever its source, to the believer in such things transformative energy is somehow generated and accessed at the crossroads which somehow harnesses and distributes power. The spells and rituals that in various times and places have been performed there have the simple aim of accessing this potential in one form or another. The character of magical rites varies of course with their authors, but all crossroads rituals are aimed at producing a transformation of some kind, either directly in the fortunes of the performer or caster or indirectly through the exercise of influence over another person, and in this they attempt to employ the most powerful symbolism. In these processes certain elements are commonly found: the seeking out of liminal places like crossroads, the echoes of gods associated with such places, a combination of holy and unholy words, auspicious timing, sacrifices and the burial of objects.[39] In a handwritten and untitled early seventeenth-century book of spells in Oxford's Bodleian Library, is the ritual hex, 'An experiment for love', which involves just such a magical ritual performed at a crossroads. As a precise example of the kind of ritual we are discussing here, it is worth citing in full:

> Take a thinne plate of virgine waxe. & make it 4. square. drawe a picture of a woman theron. & wryte in yᵉ fore pte of yᵉ head wᵗʰ a needle this worde Ascariell. & in yᵉ brest the womans name. & at yᵉ nether ende of yᵉ picture yᵉ mans name, & on ye right syde of ye picture make this caracter. ○⊤○ ♀ .& on ye left syde this caracter ⚶ then burye this plate in a crosse waye wher 2. wayes meete. halfe a foote in yᵉ ground on yᵉ day of ♀ after sonne setting wher you shall lett it remayne 3. dayes & 3. nights. & goe rounde about yᵉ place sayinge I Conjure. & adiure thee thou sprite Ascariel. wᶜʰ hast power over yᵉ love of women. by god yᵉ father. yᵉ sonne. & yᵉ holy ghoste, & by ye blessed virgine marye. & yᵉ love yᵗ she bare to her childe Ihesus. And by the merrits, passion, death. & resurection of yᵉ same Ihesus, & by thes holy. Fearefull. & terrible. Names of god. Agla. On. Tetragramaton. ego sũ qui sũ. Alpha et Omega, & by all yᵉ other holy names of god. & by all yᵉ holy companye of heaven. yᵗ yᵘ constrayne & cause this woman N. To burne in love wth this mã N. N. in ye name of yᵉ father. yᵉ sonne. & yᵉ holy ghost Amẽ. This beinge sayd roundeabout yᵉ place 3. nights together after sonne sett nete after yᵉ chaunge of yᵉ moone. make this Caracter every tyme upon ye grounde ○⊔○ with your fore finger & depart, & she will ether come or send for yᵉ partie before yᵉ 3. Dayes ende.[40]

Here we have both a practical crossroads ritual and one which invokes divine, demonic or angelic names.[41] It is also creative and time-consuming, requiring commitment from its performer. It specifies the precise carving of the charm plate and the depth, the day of the week, and time of its burial; it prescribes the length of time it is supposed to be left there, involves an incantation, and, albeit somewhat latterly, brings into the equation the blessing of the Holy Trinity and the Virgin Mary. One might imagine that the three nights of nocturnal mumbling involved in a rite like this would form at least occasional background noise at certain crossroads, and especially at certain times of the year, or even on certain days and nights (Wednesday was favoured from its relation to Woden). The fact that magical practices of these kinds were ongoing at crossroads throughout the early modern period suggests that they may have been encountered at some level by ordinary passers-by, including of course the writers of the time. In his play *The Witch* (1606) Thomas Middleton's Hecate is asked for such a 'love-charm' (I, i, 201) but crossroads magic rituals were largely absent from the drama of the day.[42] It is possible that, like the more élite practitioners of alchemy and magic, the urban sophisticates of the acting profession may have seen these things as embarrassingly rural superstitions which were either best ignored or turned into clownish caricature for consumption on the stage. In terms of dramatic narratives, this seems to be largely a missed opportunity for various reasons, including the sheer drama of the desires and events involved in such popular crossroads spellcasting, and from its more purely linguistic and liturgical aspects.

In his prose work *The Terrors of the Night* (1594), Thomas Nashe describes the hybrid nature of the magical conventions of the age, which we may see in the above 'experiment for love'. After establishing that the first witch was Proserpine, he describes her as dwelling 'half in heaven and half in hell' arguing that 'half witches are they that, pretending any religion, meddle half with God, and half with the devil . . . because in their exorcisms they use half scripture and half blasphemy'.[43] To this picture, he adds that 'the greatest and notablest heathen sorcerers that ever were, in all their hellish adjurations used the name of the one true and ever-living God'.[44] In early modern England, spells did frequently involve the combination of ecclesiastical idiom and occult elements, and typically expressed a mixture of Christian reference and fantasy demonism in the grammar of their necromancy. In another anonymous contemporary incantation, that gives the power 'To constrayne aney spirit', one is required specifically to call on the aid of 'both good spirits and evil'.[45] This duality may also be found in an incantation from the compilation entitled *A booke of Experiments taken out of dyvers augthors* (1622) that seems to see no contradiction in conjuring Satan by all that is holy, so that he may 'cause this woman N. Of whose heade these 3 heares belongeth to burn in my love'.[46] Nashe does not deny the power of such sorcery but, seeing no contradiction in terms, simply attributes it to God. This strange syncretism seems appropriate to the paradox of the crossroads.

Displaying the propitious cosmological timing most crossroads magic requires, the ritual described in 'To constrayne aney spirit' is crucially 'subiecte to one of ye 7 planets' which must also be in alignment or else the spirit in question 'will not obey you or come before you'.[47] In an interesting twist on the theme of planets and stars as gods and spiritual entities, Nashe writes that 'the night is the devil's black book' and describes the Devil as 'a special predominant planet of the night', surely elevating him somewhat in the process.[48] The echoes of the gods of its pagan past may often be found in the precise timing of a ritual, as in another early seventeenth-century English spell, entitled 'An experiment to see Spirits what they doe', where one is directed to 'kyll a lapwing on a Wednesday in ye houre of Mercury ... and set yt in a secret place wher no man cometh'.[49] Both of the auspicious gods referenced here, Mercury and Wednesday's Woden/Odin, are gods who are closely associated with crossroads. The time often specified for ritual in many spells is midnight, which has its own obvious liminal and magical connotations. For a spell to work, the chosen place must often also be in some sense liminal. In one incantation which aims 'To constrayne aney spirit to answer you and to fulfill yower intente', the operator is advised, 'some saye y^t ye circle shoulde be made in a waste place as wodes fenes heathes doles oar medowes'; if not at the crossroads as *The Key of Solomon the King* recommends, other desolate and liminal places are available.[50] Alongside these rudiments, such incantations often require an animal sacrifice of some kind, and cockerels and cats seem most to suffer the unfortunate favouritism of these popular occultists. As we have seen in the 'experiment for love', whose efficacy depends on the crossroads burial of its decorated 'thinne plate of virgine waxe', this conjuring often involves the burial of various objects, living, dead or inanimate as various spells following may demonstrate.

The preparation of these necessary elements involves the practitioner in a complicated set of activities that demands a kind of high theatre of self-performance which would seem to beg for a more nuanced form of dramatic interpretation than the witchcraft plays of the time offer.[51] Initially, however, in order to shift from the ordinary life towards the more dramatically charged world of metamorphic power that these spells invoke, it has been thought desirable to transform oneself fully into a committed witch. In Christian witch theory the transition to becoming a witch occurred through a physical meeting with the Devil and an individual pact in which, in exchange for 'the renunciation of baptism, services on earth and the soul of the witch at death', the Devil would bestow magical powers and other substantial rewards or whatever else the contract might specify.[52] In this process, the first steps of the journey would frequently be towards a crossroads, and often with some animal in tow. The *Malleus* reports that anyone who wants to become a sorcerer must go to a 'four-paths' with a black hen and this is always at midnight. It goes on 'then comes someone who asks: "What are you doing here?" "I have a chicken to sell", they reply. That someone (is) the Wicked.'[53] Despite the fact that the *Malleus* is critiquing these views to some extent, it still manages to reproduce the popular contemporary vision of the process. In a later tradition, dated by William Marion Miller to pre-1850s America, a French settler method for attaining the powers of a witch prescribes the following:

> Wait until a dark, moonless and starless night comes . . . Then, shortly before midnight, gather up a totally black cat . . . and go to a crossroads alone and unobserved. Precisely at the stroke of twelve cut off the cat's head with one blow . . . Then bury at once in a place known to you alone the head of the cat, putting one pea seed in each eye before burial.[54]

Eating the peas that eventually result from this gruesome propagation will confirm you as a witch. In late nineteenth-entury Russia, meanwhile, peasants from Makar'ev Province, Nizhnii-Novgorod, reported that those wanting to become sorcerers 'should walk at night to the crossroads . . . call upon Satan', then renounce 'Christ, their relatives, the earth, sun, moon and stars' and 'pledge their allegiance to the dark spirits and beg these devils for instruction in sorcery'.[55] Here, however, a further commitment was required as a 'declaration in blood to obey Satan' was necessary to seal the deal, as Christine D. Worobec recounts.[56]

It is not compulsory of course that one identify specifically as a witch in order to perform a crossroads ritual, and examples of rites applicable to anyone with a desire to radically change something about their lives are also to be found, again dating from ancient to modern times and from many different locations. Such rituals may be aimed at accessing the powers below, figured by the outcast bodies and sacrificial items buried there, or the powers above, with which the go-between gods of the crossroads offer the most certain connection. The following accounts point to similarities in practice across time, and in widely varying cultures, but this isomorphic approach does not aim to imply that these same practices carry identical cultural value, or that there is something about the rituals that transcends time and place. It is hoped rather that the act of collating the accounts of crossroads magic in this way might result in interesting parallels, or even juxtapositions, that may provide evidence for comparative cultural studies beyond the remit of this present exploration. The accounts themselves occupy a spectrum from the anecdotal or folkloric in nature to the classically historical in quality. They range from the casually sentimental to hard-wrenched confessional fictions extracted under regimes of torment by witch-hunters, and therefore may relate more to literary history, or the history of perception, than to the history of events in a more archaeological sense. Nevertheless, despite their narrativised elements, the sheer weight and breadth of the testimonies here suggest a range of physical practices which betray a deep desire to access the transformative energy they hope to find at the crossroads. These practices, or semblances of them, persist in some places to the present day.

Early classical crossroads practices involved both depositing at and taking from crossroads. Johnston recalls Plato's description of the wax figures that may be left at the parting of the ways and notes that 'one of the spells in the Greek magical papyri instructs a love-sick magician to deposit a similar figure, made of wax or dough, at the crossroads' to solve his problem, while another instructs him to 'inscribe his spell on a three-cornered sherd picked up at the crossroads and then to hide the sherd again'.[57] As we have seen, such processes were not always so simple. One Greek crossroads spell dating from the fourth century CE and entitled the 'Attraction spell by sleeplessness', invokes for its purposes the 'Goddess of the Three-Ways', and commands some fairly intricate activities, which must have proven very difficult in performance:

> Take the eyes from a bat and let it go alive. Take a bit of unmelted dough or unmelted wax. Make a little model of a dog. Insert the right eye of the bat into the right eye of the little dog, and its left eye similarly into the left . . . Put it into a new drinking cup and attach a papyrus label to it. Seal it with a personal ring with a motif of crocodiles head-to-tail. Deposit it where three roads meet.[58]

The spell to be inscribed on the drinking cup's label here is 'I adjure you by Hecate, three times over . . . that (insert her name) may lose the spark in her eye and lie awake with nothing in her mind, but me alone (insert your name).'[59] The operator of such a spell must at least have been serious about the intended outcome.

One well-attested example of crossroads ritual practices dates from the fourteenth century and benefits from a number of fairly elaborate accounts. The events in question were located in Kilkenny, Ireland in 1324, and involved a wealthy Hiberno-Norman noblewoman named Dame Alice Kyteler, who, along with her accomplices, was charged with having 'torn apart live animals and scattered their limbs about at a crossroads, as a rite of offering to a devil'.[60] As Puhvel informs us, she was furthermore alleged to have 'offered to the demon nine red cocks' and nine red peacocks' eyes on a stone bridge at a certain crossroads'.[61] St. John D. Seymour's account of the trial describes how Kyteler and her followers 'offered in sacrifice to demons living animals, which they dismembered, and then distributed at cross-roads to a certain evil spirit of low rank, named the Son of Art . . . Robert Artisson'.[62] She and her associates had apparently 'sought by their sorcery advice and responses from demons', and, in their nocturnal meetings blasphemously 'imitated the power of the Church' by excommunicating their husbands 'from the sole of their foot to the crown of their head, naming each part expressly'.[63] Richard Ledrede describes how on one occasion, 'by the crossroads outside the city', Kyteler had made an offering 'of three cocks to a certain demon . . . from the depths of the underworld':

> She had poured out the cock's blood, cut the animals into pieces and mixed the intestines with spiders and other black worms like scorpions, with a herb called milfoil as well as with other herbs and horrible worms. She had boiled this mixture in a pot with the brains and clothes of a boy who had died without baptism and with the head of a robber who had been decapitated.[64]

Despite these serious crimes, Kyteler escaped justice, possibly by fleeing to England, and thereafter disappeared somewhat inconveniently from the historical record, though one of her accomplices, a serving woman called Petronilla de Meath, from whom much of the testimony came, was burned at the stake for her part in the events.[65]

In a slightly less egregious case, just the previous year in France a Cistercian abbot had engaged a local sorcerer to recover some lost property (a common cause of such engagements) and in the proceedings a cat was buried alive in a box at a crossroads in order to prepare it for later sacrifice. All those concerned were severely punished when this was discovered and the abbot was sentenced to life imprisonment.[66] An account of witchcraft in the western Alps given in Johannes Nider's *Formicarius* (c. 1436–8) quotes a magician known as Staedelin, who confessed, no doubt under some duress, to raising hailstorms to destroy crops with the following account:

> With certain words we implore the prince of all demons, that he should send some [demon] of his, who would strike the place designated by us. Then, when some demon arrives, we immolate a young black fowl at some crossroads, throwing it high into the air. The demon takes up this [offering], obeys [us], and immediately rouses the air . . . by casting hail and lightning.[67]

Besides the sacrificial aspect of crossroads rituals that we see here, there was frequently an element which involved music, or at least rhythm of some kind, as Chapter 3 shows. But also in accompaniment to this, rituals regularly seem to include dancing and the free movement of the body. In both Wales and Germany it was believed that witches would gather to dance with the Devil at the crossroads, at midnight on the eve of 1 May, the evening which was known in Germany as 'walpurgisnacht', St Walpurga's Night. Another German example comes from Bamberg where the burgomaster Johannes Junius, taken for a witch in 1628, confessed to his tormentors that 'the day after an execution was held, he was at a witch-dance at the Black Cross, where Beelzebub had shown himself to them all'.[68] He is of course constructing this to fit the expected model and so to give his torturers what they want, but it indicates that he knows the most convincing form this must take, no doubt drawing on what must have been common modes of belief.[69] At a later witch trial in Steiermark, Austria, in 1689, one Gregor Agricola, a minister, was executed after being accused of organising just such 'crossroads revelry'.[70] Many of those accused of such gatherings and practices were of course plainly and simply innocent of even attempting any such thing, but where there may have been involvement in crossroads or other rituals, agonising death or life imprisonment seem high prices to pay for what might amount to schemes of practical self-improvement. This is especially the case since these, in a sense, reinforced significant elements of the dominant religious narrative: the reality of spirits, the blessing or transformative power of God, or the saints, and the power of invocation. It may of course be that the issue playing the most significant part in the harshness of the punishments visited upon individuals looking for personal transformations, and more regular practitioners of crossroads rites, is simply the implied annexation of the power normally enjoyed by the clergy.

More recent accounts of crossroads rituals again hail from many and various locations. Tracking these ancient practices through the nineteenth century, one may find remedies for illnesses, hexes for assassination, formulae to promote the transformation of one's abilities, plus rites which tend towards the apotropaic. One of this kind took place in Marlborough, England, in 1831 and followed a heated debate about the Reform Bill at which one Mr Estcourt boldly but unwisely assured a restive crowd that 'they were mistaken in him if they supposed him capable of supporting such a bill'; as the cry of 'reform' filled the room the 'unrepresented classes' freed themselves from restraint to the extent that 'immediately after the election, effigies of the two successful candidates were carted through the town accompanied with tin kettles and horns, and burnt at the cross-roads', as Waylen describes it. For extra ritual efficacy at that time, 'the bells of the churches were also rung backwards'.[71] The roots and associations of this ad hoc ceremony will be by now apparent, but one is left to wonder how much any of the original perpetrators of this effigy-burning might have known of these connections, besides a general sense that the crossroads is where things of significance might take place. A glance at a crossroads with dangerous associations is found in Marryat's *One Year in Sweden* (1862) which describes how the Swedish bridegroom on his wedding day is 'greatly afraid of elves, so he gathers strong-scented herbs ... a sure protection against sprites, and sews them in his wedding-clothes', and that he would be certain to avoid tarrying 'where the cross-roads meet'.[72] Marryat continues 'should you ask him why he takes these precautions, he will reply, "Against envy and malice!"'[73] With their roots in apotropaic magic and the spiritual perils of the parting of the ways, such traditional protections and precautions amount to far more than a bidding for a lucky match. Walter Keating Kelly's *Curiosities of Indo-European Tradition and Folk-Lore* (1863) meanwhile describes a tradition from the Linz district of Austria, in which the story goes that a labourer coming late from work is 'often met at the junction of cross-roads by Bertha, who offers him a black cloth. If he takes it he dies within the same year; but if he cries out Dame Bertha, dame Bertha, Throw the cloth upon the earth, the goddess will send him luck and plenty.'[74] The goddess here offers only two possibilities: death or personal transformation.

In his *Peasant Life in Sweden* (1870) Lloyd described the night before the pre-medieval festival of St John, or St Hans's Eve, 23 June, still celebrated in certain parts of Swedish Norrland as 'the most mystic night of the whole year', in which 'great fires are . . . made at the cross-roads' to repel other unwelcome visitors (John Stow's Survey 1603 mentions similar purifying bonfires in English celebrations of St John).[75] Into these flames was cast 'a species of toad-stool, called "B'dran". . . named after certain emissaries of Satan . . . for the purpose of nullifying the power of the "Troll" and other evil spirits, who on this and certain other nights are more especially believed to be abroad'.[76] It was believed also that if a troll were to come near to the crossroads fires of St Hans's Eve it must show itself, and given the possibly psychedelic properties of certain toadstools, it seems fairly likely under such conditions that they might, especially since any animal seen near the fires was believed to be the 'the evil one' in disguise.[77] On the subject of trolls, Puhvel notes a Faroe Islands tradition of gathering treasure from trolls on Twelfth Night by whetting an axe on a grey calfskin at a crossroads leading to a church.[78] The Welsh writer John Brown (under his pseudonym of Christopher Cobbe-Webbe) found his Pembrokeshire parishioners of 1882 to be similarly superstitious, believing in 'ghosts, white ladies, corpse candles, spectre funerals, witches, and the efficacy of charms' and claimed to have met old people who 'believed in fairies, or as they called them "the little people," of whom they spoke in low tones, as though they feared to be overheard'.[79] Cobbe-Webbe specified that for these people All Hallow's Eve, or 'La Hollantide', was a special season for cabalistic rites and that 'churchyards and crossroads were very superstitiously regarded towards midnight' at that time especially.[80]

In the seemingly unlikely source of *The Illustrated Guide to Bournemouth* of 1891 a traditional crossroads cure is recommended to be found at Swanage where a donkey ride to the crossroads might cure your whooping cough.[81] A cure for an inflammation of the eye recorded in the following year in Pennsylvania instructs the sufferer to 'go alone and by night to a crossroads' and incant aloud 'Sty! Sty! go out of my eye, / And go on the stranger who next passes by'.[82] This principle of transference of illness is also found in the instructions for a Suffolk cure for the ague from 1893, which also recommends the patient to 'go by night alone to a cross-roads . . . just as the clock is striking midnight', this time the prescription orders the supplicant to 'turn round three times and drive a large nail into the ground up to the head. Walk backwards from the nail before the clock has finished the twelfth stroke' and promises that 'the ague will leave you, but will go to the person next to step over the nail'.[83] Although recorded in the nineteenth century, this was attributed at the time to the seventeenth century, and might represent the traditions of all of these examples stretching back many years, as their associations with attested earlier rituals implies.

Into the twentieth century, narratives around crossroads were still resonating with the classic discourses of witchcraft, as we see in an Irish account which describes an old woman who 'by spinning yarn at a crossroads on May-Day morning – following Beltane Night, the Irish counterpart of St Walpurga's night – would "charm butter away from her neighbours"'.[84] The crossroads also figures prominently in southern American 'hoodoo' or 'rootwork' rituals of the early twentieth century, as an informant from Elizabeth City, North Carolina, explained:

> You go to the fork of the road on Sunday morning before day, go there for nine times in succession before the sun rise and make a special wish, a special desire, and whatever you want to do, if it's to be a conjuror or to be a bad person, then the devil comes there. First comes a red rooster, then after that the devil sends something else in the shape of a bear and after that he comes himself and takes hold of your hands and tells you to go on in the world and do anything that you want to do.[85]

One Mr Maddox, from Princess Anne, Maryland confirms the tradition and describes being told that you could:

> go to a four crossroad – what is called a four-way road – for nine mornings at one particular hour in the morning, and dance and sing ... and on the ninth morning the devil'll put in his appearance or some of his imps and give you the power to accomplish what you want to do.[86]

Another unnamed source from the 1930s describes a ritual for luck in gambling:

> go to a crossroads before the sunup and have the dice in your hands, and look at the sun when she start to peeping up, and ... shook them dice at that crossroads until the sun gets up where you can see it. I'll do this – thrown them out, thrown them out. I'll do this 'In the name of the Father, Son and Holy Ghost'. And every time you throw them out pop your fingers.[87]

These examples sit comfortably alongside those specifically aimed at musical transformations and these are explored in more detail later.

In India, in 1946, James M. Campbell recorded the Vishnuist Vallabhdcharya sect's marriage ceremony, which took place at midnight. In this, the bridegroom 'on his way to the bride's house . . . performs the chakla or cross-roads worship' through the following ritual:

> In the middle of the square a sweet ball is placed on a fried cake and at each corner an earthen pot with a sweet ball and a copper in it . . . After the worship is over the corner pots are given to four unmarried boys . . . to ensure a speedy marriage. A sweet ball is then set on the ground and on it a waistcloth is spread. On the waistcloth a sword is placed and the bridegroom's cart is made to pass over the sword. If the edge of the sword is broken it is considered a bad omen.

The inclusion of the weapon here is quite typical of the use of metals in ritual work of this kind. Campbell notes additionally that 'the bride also performs the cross-roads worship in company of her friends and relations'.[88] Here the crossroads is a family affair.

In contrast, a fantastical Haitian Vodun spell, also recorded in the mid-twentieth century, aims to produce an assassination and includes rites to be performed at 'the crossroads at midnight' by both the priest and the petitioner, 'with either a black or a white chicken'.[89] This spell describes what should happen next: 'suddenly in the middle of a whirlwind a man so tall that he seems to reach the sky appears. As he comes nearer he becomes smaller and smaller until he takes on dwarflike size.'[90] Condescending in this way from the gigantic heights of the skies to the ground-level proportions of the dwarf, this entity then proceeds either to grant or deny the request for another's murder. And into more recent times, the African-Brazilian religion Quimbanda offers a *trabalho* which is described as 'A work of great force . . . to eliminate an enemy.' As David J. Hess shows in an account dating from 1992, this operates as follows:

> 1) Go to a crossroads of Exu on a Monday or Friday near midnight, if possible in the company of a member of the opposite sex; 2) greet Ogum with a bottle of light beer, a white or red candle, and a lighted cigar; 3) greet Exu Sir Block-Streets-of-the-Souls by opening seven bottles of rum (*cachaça*) in the form of a circle, lighting seven red and black candles, and offering seven cigars; 4) put inside a vase (*alguidar*) and mix the following: manioc flour (*farinha da mandioca*), palm oil

(*azeite-de-dendê*), and peppers; 5) put on the ground in the middle of the circle the name of the person whom one wishes to hurt, and, using a knife, stab this with violence, asking Exu to attend to one's request.⁹¹

The Exu is the Brazilian version of Eshu Elegbara, the Yoruba god involved in the legend of Robert Johnson as we will see. A second *trabalho* which gives the performer the power to obtain a woman, dated the same year presents the following instructions:

1) On a Monday or Friday night, go to a female crossroads (T-shaped rather than plus-shaped) and greet Pomba Gira by pouring a little rum, or better yet, champagne or anisette (*anis*); 2) place two pieces of cloth (*pano*) on the ground, one red and the other black, and on top of this put five or seven red roses in the shape of a horseshoe; 3) fill a cup of good quality with champagne or anisette; 4) put the name of the desired person in the cup or in the middle of the horseshoe; 5) sing a *ponto* (song) and thank Pomba Gira.⁹²

Although the frequency of such practices for crossroads-based healing is no doubt inversely proportional to the advancement and availability of medical science, these are also documented in the twentieth century. In a Hungarian gypsy tradition recorded in 1962, the spell for healing of a sore mouth runs simply as follows: 'The wound is surrounded by ... nine dolls in the form of a man ... Then [the medicine woman] goes to the crossroads and throws the dolls among the pigs or cows passing there.'⁹³ Another gypsy hex for a sore throat prescribes that 'the lard of a bullfrog is rendered and smeared on the throat. The rest of the grease is poured on the crossroads, on a Friday or Saturday night, where nine dead persons are lying.'⁹⁴ Given what is described in Chapter 5: Terminus, a nine-body crossroads might well be the site of a historical gallows.⁹⁵

Somewhat unusually, there are also some specifically Christian appropriations of the transformative crossroads space, as in the Greek fertility rituals around St Theodore, or the Russian instance of shrines sited at crossroads dedicated to one whom William Francis Ryan describes as 'the rather ambivalent St. Paraskeva', a patron saint of women and who as 'provider of husbands' offers transformations of the marital kind.⁹⁶ This kind of love-magic is in a sense where we started with this chapter's examples. Again, not to imply the continuity of ideologies surrounding these crossroads practices, the intention was to notice their unrelenting significance to those requiring assistance or metamorphoses in certain societies. Perhaps this serves to indicate a continued need for the placebo effect of the merest possibility of skewing in one's favour the chances of winning the lottery in life, but it may also be a disturbing indicator of the lack of manifest social agency for many people, for whom alienation and social exclusion are as real today as in any other time. Through all of this, we may perceive the enduring duality of the crossroads as both no-man's *space*, whose vectors of direction and time suffuse the rituals of history with an indefinable mystical content, and the conjured *place* that is subject to the transformative agencies of the spoken word.[97]

Although witchcraft ceased to be a statutory offence in England in 1736, as Thomas authoritatively notes, 'the lynching of alleged witches remained a sporadic feature of English rural life until the later nineteenth century', and in this sense, witchcraft died hard in England.[98] Like Thomas, Christina Larner also discredits the idea that modern forms of paganism, or covens of witches, are a survival of ancient belief systems, with none of the modern groups claiming such connections dating from earlier than the 1920s.[99] Without wishing to question this orthodoxy, the conventions of magical practices aimed at effecting transformation at crossroads do, however, appear to come from a tradition stretching back at least to the religious practices of the ancient Greeks, were well theorised and practised in the early modern period, and hold certain significant connections with the similar crossroads traditions of many cultures. These connections have, it seems, been energised in recent times by a popular transformation myth that still speaks loudly to social groups immersed in the musical structures which emerged from early twentieth-century black cultures: blues, gospel, jazz, rhythm and blues, soul, and rock and roll, and their succeeding forms which still dominate the global music markets in the early twenty-first century. The story that offers instantaneous transformation at the crossroads to the disempowered is indeed a tempting prospect, as the next chapter shows.

Chapter 3

Music: Going Down to the Crossroads

> I went to the crossroad, fell down on my knees
> ... Asked the Lord above 'Have mercy, now save poor Bob, if you please'
> Standin' at the crossroad, tried to flag a ride
> ... Didn't nobody seem to know me, babe, everybody pass me by
> Standin' at the crossroad ...
> ... poor Bob is sinkin' down.
> Robert Johnson, 'Cross Road Blues' (1936)[1]

If there is a single narrative that captures the modern understanding of transformative crossroads magic it is the spurious fable of the selling of Robert Johnson's soul. When, in the paleoanthropology of twentieth-century rock and roll music, the biographers of the short-lived blues legend claimed that he had been down to the Dockery Plantation crossroads at midnight to sell his soul to the Devil in exchange for guitar skills, they were perhaps unwitting witnesses to the long history of myth and ritual that has been deeply associated with the transformative space of the crossroads.[2] They were not lacking in foresight, however, about the way in which such a claim would enhance their subject's credibility. The value of such a sulphurous reputation for a musician is not merely a recent phenomenon but also has historical precedents. A hundred years before Johnson (who lived 1911–38), the guitarist and violinist Niccolo Paganini (1782–1840) was considered such a suspiciously devilish virtuoso that his audiences were reputed to cross themselves before his concerts in hope of apotropaic protection from subtle demonic influence. One audience member even fled a concert after reporting seeing the Devil himself aiding Paganini's performance.[3] Going a little further back, Giuseppe Tartini (1692–1770) explained of his best-known sonata, 'The Devil's Trill' (1713), that he had 'written down the piece after waking from a particularly vivid dream of the Devil playing a violin with ferocious virtuosity', and claimed that it was 'but a shadow of what he had witnessed in the dream, for he was unable to capture on the page the Devil's full intensity'.[4] His long career was certainly not harmed by this youthful excursion into Hell. These devilish associations may in fact have added to a perception of the capacity that music has always had of conveying a kind of mystery, one hard-won perhaps through 'occulted' practice techniques, so lending the musician a certain aura of mystique or magic, and music itself a spiritual dimension.[5] Darci Sprengel describes the role of music during the 2011 Egyptian Arab Spring in combating a deep feeling of powerlessness, coming from a tradition where music is 'attributed with having its own agency' and is thought to be subject to 'forces . . . outside the artist's control', including the influence of jinn.[6] The attribution of extraordinary skills of any kind to a demonic or satanic source is found in many cultures and across time. Keith Thomas cites the eleventh-century writer William of Malmesbury's complaint that 'the common people disparaged excellence in any sphere by attributing it to demonic aid'.[7] The Faustian nature of these reputed dealings with powerful transformative forces has echoed through some of the foundational narratives of Western culture in ways that this chapter will explore.

Although Johnson is reputed never to have specifically claimed the venal crossroads exchange for himself, the lyrical content of his songs and his early and suspicious death at 27 did nothing to exorcise the compelling myth of soul-selling from his brief but increasingly closely scrutinised biography.[8] But by invoking such a metamorphic transaction with a crossroads god for the sake of Johnson's artistic mythology, his biographers inadvertently perhaps also helped to perpetuate a mythology that still lingers inside some of the cultural forms of the twenty-first century. The 1986 film *Crossroads* brought his myth to the attention of the wider rock music world with its inclusion of Steve Vai as the Devil's ringer guitarist. In the ensuing guitar battle the hero Willie Brown wins by outplaying him with a Paganini piece. Perhaps a still more evocative filmic rehearsal is found in the 'Tommy Johnson' character in the Coen Brothers' turn-of-the-millennium film *O Brother Where Art Thou* (2000). One reviewer of the mercurial London soul-singer Amy Winehouse, also 27 when she died, wonders what happened before the album *Back to Black* (2006): 'It's almost too good . . . did she sell her soul to the devil at the Golders Green and Finchley Road crossroads?'[9]

Despite Johnson's denial of the devilish business at hand, its repute still colours his musical legacy. His role in blues and rock mythology has been seminal and to some extent his influence is still felt. His life has been regarded as what Marybeth Hamilton calls 'the embodiment of the blues romance'.[10] To the blues revivalists of the mid-twentieth century and afterwards, the 'authentic' bluesman was supposed to be, as Hamilton describes, 'a tormented soul who found in his suffering a kind of transcendence: driven by demons, as legend held Johnson had been, but generating through his torment the blues' highest art'.[11] The ontological function of the artist's suffering itself, including the desperation implied by the crossroads transaction with the forces of evil, was thought to impart an essentially authentic quality to the music. In this vein, Eric Clapton referred to Johnson simply as 'the most important blues singer that ever lived'.[12]

But the story of Johnson going down to the crossroads as the 'primal voice of African-American suffering' only works in its most depoliticised form.[13] It is problematic that the romanticism that drives the mythology also serves to obscure what George Lipsitz calls the 'hard facts of life and labor in the segregated South in Johnson's day'.[14] In this context, there is a danger that this peculiarly African American experience may be appropriated without sufficiently acknowledging 'the factors that give African Americans and European Americans widely divergent opportunities and life chances', as Lipsitz says.[15] Luc Sante describes such white appropriation of Johnson's crossroads myth as a manifestation of 'colonial sentimentalism', and even worse than this, Hamilton identifies it as a kind of 'eroticisation of African-American despair'.[16] The extent to which this acquisitive aspect of the story is still important may be demonstrated by the rapper Eminem's insistence on acknowledging the African American origins of the musical forms he has exploited.[17] But however this recognition of roots functions it may not deliver authenticity in terms of either provenance or life experience.[18] Eminem has some claim to prior authentic distress, but this has not always been the case for such appropriations. After all, as Theodore Gracyk asks bluntly, 'How can a pampered, milkfaced, middle-class kid who has never had a hole in his shoe sing the blues that belong to some beat-up old black who lived his life in poverty and misery?'[19]

However, even in these circumstances, the very action of reaching after elements of the extremity that the crossroads transformation story implies still evidences a desire amongst artists for a personal authenticity – a kind of aspirational, if masochistic, longing for a certain kind of formative experience: one that might validate their artistic claim to have plumbed the human depths and accessed the 'soul', or the 'heart', or even the insistent note of loss that is often detected in Johnson's recordings. In this model, the persistence of the transformative myth suggests a continuing yearning for some kind of transcendent musical origin – even one which may perhaps still be accessed by an intense experience at a crossroads.

In Johnson's story, the Christian Devil is merely the current and most convenient placeholder for a multiplicity of possible gods who have been imagined to commune with applicants and supplicants coming down to the crossroads throughout the centuries. The derivation of Johnson's particular legendary transformational exchange is to most likely be found in the rituals of the Yoruba religion which originates in Nigeria and Benin – the geographical origins of much of his local Mississippi plantation's original slave community. The original deity involved in any such local tradition would most probably have been Eshu Elegba, the Yoruba god of the crossroads, of generative metamorphoses, of luck and misfortune, and ominously of death itself (see Figure 3.1). Considering this hypothetical crossroads ritual's supposed specificity to the traditions of the southern US, it is surprising how entirely in accord it is with crossroads rites

Figure 3.1 Eshu Elegbara statue. (Wikimedia Commons)

of magic and transformation that obtain throughout European and other global cultural traditions. These extremely widespread practices date back much further than the early modern period, into at least the early classical era, and have been more or less continuous in many places to the present day.

Yoruba and other West African cosmologies regard crossroads as sites of both danger and opportunity.[20] As we have seen, in many cultures, crossroads are thought of as places giving access to transformative powers beyond the realm of the merely physical and especially in Yoruba culture the crossroads ritual mediates this dangerous transformative power 'across physical and metaphysical worlds'.[21] Margaret Thompson Drewal explains that in Yoruba thought 'the otherworldly domain . . . coexists with the phenomenal world . . . and both human and other spirits travel back and forth between the two'.[22] Yoruba culture fosters both activity and imagination as the tools of its transformative processes.[23] Yoruba magical practice is based on the 'reflexive, progressive, transformative experience of ritual participation', and more specifically 'the transformational capacity of repetition itself'.[24] In this volatile combination of action and repetition, the principle of indeterminacy is deeply implicit and is often 'anthropomorphized as the trickster deity [Eshu] . . . the principle of unpredictability'.[25] Thompson Drewal describes the centrality of the crossroads to these transformative rituals:

> The crossroads . . . the juncture of three and sometimes four roads, is a physical representation of the intersection of the phenomenal world and the otherworld. Thus the crossroads is a prime spot to place sacrifices so that they will be taken to the otherworld . . . For similar reasons, the crossroads also figures significantly in funerals, as the point of transfer of the deceased's soul to its otherworldly domain.[26]

Here, as in many cultures, crossroads are seen as geographical trysting places giving access to transformative powers beyond the realm of the merely physical. Without assuming equivalence, there are many similarities between these functions of the crossroads that may be found in disparate times and places. Since their status as in-between places makes crossroads ideal for this sort of transaction between worlds, it may not be surprising that a common belief throughout the early modern period in England was of people 'mortgaging their souls' at the parting of the ways, in return for the hope of 'a temporary access of supernatural knowledge or power', as Thomas shows.[27] But this narrative of demonic soul-selling goes back much further into the human narrative experience than one might imagine, and is in fact a story whose extreme antiquity has not been appreciated until very recently. Sara Graça da Silva and Jamshid J. Tehrani's recent phylogenetic analyses have revealed that the common folk tale 'The Smith and the Devil', telling of a blacksmith who sells his soul to a demonic spirit in exchange for supernatural powers is probably at least 6,000 years old, making it older by far than any scripture of today's world religions.[28] Since the folk tale has been much adapted, there is no way of knowing whether the crossroads figures in its original narrative, but it is certain that the transformational exchange it describes has typically gravitated there throughout narrative history.

In this vein, a hagiographic source tells the story of how, in 538 CE, there lived in Adana in Cilicia, in present-day Turkey, an archdeacon named Theophilus, who, having been slandered and deprived of his offices, 'visited a necromancer, who led him at midnight to a place where four cross-roads met, and there conjured up Satan'; the devil then promised to reinstate him in exchange for his soul, and the priest forthwith 'signed away his soul with a pen dipped in his own blood, and abjured for ever Jesus Christ and His spotless Mother'.[29] Once reinstated, however, Theophilus cheated and applied to the Virgin for salvation from his legal satanic destiny, and then awoke to find his deed of sale returned to him, to be burned in public. After his confession before the people, he was forgiven, although confusingly he still died prematurely three days later.[30] In possibly what has become the most influential version of this basic story in the West, the sixteenth-century Faustus myth of demonic transformation that Christopher Marlowe adapted for *Dr Faustus*, it was 'toward evening, *at a crossroads*' in a forest called the Spesser Wald, near Wittemberg, that Faustus 'described certain circles with his staff . . . [and] thus in the night between nine and ten o'clock he did conjure the Devil'.[31] Just as it is conspicuously unspecified in Shakespeare's *Macbeth* that the witches meet at a crossroads on the heath, the crossroads does not figure directly in Marlowe's *Dr Faustus* either, where the protagonist makes the fatal deal in the much less dubious environment of his private study.[32] It may be mere conjecture to suggest anything more than purely dramatic reasons for doing this, but it is worth noting that the studious and respectable alchemical witchcraft of the curious humanist's study was regarded rather differently from the relatively quotidian domestic witchcraft of such a commonplace public arena as the crossroads at this time. It is possible that it is partly the social condescension involved in braving the parting of the ways that is so disturbing, and that there were those wishing to be seen as socially respectable even in their dealings with the Devil.

In the testimonies of those describing magical transactions at crossroads, especially in matters of love, revenge or the arts, a form of musical metamorphosis is often part of the deal. To the German polymath and occult writer Agrippa, given the correct ritual and a propitious time, music was itself materially transformational since it operated as an amplifier for the influence of the stars and planets. For Agrippa, music 'follows opportunely the Celestial bodies' and 'doth wonderfully allure the Celestial influence'.[33] Nanette de Jong and Barbara Lebrun refer to both the supposed divine origin of the natural sympathies and harmonies of this music of the spheres and its association with magic from the earliest times, noting that Plotinus (203–70 CE) described music as 'a form of sorcery that raises no question'.[34] In Agrippa's world, music is therefore in itself able to 'change the affections, intentions, gestures, motions, actions and dispositions of all the hearers'.[35] Agrippa also believed that it 'appeaseth the mind' or alternatively makes men mad, and possibly even cures many ills, allowing music many different transformative properties.[36]

Music could be an integral part of other magical rituals, including those of Sicilian witches' imagined fairy gatherings, and was sometimes used to bless houses in that vicinity.[37] It is also a significant element of the transaction in Lawrence Southerne's 1642 pamphlet *Fearefvll Newes from Coventry* that describes how one Thomas Holt, a 'Musitian in Coventry', having been made penurious by his nineteen children, had sold his soul to the Devil in a 'damnable contract'.[38] The pamphlet describes Holt as a phenomenal musician; one 'whom for his skill in his Art and profession few or none could compare . . . by which he gained not onely the love of many Gentlemen thereabouts; but also a competent estate to himselfe'.[39] Rather than allow this as evidence of the benefit of the musician's demonic transaction, the moralistic pamphleteer attributes the musician's sudden facility with his instrument to the blessing of God. Though this increased skill was the apparent cause of the prosperity that supposedly followed his soul-trading, it was Holt's 'infidelitie and miserable belief', Southerne says, that were 'the grand and sole ringleaders' to his damnation and so reinscribes the nature of the exchange within a specifically Christian moral hamartiology, the language of the 'fatal flaw'.[40] In this case, the musician, having been warned of the Devil's approach to claim his soul by a 'mightie and tempestuous wind . . . by reason whereof some had their houses blowne down', attempts in some desperation to write a will, but is cut short by a handsome visitor who, after some 'private conference', breaks Holt's neck, changes 'his assumed shape', and makes off into the night. Whatever the actual circumstances of Holt's murder or the moralistic and hortatory nature of the pamphlet's storyline, the essential elements of the myth are there: musicianship or other artistic wizardry expressed with a high degree of skill and subsequent prosperity associated with the fear or suspicion of some otherworldly exchange, here expressed in the devilish terms of popular contemporary theology. This tendency to see the Devil in all unusual things is borne out throughout the period in relation to the interactions of the sects and major religious groupings of the time, but also in the very trivia of everyday life in which the work of Satan provided an expedient explanation for 'strange diseases, motiveless crimes ... professional failure, a shipwreck ... a fall in a mine' or, as in this case, 'unusual success', as Thomas says.[41] The chest of gold the musician kept was also miraculously turned into dust, for which of course many explanations might be found, but the one the tract resorts to for its admonitory purposes is of course the deceptive nature of the love of money, with Judas Iscariot as the obvious exemplar.

Such imparting of musical skills by supernatural means has been a significant element of the crossroads mythology across cultures. There is an old Norwegian tradition that skill can be gained in music by 'sitting on Christmas Eve on a crossroads with a stick in each hand; these one would move like a fiddle and fiddle bow' in order to effect the charm.[42] This specificity of time and place accords with a crossroads tradition recorded in 1925, in Maryland, US, that stipulates:

> before sunrise for five mornings you take a fiddle and go into the country till you come to the end of one of the main roads or to a crossroads, on the fifth morning you will meet a man carrying a fiddle. He will teach you to play. He is the devil.[43]

The St Louis bluesman Peetie Wheatstraw, who called himself 'the Devil's Son-in-Law', is reported as claiming this for himself:

> you take your guitar and you go to where the road crosses that way, where a crossroads is ... get there just a little before 12 that night ... be playing a piece there by yourself ... A big black man will ... take your guitar and he'll tune it ... play a piece and hand it back to you. That's the way I learned to play anything I want.[44]

This tradition, however, certainly predates the blues, and C. Lee recorded the custom among communities in the southern US in the late nineteenth century, quoting one informant as claiming, 'If you take your banjo or violin to the forks of the road at midnight, Satan will teach you how to play it.'[45] The summoning elements these ritual spells have in common are the crossroads, the late night or early morning and playing the instrument as a musical offering. One account, from an informant in Ocean City, Maryland, 'starts in a cemetery and concludes at a crossroads' and insists that 'to play a banjo or a guitar or do magic tricks, you have to sell yourself to the devil'.[46] This requires that you

> go to the cemetery nine mornings and get some of the dirt and bring it back with you and put it in a little bottle, then go to some fork of the road ... and on the ninth morning there will come some rider riding at lightning speed in the form of the devil ... and when he has passed you can play any tune.[47]

Another specifies time: 'You go out there [to the forks of a road] about four o'clock, just commence dawning day, just about crack of day.'[48] Yet another informant specifies the required aid of a sacrificial rooster, adding:

> if he ain't blind, have some the young ones to knock his eye out ... You kill the rooster and eat him, but don't eat none of it yourself ... take the eye time you kill him and bury it under your step and let nobody know what you done with it ... take the drumstick an you go down to the fork of the road Sunday morning before day ... about three o'clock and when you go there, well, want to learn to play the guitar.[49]

The addition of an apotropaic threshold element to the spell is of interest here, with the rooster's eye presumably a prophylactic against the evil eye set at the back door of the home. French versions of the same sort of ritual sacrifice of white or black roosters are recorded in Puisayne, Auverne, Béarn and Gers, with variations on the ritual found also in Poland and Bavaria.[50]

In 1926, Newbell Puckett reported the particulars of a crossroads ritual for music in some detail when 'a New Orleans conjurer' described the procedure involved with making a contract with the Devil to him as follows, with an accomplished storyteller's eye for narrative specificity. Firstly, he says, you need to cut your fingernails as short as possible. Then take a bone of a black cat and go with your guitar to 'a lonely fork in the roads at midnight'. There you must 'play your best piece, thinking of and wishing for the devil all the while' and soon you will hear music, 'dim at first but growing louder and louder'; then after a while you will feel 'something tugging at your instrument' and at this point you must allow the Devil to take it but 'keep thumping along with your fingers as if you still had a guitar in your hands'. The Devil will swap instruments with you and accompany you on your guitar. Then, the conjuror concludes,

> he will seize your fingers and trim the nails until they bleed, finally taking his guitar back and returning your own. Keep on playing; do not look around. His music will become fainter and fainter as he moves away . . . You will be able to play any piece you desire on the guitar and you can do anything you want to in this world, but you have sold your eternal soul to the devil and are his in the world to come.[51]

To be clear, the promise and the metamorphic fantasy here, as in the Faustus myth, is that after this painful ritual 'you can do anything you want to in this world', and this huge claim perhaps is at the root of the continued fascination with this transaction, suggesting an almost divine power and following the logic of the mythology of the crossroads trickster god, which is, as Lewis Hyde says, a story of 'intelligence arising from appetite'.[52]

In modern Brazilian *candomblé* ceremonies, ritual music is seen as the embodiment of the magic life force and is not only a crucial element in appeasing the god-like *orixás* but is also thought to manifest their very voices. As Brian Brazeal notes, in *candomblé* ceremonies, 'music is not just an accompaniment; it is the means by which ritual work is done' via its significant 'transformative power'.[53] This is clearly also the case in many of the other crossroads transactions described above, with their common elements of performed or exchanged music, material sacrifice, and geographical and temporal specificities. It is arguable that the projection of desire onto magical intersections of time and space such as these is natural to a modern culture obsessed with instant transformations and the Faustian price of fame. This seems especially to be the case, however, where it is concerned with music, which, despite the depredations of the internet age, retains a sense of its own subversive power.

That these rituals might be perceived to involve the aid of a devil-figure may result from the fact that the Christian church has always been at best ambivalent about the power of music, and at worst has considered it literally demonic, being especially suspicious of its effects on the emotions. In terms of the so-called church 'fathers', Justin Martyr (c. 150 CE) condemned what he called 'subtle flutes that provoke people to lustful movements'; Clement of Alexandria (c. 190 CE) meanwhile declared that 'if people occupy their time with pipes, psalteries, choirs . . . and such disorderly frivolities, they become quite immodest . . . we must reject frivolous music, which weakens men's souls'; Novatian (c. 235 CE) was more specifically opposed to stringed instruments, asking 'Why should I speak of strings set vibrating with noise?' and declaring that 'even if these things were not dedicated to idols, they should not be approached and gazed upon by faithful Christians'.[54] Some of this negative construction may also draw upon the classical roots of the supposed disreputable nature of music, some of which describe music in operation for the gods of the crossroads. The first thing the trickster and crossroads god Hermes did when born, illegitimately (of Zeus and the nymph Maia), was to crawl from his mother's cave, make the first lyre from a turtle's shell and sing a song about himself.[55] Shortly after this, Hermes stole the god of music Apollo's cattle but won Apollo's forgiveness by playing the lyre he had made and giving the lyre to Apollo, exchanging it for the title Keeper of the Herds, 'reserving for himself the Shepherd's Pipes which he had invented also'.[56] Then he was appointed 'messenger of the gods and guide to Hades' with shrines appearing at the between-place of the crossroads.[57] Horace describes Hermes, the Greek Mercury and a crossroads deity himself, as both the god of 'all gainful Arts' and 'the Inventor of the Harp'.[58] Mercury plays the lute in Sambucus' emblem book of 1564 where he performs a transformative musical function.[59] In terms of the influential churchmen of later times, in the early modern period, although Martin Luther was broadly in favour of music, John Calvin was of the opinion that secular music could make (presumably) men 'effeminate in disordered delights'.[60] The Calvinist strain is addressed in Samuel Rowley's 1605 play *When You See Me You Know Me* as the music lecturer Doctor Tye declares that 'music is fit for kings, / And not for those knows not the chime of strings', and the Prince replies 'Truly I love it, yet there are a sort. / Seeming more pure than wise, that will upbraid at it, / Calling it idle, vain, and frivolous.' Tye responds, 'those that do are such / As in themselves no happy concords hold', argues that music is heavenly, and threatens those of such a Puritan mind with Hell itself, saying, 'those that gnash their teeth at music's sound / Shall make that place where music ne'er was found.'[61] With this background of fear over the material power of music, it is not surprising that by Johnson's time it was widely believed in many white conservative Christian circles that non-church music and, adding the obvious racist element, especially that made by black people, was the Devil's music. In Europe and elsewhere this discourse found fertile ground in the long tradition of mistrust for musicians (and other habitual travellers) generally.[62]

This suspicion that musicians like Johnson were in general up to no good, and might very likely be tempted towards the radical transformativity of the crossroads, has an extensive history then. One part of the background to this may be found in the nature of musicians' touring, which partook of the general wariness of settled societies towards wanderers. Misgivings on this score included the idea that such travellers might use their transitory status to spread heresy, or even, by their very peripatetic nature, the plague. Such things had also been suspected of earlier medieval travelling musicians in Europe, the Manichaean Cathar gnostic troubadours.[63] So, under Henry VIII's sovereignty, minstrelling in general, besides its potential for drawing people to Hell, was considered to be a cover for the religious dissent of 'sectaries and recusants' and one statute of his expressed the fear that 'songs and ballads were used by schismatics', as A. L. Beier has noted.[64] Beier also cites examples of musicians being prosecuted as recusants in Yorkshire in 1608 and Nottinghamshire in 1616.[65] Legislation for the prosecution of vagrancy included provision for 'many entertainers . . . wizards and unlicensed healers', an inclusion which indicates the kind of company travelling musicians were thought to keep.[66] Minstrels were also suspected to be thieves, with Robert Greene in 1592 alleging that 'music was helpful to pickpockets'; at least in one case, that of Richard Cokley in 1616, who went to a Chester fair 'to do singing, dancing and tricks', and was accused there of 'taking a purse containing £5', this was apparently true.[67] Elizabeth I's often-cited statute of 1572, reiterated in 1597, included minstrels among its 'rogues, vagabonds and sturdy beggars', while during Oliver Cromwell's Protectorate a law was enacted ordering wandering 'fiddlers and minstrels summarily to be branded'.[68] As Beier explains, minstrels could also be politically subversive, attacking unpopular people or policies, occasionally even to the point of provoking violent riots, as in 1584 when crowds numbering up to a thousand 'battled near London theatres', or in Walsall in 1610 when 'revellers led by a pipe and tabor fought all night'.[69]

The need for musicians to travel of course often historically had an economic imperative. Although the musicians known as town waits were relatively well paid as they toured other localities often on foot during the summer, the majority of those arrested as unlicensed vagrant minstrels were to some degree poor.[70] A musician called Robert Dorey 'played one day until midnight for some milkmaids near Reading in 1623, and travelled the next day before sun-up to perform for 1d at a gentleman's house'.[71] For some travellers it is poverty that forces them to musicianship in the first place, as Robert Burton complains in 1621: 'Homer himself must beg if he want means, and as by report sometimes he did "go from door to door, and sing ballads, with a company of boys about him".'[72] As the chief popular musicians of their day, ballad-singers above all were thought to be 'dishonest, immoral and seditious' and from around 1570 the word ballad itself is a pejorative term. One Methuselah Flower of Tewkesbury, was hauled into the Bridewell prison in 1642 as a rogue because he 'abused many in ill language and has not habitation' and was arrested again in 1654 in Bristol for 'singing of ballads, thereby contracting people together in a tumultuous manner'.[73] I predict a riot. Ballads were in fact banned from 1647 to 1656, and in 1648 the Provost-Marshal was 'ordered to seize singers and hawkers', while in 1655 a Devizes man was despatched to a house of correction 'for singing of ballads contrary to the statute'.[74] Whether wealthy or poor, musicians had a reputation for living dangerously and defying the authorities. The musician Nicholas Bennet was arrested in Wiltshire in 1614 for allegedly playing on Sundays.[75] Meanwhile, one other anonymous manuscript describes a musician called Michael Wise who was 'knocked on the head & kil'd downright by the Night-Watch at Salibury for giving stubborn and refractory language to them, on S Bartholmews day at night', in 1687.[76] Although 'police' brutality was much more common then, 'stubborn and refractory' language would probably not have resulted in his death if the swearer had been a respected member of the community. Church musicians for instance could be treated quite differently. According to the same document, John Taverner, organist at Cardinal Wolsey's college in Oxford, was 'cast into a prison within a deep cave under the ground of the same coll' with some of his canons for showing disturbing signs of Lutheranism. Unfortunately, this grotto was 'where the salt fish was layd, so that by the stench thereof being infected, some of them shortly after their release, died in their chamber'.[77] Taverner, however, survived the olfactory pescatorial onslaught and was exonerated since he was 'but a musician'.[78]

In the drama of the period, music of course accompanies the activities of the witches in *Macbeth*, as stage directions show: 'Music. The witches dance and then vanish, with Hecate' (IV, i, 147). Like

The Tempest's Ariel, Puck is also a metamorphic musical wanderer in *A Midsummer Night's Dream*; he is also Robin Goodfellow – a euphemism for the Devil. Some of the contemporary attitude to music may be summed up in John Milton's masque *Comus* (1634) where The Lady declares:

> This way the noise was, if mine ear be true,
> My best guide now, me thought it was the sound
> Of Riot, and ill-manag'd Merriment,
> Such as the jocund Flute, or gamesom Pipe
> Stirs up among the loose unleter'd Hinds,
> When for their teeming Flocks, and granges full
> In wanton dance they praise the bounteous *Pan*,
> And thank the gods amiss. (170–7)[79]

There is a musical element too in Thomas's argument that the contemporary perception that witches organise magical rituals in sabbath meetings may be attributed partly to 'the tendency of wandering beggars to milk other men's cows and sleep in large groups in barns and out-houses, spending the evening piping and dancing'.[80] The general sense of the illegitimacy of music in the early modern period feeds this narrative. If one already believes secular music in general to be morally dubious, even the most innocent of communal musical activities may be construed as potentially malevolent, and allied in some way with dark unseen forces. Associated in these ways with immorality and even satanic ritual, it is understandable that music's transformative abilities should arouse suspicion.

In a broad sense, the perception of the efficacy of transformative rituals in early modern England is still very much bound up with belief in the natural sympathies of certain materials, and fed by what is nervously recognised as the cutting edge of investigative knowledge in alchemical practices. Early modern witchcraft in England does not bespeak any lasting adherence to specific ancient pagan religions, or indeed any connection with literal devil-worship, evidence for either of which is severely lacking.[81] When ancient witchcraft beliefs have come into contact with perhaps more sceptical or culturally Christianised societies through colonialism, or in the case of the US, slavery, beleaguered communities may hold tightly to traditional belief systems, but these are still most often understood within the terms set by the ideology of the colonising or dominant group. Witchcraft in England may have followed much this pattern, and in any case by early modern times was not in any real sense a religion, as some modern revivalists might wish. Although there were pagan survivals in the church's liturgical customs, the fertility rites in local festivals, or even such things as wells long thought to possess magical properties, these did not usually involve a departure from the broad spectrum of Christian beliefs, practices, motifs and imagery.[82] However, although the Reformation may have led on one level to a greater scepticism of Catholic traditions that physical things could be fundamentally transformed by rituals of consecration or exorcism, this was balanced by the contemporary influence of Neoplatonism, which held that the world was 'a pulsating mass of vital influences and invisible spirits', as Thomas puts it.[83] Cosmology may also be a driver of transformation, as the *Malleus* asserts: 'men's characters are conditionally varied by the disposition of the stars' which can cause 'many variations in the humours and character of the soul'; it claims further that 'the influence of the stars is to some degree conducive to the wickedness of witches'.[84] The possibility of magical transformation, as Leonard Barkan puts it, 'whether in Ovid's work or later, is bound up with literary or religious implications that extrahuman powers are vividly alive in the universe'.[85] Here, the magic user might effect various real-world transformations of the self or another by the simple application of magical techniques, occult symbols, or invocations, and this without any theological training. As the influential occultist Roger Bacon argued in the mid-seventeenth century:

> some creatures we know have power to metamorphose and alter their objects. As the Bisilisk, who kils by sight alone. The Wolf, if he first see a man before the man see him, makes the man hoarse ... Mares in some Kingdoms impregnate by the smell of Horses ... If Plants and Animals, which are inferiour in dignity to our humane Nature, can emit, then surely may man more abundantly emit *Species*, Virtues and Colours to the alteration of external Bodies.[86]

It is therefore compelling to recognise at this time, at both a very popular level and that of the more elevated practitioners, the perceived efficacy of transformative rituals of one kind or another to produce real results, and the almost pantheistic acceptance of the structural continuity of the seen and unseen worlds that this entailed. As Bonnemaison says 'no identity exists without a space that sustains it' and it was as the meeting place of these realms that the geosymbolic crossroads was considered the prime location for transformative practices.[87]

The component of alchemical transformation in this narrative suggests connections, somewhat coincidentally, to another Robert Johnson who was also a songwriter and player of frets and strings, and a close professional associate of William Shakespeare. This earlier Johnson (1582–1633) was a virtuoso lutenist and composer of music for masques and entertainments who was attached to James I's court from 1604, and served the royal courts until his death in 1633.[88] He wrote music for the theatre, collaborating, among others, with Ben Jonson including for *Oberon, the Faery Prince*, a masque performed in 1611 and 'Have you seen the bright lily grow?' from *The Devil is an Ass* (1616). Johnson also wrote music for other dramatists including Francis Beaumont, John Fletcher, Thomas Middleton and George Chapman.[89] Between 1608 and 1617, he was also 'busily writing' for the King's Men.[90] Despite these public collaborations, like the later Robert Johnson, he is a somewhat elusive character, lacking any extant autograph collections of his own.[91] Also in keeping with his later namesake, he was a similarly seminal figure, a musical innovator who took a radical approach to matching 'disrupted textures [and] disorder to stage movements', as Daniel Albright describes it, with this Johnson also being 'especially attracted to the fantastic, the macabre, the grotesque'.[92] Albright suggests that the semantic codes involved in music 'arise through deviant behaviour, for only deviance is salient enough for the ear to register as *significant*', and that, in this context of deviant musicality, Johnson had 'the daring and composure to follow Shakespeare, Webster, and their comrades into the wilderness of much-meaning'.[93] Like his latter-day namesake then, this earlier Robert Johnson may also have had something of the allure of the deviant about him. Johnson's main career claim to fame is his composition of the original settings for some of Shakespeare's lyrics, writing at least two of the extant songs of *The Tempest*. This is of course an overtly, heavily magical play in which Ariel is the wandering spirit who sings of death and transformation.[94] The best-known of these are probably 'Where the Bee Sucks' and 'Full Fathom Five':

> Full fathom five thy father lies,
> Of his bones are coral made;
> Those are pearls that were his eyes,
> Nothing of him that doth fade
> But doth suffer a sea-change
> Into something rich and strange. (I, ii, 397–402)[95]

These narrative tendencies feed the transformative myths of the age, and *The Tempest* is of course a play in which nearly all of the dramatis personae 'undergo some sort of "sea-change"'.[96] Alongside this concern with transformative narratives, the 'tempest' is the alchemists' term for the part of the process in which the alembic is boiled to eliminate impurities and, hopefully to transform base materials into gold.[97] In this sense, the whole play takes its identity from this pseudo-magical transformative process.[98] This connection with the metamorphic function of the crossroads is more than merely oblique since alchemists were also in pursuit of what would transform them into gods: the elixir of life. In fact, their own continued transformation was included as a part of the purifying process. John S. Mebane speaks of the prominent alchemist John Dee's sense of spiritual mission in this as requiring the kind of profound personal transformation described by Pico della Mirandola in his *Oration on the Dignity of Man* (1486) and *Conclusiones* (1486).[99]

Johnson was also the composer of the music for 'Come Away Hecate' in Middleton's *The Witch* (c. 1613–16), a play that speaks of the common fantasy attached to the free wandering nature and the high-reaching aspirations of witchcraft:

> WITCHES: Come away, come away,
> Hecate, Hecate, come away.
> HECATE: I come, I come, I come, I come,
> With all the speed I may, . . .
> HECATE: I will but 'noint, and then I mount.
> *A spirit like a cat descends.*
> WITCHES: There's one comes down to fetch his dues,
> A kiss, a coll, a sip of blood, . . .
> HECATE, *going up*: Now I go, now I fly,
> Malkin my sweet spirit and I.
> Oh, what a dainty pleasure 'tis
> To ride in the air
> When the moon shines fair
> And sing, and dance, and toy, and kiss;
> Over woods, high rocks, and mountains,
> Over seas, [over misty] fountains,
> Over [steeples,] towers, and turrets,
> We fly by night, 'mongst troops of spirits.
> No ring of bells to our ears sounds,
> No howls of wolves, no yelps of hounds,
> No, not the noise of water's breach
> Or cannon's throat our height can reach. (III, iii, 50–3, 62–5, 75–90)

According to Albright, this extant tune to the crossroads goddess is 'lilting' and 'jingly': 'a clear crowd-pleaser'.[100] There was clearly no blue note here, and the lyrics tell us that after communing with the spirit metamorphosed into the likeness of a cat, these witches could 'fly by night', higher than cannon shot and the 'yelps of hounds', well out of reach of any hell hound that might be on their trail. It is perhaps interesting to consider how the accident of two Robert Johnsons in this history of crossroads magic and musical transformation adds shades of coincidence that the superstitious mind of the time, attuned and sensitised to perceive the sympathies of nature, might find suspicious.

The possibility of instant transformation is of course attractive to many, as a broader exploration may show. In a sense all magic is transformational in that it requires or requests a shift in the nature of things, and metamorphic rituals and beliefs perhaps require only a little more of the believer, since literal transformation was, as far as anyone in the early modern period knew, fundamental to the natural world, as the popularity of alchemy at the time makes plain. The spirits involved in crossroads rituals were themselves assumed to be shape-changers, as were those accompanying alchemical experiments, again as far as anyone knew. As the era's most authoritative book, the Bible makes it clear that spiritual beings like devils and angels can appear in other forms, spiritual, human or animal, and the existence of these transformative beings was hardly to be questioned.[101]

There are some complicating factors, however, and some notable dissension even at that time. All magic may be transformational, but not all transformative power is deemed to be magical to the early modern thinker. The authoritative Bacon is positive about the possibility of metamorphosis but opposes it to what he calls 'the unnecessary aspiring to Magick'.[102] Even in Ovid no metamorphic process is completely magical but is exercised in 'the real world of cosmos, society and human personality', in Barkan's understanding, while at the same time, no transformation of Ovid's is ever in itself 'completely "real", scientific, or logical'.[103] This complex dual nature seems to be reflected in the views of early modern commentators. Contemporary accounts of transformations side largely with the principle that matter may change, given certain conditions and conjunctions of physical nature and the mind. But the consensus is far from certain, especially when discussing demons, that this is not merely a matter of the power of illusion, albeit illusion caused by demons. When the writers of the *Malleus* quote St Augustine's reports of 'prestidigitatory transformations' they are sceptical of the witch Circe's ability to change 'the companions of Ulysses into beasts'; that those of Diomedes 'were changed into birds, and for a long time flew about the temple of Diomedes'; and that Praestantius' father 'had been a packhorse, and had carried corn with other animals'.[104] In John Cotta's, *The Infallible True And Assured Witch* (1624) he argues that it is 'the divell' who 'hath perswaded some foolish Sorcerers and Witches, that hee hath changed their bodies and substances, into Catts, Asses, Birds, and other creatures, which really and indeed without illusion . . . is impossible unto him to doe'.[105] This, for Cotta, is a case of the Devil usurping the function of the creator and he firmly asserts that there can be 'no reall or true matamorphosing [*sic*] of one substance or nature into another, but either by creation or generation'.[106] The *Malleus* is similarly sceptical, declaring that 'whoever believes that any creature can be changed for the better or the worse, or transformed into another kind or likeness, except by the Creator of all things, is worse than a pagan and a heretic'.[107] The writers are confident that demons 'cannot actually effect any permanent transformation in human bodies'; that is to say, no real metamorphosis, and they therefore 'refer the appearance of any such change to some dark and occult cause'.[108] For clarification, they add that 'when the body of a man is changed into the body of a beast, or a dead body is brought to life, such things only seem to happen, and are a glamour or illusion; or else the devil appears before men in an assumed body'.[109] Quoting St Thomas, they assert somewhat jarringly that 'all transmutations of bodily matters which can be effected by the forces of nature, in which the essential thing is the semen . . . can be effected by the work of devils who have acquired such semen', thereby asserting, however, that there must ultimately be a physical cause for the transformations they allow to happen.[110]

Whatever the debate among the learned, across the period the popular consensus appears to be in favour of the literal quality of such metamorphic possibilities, and this is ultimately based on the authority of the narratives of Christianity. Thomas Nashe is on the sceptical side of this in 1594 when he confesses that it is 'not to be gainsaid but the devil can transform himself into an angel of light, appear in the day as well as in the night', but qualifies this by adding that this is 'not in this subtle world of Christianity so usual as before'.[111] If he does, Nashe says, 'It is when men's minds are extraordinarily thrown down with discontent, or inly terrified with some horrible concealed murder, or other heinous crime close smothered in secret.'[112] Despite his psychological bent in this, he seems to recover his orthodoxy somewhat when he adds, 'nimble and sudden is the devil in shifting his habit; his form he can change and cog as quick as thought. What do we talk of one devil? There is not a room in any man's house but is pestered and close packed with a camp-royal of devils.'[113]

In some ways these might seem to be technical issues, since for our present purposes it is of no particular matter if any given transformation at a crossroads, either of the person visiting or the god or spirit encountered there, is regarded as authentic or illusory. The salient point here, however, is that, despite these sceptical assertions of learned occultists and commentators, the basic assumption of contemporaries is that transformations of one kind or another do in fact take place during these rituals and that the Devil is still involved one way or another. Still, writers across the period see even such relative scepticism as arrogant and irresponsible. In 1667, Joseph Glanville unflinchingly asserts (with his own emphases throughout) that 'to affirm that those *evil spirits* cannot do that which we conceit *impossible*, is boldly to stint the powers of Creatures, whose natures and faculties we know not, and to measure the *world* of *spirits* by the *narrow* rules of our own *impotent beings*'.[114] Glanville continues that 'the *Transformations* of *Witches* into the *shapes* of other *Animals* . . . is very *conceivable*', arguing alongside the current theory of foetal development that it is easy enough to conceive of how the power of the imagination can transform things 'with more ease then the *fancie* of the *Mother* can the stubborn *matter* of the *Foetus* in the womb' and adding that when witches 'feel the *hurts* in their *gross* bodies, that they receive in their *aëry vehicles*, they must be supposed to have been *really* present'.[115] In his *Michaelmas Term* (1604) Middleton's Shortyard asserts, on the side of the believers, 'no man is so impudent to deny that: spirits can change their shapes' (III, iii, 1–2). In early modern witch confessions, the Devil is often portrayed as a shape-changer. People who were tried in the East Anglian witch-scare of 1645–7 claimed that they had 'encountered the devil in the shape of "a great mouse" or a crabfish . . . a cat, a bear or a man'.[116] The accused witch Alice Kyteler's demon the 'Son of Art', who accompanied her at her crossroads ritual, would appear to her 'under various forms, sometimes as a cat, or as a hairy black dog'.[117] Petronella de Meath, one of her accomplices, said that 'with her own eyes she had seen the aforesaid demon as three shapes (*praedictus daemon tertius*), in the form of three black men (*aethiopum*) . . . and, while Petronella herself was watching, the apparition had intercourse with Alice'.[118]

When on Wednesday, 28 June 1628, Johannes Junius, the burgomaster at Bamberg, Germany, was accused of being on Haupts-moor at a witch-dance, after much torture he 'confessed' that 'a woman like a grass-maid' had come to him, who 'led him by seductive speeches to yield him to her will', and afterwards, 'changed into the form of a goat, which bleated and said, "Now you see with whom you have had to do. You must be mine or I will forthwith break your neck" ... [whereupon] the transformed spirit had seized him by the throat and demanded that he should renounce God Almighty.'[119] The combination of sex and shape-changing here is no doubt intended to appeal to the torturers' prurience, but also bespeaks a popular narrative of easy transformation in the world of demonic encounter.

In George Giffard's *A Dialogue Concerning Witches and Witchcraftes* (1593), the artificial dialogue which is the device of the piece describes a paranoia over the shape-changing potentialities of witchcraft at the time, as the speaker Samuell explains:

> when I goe but into my closes, I am afraide, for I see nowe and then a Hare; which my conscience giveth me is a witch, or some witches spirite, shee stareth so uppon me. And sometime I see an ugly weasell runne through my yard, and there is a foule great catte sometimes in my Barne, which I have no liking unto.[120]

Here, there is something almost theatrical in the way Samuell sees himself in relation to the viewer as he dwells on the feelings induced by the gaze of the creature, worrying 'shee stareth so uppon me'.[121] This sense of theatre is often present in narratives of the performance of ritual and what seems to be the dramatisation of the 'plot' of a transformation spell at the performative space of the crossroads. When Giffard's dialogue introduces a woman's cat accused of harming a man and his cattle, he sees this as an opportunity to discourse on the nature of the Devil's tactics, and conceives it as a theatrical device of sorts. The character Daniell says 'the cat is the beginner of this play' and Samuell rebukes him, saying 'Cald you it a play? It was no play to some'; Daniell replies 'Indeed the witch at last had better have wrought hard, than bene at her play. But I meane Satan did play the Jugler.'[122] The theatrical metaphor is soon abandoned by the narrative but the connection has been made – Satan's transformative tricks are devices like any in the theatre that may be used to deceive humans about the nature of reality. But in this case, God is also party to the deception. The Devil, Giffard explains, is explicitly licensed by God and 'can not turne him selfe into any likenesse unlesse God give him leave, as he doth in justice permit that so he may delude ignorant persons'.[123] God here acts as a kind of theatrical director, or author, directing Satan to perform certain theatrical sleights in order to fool the participant audience. These abstractions may be more or less the typical entanglements of people grappling with a text like the Bible riddled with conceptual inconsistencies and their own ignorance of the basic elements of reality, but they do of course have material consequences. The Devil's proverbial shiftiness is perceived in the person of the witch of the locality, and this is profoundly disturbing to the speakers, as evidenced in Daniell's wife's declaration, 'If I had but one fagot in the world, I would carry it a myle upon my shoulders to burne a witch.'[124] It is interesting how commentators on satanic transformations locate the ultimate responsibility for these acts with God and thus configure him as some kind of scheming plotter, a Machiavellian author who allows the Devil's dark work free rein in order that his own mysterious purposes might be advanced. The theatrical aspect of this transformative business seems to be compelling, and after all theatre itself is deeply metamorphic.[125]

Whether or not transformation is essentially illusory, following theatrical motifs, in terms of the major dramatists it is often constructed as a negative process. Mebane notes Ben Jonson's understanding of Renaissance occult philosophy and its 'widespread use of metamorphosis and alchemical transformation' as metaphors for human aspiration.[126] This, he argues, may be evidenced by Jonson's careful mocking 'deflation of the dreams of transformation' in the metamorphic characters of *The Alchemist* (1610).[127] Katharine Eisaman Maus agrees that Jonson equates Ovidian metamorphosis in general with vice of one kind or another.[128] For Christopher Marlowe too this appears to be the case, and Mebane notices that the clown in *Dr Faustus* who is scared of being transformed into 'a dog, or a cat, or a mouse, or a rat, or anything' (4.71–2) in fact references a complex of animal imagery suggesting that any magician who wants to 'ascend the Chain of Being toward godhead' is bound ironically to transform rather into a beast.[129] Such downward transformation is exacerbated by the fact that little enough is understood at the time about the natural alterations that happen in the case of some diseases. In 1572, Lewis Lavater described the transformations that accompany the condition of 'Licanthropia' in which the afflicted may 'leape out of their houses in the night, in all things imitating the nature of wolves, and that untill it ware day, they keep about the graves of dead men'.[130] He also describes one Baianus, who in 970 CE, by necromancy, 'chaunged himselfe into a Wolfe so often as he list, or into the likenesse of an other beast'.[131] The character of Ferdinand in Webster's *The Duchess of Malfi* (1613) exhibits this condition in a highly dramatic forum, and functions as a kind of moral exemplar of all that unbridled appetite and incestuous lust might produce. The prescient Bacon meanwhile equates metamorphosis with the transmission of disease, asserting that 'men of an evil complexion, full of contagious infirmities, as Leprosie, the Falling-sickness, spotted Feaver, bleer-eyed, or the like, infects those men in their company'. On the other side of the equation, however, he sees that 'men of a sound and wholsome complexion, especially young men, do by their very presence exhilerate and comfort others . . . [which] proceeds from their sweet natural colour, and from such *Species* and Virtues as they emit'.[132] These ideas swing both ways and thus hedge their transformative bets, but nevertheless testify to a world of transformative possibilities. With an Ovidian cheekiness, Shakespeare mocks transformative motifs mercilessly in *A Midsummer Night's Dream*, most especially in the person of Nick Bottom, the most unwilling of recipients of an Ovidian alteration. Here Puck is the transforming and transformative trickster playing his controlling games with the confused wandering young lovers, amateur actors, and the gods themselves, in the liminal madness of the wood. He gives Bottom his ass's head, and is himself a metamorph, who, after turning their friend into a human-donkey hybrid, also terrorises the rude mechanicals in the woods with his shape-changing:

> Sometime a horse I'll be, sometime a hound,
> A hog, a headless bear, sometime a fire;
> And neigh, and bark, and grunt, and roar, and burn,
> Like horse, hound, hog, bear, fire, at every turn. (III, i, 2–5)

Puck's ability to transform himself includes changing his voice, as when he leads Lysander and Demetrius astray. The anonymous tract *The mad pranks and merry jests of Robin Goodfellow* (1628) describes this same ever-changing figure thus:

> In severall shapes he'd gull the world,
> thus madly did he live.
> Sometimes a cripple he would seeme,
> sometimes a souldier brave:
> Sometimes a fox, sometimes a hare;
> brave pastimes would he have.
> Sometimes an owle he'd seeme to be,
> sometimes a skipping frog;
> Sometimes a kirne, in Irish shape, to leape ore mire or bog.[133]

In *A Midsummer Night's Dream*, he is, in one sense, the image of the Devil himself, administrating the manipulative witchy herbs of Oberon's prescription to effect the love spells which are often the subject of a journey to the crossroads. Glanville reports one of his witches saying that 'When the Devil doth any thing for her, she calls for him by the name of Robin, upon which he appears.'[134] But here it is to his own faery god Oberon that he delivers the lines about 'ghosts, wandering here and there', the 'Damnèd spirits ... That in crossways and floods have burial' (III, ii, 380–2), who in their translated state 'must for aye consort with black-browed night' (III, ii, 386) and in this he establishes the precise nature of their own statuses as wandering spirit-gods who are free of any sort of spiritual binding, the premise which makes possible the exercise of their transformative magic. The fact that Puck provides a musical accompaniment to his metamorphic manipulations fits entirely with the connections we are drawing here between music, desire and the transformative devilry of the crossroads narrative.[135]

In other plays, however, Shakespeare's dramatis personae seem consistently to equate the idea of transformation with negative experience and various kinds of significant loss. This is explicitly the case in *Timon of Athens* where Timon mocks Apemantus saying 'what a beast art thou ... that seest not thy loss in transformation!' (IV, iii, 345–7). In *Hamlet* it speaks of a loss of composure and self-knowledge, as Claudius informs Rosencrantz and Guildenstern: 'Something have you heard / Of Hamlet's transformation ... / that thus hath put him / So much from th' understanding of himself' (II, ii, 4–5, 8–9). *Henry IV, Part I* employs it as a way of describing the loss of honour in death with the Earl of Westmoreland seeing the posthumous punishment of the defeated Mortimer as a metamorphosis: 'Upon whose dead corpse there was such misuse, / Such beastly shameless transformation / ... as may not be / Without much shame retold or spoken of' (I, i, 43–6). In *Henry IV, Part 2* the word is associated with a severe loss of status from divinity to the bestial: 'From a god to a bull? A heavy descension! It was Jove's case. From a prince to a prentice? A low transformation' (II, ii, 165–7). *Troilus and Cressida* also refers to this mythical bovine transformation negatively as Thersites calls Menelaus, 'the goodly transformation of Jupiter ... the bull' and asks what form 'wit larded with malice' might turn him into:

> To an ass, were nothing – he is both ass and ox ... To be a dog, a mule, a cat, a fitchew, a toad, a lizard, an owl, a puttock, or a herring

without a roe . . . I care not to be the louse of a lazar, so I were not Menelaus! (V, i, 51–5, 57–8)

The Merry Wives of Windsor's comedic stance links transformation with the loss of dignity and social standing, as the 'cozened and beaten' Falstaff's use of the term laments: 'If it should come to the ear of the court, how I have been transformed and how my transformation hath been washed and cudgelled, they would melt me out of my fat drop by drop and liquor fishermen's boots with me' (IV, v, 88–92). There seems to be only one positive example of the term in Shakespeare's plays and even here there is some risk involved, as Antipholus of Syracuse complains to Luciana in *A Comedy of Errors*:

Against my soul's pure truth why labour you
To make it wander in an unknown field?
Are you a god? would you create me new?
Transform me then, and to your power I'll yield. (III, ii, 37–40)

In this example, the lover's soul here is dangerously vulnerable as he wanders in his unknown field towards an unknown god whose transformative power has the potential to alter his power of thought. Romantic love also drives the dramatic concord which succeeds all the discord of the lovers' confusing dealings with spiritual powers at end of *A Midsummer Night's Dream*, though this may be said to belie the emergence of another troublesome metamorphosis which the play's form hints at in the forest's transformational theatrical capacities. As a sharer in his company's prosperity, Shakespeare himself was a beneficiary of the new possibilities of meritocratic transformation. Jonson was also able to turn brick-dust to gold in the alchemy of his theatrical and social ambition in another successful meritocratic metamorphosis.

In all of these narratives of transformation, without wanting to make too much of an argument from omission it might nevertheless be notable that there is barely a mention of the infamous and auspicious location of the crossroads in Shakespeare, Jonson or almost any other dramatic writer of the time. On the contrary, it seems that besides one small mention, Shakespeare in particular avoided the crossroads all his life. It is not known how, or even whether, Jonson actually went down to the crossroads at Tyburn to receive his T-branding after his killing of Gabriel Spencer, but in any case his skills in Latin incantation were the antidote to the spell that would have bound him there as a hanged murderer in 1598, slung into one of the pits dug for the purpose as the gallows was moved around the crossroads vicinity, possibly too early in his career for his body to have been allowed removal to a less ignominious tomb. Seemingly the greatest possibility for a positive transformation, in Shakespeare's plays at least, is through abasement to romantic love and the consequent susceptibility to the very emotional manipulation that the early church fathers objected to in the experience of secular music. The fact that the pursuit of romantic love is not only the key to a positive transformative experience but also the subject of a good deal of music, and the impetus for much crossroads ritual, suggests the crucial linking role music plays as the vehicle for the transmission, and late survival, of the romantic idea of the transformative function of crossroads.

Although he must have been well aware of its general acceptance as a transformative location, the Shakespearean understanding of metamorphosis is for some reason kept well away from the idea of the crossroads. Perhaps there is something uncomfortable there, and maybe this echoes with his close association with a number of recusants who met their ends at crossroads gallows, as we shall see. Despite being fascinated with the idea of metamorphosis, the popular dramatists of the time resist depicting the most popularly settled location for this process. Maybe this arises from the difficulty of staging such a location with minimal props, but perhaps also there is a resistance to the malevolent appetite of a place which demands submission of one kind or another to the narratives of greater gods. Barkan describes the cannibalistic hunger of metamorphosis itself, and maybe this is felt keenly at the magnetic drawing together of routes where possibilities open out.[136] Burton warns against 'lust, anger, ambition, pride' and intemperate desire that causes 'incurable diseases ... hastens old age, perverts our temperature, and brings upon us sudden death' and by which 'we metamorphose ourselves and degenerate into beasts'; he argues that what 'crucifies us most, is our own folly ... our facility and proneness in yielding to several lusts, in giving way to every passion and perturbation of the mind' through which we 'transform ourselves, overthrow our constitutions, provoke God to anger, and heap upon us ... melancholy'.[137] This is best avoided.

Perhaps the one thing we do know from these transactions at the crossroads is that they will fail to deliver. Like the Faustian bargain, one famous report of a witch confession from 1681 describes an agreement with the Devil that was signally unsuccessful: 'He promised her when she made her contract with him, that she should want nothing, but ever since she hath wanted all things.'[138] This perhaps is the trick of the god at the crossroads, as Dr Faustus and others have found out: that the appetite that gives birth to transformation is in fact unlimited.[139] In the indigenous American Raven myth, the hungry trickster even goes so far as to eat itself.[140] The history of rock and roll in particular is littered with the youthful corpses of those that believed in and tried to follow Johnson's supposed path to the crossroads and beyond. In this way, the cultural in-between place of the crossroads works as one of the vacuums that nature abhors: a place perpetually hungry, for emotional content, for working performance of rituals of meaning, and for the bodies that carry those. Only the most socially or materially disempowered, or perhaps the hungriest of wanderers, is driven to the extreme measure of loitering there for long. For many musicians, their art, like the rituals of the crossroads, is born of both hopeful resistance to, and necessary acquiescence to, dominant powers of different kinds (at the intersections of commerce, censorship, fandom, or credibility, for instance). Unless one is content with powerlessness, the choice of which powers to submit to may still be the most meaningful one available, as the next chapter explores. But in this universal yearning for a meaningful transformation, or a transcendent origin, it is the music itself which remains the most potent of catalysts.

Chapter 4

Gods: Appointments with the Divine

> Where three ways meet there is a pile of stones;
> above it rises a truncated statue of a god . . .
> it must be the tomb of Mercury.
> Andrea Alciato, *Emblematum liber* or *Emblemata* (1531)[1]

Since the most ancient times, the crossroads has been viewed as a likely dwelling place not only for the spirits, magic and prophets of many cultures, but also for their gods. Both in its small local rituals and in more formulated religious practice aimed at accessing those gods, what happens at crossroads represents the outbound aspirations of an earthlocked race. Besides being the guardians, or the guards, of those spirits, the gods of the crossroads stand as agents of connection sometimes to the higher divinities and as gatekeepers to otherworlds of experience, either beyond death or otherwise somehow beyond life: the miraculous, the sublime, the instant or hard-worked conversion from one state to another. The facilitative doormen and stern concierges of the crossroads are able to open passages that lead to unusual opportunities, a word whose etymology is rooted in the Latin *porta*.[2] Proverbially of course, metaphorical doors may be opened or closed on various paths, depending on the presiding genius of the portal, and the abilities of the supplicant. The main paradox of the crossroads is that it simultaneously offers the seemingly opposed functions of opening and closing, of transformation and binding. The resolution of this divergent functionality might be found in the reciprocally metamorphic and mutually constitutive relationship between the spirits bound there, the gods encountered there and the crossroads itself.

The mediating gods of the crossroads are numerous and varied and have manifested in many countries of the world, throughout Asia,

Gods: Appointments with the Divine   85

Africa, Europe and the Americas and over at least the last two thousand years, to the present day. In looking at a selection of these, it is perhaps their functional similarities which are most striking, even when examples are separated by great gulfs of time and distance. One of those previously mentioned, on the Indian sub-continent the Hindu god Bhairava guards crossroads at the outskirts of villages where stone phalluses and eye-statues are erected to represent Bhairava as guardian of boundaries.[3] Again in Japan two crossroads deities are Chimata no kami and Dosōjin, and these are often also represented by phalluses of wood or stone, offerings of which are still made at Dosōjin shrines in the early twenty-first century (see Figure 4.1).[4] Others include Yachimata-hiko or 'eight-road-fork prince', Yachimata-hime meaning 'eight-road-fork princess', and Kunado, whose name approximates 'come-not-place': a god forbidding evil spirits to arise from the underworld. Divination was practised at their shrines.[5] Ganesha also seems to be associated with Indian crossroads, as are the Hindu goblins Rākshasas and Piśāchas.[6] These are reminiscent of Arabic Jinn, which are also found to manifest at the parting of the ways.[7] Puhvel notes some Hindu religious rituals that prescribe sacrifice at crossroads and

Figure 4.1 Dosojin shrine. (Photo: © Michael Ashkenazi, 2002)

similarly a Malawian ritual enacted there also involves sacrifices, to the god Mulungu, the creator deity in numerous Bantu cultures of Africa.[8] The term 'Mulungu' is often now used to translate the Bantu word for the Islamic and Christian Gods.[9] Puhvel documents similar rituals also in Central and South America, where the Mayans worshipped four wind gods at crossroads and offered them human sacrifices.[10] Another Indian deity associated with crossroads is Rudra, 'lord of ghosts and multiple evil powers'.[11] In passing over a crossroads, one is wise to incant the words 'adoration to Rudra who dwells at the cross-roads. Make me arrive safely.'[12] In his journey through China in the late nineteenth century, Thomas Stevens describes many buddhas that were 'presiding over the cross-roads and village entrances', wearing calico bibs significant of religious observance.[13] In Belize, El Salvador, Guatemala and Mexico, the old Mayan god of the underworld, Lord Maam, in his modern Catholic form of Saint Simon (or 'Maximon'), is worshipped as a statue seated at a crossroads, in black and red clothes and hat.[14] In Haitian Vodou, Papa Ghede is the 'eternal figure in black' who controls 'the eternal crossroads at which everyone must someday cross over'.[15] Here also, the god Kalfu controls the in-between points of the crossroads, where his ceremonies are often enacted.[16] There, Kalfu also regulates the 'gate comings and goings' of the 'malevolent spirits of the night' that cause 'the crossing of bad luck, deliberate destruction, misfortune, injustice'.[17] Crossroads are important too in Brazilian Umbanda and Quimbanda Magic, where the spirit Ogum, the orisha of warfare is also known as the 'Lord at the centre of the crossroads'.[18] Also in the Brazilian context, they feature in *Santeria* mythology as the place where offerings are made to the angelic orishas and of manifestation for the gods named Exus. These in turn are related to the most important and popular modern-day crossroads deity whose chief African and diasporic African names are Legba, Elegba, Elegbara, Ellegua, Elewa, Eshu, Exu, Nbumba Nzila, and Pomba Gira.

In many cultures of the African diaspora, Legba is the god who presents opportunities, opens the way, and gives wisdom and insight. He lives at the crossroads, which Lewis Hyde identifies as 'the classic focal point of true coincidence'.[19] As described earlier, this is most likely to be the god who is at the heart of the blues legends of soul-selling at crossroads, and whose roots are ancient and widespread.[20] In his *Santeria and the Orisha of the Crossroads*, Baba Raul Canizares argues that Eshu and Legba are derived from the same African god, despite their differing attributes in various cultures. Showing the breadth of the spectrum of belief around this deity, he explains that in Haitian

Vodou, Papa Legba is considered closest to the Christian Saint Peter, whereas in Brazilian Quimbanda, Exu is more likely to be associated with 'demonic entities such as Lucifer, clad in Mephistophelean attire and bearing a trident'.[21] In Haiti, he is known also as the old man who controls 'the cardinal points of the crossroads' and 'the crossing over from one world to the other' and is the god who is able to make contact between 'the worlds of spirit and of flesh' as Jan Chatland describes.[22] He is not only the god of destiny but also delivers the messages of the gods and interprets their will to humans.[23] As the principal doorkeeper god, Legba rules over every road and conduit in the corporeal and spiritual spheres and is thus the first to be called in any ceremony, where foods are offered to him 'so that he will open the gates to the spirit world' and allow them connect with other forces.[24] It is at the crossroads that he receives these magical offerings.[25] Since he is the god of every parting of the way, Vodouists believe that through Legba they can access all the various forces of the universe.[26] But also his concerns may be highly practical, of the usual magical kind, in helping with things like the seduction of an initially reluctant significant other.[27] In cultures including those belonging to Benin, Nigeria and Togo, Legba is known as a trickster deity.[28] He is typically depicted there either as a child or an old man whose clothes, jewellery and candles are red and black, and his cement head shrine is used to contact spirits for Obi and Diloggun divination.[29] To the Yoruba people, Eshu Elegba is universally recognised as 'responsible for all troubles among men, and between men and gods'; since he is regarded by them as a 'homeless wandering spirit' as Joan Westcott expresses, he might well find his home at the crossroads.[30] The similarities between Yoruba and ancient Greek mythologies has led to the designation of the Yoruba as the Hellenes of Africa, and Westcott has argued cogently of the connection between Eshu-Elegba and the Greek god Hermes, whose Roman form is of course Mercury and whose mythology is also intertwined with European narratives of crossroads encounter and transformation.[31]

These traditions suggest connections with possibly even older rites of ancient Rome relating to the gods called Lares, who were worshiped as crossroads deities in early times and whose reputation persisted into the early modern period. In the chapter of Reginald Scot's *The Discoverie of Witchcraft* (1584) entitled 'That the Idols or Gods of the Gentiles are Devils', Lares are identified as spirits that 'trouble private houses, and are set to oversee Cross-wayes and Cities'.[32] These were not of course originally devils in their Roman contexts; the Lares Compitales, or Lares of the Crossroads were revered at a yearly agricultural festival called simply Ludi Compitales or Crossroads Festival. Lares may possibly have originally been the deified spirits of celebrated ancestors, but since they were often perceived as protectors of field boundaries Puhvel speculates that they may have originated as field spirits that, as guardians of important property boundaries, 'came to be associated with crossroads since boundary and road often coincided'.[33] It is possible of course that they might have been both. In John Bell's 1790 dictionary of the divinities he speculates on their origin, describing the 'lararium' of Roman houses, 'where were deposited the images of their domestic gods, Lares, and statues of their ancestors'.[34] Bell cites Tertullian's theory that the Roman Lares arose from 'the ancient practice of interring the dead in their houses, whence the credulous supposed that their souls continued there also, and proceeded to pay them divine honours', noting that 'afterwards burying in cross-roads, the Lares might, for a similar reason, have been regarded as gods of them'. Like Hecate, their symbol was a dog, which Bell sees as denoting 'their fidelity . . . in preserving and watching over the places allotted to their charge'. He recounts that although the Romans at first sacrificed young boys to the Lares, this was later altered to offerings of 'wine, incense, heads of poppies, an hog, a bandage of wool, and images of straw . . . violet, myrtle, and rosemary'.[35] Aside from their local uses, these gods had a much wider symbolic function, and Bell notes that their oversight as the keepers of the highways meant that they 'did not only watch for the preservation of private men, but also for the safety of the empire'.[36]

One talented crossroads god was Mercury, the Greek Hermes, who was supposed the inventor of the harp and of wrestling, the patron of all gainful arts, and things found by chance.[37] He often acted as a messenger between the gods and humankind and, as the god of thieves, he stole various items from his fellow gods. Hermes was at first the god of sheep and cows, which led to him being god of agricultural wealth and, in turn, of commerce. As such, it was his job to oversee the roads along which that commerce was undertaken. Hence he was worshiped at crossroads all over the Hellenistic world at a cairn or 'herm' like that in *The Odyssey* called the 'Mound of Hermes'.[38] Here also you would leave a food offering, or at least contribute a stone to the cairn, a tradition with cairns that survives into the present. Barbara C. Bowen sees the origination of the god's name from the other side, as perhaps deriving from both his function as guardian god of roads and from 'the stoneheaps that marked their boundaries'.[39] In the first printed emblem book, Andrea Alciato's *Emblematum liber* or *Emblemata* (1531), there is an emblem of Mercury emerging from a roadside cairn at a three-way crossroads (see Figure 4.2) and this is subscribed with

Figure 4.2 Woodcut – Mercury cairn. (Andrea Alciato, *Emblematum liber*, Augsberg, 1531)

an accompanying Latin epigram which may be translated as 'Where three ways meet there is a pile of stones; above it rises a truncated statue of a god ... the tomb of Mercury.'[40] Borlase notes Xenophon's description of the 'erected Symbols of the God Mercury' which consisted of 'three Stones; two large Stones were pitch'd on end, over which another Stone was laid which covered the rest, bearing with its middle upon the Stones underneath' and here he says 'It was a piece of Religion among the Heathens to throw certain other small Stones, as a kind of Offering to the Idol.'[41] The Greek geographer Strabo, in his travels through Egypt in the first century BCE describes several such stone-heaps which consisted of 'three circular Stones piled on one the other, the largest underneath, and 12 feet diameter; the other two smaller in proportion, but the smallest exceeding six feet diameter', calling them 'Hermaea', since to him they brought to mind 'the Heaps near the Highways erected to the honour of Mercury'.[42] The use of cairns in religious practice and worship has resonances in various cultures, and is evident in communities from the traditional inhabitants of the Scottish Isles to the Māori of Aotearoa New Zealand.[43] For historic Māori, the *tuahu*, 'a heap of stones which had been made *tapu*' was 'the greatest *karakia* place', that is the place for 'an address to the gods in a regular form . . . a sort of charm or spell'.[44] The renowned Māori rangatira or elder Teone Taare Tikao, interviewed before his death in 1927, affirmed that 'no other spot near a village was so sacred'.[45]

In his homily *On the False Gods* (c. 996–7 CE) the English monk Ælfric, later Abbot of Eynsham in Oxfordshire, describes this god as 'a man called Mercury in his life' who was 'very full of crime and treacherous in his deeds and also loved stealing and dishonesty', asserting that the heathens made him a god and 'æt wega gelætum him lac offrodan', that is made offerings to him at crossroads', and adding 'he is called Óthin . . . in Danish'.[46] The Old Norse *Óðinn* is equivalent to Old English *Woden*, and Ælfric's interest in this is no doubt local to the politico-religious issues of the recently unified England of his time.[47] Christopher P. Jones sees an influence for Ælfric's concern over Mercury in a late sixth-century sermon by the Gallaecian monk Martin of Braga condemning Christians for continuing pagan practices, expressing concern with how converts who have renounced 'the devil, his angels, his worshipers and his evil deeds', revert to worshiping him. Specifically, Martin asks, 'lighting candles . . . at cross-roads – what is that if not worship of the Devil?'[48] This is an early example of the deliberate association of crossroads gods with the demons and devils of the coming dominant faith.

Since Mercury-Hermes was revered at the crossroads as 'an averter of evil', however, this late imposition was not always easy to maintain.[49] Subsequent writers in the early modern period took the contrary stance, that Mercury shows us the way at the crossroads, and tended to see this rather as an anticipation of messianic guidance. Throughout this later era Mercury is depicted at the crossroads in the work of various emblematists, where he is pictured presiding over beneficial literature and hard work to 'redress the defects of nature' and prove that 'God must show us the right way.'[50] Bowen paraphrases a French emblem book of 1638 which explains that 'Since Mercury was the messenger of the gods, this Mercury must mean either Holy Scripture, or the Prophets and Holy Doctors who interpret it for us.' This concludes piously that 'We all need a Mercury, that is a guide, to help us through life, so we must take Christ as our Mercury.'[51] Bowen also notes similarities in this to the moralistic trope of Hercules at the crossroads.[52]

In his 1767 enquiry into improving public roads in England, Henry Sacheverell Homer praised the Appian Way to Rome, which he noted was 'adorned with terminal Statues of Mercury, Apollo, Bacchus, Diana, Ceres, and Hercules' which were set 'at Cross-Roads and Boundaries'.[53] At one time, the Roman roads of Britain will have echoed this more magnificent example in their own crossroads worship at the frontiers of the Empire. As the most northerly imperial outpost, the UK offers plentiful archaeological evidence of Roman plinths dedicated to crossroads gods and the trivii, and it is apparent that there were still traces of such structures extant until relatively modern times.[54] Some of these may have been adapted from earlier markers by the ever-practical Romans, who might inscribe such pillars with the current emperor's name, and sometimes the distance to the next town. There were many Roman inscriptions on plinths to both Mercury and Diana in Britain: to Mercury at Colchester, Leicester, Lincoln, Carlisle, Chesterholm, Birrens, York, Castlecary, Corbridge, Wallsend and Falsa; and to Diana at Bath, Caerleon, Corbridge, Risingham, Newstead and Auchendowy.[55] In Aldborough, Yorkshire, until recent times there was a stone-carved representation of Mercury still sited at a crossroads, a historical artefact which now rests within the nearby parish church of St Andrews.

Here and elsewhere, Mercury is often pictured alongside a cock for a sacrifice, and once in these above examples he is depicted beside a man sacrificing to him at an altar. In this case he suspends what looks like a purse or a bottle over the man's head and this seems to suggest a speedy answer of blessing or favour of some kind.[56] This may imply that supplication to Mercury at a crossroads was considered particularly effective. At the most basic level, as S. I. Johnston notes, 'herms . . . erected at crossroads and other liminal points . . . undoubtedly served much the same function as Hekate and *hekataia* did', which was primarily to offer guidance on a particular path.[57] Alciato's *Emblematum liber*'s subscription to the picture of Mercury takes this theme up for the sixteenth century as it continues, 'Oh traveller, hang up garlands to the god so that he may show you the right way. We are all at the crossroads, and in this path of life we err, unless the god himself shows us the way.'[58] As Johnston suggests, his 'familiar portrayal as a god of travellers' is linked to his reputation as 'a god who aided during transition and at liminal points'.[59] Besides crossroads, Mercury has at times been associated with other forms of liminality, as Maggie Kilgour sees for instance in John Selden's notes to *Poly-Olbion* (1612), where he associates Mercury with the etymology of the word 'Marches', the dubious and dangerous border area between England and Wales.[60]

In other emblems contemporary with Alciato's, Mercury is pretty unambiguously depicted as the patron of education, which is another form of transition and transformation.[61] Of all his attributes and patronages, the association with significant transformation is the one that persists most strongly. The alchemists of the early modern period may have been somewhat responsible for this continuation in their obsession with the substance that bears his name. In a Bodleian manuscript, the alchemist and physician Simon Forman, a contemporary of Shakespeare, describes mercury as being unsurprisingly mercurial: it is 'the hottest the coldest, a true healer, a wicked murtherer, a precious medicine, a deadly poyson'; it is, he says, 'a worthy medicine of true artists'.[62] It is interesting how the alchemical crosses over into artistic narratives of transformation in this way. With reference to another significant three-way crossroads of a kind, the trivium of the liberal arts: grammar, logic and rhetoric, Bowen describes Mercury reigning over these pursuits.[63] In Ben Jonson's masque *Mercury Vindicated From the Alchemists at Court* (1615), Jonson plays with the idea of mercury as both the transformative element without which the alchemical work cannot be performed and as a metaphor for social transformation.[64] Here courtiers are satirised for their own particular alchemy: the attempt to make new men out of old (this masque was possibly a vehicle for the promotion of the desperately unpopular Duke of Buckingham, George Villiers, as a rival for Robert Carr in the king's affections and thus in courtly influence).[65] In Jonson's commendatory poem to the 1623 Shakespeare Folio, 'To the Memory of My Beloved Master William Shakspeare, and What He Hath Left Us', Jonson plays with the image further, suggesting that Shakespeare came 'like a Mercury to charm!', and treads the metaphor of the roads when he protests 'these ways / Were not the paths I meant unto thy praise'. For Jonson, Shakespeare is a restless spirit: 'Soul of the age! / . . . My Shakspeare rise! . . . / Thou art a monument without a tomb, / And art alive still, while thy book doth live', and an influencing star:

> I see thee in the hemisphere
> Advanced, and made a constellation there!
> Shine forth, thou star of poets, and with rage,
> Or influence, chide, or cheer the drooping stage,
> Which, since thy flight from hence, hath mourned like night,
> And despairs day, but for thy volume's light.[66]

For Shakespeare, his own associations with Mercury tend to centre around the idea of speed, as his mercurial Mercutio describes the folkloric Queen Mab driving her chariot of dreams and desires across the bodies of sleepers as she 'gallops night by night / Through lovers' brains' (I, iv, 70–1) causing her victims to dream of their particular desires. As ever, the narratives of the crossroads seemed to haunt rather than manifest in the minds of the dramatists.

Mercury is one of a number of deities who act as mischievous troublemakers, 'simultaneously attempting to help and hinder', as Joseph Maurone says, the so-named tricksters who are most often found 'at boundaries or crossroads, sometimes navigating them, sometimes creating them'.[67] The trickster is an unpredictable creative deity, described by Farris Thompson as 'the ultimate master of potentiality'.[68] Perhaps because of these factors, this figure has had a troubled narrative history in the West that sees people 'mortgaging their souls' at crossroads in return for 'a temporary access of supernatural knowledge or power'.[69] As Thomas describes, this produces 'excellent cautionary tales, revealing Satan as a trickster'.[70] In search of the deep structures of the psyche, Carl Jung conceived of the trickster archetype 'Mercurius' as consisting of 'all conceivable opposites'; he is 'the process by which the lower and material is transformed into the higher and spiritual, and vice versa', and he is also 'the devil, a redeeming psychopomp, an evasive trickster, and God's reflection in physical nature'.[71] This attempt at assimilation or appropriation mirrors the traditional Christian response to the trickster gods. In modern Yoruba language Bibles, Eshu and Legba have been disingenuously recast as the Devil just as the new Christian context of the Norse mythos in the thirteenth century demanded a similar misinterpretation of the trickster god Loki.[72] The obvious desire for a simple duality leads to the bastardisation of relatively complex divine characters. The invocation and imposition of Satan and the Devil here is at best misleading: the trickster is not evil or immoral but resolutely amoral.[73]

Jung's argument is that the figure of Mercurius 'appeared in European thought to compensate for an overpurified Christ'.[74] In line with Milton's Satan, trickster mythology seems to persist as a story of 'intelligence arising from appetite' as Hyde says, and the trickster typically operates through 'creative fabulation, feigning, and fibbing'.[75] In his role as the primary mediator at the crossroads, the god Legba often works his transformations 'by means of a lie that is really a truth, a deception that is in fact a revelation'.[76] This is of course the role of the artist, and the nature especially of the writer of fiction. In Vladímir Propp's 'Misfortune or Lack' model of narrative analysis 'the mischief-maker and thief is one of the prime movers';

as the 'plotter of plots, he gets the story moving and it comes to an end only when he and his mischief have been dealt with'.[77] As Shakespeare's Touchstone says, 'the truest poetry is the most feigning' (*As You Like It*, III, iii, 15). Such duality again suits the dweller at the crossroads.

Alongside Mercury, the other crossroads god revered in Roman Britain and throughout Europe was Hecate, the Roman version of whom was Trivia, or the 'Diana of the Crossroads'.[78] Her name may also instance the feminine form of one of Apollo's titles: 'the far-darter'.[79] Though specific traditions vary, Hecate was widely seen as part of a composite divinity, almost but not quite a trinity, that manifested in three forms, as Northrop Frye describes, 'one in heaven, where she was the goddess of the moon, and was called Phoebe or Cynthia or Luna; one on earth, where she was Diana, the virgin huntress of the forest . . . and one below the earth, where she was the witch-goddess Hecate'.[80] These locations and names sometimes vary, but her tripartite nature persists. In magical incantations, women are often protected by female nocturnal divinities like the moon, Diana, or 'the terrifying crossroads figure of Hecate' in relation to whom, 'witches possessed a power of coercion and . . . conjuration' as Bengt Ankarloo and Gustav Henningsen describe.[81] Richard Linche's *The fountaine of ancient fiction* (1599) recounts how, 'in Arcadia was a Statue made of Diana . . . Romanes they did commonly sacrifice a Hind vnto her, adorning their holy sanctuaries and temples with the hornes thereof'; he continues 'for the description of the Moone as she is Diana, who was oftentimes also among the auncients called Triuia, and depictured with three heads, which indeed rather belongeth vnto her as Hecate'.[82] William Harrison notes her tripleness: 'as trivia or triformis (threefold), she is also identified with Diana and Luna . . . and rules over sky, earth, and underworld'.[83] Bell meanwhile notes that in Virgil's *Aeneid* she is 'supreme both in heaven and hell' (VI.242) and that the Greeks connected her with Proserpine, the Earth and Death.[84] In Hades, he continues, she was 'Prytania of the dead, or the Invincible Queen . . . She had three bodies and three heads, those of a lioness, a bitch, and a mare.'[85] Her tripleness is of substance or manifestation as well as being an emblem of the tripleness of crossroads on their horizontal axis and a representation of the planes on the vertical.

Her statues were sometimes situated in front of the doors of houses, while others 'were erected to her in public ways, and in little cells' as Bell notes.[86] Aristophanes also indicates that such hekataia – shrines or statues of Hecate – were erected at doors or gates and confirms their association with liminal places.⁸⁷ Hecate was also known as λιμενοσκόπος (limenoskopos), literally, the watcher of the harbour, the place of transition between the land and the sea.⁸⁸ Most often, however, her shrines were found where three ways met. Plutarch, Hesychius and Harpocration specifically mention that hekataia were situated at crossroads. Philemon Holland's 1609 translation of Marcellinus describes how Hecate-Diana was called Trivia 'because she was President over the crosse waies; whereupon she is said to have three faces, and to looke three wayes'.⁸⁹ Her columns' three faces extended her protective and guiding presence along the several ways she faced. Pausanias attributes Alcamenes with creating the first statue of Hecate in c. 450 BCE, giving her 'three faces and three bodies, back to back' and placing in her six hands 'a sword, poniards, whips, cords, torches, a crown of laurel, and a key', as Robert Graves cites.⁹⁰ She sometimes also wears a dragon on her head, and at her feet there is often 'a dog, whose figure she assumes'.⁹¹ John Roberts describes how 'representations of Hecate in art . . . are either single-faced or three-faced'.⁹² After c. 430 BCE, she is often shown 'as a standing female figure with three faces or bodies, each corresponding to one of the crossing roads'.⁹³ According to Stow's Survey of London, as late as 1603 the cross at Westcheape boasted its own statue of Diana.⁹⁴ In *All's Well that Ends Well*, Bertram refers to the character Diana as 'Fontibell' (IV, ii, 1), a bawdy reference to her having good sexual organs but one that also references a Diana statue at a London fountain.⁹⁵

The obvious appeal of the crossroads may be found in its function as a reification of the hopes and aspirations of a human life predicated on movement, but in every culture this is couched in myth. In Hecate's case, one Greek tradition tells that she was abandoned to the elements at the crossroads by her mother Pheraea, the daughter of Aeolus who controls the winds, and hence crossroads were consecrated to her.⁹⁶ Another possibility is that Hecate becomes progressively associated with crossroads through their pre-existing association with ghosts, of whom Hecate was supposed to be in charge and whom she could be persuaded to influence in the favour of the supplicant through the offering of food in a 'Hecate's Supper', including 'cakes set around with candles, fish, eggs, [and] honey'.⁹⁷

A particularly active god in the business of human interaction, Hecate seems always to be busy influencing and haunting the human world throughout medieval and early modern Europe. It was believed that she would appear at the dead of night, at crossroads, tombs and crime scenes, accompanied by her infernal dogpack.⁹⁸ A fragment of

Greek tragedy offers advice 'if a night-time vision should frighten you, or you have received a visit from chthonic Hekate's troop'.[99] Like Legba, her characteristics and powers were many and varied, and according to Hesiod her influence extended 'over the heaven as well as over the earth and the sea'.[100] In 1599, Richard Linche asserts that,

> her vertues and effects are powerfull and working, not onely in the heauens where shee is called Luna, and on the earth where shee is knowne by the name of Diana, but also extend down euen to the bowels of Erebus, where shee is called Hecate and Proserpina, where it is supposed shee remaineth during the time of her lights absence from the worlds view and illustrement.[101]

She presided over purifications and expiations, sent demons to torture people and had the ability 'to give or to withhold any gift'.[102] She granted political power, victory in battle and athletic competition. Bell describes how she 'sits by kings whilst administering of justice, and hears the prayers of horsemen, hunters, and sailors ... is the dispenser of riches, and the augmenter or diminisher of flocks'.[103] Her crossroads situation gave her the broad ability to guide people 'through liminal points and during transitions of many types'.[104] Linche describes her as 'she that had the guard and keeping of all crosse waies, and such lanes as in the end concurred and conioined themselues in one, and for that cause [the ancients] depictured her with three heads', and he quotes Ovid as saying:

> If in thy trauels thou doe misse thy way,
> Doubtfull and wauering how to guide thy paces,
> Enquire what Hecate to that will say,
> Who for three seuerall waies hath seuerall faces,
> Inuoke her aid, and she will guide thy feet,
> Which alwaies after the true path shall keepe.[105]

Given this role in general guidance, she was worshiped also as the guide of newborn babies into the world, and similarly of souls to the land of the dead.[106] The Orphic Hymn to her describes her as 'mystery-raving with the souls of the dead'.[107]

This sense of activity is clearly felt in early Christian writings about the gods with which the new religion was competing. In his critique of deities other than his own, Eusebius of Caesarea taught the early Christian church how pagan gods were able to give information to worshippers about what sort of things they were pleased with or compelled by, 'what one ought to sacrifice, and what day to avoid, and what sort of figure should be given to their statues, and in what shapes they themselves appear, and in what kind of places they abide'.[108] Eusebius concludes of course that 'of all the things whereby men thus honour them there is not one which they were not taught by the daemons themselves' and then goes on to quote Hecate herself doing exactly this by specifying her own forms of worship:

> My image purify, as I shall show:
> Of wild rue form the frame, and deck it o'er
> With lizards such as run about the house;
> These mix with resin, myrrh, and frankincense,
> Pound all together in the open air
> Under the crescent moon . . .
> Then to my image offer many a prayer,
> And in thy sleep thou shalt behold me nigh.[109]

The direct action and response suggested here are portrayed perhaps with involuntary relish for the corporeal nature of the transaction. In the course of his disapprobrium, Eusebius quotes verses by the oracle of Apollo at Branchidae, in the voice of the interlocutor Porphyry: 'What need of thine, by spells that bind the gods, / Calls Hecate from swiftest ether down?' and continues:

> Some from their lofty home above the sky
> Down through mid air with Harpies swift descending
> Bow to the mystic spells that bind the gods,
> And rushing swiftly down to Deo's earth
> Bring messages to man of things to come.[110]

The proud god he depicts then asks, 'What god loves not this pedestal, whereon / I weave the tangled web of human fates?'[111] This is a god who loves her job and gets involved. In Christian discourses around paganism of course the figure of the witch often arises, and though the figure of Hecate-Diana may seem to offer protection, the association can be dangerous.[112] In the ninth-century *Canon Episcopi*, the Benedictine Abbot Regino of Prum warns priests to preach against the idea that 'certain women, perverted and dedicated to Satan, seduced by diabolical fantasies and deceits, believe and profess that they ride at night-time with Diana, goddess of the pagans . . . traversing immense spaces and obeying Diana's orders'.[113] Meanwhile, the *Malleus* describes 'certain wicked crones who believe and profess that in the night-time they ride abroad with Diana, the heathen goddess... and an innumerable host of women, upon certain beasts, and that in a silent covey at the dead of night they pass over immense distances'.[114] This idea of the marauding gods of the sky contending with or including humans in their anti-gravitational travel in the clouds is what came to be known as 'the wild hunt', and is one of the fantasies of the age. Alan Bernstein describes how such ghostly companies were thought to 'frequent the well-travelled and polluted roads'.[115] The *Malleus* also notes the transformational aspect of this encounter, that 'they declare that they have the power to change human beings for better or for worse, ay, even to turn them into some other semblance or shape', concluding that 'concerning such women I answer according to the decrees of the Council of Alexandria, that the minds of the faithful are disordered by such fantasies owing to the inspiration of no good spirit but of the devil'.[116]

Through the early modern period, it is apparent that the categories of 'god' and 'spirit' must be regarded as fluid (it was possible for Scot to state that 'Quintus Sertorius had Diana her self for his familiar').[117] Since the Bible makes it clear that non-Christian gods are demons, it should follow that their places and forms of worship must also be demonic.[118] The evidence here, however, seems to suggest something more benign. Francis Rous's, *Seaven books of the Attick antiquities* (1654) describes Hecate as having been worshipped 'in triviis, where three ways met, supposed to be the Moone in Heaven, Diana on earth, and Hecate below'; therefore as partly a lunar goddess, propitiatory offerings were taken to the images of Hecate at the full moon.[119] Some placed garlic on her cairns at crossroads, for apotropaic protection.[120] To her, Rous says, it was principally 'the richer sort' who 'every new Moone made a feast in the crosse wayes setting bread & other provision, which the poore greedily fed on, and were so ravinous... that they snacht it, before it could be laid downe'.[121] Bell tells us that this ceremony was named *roxas*, and that 'everything practised in it was a kind of expiation'.[122] Earlier historical authors and commentators like Demosthenes, Aristophanes, Apollodorus and Plutarch, confirm that foods were sent to crossroads hekataia at this time.[123] Bell confirms Rous's assertion that, although it was Hecate who was supposed to consume the bread, eggs and other foodstuffs, 'it was well known that they served as food for the indigent'.[124] He adds how Lucian 'represents a cynic as devouring with avidity these several kinds of food, puppies perhaps excepted, which were included with the rest'.[125]

It is apparent also, however, that dogs were sacrificed to Hecate, and in Rome, 'their entrails were employed in purifications to her honour', as Ovid describes 'To Trivia Queen infernal saw my eyes / Entrails of dogs become a sacrifice / Crackling within the flames of hallow'd fire'.[126] In his *King Jesus*, Robert Graves sees Hecate as one expression of 'the Great Goddess who inspires the oracles'; she, he says, is also a dog,

> both because of her promiscuity in love and because she is an eater of corpses . . . as lovely Isis, or Astarte, her initiates wear dog-masks, and . . . as deathly Hecate . . . dogs are sacrificed where three roads meet. The Dog-star shines in the most pestilent season of the year. And dogs have always guarded the land of the dead for the Great Goddess. Witness Cerberus, and Egyptian Anubis, guardian of the Western Paradise.[127]

Graves's Romantic syncretism may be an oversimplification, but it nevertheless captures something of the universality of these mythological divinities and perhaps also something of the reason for the ubiquity of the tropes and functions they embody in many cultures worldwide. This testifies to a cultural influence perpetuated not merely in the shrines and temples of the ancient world, but in the continuing desire for meaningful spiritual encounter that we may read in Western literature from the early modern period onwards.

In Arthur Golding's influential 1567 translation of Ovid's *Metamorphoses,* the witch Medea invokes the powers of Hecate when the returned Jason, grieving his father's incapacity due to age, asks her to 'take from my life some years that I should live / and add them to my father's ending days'. Medea refuses the exchange but calls on Hecate to extend Aeson's life, 'Oh grant the power, / great goddess of the triple form, that I / may fail not to accomplish this great deed!' As she continues the interaction, the poem makes further references to Hecate's three-ness, witchcraft herbal practices, the walking dead and the possibility of transformation, all of which tropes are associated with the crossroads:

> Three nights were wanting for the moon to join
>   her circling horns and form a perfect orb.
>   When these were passed,
>   . . . Through the still night
> alone, Medea stole forth from the house
> with feet bare, and in flowing garment clothed

> ... Now thrice around she paces, and three times
> besprinkles her long hair with water dipt
> from crystal streams, which having done
> she kneels a moment on the cold, bare ground,
> and screaming three times calls upon the Night, –
> ... O Hecate! grave three-faced queen of these
> charms of enchanters and enchanters, arts!
> O fruitful Earth, giver of potent herbs!
> ... from her granite tombs
> the liberated ghosts arise as Earth
> astonished groans!
> ... With 'ceaseless diligence in quest of charms'.
> ... she observed the herbs by Ossa born,
> the weeds on lofty Pelion, [and]
> ... plucked the needed roots
> ... a secret grass, from fair Euboean fields
> life-giving virtues in their waving blades,
> as yet unknown for transformation wrought.[128]

As Medea supplicates Hecate here, we can assume that when she kneels it is most likely upon the 'the cold, bare ground' of a crossroads. The details of this passage – the repetition of 'three', the 'needed roots', the 'transformation wrought' – bear significant resemblance to the crossroads rituals described earlier in this book and the aspirations of their performers.[129] Hecate appears also in Spenser's religious and political fantasy of 1590, *Faerie Queene*, where he links her with Proserpina, Queen of Hades, and references 'the dreaded name / Of Hecate' (1.1.43) when Archimago's sprite uses her as a threat to Morpheus.[130] Spenser's text also associates her with Heaven and Hell.[131] She attains the 'Great power of Jove, and high authority' after the victory over the Titans, when into her 'almighty hand / He plac't all rule and principality, / To be by her disposed diversly, / To Gods, and men, as she them list divide (7.6.3-7).[132] In this Spenser follows Hesiod, seeing Hecate as a personification of fate or divine will.[133]

In Shakespeare's employment of the goddess, Lear's boorish invocation of 'The mysteries of Hecate and the night' (I, i, 111) in his rejection of Cordelia, and Lord Talbot's sexist metaphor of 'railing Hecate' (III, ii, 63) for the challenging French peasant Joan Puzel in *Henry VI, Part I* show two sides of the writer's understanding of the goddess in question. Principally, however, the mention of Hecate evokes the trials and manipulations found in *Macbeth*. When Macbeth sees his 'dagger of the mind, a false creation', he mentions her as context when he muses on the bloody deed, declaring:

> Now o'er the one half-world
> Nature seems dead, and wicked dreams abuse
> The curtain'd sleep; Witchcraft celebrates
> Pale Hecate's off'rings, and wither'd Murder,
> ... towards his design
> Moves like a ghost. (II, i, 49–52, 55–6)

Macbeth associates her with the intent to murder again as he introduces her allusively for a second time to determine that, 'ere to black Hecate's summons / The shard-born beetle, with his drowsy hums, / Hath rung Night's yawning peal there shall be done / A deed of dreadful note' (III, ii, 41–4). Primarily, Hecate is of course the goddess of *Macbeth*'s three Weird Sisters. We may presume that Macbeth and Banquo are riding on a road or ancient trod of some kind across the heath when they come across the witches *in situ*, prophetically primed to receive them. For the practical reason that the implied native heather is treacherous to ride through, and on horseback some path is therefore necessary, a crossroads is the most logical setting for this encounter, and though none is mentioned in the play it is implicit in the context. Lisa Hopkins also notices that when Macbeth asks them 'why / Upon this blasted heath you stop our way' (I, iii, 76–7) it implies that they are all on a track or path of some kind and that at this point in the narrative they 'stand poised at a metaphorical if not a literal crossroads'.[134] Laura Annawyn Shamas agrees that Macbeth is at a psychological crossroads here, and also suggests the possibility that 'physically, he and Banquo are at a charmed crossroads site as well since the Weird Sisters have just danced and spun three ways upon the intersection'.[135] When later in the play the three witches meet Hecate she is 'angerly' (III, v, 1) over being left out of proceedings thus far. She asks.

> How did you dare
> To trade and traffic with Macbeth,
> In riddles, and affairs of death;
> And I, the mistress of your charms,
> The close contriver of all harms,
> Was never call'd to bear my part. (III, v, 3–8)

She is not only involved in the magic, but in reminding the witches that 'security / Is mortals' chiefest enemy' she promises transformation for Macbeth in the form of the 'dismal and . . . fatal end' she has planned (III, v, 21). So the outdoor activities of the witches in *Macbeth* are by implication manifested at a crossroads – as their own tripleness, and the presence of 'triple Hecate' implies.

In *Hamlet*'s inner-play meanwhile, Lucianus describes the poisoning in terms soaked in natural magic:

> Thoughts black, hands apt, drugs fit, and time agreeing;
> Confederate season, else no creature seeing;
> Thou mixture rank, of midnight weeds collected,
> With Hecate's ban thrice blasted, thrice infected,
> Thy natural magic and dire property
> On wholesome life usurp immediately. (III, ii, 257–62)

Here again Hecate is associated with murder, and a visit to her crossroads shrine is implicated in the multiple three-ness of her blasting and infecting ban. *A Midsummer Night's Dream*'s Puck invokes this too when he imagines 'the screech-owl, screeching loud' that 'Puts the wretch that lies in woe / In remembrance of a shroud' (V, i, 370–2) and declares:

> Now it is the time of night
> That the graves, all gaping wide,
> Every one lets forth his sprite,
> In the church-way paths to glide:
> And we fairies, that do run
> By the triple Hecate's team,
> From the presence of the sun,
> Following darkness like a dream
> Now are frolic. (V, i, 373–81)

The spectral journey back to the 'crossways' (III, ii, 383) resting places of the wandering spirits of the 'church-way paths' is entirely in accordance with the purgatorial wanderings of the ghost of old Hamlet, with Hecate standing in as a proxy deity charged with the keeping of the unquiet dead.

Ben Jonson also alludes to the crossroads worship of Hecate when, at the end of *Cynthia's Revels* (1600), the judge figure Criticus sentences the other characters to make sacrifices in specific ways:

> March to your several homes by Niobe's stone,
> And offer up two tears a-piece thereon,

That it may change the name, as you must change,
And of a stone be callèd Weeping-cross:
> *Because it standeth cross of Cynthia's way,*
> *One of whose names is sacred Trivia.*
And after penance thus perform'd you pass
. . . to the well of knowledge, Helicon;
Where, purgèd of your present maladies,
. . . you become
Such as you fain would seem, and then return,
Offering your service to great Cynthia. (V, v, 232–8, 241–5; my italics)

They are thus sentenced to be themselves transformed by the sacrifice into loyal servants of the goddess and in the course of their actions to transform 'Niobe's stone' to 'Weeping-cross', which is by implication at a crossroads. Cynthia, who is of course one of the manifestations of the Triple Goddess, adds 'We do approve thy censure belov'd Crites; / Which Mercury, thy true propitious friend . . . / Will undertake to see exactly done' (V, v, 249–50, 52). Throughout this period, of course, Elizabeth I has encouraged her own imaging as divine Cynthia-Diana and thus references to both abounded, but although she is therefore Hecate by implication, poets perhaps wisely 'always ignored Hecate in such contexts' as Northrop Frye suggested.[136] Despite this, Lynn S. Meskill sees Elizabeth's portrayal in Jonson's *Masque of Queens* (1609) as including aspects of both Cynthia and Hecate.[137]

In Fletcher and Massinger's *The Prophetess* (1622) the titular character Delphia almost casually performs rites to Hecate and Ceres (II, iii, 145), suggesting a general awareness of what this might mean. An empowered figure in this play, she appears variously to combine 'the Delphic oracle, the Virgin Mary . . . Jupiter, Juno, and Cumaean sibyl' and is called a witch (I, iii, 113–20), a 'holy Druid' (I, iii, 95), a 'blessed mother' (III, i, 48) and a dealer with devils (I, iii, 103).[138] She, however, 'commands deities, not simple daemons' as Molly Hand has noted.[139] The Delphic Oracle was also situated at a crossroads.

Throughout the period, the many popular and influential translations of classical works also include references to Hecate. Robert Stapylton's 1634 translation of Virgil's *Dido and Aeneas* is exemplary in refering to 'threefold Hecate', and 'triple-faced maiden Diana', and here he has Dido intone 'O Hecate howl'd-for in crosse wayes!'[140] Also in 1634, Milton's *Comus* evokes the mystery of the rites of Hecate and gives them a sense of liminality and secrecy. Here an attendant spirit warns two brothers pursuing their lost sister that 'Within the navil of this hideous Wood, / Immur'd in cypress shades a Sorcerer dwels' (520–1). The spirit then describes the 'bottom glade',

> whence night by night
> He and his monstrous rout are heard to howl
> Like stabl'd wolves, or tigers at their prey,
> Doing abhorred rites to Hecate
> In their obscured haunts of inmost bowres. (532–6)

The masque has Comus himself hail the 'Goddesse of Nocturnal sport', and ask, 'Stay thy cloudy Ebon chair, / Wherin thou rid'st with Hecat' and befriend / Us thy vow'd Priests' (134–6). Lamenting the loss of his sister, the second brother alludes to the requisite threeness when he cries 'O night and shades, / How are ye joyn'd with hell in triple knot / Against th' unarmed weakness of one Virgin' (580–2).

John Gay's poem 'Trivia' (1716) meanwhile carries on the tradition for another century and in another genre, as he notes the goddess's connections with her lunar manifestation:

> Trivia Goddess, leave these low abodes,
> And traverse o'er the wide ethereal roads
> Celestial Queen, put on thy robes of light,
> Now Cynthia nam'd, fair regent of the night.[141]

It is significant here for Cynthia-Hecate's propensity for travel as the transformative moon-figure that Gay not only places her on the heavenly road but also reminds the reader of the trivia, the crossroads of her origin.

It appears then that the significance of the gods and the crossroads are mutually constitutive and in a sense the location of such figures as Hecate at the outward places, the heath, the hidden valley bottom, the road or the crossroads, is an indication of the paradox in which the vibrancy and strength of any culture to some extent requires 'space for figures whose function is to uncover and disrupt the very things that cultures are based on', as Hyde says of Hermes.[142] The culture which demands this externalises the transformative chaos of the witch, the criminal or the restless dead, who are thereby made liminal to the identity of the mainstream. Forbidden but still accessible. Hermes steals cattle and fire from the gods and thereby his disruptive and creative energies establish human culture, though he will always remain liminal to both camps. Plato even suggests that Hermes invented language itself to facilitate his propensity for bargaining and Hyde takes this up to consider the nature of the marketplace, which for him is 'another place where we are likely to meet strangers with strange goods, and, crossroads-wise, find ourselves forced to articulate newly'.[143] In this respect Hyde associates the crossroads metaphor as concerned with actively engendering language itself.[144] Since the trickster god is a go-between, this also works at a linguistic level and Hyde points out that 'both translation and sacrifice ... are situated ... at the points of articulation' of which the crossroads is one.[145] Like our other crossroads deities, trickster gods are dwellers at the joints of things where articulation happens, and the etymology of the word, from Latin *artus*, suggests both the arts and 'a flexible joint or the boundary that is a permeable membrane'.[146] This permeability suits the dual nature of crossroads and contextualises what is anticipated to occur there. This may begin with the supplicant's own narrative, but this is the case even for the gods. The crossroads god Eshu told humans that 'as long as they sacrificed at the crossroads he would always be with them' but then he himself was 'banished to the crossroads for bad behaviour in heaven'.[147] It is precisely because Eshu is 'the god of uncertainty' at the crossroads that he is also 'the god who can tear a hole in the fabric of fate so a person might slip from one life into another'.[148] Just as the god is the anthropomorphic representation of the physical and metaphorical implications of the parting and joining of the ways, somehow the nature of the crossroads permeates the material of the god who lives there. In this transaction, both the locality and the god itself are transformed.

Chapter 5

Terminus: The Night, the Crossroads and the Stake

> I'm goin' down to the crossroads, gonna flag a ride,
> The place where faith, hope and charity died.
> Bob Dylan, 'Murder Most Foul' (2020)[1]

Although the treatment of the remains of the victims of suicide and hanging varied with the circumstances of their crimes and their places of execution, their ceremonies were often designed to arrest the unquiet spirit, their most common elements being the night, the crossroads and the stake. In 1977, during excavations for a new flyover on the A14 in Cambridgeshire, twelve skeletons were discovered beneath a crossroads between the old villages of Dry Drayton and Oakington.[2] Since a nearby field had long been known as Gallows Piece, and medieval records showed that Crowland Abbey kept a gallows at the same crossroads (as was common for abbeys of the time), this suggested that the bodies were those of executed criminals (though some may also have been the victims of suicide).[3] One gallows at a crossroads is clearly depicted on the Agas map outside the Postern Gate of the Tower of London (see Figure 5.1). The execution of criminals at such crossroads sites dates back at least to Plato's *Laws* (348 BCE) where it is stated that murderers of their own family members should be dispatched 'at an appointed place without the city where three ways meet'.[4] Plato directs of certain murderers: 'the magistrates who are servants of the judges shall kill him; then they are to throw him down naked at a specified crossroads outside the city'.[5] In Roman times, crucifixion also often took place at crossroads, or by roadsides. In his history of crossroads burials in England, Andrew Reynolds records that, of twelve Anglo-Saxon boundary burials studied, ten were 'either beside or adjacent to routeways'.[6] Anglo-Saxon execution cemeteries in general were 'often associated with a hundred meeting place, a

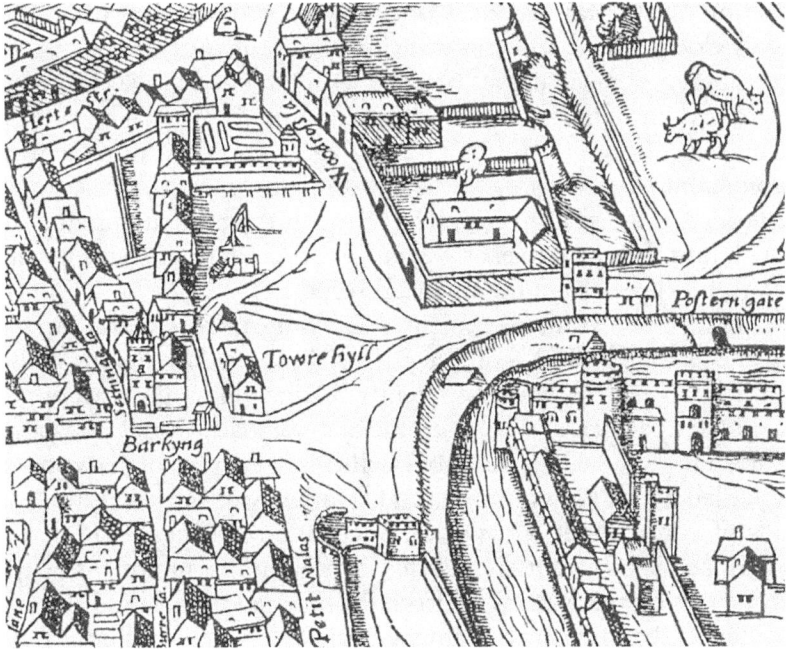

Figure 5.1 Gallows outside Tower of London, Postern Gate, c. 1562. (Janelle Jenstad, ed. The Agas Map, image © London Metropolitan Archives, City of London)

market or major highway'.[7] Though identified from at least the Middle Anglo-Saxon era, it is the ninth to twelfth centuries that see the major development of crossroads burials in England.[8] This lasts until the early nineteenth century, when they are finally banned.

As Johnston suggests, it was crossroads' status as 'unclaimed "nowheres"', that meant they were considered 'appropriate places to leave materials expelled from society', including 'the polluted remains of household purification rituals' or ὀξυθύμια.[9] Johnston notes that this word could also refer to a 'scaffold erected for the purpose of hanging or whipping criminals', as could the word 'hekate', adding to the complex of interwoven concepts around crossroads.[10] As we have seen, Hecate has a close relationship with the crossroads, and to add to this narrative, Thomas Rogers Forbes speculates that some examples of crossroads burial, particularly 'burial of suicides at night' may well have begun 'as a rite in honor of Hecate, goddess of darkness'.[11] Since the unfortunate victims of suicide were considered a species of criminal in earlier times they were often buried at the crossroads like those executed by hanging. Due to the nature of the crime, historical instances of this form of burial are often thoroughly documented and sometimes memorialised at the place itself, remembered in place names or even with a tended grave.[12] The very fact that these burials may be commemorated, one might even say celebrated, in popular forms might suggest that such interment can become almost auspicious to the culture that orders it, transforming the nature of the gesture entirely. Although the more dominant view of such burials is negative, as we will see, this alternative line of interpretation expresses a more nuanced response.

The earliest extant document specifying a crossroads burial in England is dated 1510 – of one Robert Browner, a religious of Butley Priory in Suffolk, who apparently 'hanged himself on account of fiscal incompetence'.[13] The last official crossroads burial in England occurred in June 1823 when Abel Griffiths, a 22-year-old law student who killed himself after murdering his father, was buried at the crossroads of Eaton Street, Grosvenor Place, and the Kings Road in London. Since the crowd attending this dishonourable interment held up George IV's carriage, pressure from the king led to the 1823 Burial of Suicide Act, banning such highway burials.[14] It was the Burial Act of 1880 that finally removed all penalty for suicide.[15] A short account of one such crossroads interment in 1573 may serve to indicate its popularity. This was the case of Thomas Maule of Pleasley in Derbyshire who hanged himself 'on a tree by the wayeside after a druncken fitte April 3'. Two days later the coroner's inquest was held in the church porch, and the parish register tells us that Maule was the 'same nighte at midd nighte burried at the nighest crosse roads with a stake yn him', and in attendance were 'manie peopple frome Manesfeilde'.[16] Forbes meanwhile recounts the Coroner's report for 28 November 1595 on Elizabeth Wickham who 'hanged her selfe upon a garden pale in her aperne stringe' which reports that she was buried that day 'in the aley where she hanged her selfe according to her dezarts having a stake driven thorowgh her in Remembrance of her wicked [act?]', adding helpfully, 'an Alye being comon thorowghfare or highway'.[17] The 1731 Great Thurlow parish register records a crossroads burial thus: '*Elizabeth Rawe sepulta fuit in trivio loco, vulgo dicto Sowley Green, quia dextra occidit ipsa sua*' [Elizabeth Rawe was buried in the three ways in this place commonly called Sowley Green because with her own right hand she killed herself].[18] The nineteenth-century historian Alfred Kingston records two instances from the reign of George III. In the first from 1765, the coroner's inquest sat upon the case of one Ploward, a schoolmaster from Litlington, who, 'after shooting Mr. Whedd, of Fowlmere, cut his own throat', and it came to the verdict of *felo de se*, 'upon which he was ordered to be buried in the high cross-way'.[19] And in the second, in 1779, 'John Stanford, who hung himself at the Red Lion, Kneesworth, was found to be a *felo de se*, and was "ordered to be buried in a cross-road".'[20]

The operation of the law around this issue evolved over time, as R. A. Houston explains, since antiquity, 'burying a suicide in unconsecrated ground with a stake through the heart had no authority at law, but was a "customary" or local usage sanctioned by warrant of an English coroner'.[21] By 1603, with the institution of the 68th Canon, clergy could not refuse or obstinately delay burials, but the characteristics of the burial, including the location and the ritual, were still often subject to the operation of the 'micro-politics of the parish'.[22] Houston gives the example of a burial at Thirsk in North Yorkshire on 23 July 1603 when John Bradley was buried '*non per ministrum* having drowned himselfe'.[23]

For the reasons we have explained which most obviously connect them, crossroads, and therefore the gallows and outcast burials of the deviant dead, were often sited at boundaries from ancient times.[24] In a society used to performing the 'beating of the bounds' over the days of 'rogation' in the church festival calendar in which the party on three successive days walked the parish boundaries 'to drive away the devil . . . [in] an annual exorcism of the parish', the roads which lay between these might be the only neutral space.[25] If the most neutral between-spaces of early modern Britain are highways and roads lying between boundaries of estates, parishes or other geographical authorities of oversight, then the ultraliminal place, the place between the edges, would be where such highways crossed, the 'transitional gaps between defined, bounded areas, that is, between roads or between the areas of land that roads define' as Johnston has described.[26] Reynolds describes a shallow burial at Broad Hinton in Wiltshire of a male aged 35–40, dated to 540–680 CE, 'at a crossroads formed by the intersection of two hollow ways' that lay near the boundary of the Domesday hundreds of Kingsbridge and Selkley and notes a land charter of 1008 CE which designates one boundary mark as 'where the thieves lie'.[27] Other ancient boundary burials were found at Felpham, Figheldean, Singleton, Brough and Perth.[28] A further recent archaeological example of a burial at an early boundary crossroads came from the excavations for the Channel Tunnel Rail Link at White Horse Stone in Kent, which revealed the intersection of the old Roman road leading south from Rochester with another ancient road, the Pilgrims Way. The boundaries between the parishes of Aylesford and Boxley, and between the old hundreds of Maidstone and Eyhorn, ran over this intersection, where the burial of a female aged 25–35 and dated to 680–980 CE was found 'just 5m north of the boundary line in the south-east quadrant of the crossroads'.[29]

The northern German Rügen Customary of 1530 enjoins specifically that 'a suicide should be buried at a road junction, at a place where several boundaries meet'.[30] There are plenty of examples in the historical record of such burials ordered to take place at a boundary. In 1665, the teenager Henry Apes hanged himself in a barn and 'was buryed between the two parishes of Staunton ... and Alton Barnes, with two stakes thrust through him', which suggests that poor Apes was twice as threatening as similar corpses. The record adds helpfully that 'Mr Budd would not suffer him to be buryed in the churchyard nor is hee enterd into the booke of burials.'[31] Charles Harper describes a mound on the Icknield Way known as Marman's Grave, which is reputed a suicide burial and marked by a post bearing the letters of B and E denoting the boundaries of the parishes of Barnham and Elveden. Another known as Cannard's Grave was also originally the site of a boundary dyke.[32] Meanwhile, at Kelsale in East Anglia, in 1733 there is a parish register entry which reads simply 'Robert Balls at the White Cross was buried February 4th'; White Cross was a crossroads at the parish boundary.[33] Taking this further into the macabre, there is a Scottish folk tradition in which the traditional fairies of the lowlands were supposed to carry bows 'made of the ribs of a man buried where three laird's lands meet', that is, at just such a place, a crossing of the tracks between the boundaries.[34] This hints further at the supernatural qualities associated with such places and the burials that occurred there.

In addition to indicating interment at the limbus of the crossroads, Puck's 'crossways and floods' of course include burial in another kind of borderland: that disputed between the land itself and the flowing waters of the earth in the floodplains of rivers and within the high-tide marks of the sea.[35] An Anglo-Saxon burial was identified on the foreshore of the Thames, in which the corpse's feet were found to be 'crossed at the ankles' and an iron peg was recovered 'from between the legs, suggesting perhaps that the body had been staked to the foreshore'; a land charter records that this was also at the edge of an ancient 'hundred' boundary.[36] Crossing the ankles of a corpse in this manner may be another form of apotropaic precaution.[37] Houston recounts one poignant entry in a parish register from near to Edinburgh from 31 January 1648 which states that 'Janet Blane spouse to John Cleland betwixt 6 and 7 hours at night did drown herself and her daughter being about the age of five years in Duddingston Loch'; it notes further that Janet having 'wilfully killed herself . . . was buried next to the loch', whilst her daughter, because 'innocent of the deed, was laid to rest in the churchyard'.[38] Water margins were thought appropriate to suicides of this kind.[39] In this vein, Robert Halliday describes a case reported in *The Gentleman's Magazine* of 1784 in which Thomas Williams of Aberystwyth had been 'poisoned by a woman who shared his house, who then took poison herself and was buried on the sea shore'. In this case the intention is made very clear – it was 'to prevent her joining a band of ghosts who had terrorised a nearby village'.[40] Halliday sees the perception of the added apotropaic efficacy of water in the fact that when the coroner suggested 'burying her at a crossroads with a stake through her heart . . . the seashore was considered a safer option'.[41] In the medieval period and afterwards, water in general was regarded as a potential barrier to the undead and may have been poured behind a funerary procession to stop the corpse from walking back home.[42] Such a place was possibly identified in the 1930s at Morgan's Grave, on the seashore at Porteynon, Gower Peninsula where there was 'a considerable mound of earth and stones' as C. Wanklyn notes.[43] A further example splits the difference between water and road when Walter Oswald Wait describes how a little beyond the road to Dunchurch there was at that time to be found 'a mound raised over the grave of a poor girl, who about 100 years ago poisoned herself, and was buried where the brook crosses the road at right angles, because there were no cross-roads in the parish'.[44]

Besides these examples of suicide burials, there were also many cases of burial at crossroads simply because gallows were often sited there (as were other instruments of judicial punishment like the stocks or pillory, and sometimes small cages).[45] Tradition dictated that unless the bodies of the hanged were claimed by relatives they should be buried under the gallows.[46] In the British Isles, such burial practice may have begun in the Anglo-Saxon era, and one example of this is the Bran Ditch at Fowlmere dating from that period where, in the 1920s, sixty skeletons were found buried in haphazard and shallow graves at a crossing named Gallows Gate. Some of these, Halliday notes, 'were decapitated, while others had distended necks', undoubtedly it seems from execution at the gallows.[47] In our exemplary period, three men were hanged in 1555 at the 'gallows in Charing-cross . . . for robbing of certain Spaniards of a treasure of gold'; one of them 'having hung four days was . . . cut down and buried under the gallows'.[48] Richard Challoner describes such gallows burials, in this case of religious deviants – both Catholic priests and laymen – including those of Robert Grissold, a layman executed in 1604 at Warwick, and Fathers Thomas Maxfield, in 1616 at Tyburn, and Hugh Green in 1642, at Dorchester gallows, another scaffold sited at a road junction.[49] A further, and very prominent, example serves to show the continuity of these burial practices throughout the early modern period when on 30 January 1661, the twelfth anniversary of Charles I's execution, the bodies of the regicides Cromwell, Ireton and Bradshaw, were disinterred from their resting places in the august surroundings of Westminster Abbey, taken and hanged at Tyburn and then reinterred like common criminals underneath the notorious gallows.[50]

Throughout the medieval and early modern periods the most pre-eminent and infamous crossroads gallows in the country was without doubt the notorious scaffold at Tyburn (see Figure 5.2). This long-used gallows was based at various locations upon the crossroads of what were Tyburn Road and Watling Street, now Marble Arch and Edgeware Rd, in the environs of London. Like many other gallows sites, the original location of Tyburn was at the outskirts of the town. The name 'Tyburn' derives from 'Teo Bourne' meaning 'boundary stream'.[51] An Anglo-Saxon boundary clause of 1002 CE also signals its liminal origins.[52] The great age of Tyburn spanned

Figure 5.2 Tyburn execution, c. seventeenth century

687 years, from its beginning in 1196 as the 'King's Gallows' of Henry II, to 1783, when the gallows were finally moved to the relative privacy of Newgate Prison. The original gallows was an elm tree, and this may have initially been a pagan site of the kind often favoured for executions by Christian monarchs.[53] After the demise of the elm tree, a larger structure with a six-person capacity was built and this was subsequently expanded by Elizabeth I into a triangular structure which could dispatch eight people per side at the same time. Public executions could pull many thousands of people, especially to watch simultaneous hangings. A crowd of 3,000–7,000 people would have been more or less standard in London later in the eighteenth century, with up to 100,000 claimed occasionally (see Figure 5.3).[54] V. A. C. Gatrell calculates that 75,000 people may have been executed in this manner in the century spanning 1530–1630 alone, and adds accurately that 'nothing like this was seen again'.[55] Until the 1780s, 'after each of the eight annual Old Bailey sessions anything between a couple and a dozen . . . were hanged' at Tyburn, and up to the 1830s there were hangings 'once or twice a year in many assize towns'.[56] In the 1820s, Gatrell notes, 'two-thirds were hanged for property crimes'.[57] Tragically, perhaps as much as

Figure 5.3 The execution of the idle apprentice at Tyburn. (Engraving by T. Cook, 1795, after W. Hogarth, 1747; Creative Commons)

'90 percent of the men hanged in London in the 1780s were aged under 21', a high proportion of which were 'recent immigrants to the city'.⁵⁸ The corpses of these luckless people not claimed by friends or relatives were simply buried at the site, with the gallows moving to another part of the crossroads once the pits were full.⁵⁹ Tyburn itself is still a great crossroads and a place of transit, covered as it is by one of the main sites of Paddington Station.⁶⁰

Tyburn is of course only one example of such a site among many in London and in all other localities in the era. Even up to the end of the eighteenth century gallows sites of this kind were only expanding. A history of London from 1878 recalls a report in *The Morning Post* of 1776 of a planned 'second Tyburn'. It recounts the order of the office of the Secretary of State that 'criminals capitally convicted at the Old Bailey shall in future be executed at the cross road near the "Mother Red Cap" inn, the half-way house to Hampstead'. Interestingly it adds that 'no galleries, scaffolds, or other temporary stages be built near the place', giving perhaps some idea of the potential scope for spectatorship of such a place.⁶¹ There are many other examples of historical gallows at boundaries and crossroads which now may be traced by archaeological investigation, or by the study of location names. One example, Gallow Howe in North Yorkshire, has been the subject of study based on its name and on a large stone marking-post, dated 1833. It has been confirmed by locals as an old hanging place at a crossroads.⁶² Raymond Hayes asserts its possibly pagan or pre-Christian roots and claims that Gallow Howe 'was once an impressive cairn of stones with a walled cist 5ft by 3ft but is now destroyed'; its antiquity perhaps indicated by artefacts found nearby, including a flint arrowhead and pieces of urn of uncertain date. Describing the nature of the site, Hayes cites various characteristics of the crossroads we have been exploring: 'on the north end of the rigg was an important junction of old roads called Shaw End by the locals. There is a massive block of stone inscribed Gallow Howe 1833 D (for Danby). Here the parish boundary turns west.'⁶³ It is very likely then that this is an early gallows site located on a ridge above a fork in a significant ancient roadway. The fact that the place once also incorporated a cairn of indeterminate age and function, perhaps indicating the presence of older gods, also suggests that its ancient significance was greater than merely to mark the boundary of the parish. Its position here at the edge of the functional spiritual safety of parochial authority also indicates that it fits the traditional psychogeography of the crossroads.⁶⁴

It is difficult to estimate the prevalence or frequency of gallows in the medieval to early modern periods, but one study of medieval Lincolnshire shows that on average, in that county at least, 'no more than about five miles separated any two sets of gallows'.[65] It was here, in the popular vernacular of the time, that criminals were 'launched into eternity'.[66] This innocent-sounding and poetic phrase perhaps expresses the almost casual nature of the perception of hanging and crossroads burial in the period. Both hanging and burial at crossroads, however, contain a formal anomaly: in order to be launched upwards into eternity to receive the judgement of God, one must first undergo two falls. To be dropped to the end of a rope and then thrust unceremoniously into the ground seems much more like a two-stage concealment than an offering up to God. It smacks somehow of a kind of spiritual embarrassment, a compounding of the original sin. Crossroads then might be just as much meant to confuse the judgement of the God who looks down upon them as the intersection might confuse other linear spirits. One might wonder also at the choice of such a place for gallows given its history of human sacrifice.

In another sense, the burial of unwanted corpses of the hanged at the crossroads site has a certain cold logic to it: the corpse is simply abandoned at its place of final ignominy. In the case of the victims of suicide, however, the nature of the crime itself necessitated a more complex response. Historians have recorded the merciless procession of religious councils keen to establish ecclesiastical practices to deny suicides burial honours and to mark their deviancy from the respectable community of Christian dead. Such deliberations took place as early as 561 at the Council of Braga, in Geneva.[67] In England, a canon denying suicide victims normal funerals and burials was adopted in 672 at the Council of Hertford, and a canon attributed to King Edgar reiterated the prohibition and exempted 'madmen' soon after the year 1000, denying them burial 'with hymns and psalmody or any rites of honourable sepulture'.[68] In France in 1284 the Synod of Nîmes 'forbade the burial of all suicides in hallowed ground', as Janet Clare relays.[69] Houston notes the Henrician canon that 'restated that clergy were not to bury suicides "in their churches or churchyards, and that if they have in fact buried such people, they shall throw their remains out of the church or churchyard at the command of their ordinaries"'.[70] It is possible however that even in Anglo-Saxon England the processes dictating burial of undesirables was driven by 'a deeper level of age-old superstition and belief'.[71] If this is so, these prohibitions were merely confirmations of the mores around suicide which may have prevailed over many centuries. On top of the denial of burial ceremony arose rites of desecration around suicide burial in which the crossroads featured prominently; these, as Michael MacDonald and Terence Murphy show, were 'genuine popular customs, accepted by the church and the state as an essential part of punishing suicide'.[72] Although mysterious in origin, they seem to express the belief that self-murder was somehow evil on a supernatural level.[73] Although they attacked many traditional rituals as pagan in origin, in general the Protestant clergy encouraged rites of desecration for suicides.[74] Though the Reformation resulted in priests losing many of their magical and sacramental abilities, like exorcism and prayer for the souls of the dead, in many ways the reformers intensified such customary practices, heightening the popular anxieties over witchcraft and demonism.[75] In this world view, suicide was seen as a manifestation of God's disfavour, with Satan, as ever ambiguous in the hierarchy of divine intention, acting as the 'sword of God's wrath'.[76] The prominent Protestant divine and later martyr Hugh Latimer saw a very busy Devil who often tormented people until they 'rid themselves out of this life'.[77] Another reformer, Richard Gilpin expressed how 'Satan . . . tempts Men often to Self-Murther'.[78] This demonic instigation, however, produces little mercy for the victim and it is the case that, between about 1500 and 1660, suicide was penalised more seriously than any other time.[79] Michael Dalton said of suicide in 1626, 'For the heinousnesse thereof . . . it is an offence against God, against the king, and against Nature.'[80] The problem here may have been partly to do with terminology, since word 'suicide' itself did not appear until the 1630s, and did not become popular until the eighteenth century, before which time, as MacDonald points out, 'there were no terms with which to describe self-destruction that did not brand its perpetrators as criminals or madmen'.[81] Besides the demonic influence, suicide was also imagined to happen at the instigation of witchcraft.[82] Other examples of this religious attribution of evil agency abound in early modern writing and in a sense these underwrite the disgusting nature of the resulting corpse's treatment after the fact.[83]

The siting of the desecration process seems always to have tended towards the liminal. In ancient Thebes and Rome, those committing suicide by hanging were simply left unburied.[84] In medieval Metz and Strasbourg, they were set adrift in barrels on a river, as a physical representation of the eternally wandering nature of the suicide's soul.[85] But by the later Middle Ages many Western European regions had adopted more elaborate rituals for desecrating their corpses.[86] Jeremy Harte gives instances of bodies being 'dragged on hurdles, hanged, beheaded, staked, and weighed down with stones before they were buried beneath the gallows, in the knacker's pit, on the seashore, or at a crossroads'.[87] MacDonald and Murphy describe the typical ritual of desecration that developed in Europe, variations on which we have already encountered, in which on the night following the coroner's inquest,

> officials of the parish, the churchwardens and their helpers, carried the corpse to a crossroads and threw it naked into a pit. A wooden stake was hammered through the body, pinioning it in the grave, and the hole was filled in. No prayers for the dead were repeated; the minister did not attend.[88]

An unusual example of the treatment of the corpse of a suicide occured on 20 February 1598, when 'Thomas Dobie drounit himself in the Quarrel holes besyde the Abbay [at the eastern foot of Calton Hill], and upon the morne, he wes harlit [dragged] throw the toune backward, and ther after hangit on the gallows', as the Edinburgh burgess Robert Birrel's diary records.[89]

As a significant element of this form of crossroads burial, the stake was intended both as a precaution against wandering of the spirit and an object of horror to those who passed by: a deterrent to succumbing to the Devil's temptation in this way.[90] Daniel Ogden describes this practice happening before the fourth century CE in a reference to the pinning of a corpse of a potentially restless ghost with 'swords being driven down into the grave'.[91] Burchard of Worms's *Corrector* (c. 1025 CE) directs that 'when any child has died without baptism [the townspeople] take the corpse of the little one and place it in some secret place and transfix it with a stake [lest it] arise and injure many'.[92] This sickening practice may be confirmed as recorded in a place name near the town of Moneycusker in Cork, Ireland, which is a field known by locals as 'Crossnalanniv' or 'Cros na Leanbh (children's crossroads), burial place of unbaptised infants'.[93] Christopher Daniell claims staking was rare until the latter part of the fifteenth century, but 'not uncommon' in the sixteenth.[94] By Elizabethan times it had become normal. William Harrison described in 1577 how 'such as kill themselves are buried in the field with a stake driven through their bodies'.[95] Robert Pashley is I think incorrect in asserting that the stake was 'not at all meant as an indignity, but simply as a precaution' and is overly generous in assuming it is 'to contribute to the mutual benefit of both the dead man and his survivors, by ensuring, to the former, the quiet occupation of his tomb, and, to the latter, freedom from molestation by his nightly rambles'.[96] He is right, however, in expressing this last fear of the returning spirit of the perturbed and restless dead. When Amy Stokes killed herself in 1590, the coroner commanded that her body be taken to 'some cross way neare the townes end and theare that she should have a stake dreven thorowgh her brest and so be buried with the stake to be scene for a memoryall that others goinge by seeinge the same might take heede for comittinge the lyke faite'.[97] John Weever in 1631 also describes suicides buried 'with a stake thrust through their bodies, to terrifie all passengers, by that so infamous and reproachful a buriall, not to make such their final passage out of this world'.[98] The Swiss traveller César de Saussure wrote in 1726 that English law against suicide ordered 'the burying of the corpse with a stake thrust through it, and without a bier, at the crossing of two high roads'.[99] A staking of a suicide has been found in the records of Berwick-upon-Tweed in 1765, when a small docket records in grimly specific detail the money paid to Mr William Wilson for burying a *felo de se*.[100] In this distasteful process, some incentive was apparently requisite, and a total of 11 1/2 d was paid 'to licker drunk' for the gravediggers.[101] The receipt shows that 'the stake was far from a crude bludgeon, being carefully fashioned of durable timber and tipped or shoed with iron. It was designed to be seen, because ironwork was also fixed to the top and it was painted.'[102] William Dimond's, 'Fragment in Blank Verse' from 1800 shows that such deterrence was a persistent motive of the process in Western culture: 'Observe that stake! 'Twas in the midway plac'd . . . / To draw the glance abhorrent, and the scoff / From vulgar passengers'.[103] Thomas Hardy describes one such case persisting in his memory, where earth was heaped round the stake at the crossroads 'like an ancient tumulus'.[104] A deterrent display was often part of the theatre of death for such unfortunates. W. Fulbecke's, *A parallele or conference of the civill law, the canon law, and the common law of this realme of England:* (1601), on culpable suicide directs that, of the bodies of suicides,

> for the terror of them that liue, they are thus ordered. The body is drawne out of the house, wherin the man did kil himselfe, with ropes, not by the dore, but through some hoal or pit made under the threshold of the dore, because it is unworthy to be brought out the same way, which the man whilest he liued, did use: and hee is drawne by a horse to the place of punishment or shame, where he is hanged upon a gibbet, and none may take the body downe, but by

the authoritie of the magistrate: and none may weare any mourning roabe for such an offendour.[105]

Michael Dalton's *Countrey Justice* (1618) meanwhile, described by Houston as 'one of the main handbooks for seventeenth-century judges', prescribes the procedure so:

> their dead bodies (for the terrour of others) are drawne out of the house, &c. with ropes, by a horse, to a place appointed for punishment or shame, where the dead bodie is hanged upon a Gibbet: And none may take downe the bodie, but by the authoritie of the magistrate.[106]

As late as 1812 an elaborate desecration ritual is described in the *Edinburgh Annual Register* for an alleged murderer and suicide called John Williams, involving the display of the body, a procession stopping at victims' houses, the use of murder weapons to drive in the stake and the destination being 'a crossroads, where a grave deliberately too small to allow the body to repose in an attitude of sleep awaited'. This grave was dug where four roads met in East London: 'the New Road into Whitechapel; that into Sun Tavern Fields; the back lane to Wellclose Square; and Ratcliffe Highway' (see Figure 5.4).[107] The precise process was as follows:

> At about ten o'clock on Monday night, Mr Robinson, the high constable of the parish of St George, accompanied by Mr. Machin, one of the constables, Mr. Harrison, the collector, and Mr Robinson's deputy, went to the prison at Coldbath-Fields, where the body of Williams being delivered to them, was put into a hackney-coach . . . and about twelve o'clock the body was deposited in the blackhole, where it remained all night. Yesterday morning, about nine o'clock, the high constable, with his attendants, arrived at the watchhouse with a cart, that had been fitted up for the purpose of giving the greatest possible degree of exposure to the face and body of Williams. A stage, or platform, was formed upon the cart by boards, which extended from one side to the other . . . on which the body rested, with the head towards the horse, and so much elevated, as to be completely exposed to public view . . . On the right-hand side of the head was fixed, perpendicularly, the maul, with which the murder of the Marrs was committed. On the left also, in a perpendicular position, was fixed the ripping chissel. Above his head was laid, in a transverse direction upon the boards, the iron crow; and parallel with it, the stake destined to be driven through the body. The hole, about

Figure 5.4 John Williams burial, London, 1811

four feet deep, three feet long, and two feet wide, was dug precisely at the crossing of the roads, four or five feet from the turnpike house. About half past twelve o'clock, the body was pushed out of the cart, and crammed, neck and heels, into the hole ... so formed, as not to admit of being laid at full length. The stake was immediately driven through the body, amidst the shouts and vociferous execrations of the multitude, and the hole filled up, and well rammed down.[108]

The writer notes that 'the concourse of spectators, on this awful occasion, was immense'.[109] It is interesting to consider this vast crowd, in a major European city, at the dawn of the industrial age, witnessing a ritual desecration, a staking through the heart, and a profane burial at the anciently significant site of the crossroads. This was a modern example, in the early nineteenth century, of a spontaneous mass popular enactment of a ritual thousands of years old and with known roots in pagan worship and beliefs.

It is perhaps also somewhat surprising that such execution gave rise to a macabre trade in the remains of its victims, and a superstitious ideology of ritual and magic which surrounded its trappings. Although there is no evidence that the executions themselves were thought of as 'purification rituals which made use of body magic', the exception to this might be the contemporary belief that attributed magical powers to 'blood, parts of the dead bodies of the executed and to the noose of the gallows', as Floricke Egmond notes.[110] In the doubly unhappy Williams's case, souvenirs sold to spectators included slivers of wood taken from his stake.[111] This might be thought to simply instance keepsake collecting, were it not that it takes place within a popular contemporary network of belief that also included the idea that healing could occur merely from touching the dead hand of a person newly hanged.[112] This was thought to cure a variety of diseases, tumours and skin complaints.[113] The practice sits within a long magical tradition associated with the places and the victims of execution. In order to cure a form of malaria known as 'quartanes', Agrippa's *Of Occult Philosophy* (1509–10, trans. 1650) prescribes 'a piece of a naile from a Gibbet, wrapt up in Wooll, and hanged about the neck . . . also a Rope doth the like that is taken from a Gallows, and hid under ground, that the sun cannot reach it'.[114] Describing eyewitness accounts of these practices, Clare Gittings suggests that 'a reversal seems to have taken place in the popular imagination at the moment of execution, causing that which had been, while living, harmful and threatening to society, to take on healing and beneficial powers instead'.[115] Such a reversal is perhaps made possible by the fact that generative and positive transformations are part of the lore of the crossroads, the traditional scene of spiritual metamorphoses. As we have seen, many other examples of magic are made possible at crossroads and these are often intended to be beneficial. There are other supernatural associations between execution and magic, however, which might more obviously tend towards the dark.[116]

In a world where the supernatural is thought real and accessible, various afterlives are also thought possible in the hinterlands of death (for instance, in the Catholic tradition, in Purgatory and Limbo), the liminal zone just beyond the grave, and in this context, staking the corpse may not be as illogical as it may seem. Gittings notes in the medieval period there being 'a greater perceived continuity . . . between the states of being alive and being dead' and this could lead to some ambiguity.[117] In cases of murder, there was 'a widely held tradition, believed even by James I, that the corpse would bleed if its murderer approached or touched it' and Gittings quotes a sworn statement made at a murder trial heard at the Hertford Assizes in 1629:

> That the body being taken out of the grave thirty days after the party's death . . . the four defendants . . . touched the dead body . . . the deceased opened one of her eyes, and shut it again three several times . . . thrust out the ring or marriage finger three times . . . and the finger dropped blood on the grass.[118]

The perception of life and death that this attests to – giving rise to myths of the undead, the living dead, the walking dead – is traditionally resolved by a decent burial, preceded by a dignified funeral, the opposite of which we have just observed taking place at a crossroads in East London in 1811. Gittings describes how 'the funeral marks the ritual separation of the living and the dead'.[119] As Thomas Sparke's *A brotherly perswasion to unitie* declares in 1607, 'burials are in some sort civil, human, and politic things'.[120] In late medieval times, the moment of actual interment was less significant than what might be up to three burial services that led up to it.[121] In the contemporary religious context the integrity of the body meant a better possibility of bodily resurrection and hence even felons wanted 'to be buried *decently*, preferably in the home churchyard; "decently" was always the word used', and since this was the case, Gatrell explains, 'authorities knew how to thwart these expectations cruelly [and] . . . struck at popular anxieties deliberately'.[122] Conventions in funeral rituals were adhered to very strongly and, in this, the precise orientation of the body was significant; Francis Tate describes in 1771 how the body was 'laid with the face upright, and the feet towards the door'.[123] In the grave the orientation would be with 'the head lying to the west . . . that he may rise with his face to the east'.[124] Various conventions were enacted in various localities, and even these decencies could include a genuflection to the power of the crossroads: one Irish tradition practised in Carlow as late as 1940 was that 'during funeral processions the coffin was placed on the ground at every crossroads and "de Profundis" [Psalm 130] was recited by four venerable laymen'.[125]

Attitudes to suicide and hanging have of course evolved, but even at the time there were some noteworthy contrasts and contradictions in the perception of these. Houston notes that in both England and Scotland 'the corpses of self-murderers were the sites of complex meanings and contested understandings', and that they were 'seldom the objects of universal revulsion or generalized sympathy'.[126] Thus popular cultural responses could be not merely complex but nuanced. Throughout the eighteenth century especially, songs known as 'flash ballads', reveling in 'drink, devil-may-care heroism', and exactly the kind of 'bleak endings at Tyburn' that led to crossroads burial were incredibly popular; so popular in fact that in 1750 the Bishop of London lay the blame for a recent earthquake on what he called these 'infamous and obscene songs and ballads that are openly sung on our public streets, to the great uneasiness of all modest and virtuous persons who are passing by; to the great corruption and depravity of our servants and children'.[127] At the same time as its celebration in lyric form, however, sometimes even the desecration of a crossroads burial was not enough to assuage popular social rage, as *The Gentleman's Magazine* reported in 1735: 'a London mob were so incensed by the suicide of a murderer named James Newth that they exhumed his body from the crossroads and mutilated it'.[128]

The place of outcast burial itself was also subject to certain ambiguities which develop especially over time, as the next chapter explores more fully. On the one hand, as Terence Murphy says, both 'the site of a suicide and the place of burial ... were popularly regarded as accursed, ritually polluted, and subject to haunting'.[129] On the other, such sites of outcast burial could become the grounds for public sympathy, even deliberate memorialisation. This process may be illustrated in the history of the Cross Bones cemetery in Southwark, London, which was established originally as an unconsecrated outcast graveyard for prostitutes, presumably principally those working the area of the sinful suburbs around the public theatres and within the Liberty of the Clink.[130] Stow notes the function of this 'Single Woman's churchyard' in his Survey of London in 1598 as being for women who were 'forbidden the rites of the church, so long as they continued that sinful life, and were excluded from Christian burial'.[131] As with much church history, the quality of mercy is singularly lacking in this response, which obviously proved ineffective – Cross Bones was closed in 1853 because it was 'overcharged with dead'.[132] In 1883, when the land was sold to be used for building, Lord Brabazon, an interested party, sent a stiffly worded letter to *The Times*, requesting successfully that the land be saved from 'desecration'.[133] Locals also repelled later attempts to develop the place and to use it as a fairground. Once the immediate context has passed, a longer view allows for more compassion perhaps and for the lives lived to pass into respected memory despite their perceived moral choices. But importantly, the potential for desecration suggests that the place possesses a consecration of its own.

The mutilation of corpses was also, perhaps unsurprisingly, fraught with contradictory impulses. Of course the relatives would wish to avoid the shame of such damaging rituals.[134] Even its cautionary and exemplary functions were questionable. Houston cites the eighteenth-century Milanese writer of jurisprudence, Caesare Bonesana, in whose opinion punishing the dead 'would make no more impression on the living than whipping a statue'.[135] In fact, such 'retributive rather than reformatory' justice was itself becoming less than socially respectable.[136] As Houston outlines, by 1700 in Scotland 'punishments that had been judicial or para-judicial, including dragging bodies through public streets and hanging them on gibbets' lost their judicial status and became merely popular.[137] Since the mistreatment of corpses was meant to reaffirm a certain social order this would require an authoritative basis and without legal sanction it was bound eventually to fall away.[138]

Also, the fact that the practices of mutilation and outcast burial were not universal suggests the possibility of sympathies offered the victims of suicide, if not quite those of hanging. Gittings records an instance in 1597 at Drypole, Yorkshire, where 'Anne Ruter a single woman drowned herself and was buried the 4th day of July on the north side of the church', which implied a slight dishonour but not an outright rejection.[139] Houston mentions that in fifty years of *Ware's Whitehaven Advertiser* from the late eighteenth century, eighteen suicides are reported over the six northern counties. Of these, three mention unusual burials and these all involve convicted criminals: one of these is interred at a crossroads, one on Lancaster moor (both staked), and the third was 'ordered to be buried at low water mark'.[140] Houston may be correct therefore to suggest that English burial practices are not particularly severe, or at least become less so over time, though incorrect in suggesting that the practice of staking was confined to south-east England.[141]

Arguments for leniency start fairly early in this history. In his *Biathanatos* (1608) John Donne pleads for mercy for the victims of suicide and cites More's *Utopia* (1516) in which only those who 'killed themselves without giving an account of their reasons ... were cast out unburied'.[142] He cites the biblical examples of Jesus, Samson, Saul and Judas, and quotes church law which stipulates only the denial of oblations and the singing of psalms for the burial services of suicides.[143] Donne points out that in true canon law 'Cristian Buriall' is also denied to 'men slaine at Tilt', and mentions that the Romans treated those killed by lightning similarly; he quotes Pope Gregory's dictum that 'so much as a sumptuous funerall profits a wicked man, so much a base, or none at all hurts a godly'.[144]

Despite Plato's early injunctions about crossroads, highway burial appears not to have been a necessary indication of disapprobation by classical societies; the tombs of aristocratic families line the ancient Appian Way, for instance. Realino Marra and Marco Orrù have even suggested that in ancient Greece and Rome 'sanctions of suicidal actions were tenuous at best' and even after this, they were not universally applied, and only became common in the medieval period and afterwards.[145] Even then, as we see, ambiguous attitudes to suicide were possible. Harte gives the example of one Richard Wolph who killed himself in the1680s; initially Wolph 'was buried on Myddle Hill, att that crosseway where the roadway from Ellesmeare to Shrewsbury, called the Lowerway, goes over crosse the way that goes from Myddle toward the Red Bull' but although this was an 'exemplary location for a suicide burial' it was contested by those who knew his circumstances such that 'by the next night he had been dug up again and was resting unobtrusively in a field nearby'.[146]

But beyond these considerations, given its associations with the divine, the crossroads could also function as a sacred space in its own right, either as directly auspicious, or at least as the next best thing to consecrated ground.[147] Puhvel notes certain Greek, Slavonic and Indian traditions that 'counted interment at crossroads as particularly auspicious and indeed beneficial to the world of traffic passing by'.[148] One otherwise horrendously colonialist reading of indigenous Angolans describes their 'curious hankering after cross-roads as a place of interment', and even when the crossroads burial was prevented by the Portuguese colonial powers, the inhabitants 'succeeded in digging the grave by the side of the path'; its ritual significance evident from the practice that 'on and round it they plant certain species of euphorbias, and on the grave they lay various articles, such as cooking-vessels, water bottles, pipes, and arms'.[149] As late as 1852 it was reported that shamans in Siberia were 'by their own desire buried in cross-roads' so as to attempt to exert influence upon the locals after death.[150] In Sweden, duels were fought at crossroads so as to best invoke divine justice over the proceedings, which speaks to a more orthodox possibility of finding there the benign influence of the Christian God.[151] In the eighteenth century, Borlase asks why the place 'commonly chosen for the English suicide's burial was not simply by the way-side, but where four roads meet', concluding that it was because these locations 'were ordinarily regarded as *the most holy* that existed out of consecrated ground'. Borlase sees some human mercy in this, suggesting that 'it was especially at cross-roads that sepulchral monuments were erected, by the piety or superstition of our Roman Catholic forefathers, who thus secured the prayers of passers-by in favour of the dead'.[152] Noting that early Christian burials were not allowed in towns but had sometimes taken place on highways, the Victorian historian Philip Alexander Prince cites it as a curious fact, that 'those who now by our laws have been pronounced to have died (not being insane) by their own hands, are interred in the very spots where alone Christian burial was formerly allowed'. He argues that 'the *cross-roads*, those points where four roads meet, were considered sanctified by the accidental mark of the cross; and not even the consecrated ground of the churchyard was for ages considered equal in sacredness to those spots'.[153] Oral histories of crossroads burial that emerged in the early 1930s seem to show some agreement on the nature of the event which accord with these views in twisting the usual narrative of rejection and exorcism. E. S. Chalk describes the fate of an old couple called John and Mary Watts who suffered under enclosures and committed suicide together. Chalk asserts that they were buried and staked together at a crossroads because it was the 'holiest place possible outside the churchyard'.[154] A respondent called V meanwhile recounts how he was taught as a boy that the reason people might be buried at crossroads was that 'those were the places most likely to be avoided by the devil, and that the fastening of the body to the ground by a stake was a further protection against the devil snatching it away'.[155] J. P. Bacon Philips goes further in suggesting that this was so their bodies 'always had the shadow of the Cross resting on them', an image which is highly suggestive of the vertical axis of the crossroads and what lies beneath.[156]

It seems that, despite the intentions of religious authorities and the pressures of parish micropolitics, there exists a certain amount of pity for the victims of these harsh practices. But more than this, their identities are not only not extinguished by the process, they may even be inscribed into the very landscape, their names descending through the years as memorial place names even as those of their desecrators may be lost. A brief exchange on the matter in *Notes and Queries* in the early 1930s gives a flavour of the proliferation of this geographical act of memory. C. Wanklyn requests information on Morgan's Grave, which is 'at a point where three roads meet'.[157] H. Askew responds by listing eight other examples of such a thing, all at roads and most at intersections, within a mere twenty-mile radius: Cannards Grave (Shepton Mallet), Comber's Grave (Midsomer Norton), Hellicar's Grave (Frome), Mary's Grave (Chantry, Mells), Millard's Grave (Frome), Nan Bull's Grave (Crewkerne), Pain's Grave (Doulting) and Tucker's Grave (Norton St Philip).[158] H. Askew recounts Selby's Grave near Spennymoor, which is a known crossroads suicide burial site dating to 1660.[159] Joseph E. Morris adds Mather's Grave, commemorating a documented suicide crossroads burial in Derbyshire in 1716.[160] W. Bradbrooke submits Mucklow's Grave, marking another documented suicide burial in Worcestershire in 1773.[161]

Charles Harper notes a further eight examples: Chunk Harvey's Grave, Geoffrey Lagden's Grave, The Boy's Grave, Farley's Grave, Deacon's Grave, Gilbert's Grave, Betty's Grave, Snook's Grave – the last being a documented site of a person hanged in 1802 for robbing a postboy.[162] Joseph E. Morris then introduces Kitty Jay's Grave on Dartmoor, which dates to around 1802–40. This suicide burial spot is not only memorialised in the place name, but Morris is able to describe the care with which the site is treated, reporting that 'one day last summer [of 1933] a char-à-banc was seen to stop . . . while a lady alighted and placed a beautiful bouquet on the grave'.[163] Kitty Jay's Grave seems to continue to be carefully tended up to the present day in 2021 and even features in Dartmoor's tourist guides (see Figure 5.5).[164] Given these few examples, it would be difficult to argue that the memories of the victims had been expunged from the community and their names cursed as perhaps we imagine the original desecrators might have intended.

Figure 5.5 Kitty Jay's Grave, Dartmoor, at the crossing of the road from Batworthy to Widecombe in the Moor and the track from Manaton to Grimspound. (Image Capture: April 2009, Map data ©2021 Google)

In modern terms we might say that responses to suicide and hanging were conflicted, but it would be a beautiful irony if the latter few historians and lay people were correct in their interpretation of the crossroads as the second most holy place after the consecrated ground of the churchyard. Far from working as Richard II's abhorred common grave, with the cursed outcast resting under the feet of passengers and horses alike, burial at the crossroads may, in some cultural traditions at least, have been associated with the symbolism of eternal salvation, or have resonated with thoughts of sanctuary and protection from evil. Whether or not the origins of crossroads burial can support these themes, the historical narratives that develop around the practice result in forms of sympathetic memorialisation that may certainly have caused the original desecrators some dismay.

Chapter 6

Literature: Liminal Ground in Early Modern Drama

Where black roads cross in the white of the moon,
Dig her grave, to the stout old tune . . .
Hammer the pointed white-ash stick
Into her heart – Now there's the trick.
Earl Daniels, 'Crossroads Burial' (1937)[1]

No rest she had in the old town church,
No grave by the lake so sweet,
They buried her in unholy ground,
Where the four cross-roads do meet.
Dora Mary Shorter, 'The Fetch' (1899)[2]

With downward face, now mark him well.
As if to view his native hell!
Nail'd fast with knotty stakes: –
Where cross the roads they dug his grave;
There howls his ghost! – unlucky knave.
Taliesin Williams, 'Doom of Colyn Dolphyn' (1837)[3]

A dozen men sat on his corpse
To find out why he died
And they buried Ben in four cross-roads
With a stake in his inside.
Thomas Hood, 'Faithless Nelly Gray' (1828)[4]

'Tis here three cross-roads meet –
Observe that stake! 'Twas in the midway plac'd . . .
To draw the glance abhorrent, and the scoff
From vulgar passengers. It marks the grave
Of one self-slaughter'd! Miserable wretch!
William Dimond, 'Fragment in Blank Verse' (1800)[5]

As these epigraphs suggest, the pejorative burial and staking of people at crossroads has registered in Western popular poetry and ballads for centuries. In prose literature too, the popular imagination ranged over such matters and preserves the familiar refrain. The character of the Earl in the 1798 thriller *The Sicilian*, at the reading of a suicide note, swears that 'such an infernal monster' should not be allowed to be buried 'as if he had died a natural death'; the Captain, meanwhile had 'shuddered several times while reading the horrid scrawl', and opines that 'such a confession entitles him to be laid between four crossroads, with a stake driven through his body'.[6] It was said of one character in James Samuel Stone's 1887 *The Heart of Merrie England*, that 'had he lived to see the day when gallows should not be erected by the highway, nor suicides buried in the cross-roads, nor ghosts haunt the uncanny corners, he would have given up his spirit in despair'.[7]

The scene of the crossroads has been a compelling literary subject for many years, and given the cultural significance of the crossroads in the sixteenth and seventeenth centuries it is a very strange circumstance that the drama of that time seems on the whole to give it a wide berth. This may be because the aspirations of the writers tended rather towards the life of the city and the machinations of the royal courts rather than the more rural aspects of common experience. Where these are depicted there is a tendency to concentrate on the simplicity or stupidity of the rural populace rather than on the details of their domestic and spiritual practices. Where there is a sense of interest in the non-urban environment, it tends towards a pastoral idyll of some kind: one that draws its idyllic quality from its sense of freedom from the shackles of puritan urban moralities, rather than from a celebration of the ways of country life per se. The fact that the crossroads of dramatic ritual requires a certain liminality means that most of the focus of these practices would be on crossroads outside major urban developments, and indeed any crossroads chosen for these purposes would tend to be on the outskirts of even small settlements.

However, as the London of their focus is expanding, the burgeoning city is increasingly becoming a stage for once-liminal crossroads ceremonies and debates about what should be sited there. Also any writers and players on the road must have come across evidence of various crossroads practices, especially those of hanging and outcast burial. On any journey around the country at this time, the traveller would have passed over many crossroads, some being the sites of gallows.[8] If medieval Lincolnshire is a measure for early modern England, there being no more than five miles between any two sets of gallows, William Shakespeare's route from Anne Hathaway's cottage in Stratford to his lodgings near the Globe at Southwark might have taken him by as many as twenty separate highway gallows.[9] It is highly likely also that some of these were the burial places of suicides, with evident freshly turned earth or even the protruding butts of stakes, rooted in the unfortunate corpse's heart, to warn the passing traveller of the social shame of suicidal despair. Perhaps the sharp-eyed might have discovered lingering signs of other crossroads rituals performed there. Yet when Shakespeare writes the witches scene of *Macbeth* the setting is merely a 'heath' with no useful indication of the tracks that must have crossed at such a meeting place, tracks which Macbeth and Banquo must in all likelihood be following, and which could have deepened the dramatic moment of the encounter.

Christopher Marlowe's journeying around the south of England also apparently provokes no compulsion to employ the crossroads setting of the original devil-dealing tale and he chooses rather to resituate Faustus's pact within the more civil confines of his own study. Perhaps also these are attempts to avoid what must already have been a cliché: the crossroads working as a metaphor for the point of decision-making in a tired 'journey-of-life' narrative mode. The Oedipus and Hercules models suggest that employing the crossroads as a dramatic device might have been just too obvious to justify. A further consideration might be that the crossroads may resist dramatic staging, in the simple sense that the very scene might be difficult to depict easily. It might be argued that a simple signpost on the stage pointing in different directions could signify the crossroads adequately. However, this seems not to be the case: signage in this most obvious place at the time was apparently conspicuous by its scarcity, perhaps especially outside towns. Stow and Dekker complain of its absence and desire that such a thing be instituted, at crossroads at least, for the facility of the unfamiliar traveller. A fingerpost-style signpost of the kind later times made familiar might thus have seemed a modern anomaly to an audience of the late sixteenth and early seventeenth centuries. This deficiency may be indicated in Daniel Defoe's desire not to lack 'Directions for his way' in his 1697 *Essay Upon Projects* which deals with road improvements.[10] He is not the only social commentator of the time to suggest that signposts should be placed 'at every turning ... for the Direction of Strangers'.[11] It was not until 1698 that parishes were required to set up signposts at crossroads in England, although the French had been doing this since the early seventeenth century.[12]

As we have seen, in Shakespeare's lifetime and long after, to live or to die in certain proscribed ways, as a traitor or a suicide for instance, meant, *post extremis*, to be treated as public refuse and buried in or by a roadway, the detritus of a social and religious construction of the world which could admit no incoherence in death. Claude Lévi-Strauss offers a description of two contrasting societies: those which practise cannibalism, that is, those 'which regard the absorption of certain individuals possessing dangerous powers as the only means of neutralizing these powers' and those which 'adopt what might be called the practice of *anthropemy* (from the Greek *emein*, to vomit).[13] Shakespeare's was of the latter kind. When Nashe suggested in 1589 that the rebellious authors of the Martin Marprelate tracts, once dead, 'should not be buried in any church . . . chapel, nor churchyard . . . but in some barn, outhouse . . . field [or] . . . dunghill', the sentiment expressed this commonly held belief about the rightful interment of the remains of those who troubled fundamental social or religious norms.[14] This was not the case, however, for the majority of the victims of execution, who were typically buried in the churchyard of the parish where the gaol or gallows stood. Gittings notes the parish register for St Mary's, Reading, for 26 March 1679, which records four men 'hanged and buried' there on that same day.[15] Even after the notoriously draconian 'Black Act' of 1723, Christian burial rites were denied only to the most serious offenders.[16] But nevertheless, throughout the period there were quite a number of people who were considered to be in this category of the worst of the worst and it is probable that, like many in his community, Shakespeare was familiar with some of them.

Indeed, it is highly likely that in the five years between 1582 and 1586, that is between the formative ages of 18 and 22, Shakespeare knew of at least five people, either related to his family or close local contemporaries, regarded by many as the direst of society's delinquents: Thomas Cottam, Edward Arden, John Somerville, Francis Throckmorton and Robert Dibdale. Their final resting places are unlikely to have been proximate to the consecrated ground of church, chapel or churchyard. Indeed, rather than a barn or dunghill, their graves would most likely have been beside or beneath some sort of public road, most likely a crossroads.

The first of these, Thomas Cottam, was the brother of one of Shakespeare's schoolmasters at King's New School in Stratford. Having been trained in the Catholic priesthood at Douai and ordained in 1580, Cottam was arrested upon his return to England as a missioner and eventually executed as a traitor at Tyburn on 15 May 1582. The fact that, soon after this, his schoolmaster brother John Cottam left both the school and the Stratford area points to local knowledge of the facts surrounding his execution.[17] In the following year, the second, Edward Arden, a possible kinsman of Shakespeare's on his mother Mary Arden's side, was arrested after being implicated in his son-in-law John Somerville's mad plot to assassinate Elizabeth I. He was hanged, drawn and quartered, at Smithfield on 20 December 1583.[18] Some years later, in 1599, Shakespeare applied to the official herald for the authority to 'quarter his arms with those of Arden', indicating a continuing relationship with the family over the intervening period.[19] Opinion differs on whether the third troubling person, the would-be assassin Somerville either 'hanged himself in Newgate' or was otherwise found suspiciously strangled in his cell.[20] Either way, if Somerville were not known to Shakespeare it would be a curious coincidence that the name 'John Somerville' appears in *Henry VI, Part 3*, one of Shakespeare's earliest plays and written only a few years after Somerville's death in 1583.[21] Edward Arden's wife, Mary Throckmorton, meanwhile, was a probable kinswoman of the fourth of these locals, Francis Throckmorton, who was arrested in November 1583 as an agent for a conspiracy in which England was to be invaded by a French army under Henri, duc de Guise, which was aimed at freeing Mary Queen of Scots and restoring the authority of the Pope.[22] Shakespeare's local acquaintance with this family also is very likely, and Throckmorton's execution as a traitor at Tyburn on 10 July 1584 would have certainly been 'common talk in Stratford-upon-Avon' that year, as Charlotte Carmichael Stopes argued.[23] Fifthly, and perhaps most significantly however, in October 1586 another Catholic missionary priest, Robert Dibdale, also ended his days at the Tyburn tree as a traitor. Dibdale was not only an associate of the schoolmaster's renegade brother Thomas Cottam but also an exact local contemporary of Anne Hathaway. Anne must certainly have known Dibdale and his family, and Frank Walsh Brownlow cites the fact that his brother-in-law had witnessed Anne's father's will, of which she was a beneficiary.[24] By extension it is extremely likely that Shakespeare would also have known, or at the very least known of, Dibdale, and his fate at the time. Edgar Fripp speculates about an even closer possible relation between the two through their respective maternal lines.[25] This connection is of particular interest since Dibdale had also been central to the notorious case of the 'Denham exorcisms', an episode of spurious priestly practice and Catholic propagandising in Denham, Buckinghamshire, later the subject of Harsnett's influential *Declaration*.[26]

Harsnett's *Declaration* is a book that Shakespeare is known to have read sometime before 1605, after which it seems to influence his writing of *King Lear* and other plays.[27] It also offers some conceptual and geographical associations of the crossroads that we will come back to. However, despite the various possible connections between the fate of these contemporaries and the author's own background, in the main Shakespeare's drama tends to skirt around the issues of imprisonment and execution, and what happens at crossroads is largely unacknowledged in his imaginative world. Richard Wilson has pointed out his relative 'effacement of contemporary violence' and others have noted that Shakespeare's project seems to 'occlude the barbarity of Tyburn and the Tower', especially where this is connected to any hint of religious controversy.[28] This may have been a self-protective measure, and was perhaps a symptom of the taboo nature of his early connections with the conspiratorial Catholicism of such outcast dead. Tyburn, 'that other great London stage', might also conjure some uncomfortable connections when someone as familiar as the ex-playwright Anthony Munday could be found haranguing unfortunate Catholic prisoners there.[29] But nevertheless, despite Shakespeare's relatively light handing of these weighty contemporary issues, the specific question of the burial of such dubious subjects emerges in various hints and allusions found in the plays, occasionally wandering onto the stage themselves like the shadowy revenants of unquiet thoughts.

One such intimation is found in the phrase Hamlet uses to reply to his father's ghost, '*hic et ubique*' (I, v, 156), or 'here and everywhere', which is an extract from a liturgy that may be used to refer to those buried in unconsecrated ground, as John Klause notes.[30] This would be an important usage because it functions to express Hamlet's uncertainty about the ghost at this point in the play, since an uncertain burial would imply that it might indeed be merely a typical wandering spirit rather than the authentic ghost of his murdered father. Another allusion, in *All's Well That Ends Well*, has Parolles refer to the same trope of unconsecrated burial among the sophistry of his comedic discourse on the nature of virginity: 'He that hangs himself is a virgin: virginity murders itself, and should be buried in highways out of all sanctified limit, as a desperate offendress against nature' (I, i, 120–2).[31] This appears to be delivered with some irony – the hanging of virgins possibly alluding to the perceived innocence of the Catholic priests who may be hanged, and afterwards buried 'out of all sanctified limit', in the 'highways' he mentions. Shakespeare mentions the gallows twenty-one times, but Tyburn in direct reference only once.[32] Here, Berowne of *Love's Labour's Lost*, also refers obliquely to the hanging of innocents in reference specifically to Tyburn's triangular construction, as the scene's three watching lovers make up what he describes as 'the triumviry, the corner-cap of society, / The shape of love's Tyburn that hangs up simplicity' (IV, iii, 50–1).[33] 'Simplicity' was again synonymous with innocence at the time, and thus this may again refer to the perceived innocence of the religious victims of Tyburn. Tyburn is certainly on other Londoners' minds throughout the period, and positively proverbially so. The medieval *Interlude of Youth* is darkly ominous in its use of the place as one character declares 'The Mayor of London sent for me / Forth of Newgate for to come / For to preach at Tyburn' (253–5) as Darryll Grantley writes.[34] And in *Like Will to Like*, Grantley notes how Ralph Roister and Tom Tosspot are 'offered the potential patrimony of St Thomas-a-Waterings and Tyburn Hill as a reward for proving themselves as thorough knaves (380–4), not realizing the implications of being offered these gallows locations.'[35]

Highway burial outside a 'sanctified limit' is described in *Richard II* where the deposed king offers to exchange his large kingdom for an obscure and trivial grave, or even worse as he petulantly complains,

> I'll be buried in the king's highway,
> Some way of common trade, where subjects' feet
> May hourly trample on their sovereign's head;
> For on my heart they tread now whilst I live;
> And buried once, why not upon my head? (III, iii, 155–9)

Richard's concern here with the public nature of the putative grave indicates partly the form of punishment such burial is intended to perform. Shakespeare's understanding of the dishonour of such burial is shown when Henry V, begging a blessing before Agincourt, feels the need to assure God, 'I Richard's body have interrèd new / . . . and I have built / Two chantries where the sad and solemn priests / Sing still for Richard's soul' (IV, i, 288, 293–5), though the fact that God appears so far to have missed this suggests a certain level of irony. There are echoes and hints of contested burials also in *Titus Andronicus*, in which George Peele is highly likely to have had a hand.[36] This play begins at the tomb of the Andronici and is obsessed with legitimate and illegitimate holes – wombs and tombs – and graves whose corpses 'walk', as in Aaron's confession: 'Oft have I digg'd up dead men from their graves, And set them upright at their dear friends' doors' (V, i, 137–8). The first contested burial is of Mutius, one of Titus's sons who survives Rome's war with the Goths, but is killed by Titus himself for trying to help Bassianus run off with Lavinia. Lucius pleads: 'But let us give him burial, as becomes; / Give Mutius burial with our brethren' (I, i, 352–3); Titus replies 'Traitors, away! he rests not in this tomb / . . . Here none but soldiers and Rome's servitors / Repose in fame; none basely slain in brawls: / Bury him where you can; he comes not here' (I, i, 354, 357–9). It is to no avail that Marcus Andronicus responds, 'My lord, this is impiety in you' (I, i, 360). The second dishonourable burial is at the detestable pit in the forest (attributed most likely to Shakespeare), where Bassanius's corpse is thrown when he is murdered, and where Lavinia is raped with Tamora's approval, who has 'wander'd hither to an obscure plot' as Bassanius says. The pit is described as an 'unhallowed and bloodstained hole' (II, iv, 19), 'detested, dark, blood-drinking pit' and a 'swallowing womb /. . .poor Bassanius' grave' (II, iv, 19, 33, 48–9). Marjorie Garber sees this as a 'graphic and nightmarish . . . image of female sexuality' and the geography here as a 'living metaphor, a dream landscape' which represents the plays vile events.[37] In these passages, Peele and Shakespeare's precise modes of collaboration are disputed but include the probability of each influencing the other's style whatever the division of labour.[38] It seems also that there is a shared sense of the visceral horror, and quite possibly a fear, of dishonourable burial which manifests in this play as deeply misogynistic geographical imagery.

Typically, the bodies of those executed for treason, or their recoverable pieces, would be laid to rest 'near or under the gallows', and the public gallows, as we have seen Tyburn included, were most often sited at a common crossroads.[39] Burial at such places implies an attempt at utter rejection, the ousting of the unclean spirit from the community's bosom and from rest with the revered dead. It also suggests the permanent outing of private space, placing the ultimate privacy, the grave, by that most public of passing places, the confluence of roadways. It may be argued that crossroads burials were a signal not so much of the simple difference between the public and the private, however, but rather of an association with a particular kind of publicness: one denoting liminality and a lack of Christian oversight. Such places may be suitable for the things no one wishes to claim, for dishonourable graves and gibbets. Burial at the public crossroads, then, implies both an exorcism and an enforced liminality that no doubt adds to the troubling ambiguity of the status of the corpse. The crossroads thus operates as a kind of public caging area for the netherworld, in comparison with which even a marketplace has a certain privacy, delineated by its boundaries.

Aside from the function of social exorcism actioned by its very public nature, a question remains over why many societies specifically chose the 'crossways' as an appropriate place for the burial of outcasts. Early modern graveyards were also notoriously public places, so much so that concerned bishops issued injunctions, one against the 'feeding of cattle ... the playing of games, depositing dung, the emptying of chamber-pots or "easing of nature", fighting, performing plays and hanging out washing', all of which were apparently taking place in early modern churchyards.[40] Some greater privacy was promised with burial inside the church itself, but this became so prevalent that churches were often overcrowded with underfloor corpses, and thus strong discouragement was offered to this option.[41] Crossroads, therefore, must have offered some deeper level of public disgrace, connected with their particular geography or historical associations.

Since they were equally disruptive of the natural order of things, the corpses of traitors and suicides were often similarly punished by being dishonourably buried in roadways as the worst of social offenders. In fact, the self-destructive act itself was portrayed as another species of treasonous revolt. In dealing with the estate of Sir James Hales, who drowned himself in 1554, Lord Dyer described suicide as 'an offence against nature, against God, and against the King'.[42] Arnold Van Gennep outlines how mortuary rites 'proceed through three phases: separation, transition, and integration'; suicides were perceived as disrupting this process and therefore not making this transition into integration.[43] It was thought that they could not 'fully enter the realm of the dead, since they did not await Death's summons [and] their ghosts are dangerous and intrusive', as MacDonald and Murphy put it.[44] They were, as Victor Turner says, 'transitional beings ... particularly polluting'.[45] By burying the body by a road, in a highway or at a crossroads at night, the community was able to remove the spiritual pollution that the suicide attracted and to protect itself against the unfortunate person's malevolent revenant.[46] The clearly insane Somerville, for instance, if suicide was indeed considered to be the cause of death, would in all likelihood have been barred from having his remains interred in consecrated ground even if he were found innocent of his treasonous assassination plot. Sixteenth- and seventeenth-century courts were very rarely in favour of returning the *non compos mentis* verdict that would have excused the act as the result of madness rather than badness and allowed the full rites of burial in sanctified earth.[47] In fact between 1487 and 1660, only 1.6 per cent of suicides in total were returned *non compos mentis*.[48]

The pre-eminent discussion of these issues in Shakespeare is of course that surrounding the case of Ophelia in *Hamlet*, a play entirely premised on the idea of a troubled, walking spirit, though its gravity is somewhat lightened in the play by its introduction through the misprision of clowns. The Gravedigger asks, 'Is she to be buried in Christian burial, when she wilfully seeks her own salvation?' and the Second Man replies, 'I tell thee she is. Therefore make her grave straight. The crowner hath sat on her and finds it Christian burial' (V, i, 1–5). However, he concedes 'if this had not been a gentlewoman she should have been buried out o'Christian burial' (V, i, 22–5). Social rank was indeed a factor in these matters. When Francis Norris, 1st Earl of Berkshire shot himself with his crossbow in 1622, the court ordered the coroner that 'the evidence touching the earle of Berkshires manner of death must not be urged, but the matter made as fair as possible'; 'fair' in this context of course meant a whitewash, and the Earl was ruled *non compos mentis*, a verdict five times more likely for the wealthy than for commoners at this time.[49]

A staked burial at a crossroads was meant to remove the supernatural pollution caused by suicide, protect a society against the return of the evil and restore good spiritual order.[50] In terms of contemporary received wisdom on the matter, although both Luther and Calvin had argued that suicide was caused by demonic attack or possession, Augustine and Aquinas had not.[51] Luther in particular asserted that this freed the cleric from worries about punitive burial. In *Hamlet*, Shakespeare does not imply Ophelia's suicide is demonic in origin and thereby leaves the question of legitimate burial open. Her right to 'Christian burial' in consecrated ground rather than under or beside a road or crossroads therefore is uncertain, although the Priest accompanying her burial party ends the matter by admitting that 'Her death was doubtful / And but that great command o'ersways the order / She should in ground unsanctified been lodged / Till the last trumpet' and declaring that instead of 'charitable prayers /, Flints and pebbles should be thrown on her'. One can feel the brooding resentment in his conclusion: 'Yet here she is allowed her virgin crants / Her maiden strewments, and the bringing home / Of bell and burial (V, i, 216–23).

Forbes gives a contemporary report of the burial of one lacking Ophelia's wealth and influence who 'wilfully' sought her own 'salvation', in the coroner Thomas Wilbraham's report in 1590 of Amy Stokes mentioned previously who, not 'having the fear of God before her eyes . . . hanged herself from a beam in a bedroom' with a ha'penny cord. Since the jury returned a verdict of *felo de se*, she was buried at night at a crossroads and a stake was driven through the corpse's chest.[52] A renegade priest was buried at a crossroads in 1614 with a stake through his stomach after his death was represented as suicide, although he may have fallen from a roof while being pursued by co-religionists.[53] A later and more prominent example, with some similarity to the case of John Somerville, is of the body of one Miles Sindercombe, who was indicted and sentenced to death for treason for trying to kill Oliver Cromwell, but somehow contrived to poison himself in prison. His corpse was ordered by the coroner on 17 February 1656 to be buried 'according to Law, in the next Common High-way', and according to the anonymous author was, thus,

> drawn to the open place upon Tower Hill . . . and there under the Scaffold of Common execution a Hole being digg'd, he was turned in stark naked, and a stake, spiked with Iron, was driven through him into the earth; That part of the stake which remaines above ground, being all plated with Iron; which may stand as an example of terror to all Traytors for the time to come.[54]

The scaffold on Tower Hill was on a rise overlooking what was at the time a crossing of obscure roads leading to Chick Lane and Tower Street, just outside the Tower of London's Postern Gate, where passers-by would have had ample opportunity to consider the iron-plated butt of the stake which pinned the corpse below (see Figure 5.1). Failing the privilege of wealth and influence, Ophelia's 'ground unsanctified' would most likely, or at least conventionally, have been at such a crossroads, where the body would be roughly and unceremoniously dumped into its hole at night, and possibly staked with a long enough piece of wood that its end might be left protruding above ground. As we have seen, the visible stake is meant as a warning to the living. Weever reports in 1631 that suicides were buried 'in or near to the highways, with a stake thrust through their bodies, to terrify all passengers, by that so infamous and reproachful a burial, not to make such their final passage out of this present world'.[55] Such a protruding stake, possibly with its butt bound in iron, must in fact have been a fairly common thing to have seen at various crossroads throughout the land during this period and may therefore be threateningly implicit in the priest's invocation of Ophelia's 'ground unsanctified'.[56] Perhaps local children would dare each other to kick it.[57]

But the provocation to terror, however socially useful it may have been, was not the stake's only purpose. Besides its evidently cautionary role, there is another function of the stake that is also important to early modern societies, which accords with the location of a burial at a crossroads and which relates to what was obvious to many throughout the period: that the spirits of the unquiet dead walked the earth after death.[58] This superstition was not restricted to the fanciful imaginings of dramatists, but was one which many funeral rituals and traditions of the day, and of long afterwards, were designed to guard against. In early modern Lincolnshire one funerary practice involved tying a thread around the corpse's ankles to stop the ghost of even an entirely innocent deceased from roaming and finding its way back.[59] The preparation of the corpse by spreading it with salt was also supposed to prevent the same thing.[60] In his poem 'To Perilla' (1648) Robert Herrick, whose father's own suicide clearly exercised continued influence over his poetry, writes, 'Dead when I am, first cast in salt . . . / Then shall my ghost not walk about, but keep / Still in the cool and silent shades of sleep.[61] Prevention of a corpse's walking could also be effected by employing a person known as a 'sin-eater'. As John Aubrey explained in 1686, these were 'poor people, who were to take upon them all the sinnes of the party deceased . . . the Corps was brought out of the house and layd on the Biere', then a loaf and a maple bowl full of beer and 'sixpence in money' were delivered to the sin-eater 'in consideration whereof he took upon him . . . all the Sinnes of the Defunct, and freed him (or her) from walking after they were dead'.[62] These various ways of stopping a ghost from returning to trouble the community help to explain the necessity for the stake in cases of particularly troubled revenants, who might want to 'rise again . . . / And push us from our stools' (*Macbeth* III, iv, 81, 83).

Probably written shortly after Shakespeare read Harsnett, *Macbeth* plays around with these issues of superstition, spiritual credulity and the walking of the unquiet dead. Lady Macbeth dreams and herself walks like one dead, talking to reassure her disturbed self, 'look not so pale: I tell you yet again Banquo's buried; he cannot come out on's grave' (V, I, 60–1).[63] But it is dawning on this sceptic, at least in her unquiet dreams, that Banquo already has. Macbeth's own concern is with the implied disturbance of the natural order, as he states, 'If charnel-houses and our graves must send / Those that we bury back, our monuments / Shall be the maws of kites' (III, iv, 71–3). The strong imagery of these emetic resting places, spewing sepulchres, seems to follow strong sentiment on these matters. In terms of his depiction of the returning ghost, rather than reproducing the typical Senecan gibberers of a classical underworld, Shakespeare offers something closer to 'superstition drawn from native ghost-lore' as F. W. Moorman shows, and this is linked syncretically to both pagan deities and the satanic cloak that Christianity threw over them.[64]

In the case of roadside burials, not only were the crimes or traumas of these outcast dead enough to disturb their eternal repose but because a proper funeral was required 'to assist the passage of the soul to the hereafter', as Gittings says, merely withholding this ceremony alone might cause the soul to walk.[65] Proper burial rites withheld or interrupted in a Hindu ceremony may cause the soul automatically to take residence at the place of the funeral pyre or at a crossroads.[66] Denying these literal rites of passage then, as was the case when the community exorcised itself of the remains of a suicide or traitor, in refusing the dead integration, compounded the potential spiritual predicament in a way which needed rectifying in its own turn.[67] Thus, the stake comes to seem like a reasonable insurance policy against the almost inevitable return of the dead. In other words, without the stake to hold her troubled spirit in place, an Ophelia bereft of rites might well have become as one of Puck's feared 'ghosts, wandering here and there, / ... Damned spirits all' who must 'troop home' in this case to the 'crossways and floods' where they 'have burial'; one of those who, since they 'willfully themselves exil'd from light ... must for aye consort with black-brow'd night' (III, ii, 380–3, 386–7).[68]

In early modern culture, and in some places still, the crossroads is not only a liminal place, but also a nexus where paths, movement and points of decision simultaneously converge and part. For many, as we have seen, crossroads were haunted places, echoing with folk memory of forbidden religious and magical rituals. Puck's crossways-buried spirits reference this history of the crossroads as a place with an apotropaic function, to guard against evil. Since the geographical confluence of roadways itself was supposed to confuse the restless spirit, 'to diffuse the evil influence of the body in several different directions' as Gittings describes, its effective power was to arrest the movement of turbulent ghosts who might otherwise walk the roads of the night home to the scenes of their particular traumas.[69] Here at the crossroads they may be fixed, their movement arrested, paradoxically, in a place of permanent transit and transition. This arresting ability of the crossroads may be related to the idea, as many myths have it, that spirits move in straight lines.[70] Staking added some insurance.

This was the context in which Harsnett's *Declaration* was offered against Catholic superstitions he adjudged to be haunting the nation. In this he emphasised his scepticism over things such as demons and the walking dead by lamenting the fact that 'our children, old women and maides [are] afraid to crosse . . . a three-way leet'.[71] A 'three-way leet' is a Y-shaped crossroads, of the kind that has been particularly associated with Puck's 'triple' Hecate.[72] The felt necessity to beware where one might walk that Harsnett describes speaks of places clearly haunted by the presence of the unknown and, in a period when place was tightly connected to a sense of belonging and spiritual oversight, to consign a corpse to such a place as the crossroads was to abandon it to a kind of primal chaos. One can only wonder at Shakespeare's reading of this critique of the notoriously egregious exorcisms carried out in the 1580s by his associate Dibdale as Harsnett connects the credulity of believers in folk religion and even a basic paganism with Catholic sympathies. Shakespeare must have been aware of the superstitious nature of attitudes to the physical crossroads and must himself have made the connection between these superstitions and those buried there. In de Certeau's 'determination through objects' in stories, which is as he says the 'law of a "place"', he notes that 'an inert body always seems, in the West, to found a place and give it the appearance of a tomb'.[73] A question remains then around the relative absence of this deeply dramatical social space from the work of the most accomplished dramatist of the age.

Any narration of geography involves what de Certeau calls 'procedures of delimitation' and as such marking of boundaries consists of 'narrative contracts and compilations of stories' which have the function of 'founding and articulating spaces'.[74] The placing of a body at a boundary then is to write it into the margins of a story as an element in the parergon, forming part of the defining frame. Refusing this interment is to refuse the influence of the marginal on the dramatic stage. De Certeau determines that 'it is the partition of space that structures it' and that 'there is no spatiality that is not organized by the determination of frontiers'.[75] This is of course not precisely applicable in respect to crossroads, which are polyliminal spaces dependent to some extent on the indeterminacy of their own sense of place. However, if as de Certeau says the 'role of stories in delimitation . . . is to *authorize* the establishment, displacement or transcendence of limits', what may be pushed to the boundaries of Shakespeare's work is precisely the boundary itself.[76] In as much as its margins define the story a society is able to tell itself about itself, this may be read as a gesture towards an open narrative on the important contemporary matters surrounding the crossroads. It may also be futile. As we have noted, any parting of ways is also a coming together of ways, seen from another perspective. This is seen by de Certeau too as a 'paradox of the frontier': that it is created by its contacts and hence 'the points of differentiation between two bodies are also their common points. Conjunction and disjunction are inseparable in them.'[77] In other words, although bound and obstructed by the crossroads and the stake, the outcast dead on the outskirts of Shakespeare's imagination will by their very persistent nature still troop home to us as spirits, 'doomed for a certain term to walk the night'. Despite the urge to exorcise such delinquents, they are often surprisingly incarnate, as, interred within cultural forms, they outlast monuments.

In avoiding the direct dramatic representation of crossroads, Shakespeare is in accordance with most of his contemporary writers, in whose plays the presence of the crossroads seems to haunt dramatic characters obliquely through linguistic and cultural associations. Like Shakespeare, for Ben Jonson being 'crossed' is most often a cipher for frustration. Their theatrical associate William Kemp uses it so in his road trip narrative *Kemp's Nine Daies Wonder* (1600): 'Crosse me no more I prethee with thy rabble of bald rimes, least at my returne I set a crosse on thy forehead, that all men may know thee for a foole.'[78] In Jonson's *A Tale of a Tub* (1633), Turfe links this frustration with crossroads when he asks 'Passion of me, was ever man thus cross'd? . . . / How should we bustle forward? Gi' some counsel, / How to bestir our stumps i' these cross ways' (III, i, 1, 18–19). Two lines previously, the shadow of the crossroads gallows falls to express determination to keep a secret: 'or let me be trussed up at Tyburn shortly' (II, vi, 52) and six lines on the 'hang-man's stomach' for hangings is invoked (III, i, 25). This is not a mere coincidence but rather evidence of a field of discourse around crossroads which is both subterranean to the narrative and central to the depiction of these constables.

An exception to this obliquity and insinuation is found, however, in George Peele's *Old Wives Tale* (1595) where an onstage crossroads is presented directly and which echoes with many of the themes of this book – improper burial, restless spirits, crossroads magic and transformative experiences at crossroads – albeit with a very light touch. This is a crossroads within a smithy within a forest and it therefore occupies a location within a location within a location. The theatrical presentation adds a further potential liminality. It is therefore multiply and exponentially liminal.[79] Without suggesting any intent on Peele's part, the tripling of this location, location, location seems to echo the proverbially triple nature of the crossroads itself, which is the source of its numinous and transformative reputation.

The liminal places here – crossroads, smithies, forests and theatres – have long been places associated with the power of transformation. Crossroads, as we see, have been the home of many of the gods of transformation. Forests are very often the scene of transformative narratives in literature generally, but especially in early modern drama, as Shakespeare's *A Midsummer Night's Dream* and *As You Like It* attest. Smithies, as the transmutational side of the job of ironworking implies, have been culturally significant places since the ages of metal and here, where 'Vulcan' (44) presides, there is an echo of that supernatural past. The fact that the Faustian folktale of 'The Smith and the Devil' has recently been proven to date back to the Bronze Age might give us to understand the depth of these associations in an oral heritage that predates what we call literature, or for that matter, scripture.[80] Not only is the crossroads in Peele's play transformational, but so are all of its outer settings and diegetic strata. We have a crossroads (in an inner play-narrative) within a smithy (in an outer play stratum), within a forest (within a theatre). This metadramatic form draws attention to these liminal strata through structures whose very business seems to be to disturb a sense of narrative stability. In early modern metadrama, structures of narrative are also structures of authority and oversight, and this is almost always at this time invested with the insidious presence of the informer, a connection about which I have written extensively elsewhere.[81] The usual early modern tendency to reproduce the structures of informing in a play's metadrama, as is the case in almost all other instances of early modern metadrama I have studied, is lacking here, except perhaps in a hint here and there. Unusually for the time, this metadrama does actually seem to offer a depoliticised setting of story within story, working merely as a convention maybe, but also, and this I resist admitting of almost all other examples of metadrama from the period, as a way of playing with the rules and parameters of the dramatic art, for its own sake. It still does toy with ideas around authority, agency and protection from evil, especially in the figure of dead Jack, the unburied and unquieted revenant, but instead the focus is on transformation and, although the play often hints at what may lie hidden beneath, it studiously avoids narrative depth in any form.

Given the recent loss of Christopher Marlowe to the writing community (possibly only a few months dead and buried at the time of writing), Peele may have felt keen at this time to avoid any suspicion of modes of theatre reminiscent of the structures of informing in his play.[82] On this count, Peele must certainly have known Marlowe, whose own combined careers of writing and informing may have been salutary, and he eulogised him in his 'The honour of the garter' (1593) as 'unhappy in thine end, / *Marley*, the Muses darling for thy verse; / Fitte to write passions for the soules below.'[83] Here he also laments 'The wrongs that learning beares of couetousnes / And Courts disdaine, the enemie to Arte.'[84] Peele himself may not be too familiar to us, but he was fully involved in the transformative business of theatre as a writer, although his involvement as an actor may be contested.[85] It has been suggested that Marlowe and Peele may both have contributed to *The First Part of the Contention betwixt the two famous Houses of Yorke and Lancaster* (1594).[86] Though named by Francis Meres's *Palladis Tamia* (1598) as the English Ariosto, alongside Marlowe, Kyd and Greene, he also apparently came across to his contemporaries as something of a 'shifty cozening companion', or as A. W. Bullen notes in the idiom of his own time 'a sharking tosspot'.[87] Apparently his writing did not afford him the transformation he might have desired. Greene's *Groats-Worth of Wit* describes him as having been 'driuen . . . to extreme shifts' and, as David H. Horne points out, besides being a possible reference to being driven to the expedient of writing for the public theatres, in the sixteenth century a 'shift' could also be 'a fraudulent device, an evasion or subterfuge'.[88] Despite this disreputable shadow to Peele's life, which might lead us to see him in Marlowe's world, Horne asserts that Peele was 'like his fellow Elizabethans, morally neither better or worse'.[89] More significantly for this present argument, Peele's links with Shakespeare are many. Peele was one of the University Wits implicated in the early 'upstart crow' reference to Shakespeare in Greene's *Groats-Worth of Wit*, which was not written by Robert Greene, but very probably by Henry Chettle.[90] Duncan Salkeld sees a further personal connection between the men in the diary of Philip Henslowe through a certain Clerkenwell brothel.[91] Brian Vickers meanwhile has described in convincing detail Peele's collaboration with Shakespeare on *Titus Andronicus*, with all of its wombs and tombs.[92]

In *The Old Wives Tale*, a daft, romping gallimaufry of fairy-tale motifs and a mad admixture of metadramatic forms and social issues are at play. Its fast-paced, possibly hour-long format encourages a dramatic experience of skimming over the surface of narratives of both high drama and quotidian folksiness without allowing us to settle into any given narrative with real sympathy. Nevertheless, it has some charm. The story involves three young pages who, after losing their way in a forest, happen upon the house of a smith named Clunch who offers them comfort in the form of food and beer. At their request, the play's eponymous 'old wife', Gammer Madge, then tells them a story. Clunch meanwhile persuades one of the pages to follow him upstairs for what he calls an 'unnatural rest'. As Madge tells of a king's daughter stolen away by a magician transformed into a dragon, and the brothers that try to rescue her, the characters of the story she is telling begin to materialise on the stage and the woman and her audience of guests then become the outermost frame of a metadrama which plays on various power structures, and significantly for our purpose, sites them at a crossroads. Here, marriageable girls each find a partner that fits them, time is disrupted as characters magically age prematurely or see their years reduced, the ghost of an unburied corpse appears, and the spirit of a well emerges from beneath, until ultimately all is resolved back to the outer frame in which Madge has fallen asleep and nothing significant has occurred.[93]

As he has adapted them for this play, Peele has transformed sources which are often themselves folk tales of journeys of transformation, including Apuleius' *The Golden Ass* which tells of 'men's forms and fortunes transformed' and the 'Three Heads of the Well' in which marriageable girls each find a partner that fits them, carrying shades of Dante.[94] He also adapts more 'literary' texts like Greene's *Orlando Furioso*, and his *Perimedes the Blacksmith* which fits with the initial setting of characters and also employs a metafictional frame narrative device partly involving a storytelling wife. Besides those of its sources, the play's narrative also contains various metamorphoses of its own. Binnie lists some character transformations for us: 'Erestus is transformed into a bear and an old man; Venelia into a mad, mute woman; Sacrapant transformed himself into a dragon, then into a seeming youth; Jack appears to be a live man.'[95]

The play hints at its own superstitious underpinnings at the outset, if again it skims only a surface. After their initial meeting of Clunch, the companions are taken inside the smithy over the threshold, upon which they are warned not to stumble (57), to the hearth and its 'good fire to sit by' (51). There is a cultural formality to this small moment which goes far beyond the 'bad luck' with which it is glossed in the Binnie edition. It would be typical of the time for the threshold and hearth of a house to be protected from evil influence by iron artefacts of some kind, or by buried apotropaia such as witch-bottles, dead cats or discarded shoes. A stumble at such a spot might indicate that the charm had tripped them and that therefore they must pose a threat to the household. In this way also the home hearth setting of the narrative offers a kind of protection from malign influence in which its drama might play upon disturbing issues around transformations of essence without fear of real evil consequences. This small hint at something lying beneath may be typical of the play's approach as its speedy presentation encourages an almost postmodern dramatic experience of skimming over the surface of narratives of both high drama and quotidian folksiness without allowing us to settle into any given element with real sympathy. Surfaces may be quite the issue here in many ways, or at least depths not quite penetrated; the Head's advice to the sisters at the well is 'Gently dip, but not too deep' (664), and this may be mirrored in the play's swiftly shifting restitutions of unwanted transformations.

The initial location within the smithy is where the wandering pages of the story, Antic, Frolic and Fantastic, who have lost their way in the wood (48–9) find refuge and a narrative. The dangers of the forest are treated lightly as Frolic declares that unless Clunch rescues them they are 'like to wander with a sorrowful heigh-ho, among the owlets and hobgoblins of the forest' (42–3). This is mirrored in the Two Brothers of the inner narrative, Calypha and Thelea, who wander looking for their sister. Other wanderers of the play include Venelia, who is beloved of Erestus and who 'runs madding all enraged about the woods' (203), the braggart knight Huanebango and his servant Corebus who are uncertain of their direction and ask Erestus the way to the conjuror's house (317–8), and Corebus again, who is blinded by Sacrapant to 'wander up and down / In naught but darkness and eternal night' (589–90), just as he has himself threatened the churchwarden 'We shall have you turned out of the parish one of these days, with never a tatter to your arse. Then you are in worse taking than Jack!' (530–3). To wander in this way is apparently worse than death, as we will explore later in this book.

Inside the smithy of course is the crossroads of the narrative, and wanderers are drawn to crossroads here and historically just as tales tend to wend their ways towards inner tales. Gammer Madge, who, it turns out, is a terrible storyteller, tells us that the conjuror Sacrapant 'turned a proper young man to a bear in the night and a man in the day' (129–30) and that this young man, Erestus, the

'White Bear of England's Wood' (169) 'keeps by a cross that parts three several ways' (130–1). That is, he lives at the 'three-way leet' of Harsnett's warning and of Hecate's favour, a type of crossroads feared as an extremely dangerous place to wander at night.[96] If there is also a cross at this crossroads, this is simply ignored as a sign of any kind. As she continues, the two brothers of the story materialise on stage and carry on the narrative themselves. Hence, the teller of the tale is now transformed into an onstage audience, as Frolic says 'Soft, gammer, here some come to tell your tale for you' and Fantastic adds 'Let them alone; let us hear what they will say' (134–5). This transition to metadrama then comes initially at the transformational crossroads.

Next, as the stage directions tell us, Erestus enters: *Senex at the cross, stooping to gather* (S.D. 144). He is gathering 'Hips and haws, and sticks and straws' as indications of his poverty, but the hawthorn fruit also hints of witchcraft, in keeping with the numinous location.[97] Crossroads were often sites for 'the ritual gathering of stones or herbs to be used in sorceries' as Francisco Bethencourt shows.[98] There is an association also of the mandrake-root element of many charms with crossroads.[99] Here at the three-way crossroads Erestus casts a spell for the two brothers aimed at finding the lost sister Delia. This charm for finding lost things begins with a triple rhyme 'hark well, and mark well, my old spell' (161) and asserting that 'things that seem are not the same' (164). He then sits at the crossroads to tell his 'heavy tale' (182) of his youth having been stolen by Sacrapant, 'Seeming an old and miserable man', while yet 'I am in April of my age' (200–1). He is therefore the subject of two forced transformations: one bestial and the other senile.

After giving his discontented neighbour Lampriscus some life-changing advice about his unmarried daughters, Erestus then 'Withdraws' (S.D. 249); he does not leave the stage, but remains a hidden audience at the crossroads, firstly of the harvest-men's song and then of Corebus and Huanebango. Here, in a crossover of metadramatic structure and crossroads imagery we have an onstage audience watching an onstage audience. This metadramatic moment draws attention to the experience of watching, although it tends to obscure the outer frame by a process I have called frame-blindness, where one may be drawn into a common perspective with the inner audience. It is interesting that, while such hidden oversight almost always expresses a relation of power, in this case that would be a fairly benign view. Momentarily, however, Erestus is nevertheless an unseen and empowered presence at the crossroads and one able to perform works of transformation.

Upon his entry at the crossroads where Erestus is still watching, Huanebango evokes the names of pairs of gods: 'by Mars and Mercury, Jupiter and Janus, Sol and Saturnus, Pallas and Proserpina' (268–70). Three of these are associated with crossroads: Janus whose double prospect is horizontal, Mercury who looks heavenwards to connect with the gods to whom he is messenger, and Proserpina, who is interchangeable with Hecate and whom we might find by looking down to the underworld. Despite this comprehensive invocation of the divine, he leaves without transacting charitably with the newly emerged Erestus and so receives no benefit at the crossroads but a curse of deafness. There is a ritual of exchange familiar from folk tale here which has clearly failed. In exchange for Corebus's gift of cake (346–9), however, Erestus prophesies over the clown favourably that his wealth might be transformed and though he is made blind by Sacrapant, he subsequently marries Celanta, the recipient of the fortune from the magical head in the well.

The succeeding interlude in Sacrapant's study might prompt a thought about crossroads and the possibilities of staging. Binney suggests that 'an "inner stage", or some kind of alcove with curtains before it, was commonly used as a conjuror's "study" or cell'.[100] When the two brothers again enter to catch a glimpse of Delia as she is dismissed from the study, however, they ask where to go, 'that or this?' (423), suggesting a level of confusion about place and direction that the play might well be founded upon. A more logical staging here might find them back at the 'cross that parts three several ways' (130–1), and this would imply that when Sacrapant *'removes a turf, and shows a light in a glass'* (S.D. 444) this is also at the crossroads, a magical device which would certainly fit with the history of place magic associated with crossroads. It would also seem to fit with the stage directions telling us that Erestus soon after re-enters 'at the cross' (S.D. 456) to meet the wandering knight Eumenides.[101] The crossroads works in this case as a convenient dramatic device, but also more than this it could easily be used to define all the movement spaces of the stage. Whatever the choice, if three locations are chosen as static positions on the stage, then the mound where the conjuror's life-light is buried and his study are still very much in the vicinity of the crossroads, and each shares the magical and transformational implications of the others.[102]

Although the play's repeated motifs of ground and burial go to work alongside the implied vertical axis of the crossroads's notoriously 'thin' place of ritual and metamorphoses, we may note that despite the digging, any promise of depth or permanence is at best illusory. Also, significantly, this place requires only a little digging to access the powers it promises. After asking to have his fortune told, Eumenides is told by Erestus to 'Bestowe thy alms, give more than all, Till dead mens bones come at thy call' (470–1), before lying down to sleep (possibly in the dust of the crossroad, a vulnerable situation to be in). Next to enter are the debaters on the issue of poor Jack's burial, and it would be entirely appropriate to the subject matter if this were at the crossroads too. Corebus's demand for 'Christmas burial' (488) for Jack is a clown's malapropism for the 'Christian burial' which he is outraged the churchwarden and sexton will not perform without payment. The linguistic play recalls that of the gravediggers from Ophelia's case. This central concern with burial recalls other instances in Peele's play where the ground is at issue. As we have mentioned Erestus is *stooping to gather* (S.D. 144) hips and haws. Erestus and Lampriscus at another point are looking towards the ground of the crossroads (206–7) and we might ask whether Lampriscus is looking down towards his two buried wives with whom he lived 'unquietly' as he says (219).[103] There may be some underlying anxiety that these unquiet wives might stand for the 'unquiet' souls crossroads were meant to contain. Also, their burials were on saints' days – St Andrew's (30 November) and St Luke's (18 October) – festivals whose survivals of folk celebrations included efficacious love prayers which may originate in the kind of fertility rites often enacted at crossroads.[104] That the harvest-men sing of sowing at the crossroads (262) also speaks of fertility rites. Later we also see Sacrapant digging for his life-light, either in the ground of the crossroads or as close as makes no difference (444). Then the two brothers are forced to dig for gold (S.D. 613), until they accidentally uncover the life-light (S.D. 629). Things buried at crossroads were often supposed to have magical efficacy, possibly derived from the gods who also dwelt there both above and below. Also, when the two heads rise from the well they reference Dante, whose own liminal well is at found the boundary of the eighth and ninth circles of Hell. The eighth circle is named Malebolge, the only one to be named – it means 'evil ditches'.[105] In the *Old Wives Tale*, Jack's friend Wiggen enquires of the churchwarden who is reluctant to bury the corpse of poor Jack 'whether will you have the ground broken, or your pates broken first?' (524–5), offering to do a little digging where it is least welcome. All of this points to power or possibly fear of power accessed somehow by directing the attention earthwards at certain significant places.

The chief fear expressed in this play is both of the magician and the dead, and for each, burial is the origin of their perilous influence. This dark undergirding of the play is handled lightly but persists nevertheless in subterranean hints. The kindly knight Eumenides pays for Jack's burial (545) but in ancient Greece the name 'Eumenides', or 'the kindly ones', was a euphemism for the furies, the deities of vengeance.[106] Mary Ellen Lamb points out 'the malice of the actual furies assisting the evil conjuror Sacrapant who was . . . born in Thessaly to a famous witch', although his magic is 'more folk than classical'.[107] After Eumenides has paid for the burial, Corebus mentions digging and crossing again when he tells the reluctant churchwarden to 'thank God the long staff and bilbow blade crossed not your cockscomb' before he votes for going to the 'church-stile' (549–51) for a pint. Though this is in all likelihood the name of a pub, it is worth noting that the church stile was regarded as another liminal and possibly magical place of encounter with the supernatural.[108]

Focusing in more closely on matters close to the crossroads, the play's anxiety over the proper burial of what Lamb calls Jack's 'indigent corpse' is echoed in Sacrapant's command to his furies to bear the presumed dead body of Huanebango 'away . . . into the open fields / To be a ravening prey to crows and kites' (587–8) rather than being properly interred.[109] His unquiet spirit then can only be expected to wander and he is raised from the dead (or merely revived) by the lightning that occurs when Zantippa attacks the head in the well (674). The apparition of the head from below, the raising of Huanebango, the granting of Zantippa her wish, each transformative encounter is the result of proximity to this enchanted space in the vicinity of the crossroads.

When dead Jack at first meets Eumenides (724) the former is invisible. Since he is improperly buried he is therefore an unquiet spirit, as Eumenides suspects in an aside (746) and accordingly Jack pinches him, in a manner reminiscent of the mischief of *Tempest*'s Ariel, *A Midsummer Night's Dream*'s Puck or of the 'fairies' set to torment Falstaff in *Merry Wives*. Despite this assault, Eumenides seems charmed by Jack and follows him where he wanders (832). Jack's status as an unquiet spirit gives him access to knowledge about the supernatural which plays on some of the same discourses which surround the idea of the crossroads. When Eumenides asks Jack 'they say it is good to go cross-legged and say his prayers backward, what sayest thou?' (832–4), this addresses the banning or binding nature of the saltire X. To depict someone as going 'cross-legged' is another apotropaic device. In the tarot-card tradition the Hanged Man is cross-legged and may be a depiction of the Norse god Odin, another crossroads deity imagined to be associated with Mercury.[110] But here Jack is impatient with his own supernatural status and wants nothing to do with these questions, keeping to surface matters and silencing the good knight: 'Tut, never fear, master; let me alone. Here sit you still; speak not a word' (835–6). The Jack and Eumenides folkloric story-type of 'The Grateful Dead' is, as Jackson I. Cope says, 'a ritual resurrection focused upon burial', a comedic form of mankind's role as a 'functionary of nature's renewal' and is thus another fertility narrative in accord with the others we have already seen at the crossroads in this play.[111]

Finally, the entire denouement of the play turns upon 'the unnatural wakefulness of the dead'.[112] This sees Jack protect Eumenides from the magician's enchantments (S.D. 838) and, as the unseen agent of this transaction of power, he 'invades the head of Sacrapant' (846) who screams 'What hateful Fury doth envy my happy state?' (847) and dies confessing moralistically, 'He in whose life his actions hath been so foul, / Now in his death to hell descends his soul' (852–3). Here we pass from folk tale to echoes of stage morality plays as Sacrapant's foul soul descends into the earth, and appropriately the vice-like Jack immediately looks to the next trouble he can instigate: 'O sir, are you gone? Now I hope we shall have some other coil' (854–5), echoing with the briefest resonances of the devilish informer figure. After being the catalyst for the resolutions of the play's ending, the restoration of Delia to her brothers, their release from Sacrapant's slavery, Erestus's renovation and his reuniting with Venelia, the menace of this unquiet spirit is still displayed in his demand for Eumenides to slice Delia in half to pay his promise of Jack benefiting by half of whatever Eumenides gained in their compact (an arrangement which is typical of the early modern informer). This echoes with the biblical Solomon and Abraham and Isaac, but also the troubling demands of a twisted contemporary mechanism of authority.[113] When Jack's catalysing and troublesome spirit exits to where he belongs it is the effect of Eumenides having paid for his proper burial – he leaves as a benign agent of the unseen worlds 'thank that good deed for this good turn. And so, God be with you all!' (949–50). When he 'leaps down in the ground' (S.D. 950) the unquiet spirit is laid to rest in the crucial earth of this play and God himself is set right in his heavens again, ultimately by the simple charitable exchange of the wanderer at the crossroads. De Certeau speaks of such narratives which operate by 'putting into a landscape . . . heroes who transgress frontiers and who, guilty of an offence against the law of the place, best provide its restoration with their tombs'.[114]

Back in the play's outer frame, Madge makes clear that 'this was the ghost of the poor man that they kept such a coil to bury, and that makes him help the wandering knight so much.' After all this disturbing metaphysical and mythical coil it is appropriate that they should seal the return back to reality with the physical sharing of 'a cup of ale and a toast ... bread and cheese' (964, 969) the staples of a breakfast that promises a day of non-supernatural normality ahead.[115]

Where Shakespeare takes a wide berth and skirts around the crossroads, Peele's play puts it at the heart of the narrative but skims across its surface. Like the ballads of later times, *The Old Wives Tale* trivialises the potentially fearsome activities at crossroads. Although the crossroads invites trivia by its very nature, the desire to avoid depth of engagement with its narratives of power suggests a self-defensiveness perhaps rooted in some residual belief in their efficacy. The message it projects seems to be not to dabble too deeply in such matters, otherwise unquiet spirits may invade your head, unwelcome corpses may walk and life-lights may be extinguished. Or that in looking too closely at such things, meddling in that Faustian sorcery you too may fall into Hell, the ultimate end of those who dig to dangerous depths. The placing of a body at a boundary is to write it into the margins of a story as a part of the defining frame. Disregarding this interment may be to reject the influence of the marginal, but on the dramatic stage this has a way of returning despite its excision from the script.

Chapter 7

Hallowed Roads: Routes to the Crossroads

A thousand spectres moved,
In 'dread array,' along 'the church-way-path'.
George Beattie, 'The Dream' (1824)[1]

Since for much of its history humankind's natural habitat was the road, it is possible that the reverence for the road is born of a kind of nostalgia, bearing with it a sense of the sacredness of paths to known places of rest and safety. In such a mobile ancient world, those who knew the roads, and crucially the crossroads, would be unusually culturally empowered. As Cresswell says, culture is more 'about routes than roots'.[2] The status of crossroads in the popular imagination is therefore intrinsically bound with culturally specific ideas of the road, its possibilities and dangers. The roads which intersect are themselves often invested with meaning that their crossing serves to amplify and therefore the reason crossroads are enchanted begins with the reason any road might be enchanted. In looking at this delimited geography we must therefore refer 'not only to the site as a hermetically sealed space but also to those roads which lead in and out of that space', as Sanders recommends.[3] This chapter explores roads as sacred or cursed, and their liminality in relation to boundaries and borders.

The early modern was a time of new social and geographical mobility whose emerging cartographic instincts culminate perhaps in John Ogilby's *Britannia* (1675). The title page of this significant work shows a surveyor directing two men as they measure a crossroads.[4] Since this is a direct route map, all crossroads are displayed as open options with place-named directions attached. Ogilby's project functions to demystify the road networks of the country for the practical purposes of his own day. Roads in themselves, however, are often very ancient, often following the most natural routes, with each succeeding culture overlaying its own surfaces on the ones of those before them. Given their nature also as natural land borders, roads are also often literally liminal to the areas they traverse or separate.

In her detailed study of Lincolnshire, Dorothy M. Owen gives a sense of how parish boundaries often followed such ancient byways as she maps thirty-five parishes divided by the line of the prehistoric High Dyke, which forms a section of the ancient Roman road known as Ermine Street running from Woolsthorpe-by-Colsterworth towards Bracebridge Heath.[5] Owen describes these old 'great road[s] which lay between two parishes' as sites where disputes might arise over offerings given at chapels or shrines which were typically sited at such liminal places.[6] In the ancient world, roads, crossroads and boundaries often held a potentially inherent sacral quality. In Leicestershire, the Roman town of Vernemetum stood at the crossroads of the Fosse Way and another Roman or pre-Roman road, the Salt Way. The town's name means 'great/especially sacred grove' and Owen suggests that the site may have been revered as sacred since the late Iron Age. In further confirmation of this continuity, in the 1960s several Saxon barrows were excavated on the ridge of the hill, at the crossroads itself.[7]

In Shakespeare's *A Midsummer Night's Dream*, Puck introduces us to a term which may lead us further into familiar crossroads territory when he tells Oberon it is the time when 'the graves all gaping wide, / Every one lets forth his sprite, / In the church-way paths to glide' (V, i, 369–72). This seemingly innocuous reference to 'church-way paths' in fact has a rich history which to its early modern audience amplifies the perceived wandering of spirits that Puck references. In Britain especially a 'church-way path' is an often ancient countryside funeral route by which a dead body would be carried from an outlying parish that lacked permission to inter the dead to one which had burial rights. Such 'funeral paths' were often very ancient and some may have predated the very churches they ostensibly linked. Although they were quite common throughout the land, they were understandably invested with some superstitious awe, and can often be traced on maps to this day. It is perhaps testament to the persistence of the powerful phenomena attributed to such a path that, even in relatively recent times, it was believed that any part of the countryside over which a dead body was carried automatically became a public right of way.[8]

Beyond the early modern period, Thomas Gray uses this term in his 'Elegy Written in a Country Churchyard' (1751) which imagines the death and funeral of a melancholy character, declaring that it was 'slow thro' the church-way path we saw him borne' (line 114), possibly with the Shakespeare in mind.⁹ An anonymous 1759 poem written as a critique of religion also uses the term in its imagination of a corrupted Gothic muse who goes 'with meek-eyed peace to rove / Thro' church-way path or silent grove', and it invokes the metaphorical power of spirits 'to wander at the midnight hour / . . . To stalk, in garb terrifick clad / And scoul the weak and wicked mad'.¹⁰ This supernatural usage is again echoed after Gray's death in his friend William Mason's own poem '*Elegy VI*. Written in a Church-Yard in South Wales, 1787', which supposes what might have been the case had Gray himself 'pac'd this church-way path along' (line 61). As it mentions the church-way path, this imagines the dead walking, a tradition the poem speculates may be 'devolv'd from Druids old' (line 96), Wales being a traditional home of the Celtic Druidic class.¹¹ The later Scots poet George Beattie, he of the epigraph, evokes Puck in his use of the term in 1824, when he dreams of his 'thousand spectres' in 'dread array' that moved,

> . . . along 'the church-way-path,'
> All swathed in winding-sheets as white as snow –
> A ghastly crew! Methought I saw the graves
> Yawn and yield up their charge.¹²

It is clear that throughout the intervening years since Puck's declaration the idea of the church-way path has lost none of its primary numinous quality.

Examples of church-way paths may be seen in the maps and parish and town records across Britain. To give a small selection, they may be found at Headington, Noke, Little Clanfield and Iffley in Oxfordshire, Chigwell in Essex, Walthamstow in London, the Isle of Thanet in Kent, Eastington in Gloucestershire, Appleby in Cumbria, Manningford Abbots in Wiltshire, Hinton St George in Somerset, Thornton in Yorkshire, and Much Wenlock in Shropshire.¹³ This geographical spread gives a sense of this feature which was once of great significance, especially to a rural religious expression whose rhythms were locked into liturgical traditions that not only mirrored the turning of the seasons but also accommodated the ebb and flow of life and death. In the records, these paths are often found described as 'the *old* church way'; one is acknowledged as 'ancient' in 1828, while the one situated in Manningford Abbots is first mentioned in the year 987 CE, seemingly many years before the first Christian church was built there.¹⁴ The extent to which these routes were taken seriously by the local inhabitants may be seen in the following examples. In 1349, residents of Stragglethorpe in Lincolnshire had endured difficulties with flood and pestilence but it was noted that despite all this they were not to be deterred and they still carried their dead along the funeral path to be buried at the mother church in Beckingham.[15] The continuity of this may be seen when, early in the nineteenth century during one cycle of the ongoing land-grab of the Inclosures Acts, the Oxfordshire landowner Joseph Locke enclosed land including the old church-way path leading from a hamlet called Quarry. At the next funeral the new wall was broken down by the offended villagers, no doubt at considerable legal risk to themselves. Quarry parishioners said that if they were to be 'deprived of their funeral path they will not come to church at all' and instead they opted for the highly rebellious measure of having a Methodist preacher come to them.[16] One early twentieth-century parishioner of the village of Fryup in Yorkshire, told her neighbours that when she died her body was 'to be taken to burial . . . along the "old road", known locally as the corpse way, or else she would return to haunt them' as Paul Devereux recounts.[17] This moorland track was also known as the 'Old Hell Road', a usage undeniably evocative of the sense of dread and awe associated with the route.[18] Given their association with the arcane mysteries of death and its literal rites of passage, it is unsurprising that, across the span of multiple centuries, supernatural associations accrued to these corpse-paths and passed from generation to generation.

No doubt related to their practical function to aid the movement of corpses from one holy place to another where they might be buried, the further reputation these paths have is of forming a connecting route between the spirits of the dead in one place of burial and those in another. Traditions found in various countries suggest that the dead visit each other in their places of rest, and moreover that in doing so they take the most direct route, moving in a straight line. The palimpsestic nature of religious sites means that this tradition may go back further than recorded history. Many traditions indeed assert that spirits can only travel in straight lines. To begin within the Western world's most popular guide to spirits, the biblical prophecy of Ezekiel describes what to believers is normally invisible when the prophet sees a vision in a fire of spirits, or 'what looked like four living creatures. In appearance their form was that of a man' (Ezek. 1: 5). Ezekiel specifies the movement of these visionary creatures: 'each one went straight ahead; they did not turn as they moved' (Ezek. 1: 9), repeating for good measure that 'each one went straight ahead. Wherever the spirit would go, they would go, without turning as they went' (Ezek. 1: 12).[19] Following the spirit of God of course legitimises these spirits, but also their very fourfoldness, like that of the gospels, expresses a biblical notion of completeness, and they therefore act as exemplars for the very nature of spiritual creatures. This tradition extends well beyond the scope of historical Christian beliefs. Irish, Icelandic and other Celtic peoples had also long imagined the 'fairy paths' of spiritual creatures were likely to be straight and so would tend to avoid building houses on lines between burial sites.[20] Since spirits prefer to move in straight lines, dwellings in traditional societies often tended not to be sited on a direct route between these places. According to the Māori elder Teone Taare Tikao, the door of historical Māori houses in Aotearoa New Zealand faced east or north but not west in order 'to avoid the peril of the souls of the dead going through them' on their way back to the different destinations of the Māori dead, *Reinga* and the *Hawaikis*. This meant that 'when the buildings lay across their track [spirits] went over the top of them instead of proceeding straight through them'.[21] Some British church-way paths were straight and some were not, but Devereux emphasises that the Dutch version of these, known as *Doodwegen* (death roads) or *Spokenwegen* (ghost roads), were officially checked every year 'to ensure their straightness and regular width' to accommodate such straight-moving spirits.[22] This may also be at the core of a society's wish to bury troubled souls at the crossroads thereby to confuse their natural propensities with its intersectional nodality.

In Nemen, Russia, their 'corpse flight paths' (called in Devereux's German source the *Leichenflugbahn*) are straight paths that are imagined to link old cemeteries, and along which spirits may walk. These are habitually 'kept clear of fences, walls and buildings', for their ease of passage, and, as in the Māori and Irish tradition, presumably to avoid hauntings.[23] In Germany, these imagined spiritual paths known as *Geisterwege* also 'end or originate in a cemetery' and, Devereux claims, 'always run in a straight line over mountains and valleys'.[24] In this respect, of interest is the Icelandic practice of divination in which 'the seer would resort to a lonely crossroads from which a church was visible, or where one of the roads ran *straight* to a church, put on animal skin and go into a trance by staring at a polished axe blade while lying perfectly still' (italics in original).[25] This was apparently effective for the seer, who would then interrogate the spirits which had been perceived to have 'glided up to the crossroads', as Devereux, channelling Puck, describes the mantic process.[26] Such paths sacred to spirits of the dead or to spiritual creatures have been rendered in various ways throughout the folk histories of many cultures. The idea of the fairy path resounds in *The Merry Wives of Windsor*, where Mistress Page gets children 'fairy-like to-pinch the unclean knight' Falstaff and 'ask him why, that hour of fairy revel, / In their so sacred paths he dares to tread / In shape profane' (IV, iv, 55–8). Here, Falstaff is gulled by people referencing this idea of the spirit-route.

For obvious reasons, we might easily relate these to the church-ways or funeral paths referred to above, but their roots may well also go further back into the deep and equally superstitious territory of human prehistory. This might involve their possible relationship to the Neolithic earthen avenues or 'cursuses' which archaeologists have identified often running between prehistoric barrows, burial sites or sites of ceremonial importance. These earthworks can run for considerable distances in Britain, even sometimes for miles, and are often, as the archaeologist David McOmish says, 'almost obsessively straight'.[27] In August and September of 2008, a team of archaeologists from the universities of Bristol, Manchester, Birmingham, Sheffield, and others investigating the Stonehenge Cursus, in Wiltshire, which is roughly two miles long, discovered an antler pick employed in the original digging of the earthwork and used this to carbon date its age (and therefore that of the cursus) to around 3,500 years BCE, making it 500 years older than Stonehenge itself.[28] The project's spokesman, Julian Thomas, explained that the cursus appears to 'encloses a pathway which has been made inaccessible . . . and that suggests it was either a sanctified area or for some reason was cursed'.[29] He noted also that a team from Sheffield University had discovered burial cremations at Stonehenge dating to 2900 BCE.[30] Various theories have been proposed for their use or significance within Neolithic and later communities, and whether they were solstitial, processional paths or what McOmish calls 'proving grounds for young men' undergoing some kind of rite of passage, it seems likely that, like crossroads, they were regarded either as sites of transition or of transformation.[31] It is of considerable further interest here that in many cases, as McOmish tells us, 'cursuses were sited at transitional places, not only rivers but also at the crossover points of different types of geology'.[32] It also seems that 'confluences of two rivers seem to have been particularly favoured', for instance at the junction of the Thames and the River Cole.[33] The crossing point of geological formations or the confluence of rivers may perform the same conceptual function as the crossroads, especially where the connection is between sites of religious significance. Rivers were the main arterial routes in the ancient world. It is possible then that the many examples of church-way paths, funeral paths, corpse-roads or lich-ways of later times, with their reputation for walking ghosts, may be linked with earlier sacral activity around the crossing of ways, despite this explicit link having faded from cultural memory over the long centuries. But even further than this, it appears that despite their already established great antiquity many cursus enclosures in fact represent 'the formalisation of sections of [even older] long-established paths or routes'.[34] The geographical specificity of the crossroads as a place of transition seems to have partaken of this long history, as ultimately connected with the tendency for certain roads to be imbued with a sacred or cursed nature, or simply with a fearful spiritual aura, and was consequently viewed with both awe and dread.

In these interpretations, the road itself is often both a place of actual transition and a metonymy for life beyond death, also hinting at possibilities of spiritual communication. In continuity with this, roads themselves have been seen as magical or even essentially semi-demonic in construction. William Harrison's *Description of Britain* (1577) tells of how Mulmutius the ancient sorcerer-king of the Britons was supposed to have built in the country 'Highways of a beautiful and admirable Structure, from one end to the other' and he achieved this, 'which it was impossible for men to do' in just a few days, with 'the Assistance of his Art, and of Devils'.[35] It is possible that the historical and literary field of signification around roads in British culture still carries something of this ontological sense of mystery and the hint of these occult origins. As an overdetermination of these concepts, the crossroads compounds such mysterious transition with the possibility of transformation at a decision point between routes and so signifies a kind of communication between possible worlds, and by extension between the parallel universes of humans and the gods.

It was the interaction of humans and the concept of the divine in the deep controversies of the Reformation that brought the subject of crossroads practices into more urban contexts through a combination of paranoia over both iconoclasm and suspected witchcraft. In the 1530s–40s, John Leyland speaks of crosses in the town of 'Brakely' which had been 'throwne doune a late by theves that sowght for treasure'.[36] Though there had been some destruction of religious images in churches in the late 1530s, if, as Leyland suggests, this early iconoclastic vandalism was based on need or greed rather than religious fervour it nevertheless shows a broader lack of reverence for such things. In the late fifteenth-century *Malleus*, Kramer and Sprenger had blamed such cross-destruction in their own European context on witchcraft, which meant that 'hardly one in ten of the Crucifixes set up at cross-roads ... can be found whole and intact.'[37] Henry VIII's 1541 Act against Conjurations, Witchcrafts, Sorcery and Inchantments states its purpose as to address how 'dyvers and sundrie persones' have unlawfully 'devised and practised Invocacions and conjuracions of Sprites, pretendyng by suche meanes to understande and get Knowlege for their owne lucre' and have also 'used and occupied wichecraftes, inchauntmentes and sorceries to the distruccion of their neighbours persones and goodes'.[38] Pursuing this line, the Act informs us that 'for execucion of their saide falce devyses and practises' these supposed witches have made or caused to be made 'dyvers Images and pictures of men, women, childrene, Angelles or develles, beastes or fowles' and have 'dygged up and pulled downe an infinite nombre of Crosses within this Realme'.[39] James Fitzjames Stephen suggests that the real focus here was on the pulling down of crosses, which although supposed to be practised in magic rituals was really attributable to radical Protestants and that this Act was therefore primarily intended as a 'hank upon the reformers' and not to address witchcraft.[40] Although it was apparently not put into execution either against witches or reformers the Act was certainly intended to conflate both sets of crossroads vandals.

Connections between religious reform and witchcraft ritual may also be seen in contemporary controversies over the ancient stone crossroads crosses that the growing mass of London increasingly pulled into its orbit. As the city increased in size, it increasingly encompassed ancient routes and crossroads into its own urban spaces and some of these were sites of venerable and venerated stone crosses. One of these areas was St Giles-in-the-Fields, which as its name suggests was originally outside the city. Once the site of a hospital for lepers, it increasingly attracted the poor and the rich escaping the city. It was situated at the crossroads of what are now Oxford Street, Tottenham Court Road, Charing Cross Road, and New Oxford Street, and deep below its streets is another crossroads: of the Central Line and the Northern Line of the London Underground. In the early modern period it had its own gallows and holding cage, and it was also a regular stopping place for victims to drink on their way to be hanged at the more major site of Tyburn. Before this development, its crossroads cross was a small countryside affair.[41] The old liturgies around such crosses were also under increased pressure from enclosure and cultivation that led increasingly to the obliteration of such old landmarks and rights of way.[42] Although some of this pressure was merely the result of urban expansion, pressure was also exerted by the conscious promotion of Protestant religious ideologies. Lacking the inherent stability of de Certeau's *place*, the practised *space* of the crossroads is porous to these 'transformations caused by successive contexts'.[43] Elizabeth I's 1547 and 1559 Royal Injunctions banned most religious processions for instance and although the Rogation Week tradition of beating the bounds of the parish to banish evil spirits was excluded from the ban they were no longer to include 'stopping at wayside crosses'.[44] The exorcism of evil spirits from parishes in Rogation Week recalls the very ancient practice of pushing spirits to the boundaries which may have led to their inhabitation of the liminal spaces of the crossroads in the first place. Bernstein tells of William of Auverne's (d. 1249) view that, in contrast to the polluted highways, the fields repel evil spirits.[45] There was, however, some resistance to Elizabeth's own perceived iconoclasm in these matters, and local clergy sometimes proved reluctant to give up pausing for prayer at the places where wayside crosses had been, resulting in the practice of substitute crosses being cut into tree trunks to commemorate the ancient stations of the liturgy.[46]

That this is very much a religio-political issue at the time may be seen in the debate around the renovation or otherwise of the Eleanor Cross in Cheapside. In early modern London, Cheapside was a marketplace and thoroughfare at the confluence of roads. Alongside its neighbour structure, the conduit known as the 'Standard', its ancient Eleanor Cross served as a central focus for proclamations and occasional executions and enjoyed a visibility that other more marginal sites such as Tyburn lacked.[47] In Anthony Munday's *Sir Thomas More*, Lincoln is executed there, on 'a Jibbit . . . erected in Cheapside, / hard by the Standard' (7.572–3).[48] It was also a place of dramatisation for the City itself, as a crucial pageant station in the Lord Mayor's Show, forming part of a legitimating ritual journey through the city and acting as a central ceremonial space.[49] Cheapside's inner-city crossroads space was not marginal then, except in relation to the wider conurbation, but it was nevertheless a liminal place, standing as it did at the 'nexus of four city wards: Cheap, Bread Street, Cordwainer Street and Cripplegate'.[50] In his 1598 Survey, Stow locates it on the line which he uses to delineate the east-west axis of the city and also refers to what he calls its 'olde Crosse', which may refer to its continuous renovation over the centuries since it was built in 1290.[51] The cross itself was around thirty-six feet high, with its ornamentation including statues of 'a contemporaneous pope . . . four apostles, and . . . the Virgin, with the infant Jesus in her arms', while 'four standing figures filled the top niche', and to top it off there was 'a cross, surmounted with the emblematic dove'.[52] By Stow's time, the Cheapside Cross had become a very public site of contentious triangular debate between Catholics, those of the middle-way Church of England, and some militantly iconoclastic Protestants. During the night of 21 June 1581, however, matters were taken into the hands of the populace when religious images on the lowest level of the edifice were vandalised and something of the nature of the controversy may be seen in the fact that it took fourteen years before it was even partially repaired. Then, somewhat bizarrely given the cast of the arguments, around 1596, someone attached 'a gray marble tabernacle enclosing an alabaster statue of the goddess Diana' beneath the cross's now-defaced image of Christ resurrected.[53] Diana, as we have seen, is firmly in the tradition of the crossroads goddesses and, besides her associations with Elizabeth herself, is of course linked with her partners in the divine: Luna above and Hecate below, associated as she is with the triple form of Diana and specifically what Jean-Louis Backès calls her 'subterranean power'.[54]

Despite the heavy religious overtones of the continuing controversy over this crossroads-cross, shrine and beloved landmark, Stow notes some fairly typical recourse to purely bureaucratic necessity in the city's initial attempts to have the cross removed because it obstructed carriage traffic.[55] Weighing in on the debate in 1600 came the Vice-Chancellor of Oxford University, George Abbott, whose considerable objections to the existence of the cross were expressed in his tract entitled 'Cheapside crosse censured and condemned', and these are very much based around seeing this cross as a pagan survival.[56] Abbot's view was that images of the Trinity such as those that adorned the cross were forbidden by the Bible and by church tradition. Since it encouraged papist idolatry, as he said, it 'hath many in the twilight and morning early which doe reverence before it', his recommendation was that it be pulled down.[57] Abbott thought that women were particularly vulnerable to its influence as an idol.[58] The fact that it also incorporated a shrine to the pagan god Diana seems to have escaped his notice, yet his conclusion is that 'the Crosse is in no sort to be set up again ... lest we should seem to persist in that palpable darknesse of *Egypt*', that most archetypical of pagan nations.[59] The cross, however, persisted and in 1641 a satirical tract named 'The Dolefull Lamentation of Cheapeside Cross' imagined the re-vandalised cross giving testimony in court, claiming, 'I the foresaid Iasper Crosse was assaulted and battered in the Kings highway, by many violent and insolent-minded people, or rather ill-affected Brethren.'[60] This foray led to the very odd proposal that the cross with its divided loyalties 'should be convicted of high treason and beheaded', an eventuality that would of course have led to it being buried, in common with other traitors, in a crossroads: a vertiginous thought indeed.[61]

The Eleanor Crosses were not the only crosses at crossroads, which often hosted more minor examples in both rural and urban localities. When Amy Stokes 'murthered her selfe' in Aldgate, London in 1590, the corpse was condemned to be 'carried from her sayd howse to some crosse way neare the townes end' and it was buried 'in the crossway Beyond sparrowes corner neare to the place where the owlde cross ded stand'.[62] Forbes suggests that such crosses may have been erected at crossroads 'to conteract the malign spirits thought to haunt the spot and perhaps also to comfort the families of criminals and suicides whose bodies rested under the highway'.[63] Given that we are talking about more modest crosses than the Cheapside edifice, the first of these is plausible. However, the second seems too generous and would in any case actively counteract the whole point of an outcast burial, which was in the first place at least meant to fix the crime and the criminal in public infamy. Amy's body was to have a 'stake dreven thorowgh her brest' with the 'stake to be seene for a memoryall that others goinge by seeinge the same myght take heede for comittinge the lyke faite'.[64] Alongside Amy's visible stake, surely a cross could only remind the passer-by of other forms of torture: a cold form of comfort at best.

These concerns bring the drama of the crossroads ever closer to the heart of the city. Although Stow ignores the theatres, he sees London itself as a kind of stage.[65] This is not necessarily a positive image, however, which he relates to social decay he perceives to be a result of the Reformation.[66] As we have seen, throughout the early modern period many of London's dramas and public spectacles will play out at crossroads. Laurence Manley notes the many dramatic ritual observances of city life in London and in this context describes how the mayor 'led the aldermen in ritual chant' at the grave of Thomas Beckett.[67] Beside any of these urban high dramas, including the sometimes raucous local rogation celebrations, the simple crossroads ritual might have seemed minor, solitary and disturbingly individualistic. Like a crossroads in its own right, London is also at times a spiritual locus at whose many crossing places sacred ceremony and rites of execution may meet. The implication of such physical rituals leads the believer towards spiritual encounter and possible demonic manifestation. Amongst Stow's litany of topographical description of buildings and districts, the space of the city is literally marked by the action of spirits. Stow's description of St James's Church includes the story of when certain men were 'in the loft next under the bells, ringing of a peale, a tempest of thunder and lightnings did arise, and an ugly shapen sight appeared to them coming in at the south window, and lighted on the north'; in some fear of this apparition, they 'fell down and lay as dead . . . letting the bells ring and cease of their own accord'. When they came to they found 'certaine stones of the north window to be "razed" and "scrat" as if they had been so much butter printed with a lion's claw' and Stow concludes that 'the same stones were fastened there again, and so remain to this day; I have seen them oft, and have put a feather or small stick into the holes where the claws had entered three or four inches deep'.[68] This is regarded as high spiritual drama, as Stow's retelling shows, and demonstrates for us what might be thought possible at places with spiritual significance.

If London here itself appears as theatre, theatre itself is often found at the boundaries; as Dillon says of the early modern theatres, they 'stand at a cross-roads between the city and the non-city'.[69] Some, including the Cockpit and the Swan appear to have literally occupied crossroads. Though not all theatres were strictly marginal, many were. The Fortune Theatre, for instance, was located at a civic boundary of Cripplegate Without, a place 'renowned for its lawlessness'.[70] Munday describes beating the bounds of this parish in his 1618 edition of Stow's *Survey* in which the parading parishioners come up against a place where their traditional progress is impeded, an ambiguity which Munday links to the locality of the theatre in question, as if it offers some kind of spiritual barrier.[71] Early modern drama is generally equivocal on the subject of boundaries and borders. Hopkins speaks of *Hamlet, Othello, King Lear, Macbeth* and the *Henriad* in terms of the 'radical uncertainty and shifting conception in their attitude' to such liminal issues and this in a time when England's own national boundaries were fluctuating.[72]

Boundaries are there to be crossed of course, but throughout the drama of the time the idea of crossing is often used as a metaphor for frustration and for confusion, rather than transformation. In *The Merry Devil of Edmonton* (1608), derivatives of the word 'cross' are found throughout, and in one passage in particular, almost incidentally, the usage reveals some of the concerns of this chapter.[73] The intergenerational conflict which forms the main plot of the play is introduced when Sir Arthur Clare confides in his wife that he has decided to break off the engagement between their daughter, Millicent, and her suitor due to his concerns about the solvency of the latter's father. Sir Arthur's whispered exchange with his wife on the 'crosses' to which he intends to subject Millicent's courtship is interrupted by his daughter approaching within earshot, so he hurriedly switches to the seemingly innocuous topic of local topography of routes and road features:

> But there are crosses wife, heere's one in Waltham,
> Another at the Abby, and the third
> At Cheston; and tis ominous to passe
> Any of these without a pater-noster.
> Crosses of love still thwart this marriage,
> Whilst that we two, like spirits, walke in night
> About those stony and hard hearted plots. (I, i, 55–61)

The passage firmly locates the action in reference to the crosses at the Hertfordshire village of Waltham, at Waltham Abbey, and Cheston Nunnery and, as Millicent passes out of earshot, in a superstitious reality in which a paternoster must be said at such a place to ward off evil spirits.[74] At the same time, Sir Arthur curses Millicent's plans with 'crosses of love', and identifies himself and his wife with the night-walking spirits which haunt the crossroads or the graveyard's 'stony [. . .] plots', in a reversal of the activity of Shakespeare's matchmaking hobgoblin Puck. Not only might this excite a reformer's anxiety about folk belief, but the secondary pun on 'plots', as both parental stratagems and the ground upon which the devilish spirit wanders, merely reinforces the connections here drawn between arbitrary parental interdiction, the remnants of a history largely located at crossroads in the landscape, and the folkloric associations of 'walk[ing] in night'. Here we might see how this 'world of the early modern roads and highways . . . forms a kind of spectral geography' to certain early modern plays, 'shaping, shadowing, and standing behind their onstage events and actions' as Sanders has eloquently said.[75]

To speak of roads and crossroads is, and possibly always has been, ineluctably metaphorical and therefore rooted in the slippery realm of language. In Shakespeare's *The Merchant of Venice*, Salanio alludes to the crossed highway as an unsafe place of communication when he refers to a rumour about the good Antonio, that 'is true, without any slips of prolixity or crossing the plain highway of talk' (III, i, 10–12). The 'plain highway' is plainly a safe road. To cross the plain highway of talk is to obscure the honest origins of an utterance, to transform it into something self-serving. The religious debate around the crossing of roads and the ambiguities of boundaries that dominates this area of human aspiration throughout European and wider history always assumes this linguistic and practical duplicity of the other: the pagan, the witch, the fanatic or the wanderer of the next chapter. Its own particular blindness is to its own dependence on such manipulative excursions into the world of edgy, liminal areas of human experience. Without the beating of the bounds of these edges the centre could hardly hold.

Chapter 8

Wanderers: The Predicament of a Stranger

A miserable thing 'tis so to wander,
And like a beggar for to whine at door,
Contemn'd of all the world, an exile is,
Hated, rejected, needy still and poor.
Tyrteus (c. 700 BCE)[1]

I got to keep moving, hmmm, I got to keep moving,
Blues falling down like hail . . .
And I can't keep no money, for a hellhound on my trail
Robert Johnson, 'Hellhound on my trail' (1937)[2]

Iko rita meta, idamu alejo: A crossroad is the predicament of a stranger.
Yoruba proverb[3]

The disreputable or romantic figure of the wanderer of roads has occupied the world's narratives from the earliest times.[4] For de Certeau, 'every story is a travel story – a spatial practice', but the story of the wanderer perhaps carries a specific resonance of dangerous liaisons with space.[5] Since premodern communities were often policed by mutual watching, to be on the road at this time was, as Cresswell says, 'to exist on the margins . . . outside the web of obligations and duties that marked feudalism' and it was for this reason that wanderers were distrusted.[6] The effect of the enclosures of common lands and other imminent bringers of instant poverty engendered a very particular kind of fear. The fear of the settled for the wandering stranger was firstly a straightforward fear of the unknown other, but more so it reveals a deep-seated fear that one might become the other. Lewis Mumford puts it viscerally: that during the Middle Ages the 'unattached individual . . . was one condemned either to excommunication or to exile', that is to say they were in a sense perennially 'close to death'.[7] For the wanderer, this situation was to some extent self-perpetuating, as in the case of European Jews whose wandering as a result of pogroms and forced evictions led to the horrendous irony of them being suspected across Europe because of this very mobility, as Cresswell notes.[8] By the sixteenth century in Europe, numbers of placeless or temporarily transient people were soaring and these included not only the newly landless but also increasingly those travelling as merchants.[9] Some of were even forced to turn to music for a living. They were additionally frightening because of their apparent freedom to evade the significant land ties, the *adscriptus glebae* of the medieval peasant, as well as the self-policing gaze of early modernity. These 'advanced troops . . . of post-traditional chaos' not only shared the liminality of the crossroads but were often drawn there, associated with the myths and fears generated and enacted at the space of the crossroads.[10]

To begin to situate such dangerous mobility within the wider environment, it is useful to consider de Certeau's formulation distinguishing between the idea of *place* and that of *space*. A *place* is 'an instantaneous configuration of positions' that implies stability, whereas a *space* exists in consideration of 'vectors of direction, velocities, and time variables' and is 'composed of intersections of mobile elements'.[11] For de Certeau, 'to walk is to lack a place'; it is he says 'the indefinite process of being absent and in search of a proper'.[12] To wander, then, is to embody the very concept of space, which for de Certeau offers an inherent resistance to power. If our towns and cities are indeed 'a universe of rented spaces haunted by a nowhere or by dreamed-of places' then the wanderer is the original haunting revenant from that unbounded nowhere, or from the dreamed-of beyond where everything should be in its proper place.[13] Their appearance is an alarming sign that the powers of the status quo are temporarily out of joint.

It is perhaps their primary quality of lack that, for the quantifiably settled populations of humanity, has long made the ambiguity of the wanderer of roads a source of anxiety and an idea which has seeded many a narrative. In fact, the relationship between wanderers and the more static population is reciprocal as Hyde points out: 'the god of the roads needs the more settled territories before his travelling means very much'.[14] In any case, the uncertainty of the settled around the wanderer's restless desire ('Why don't they settle down?'; 'What do they want from us?') is made all the more disturbing by the long association of wandering with disreputable death. Of course for many centuries it was a commonly accepted fact that the spirits, or even sometimes the actual corpses, of criminals, suicides and murder victims wandered the earth after their physical demise. The wanderer does not simply submit 'passively to space and time', as Merleau-Ponty puts it but rather 'takes them up in their basic significance'.[15] In this light, the journeys of living wanderers seem to be on a continuum of lack and desire with the classical journey through death and beyond, lending wanderers of any kind a disturbingly supernatural aspect. As Chapter 5 described in detail, in this respect the crossroads was a place where societies might contain the unruly desires of certain wandering subjects, although even when delimited there they could still prove disorderly. But the crossroads has other functions too for the wanderer.

In *Tarleton's Newes out of Purgatorie* (1590), the wandering spirit of Shakespeare's acting colleague Dick Tarleton returns from the grave to appear to the anonymous writer of the tract and, in the course of describing his afterlife, makes a number of seemingly casual connections which are key to understanding the narrative networks of myth and belief that circulate around crossroads. He firstly identifies himself as what he calls 'one of those *Familiares Lares* that were rather pleasantly disposed' and then later came to be imbued with 'hurtfull influence, as *Hob Thrust, Robin Goodfellow* and such like spirites'.[16] It is interesting that he is aware of that shift. Explaining his spiritual journey, he figures it has a choice at a crossroads when he describes how 'after thy breath hath left thy bodye, and thy soule is set free from this vile prison of earth . . . then doth it wander forward into a faire broade waye', coming to a place where:

> at the turning of a crosse there are three passages, one on the right hand, and that is verye narowe and leadeth into heaven: The second on the left hand, is broad and faire, over a green vale, and that conduceth unto hell: now betwixt these is there a lane neither too broad, nor too narrow, and that is the high way to Purgatory.[17]

For the contemporary believer, this spiritual crossroads described here is not quite a metaphor but an actual location which accords with Catholic doctrinal conventions: the spirit is a localised entity which must be spatially sorted into Heaven, Hell or Purgatory after death, according to its conduct in life. This kind of religious narrative places the crossroads within an allegorical tradition that will to a large extent culminate in Bunyan's extended piece of road literature, in which the figure of the Pilgrim might function as the ultimate justifier of wandering road traditions, providing this with a soteriological facet which will increasingly dominate Western narratives of travel and colonial expansion. In this nuancing, Nancy Rosenfeld cites Bunyan figuring temptation as a wandering gypsy, with Bunyan being carried away like a stolen child into the world of the outsider.[18] For later Romantic or modern travellers, their journey to a Celestial City may be associated with a full immersion in the sublimity or beauty of 'Nature' or may in itself consist of 'the ultimate vacation experience'. For many wanderers of the early modern period, however, including the once-revered pilgrims, the associations their journey must bear are largely negative, and densely cluttered with shades of violence, criminality and the demonic.

Although, as noted, mobility was increasing throughout the early modern period, travel was often figured as fraught with danger and associated with death. Nashe is equivocal about travel in general in his prose work *The Unfortunate Traveller* of 1594. He accuses his fellow countryman who is straying far from England of ambitiously wishing 'to be better accounted of than other of thy condition' and refers to his voyage as 'insolent fancies … Icarus' feathers, whose wanton wax, melted against the sun, will betray thee into a sea of confusion'. The traveller is reminded that the first of his kind was Cain, the originary fratricidal murderer, 'and he was called a vagabond runagate on the face of the earth', and further warned that he must have 'the back of an ass to bear all, a tongue like the tail of a dog to flatter all, the mouth of a hog to eat what is set before him, [and] the ear of a merchant to hear all and say nothing', the speaker concluding 'if this be not the highest step of thraldom, there is no liberty or freedom'.[19] More disturbingly still, in his *Daemonologie*, King James I pronounced that devils were still, as of 1597, 'wandring through the worlde, as Gods hang-men, to execute such turnes as he employs them in', as they had been since the fall of humankind from grace in the book of Genesis.[20] Such confused theological gobbledegook no doubt helped to breed general suspicions around what a walking spirit of any kind might be capable of, and might certainly encourage the kind of funerary traditions in which the feet a corpse might be tied together to prevent it walking, a practice that persisted in some places until the early twentieth century.[21] For many of the time, such walking of the dead was assumed to be universal, and it was traditional in Yorkshire to give shoes to the poor so that one would receive a spiritual pair in return when dead oneself and therefore be able to successfully negotiate the 'stony country', 'gorse terrain' or 'needle-pointed bridge' over which disembodied spirits would otherwise have to transit barefoot.[22]

Such funereal rituals and death-oriented social practices are the physical manifestations of the idea of the wandering dead, a concept sanctified by scripture, long tradition and the highest authorities both ancient and modern. Apuleius' late second-century *De deo Socratis* describes a variety of demon that consists of 'the human soul that abandons its body when it has finished its services in life'.[23] These he says used to be termed 'lemures', some of which 'occupy houses with a propitious and peaceful attitude', as the Lares of the family, while others, 'because of their misdeeds in life, are punished with a kind of exile, namely, with the denial of a home and with undirected wanderings'.[24] Tertullian attempts to put some logic around this in *De Anima* (second century CE) where he notes, but condemns, the belief that souls that experience premature death must wander for as long as the time for which they would otherwise have lived.[25] According to Burton's *Anatomy of Melancholy* (1621), Zeno and his Stoics 'supposed the soul so long to continue, till the body was fully putrified, and resolved into materia prima' and believed that 'whilst the body was consuming, it wandered all abroad'.[26] The fifteenth-century author of *Dives and Pauper* perpetuates the typical conflation of the dead with the Devil in asserting that such haunting spirits may be either the dead sent back by God 'to have help . . . [or] to show that the souls live after the body' or simply 'fiends'.[27] Lavater, careful to refute the assumption of doubters that ghosts were 'meere trifles and old wives tales', declares plainly that 'spirites do oftentimes walke and shewe themselves unto men' and argues that this is attested by 'credible Historiographers, and aunceint fathers, and other grave men of great authoritie'.[28] In this necessarily ill-defined area, Scot's sceptical *Discoverie of Witchcraft* (1584) offers a typology of spirits also dignified by classical antiquity, declaring that 'Larvae are said to be spirits that walk only by night', while 'Genii are the two Angels, which they supposed were appointed to wait upon each man'. More disturbingly for the living early modern traveller perhaps are Manes, 'the spirits which oppose themselves against men in the way'.[29] These ideas also gave rise to other death traditions such as the practice of 'sitting up on Midsummer Eve in the church porch' in order to watch the procession of apparitions of 'those who were to die during the ensuing twelve months' that Thomas describes taking place in 1608 and 1634.[30] Katherine M. Briggs sees this tradition operating throughout rural England, where 'anyone watching in the church porch through the vigils of St John and St Mark could see all those who were going to die in the course of the year going round the church'.[31] This sits alongside other traditions that spirits may be seen walking in procession by various means at All Hallows Eve, found especially in Wales and Italy. These beliefs were not confined to the wandering of spirits only, but could also be extended to the actual physical body of the deceased. In medieval England, it was not only religious confessionals and guidebooks for preachers but also histories that refered to 'the havoc wrought by ambulatory corpses and the strategies used to keep them under control' as Stephen Gordon notes.[32] The general expectation of the appearance of a spirit at a crossroads may be seen from another example dating from the 1650s in which a 'considerable number of male and female Quakers, having a presentiment that one of their brethren, though buried at the junction of four cross-roads after a verdict of felo de se, was due again upon earth, proceeded to his grave and attempted to raise him from the dead'.[33] Of course, this is reported to have happened at the resurrection of Christ (Matthew 27: 51–2), and so was widely thought to be a factual possibility. Whatever the detail of the matter, the idea of the wandering dead became so commonplace that such deceased restlessness could become an apt metaphor even for life itself, as Macbeth states after cowering from the wandering ghosts of his own making, 'Life's but a walking shadow, a poor player that struts and frets his hour upon the stage and then is heard no more' (V, v, 19–28), the walking dead metaphor taking precedence even over life's likeness to the stage.

It was perhaps with the effect of avoiding pedestrian congestion on spiritual routes that this general deathly wandering came to require a violent backstory. So, for many centuries it has been a commonly accepted element of death-lore that it is principally the spirits, or even sometimes the corpses, of criminals, suicides and murder victims that walked the earth after death.[34] The occult writer Cornelius Agrippa was referring to this widely accepted belief when he spoke of spirits that 'want a due buriall or have left their bodies by violent death, and as yet wander about their carkasses in a troubled and moist spirit'.[35] Of course, it was particularly the spirits of suicides that were supposed to wander, and sometimes far from their place of restless interment. In *Mist's Weekly Journal* of 1726 it was reported that 'a Spectrum, in the Shape of a Weaver of Crediton, who kill'd himself' had purportedly been seen some eight miles away in Exeter, a distance which was typically about half a day's journey in 1726.[36] Of the fate of the remains of those who commit suicide, Lavater asserts that 'many wonderfull and straunge things happen about those which wilfully cast away themselves', adding that 'somtime their corpses must be carried a great way off, before they being thrust in a sack can be throwne into the sea'.[37] But most weirdly, he describes how the corpse of a suicide victim may upset the natural order of things so much that physics runs backwards: 'being laid in a waggon or cart, the horse could scant draw them downe the hill, but up the hill they need not labour at all, for the cart would runne very fast of his owne accord'.[38]

Lavater also introduces a conventional geographical element to this, where 'wicked divels worke straunge things in those places where men have exercised pride and crueltie'.[39] Such wandering spirits are for Lavater most often encountered in places associated with either the numinous aura of churches and ruins, or with the many scenes of trauma that the early modern world provides: Christian buildings, old castles, prisons, sepulchres, the sites of battles, places of execution and, significantly, 'in the bounds of countries, and buts of lands'.[40] Those spirits found wandering at such 'bounds' and 'buts' may well have been ushered there by the practical exorcism of settled property, by which the owners would 'take measures based on magic or religion to expel the more malevolent [spirits] from their land'.[41] Lavater claims that Catholic exorcists in particular were only able to 'drive away evil spirits out of houses into woods and desart places'.[42] These were thus believed to roam boundary areas, which often meant pathways, roads and crossroads.[43] And it is there that they might literally find common ground with 'the ghosts of self-murderers, who are buried in crossroads' and who were 'condemned (according to the opinion of the ancients) to wander for a hundred years, as the rites of sepulture had never been regularly bestowed on their bodies', as Bell's 1788 edition of *A Midsummer Night's Dream* puts it.[44] For the ancients, even properly buried souls were apt to be restive on the roads if not appropriately revered, as Lavater mentions of the Roman feast of Parentalia, honouring the dead, which, once having been neglected, 'there arose stormes and pestilence, and ... soules rising out of their graves, did wander with pittiful complaintes about the graves, and by the highway sides, and in the fieldes'.[45] In many places these highway malingerers found their way to crossroads. In early modern Franconia, northern Bavaria, the spirits of the dead 'unable to find peace in the grave dance[d] wild dances at crossroads by moonlight', as Puhvel notes.[46] Many Chinese, Indian, Danish, Icelandic and African traditions aim at contacting or propitiating the spirits of the dead at the crossroads.[47] There are Welsh traditions of a host of the restless spirits of sinners led by hideous spirit hounds found haunting byways and crossroads and these sightings are particularly prevalent on religious holidays such as those of St John, St David, All Saints' Day, Christmas and Good Friday.[48] Superstition and religion are equal partners in these conventions.

In this respect, crossroads were a potential meeting place of manifestation for both the restless wandering spirit and the demonic forces of Hell in one form or another. In the medieval period, it was reported that the knight Henry of Falkenstein, who had asserted a disbelief in demons, has their existence proven to him by a priest named Philip who took him to a crossroads, 'drew a circle round him with a sword [and] placed him within it', upon which a demon 'so hideous that the knight could not look upon him' appeared there.[49] A chapbook of the eighteenth century described the noisy ghost of 'John Fox of King's Lynn, who had hanged himself and been buried at a crossroads' whose spectre returned 'noisily crying out that he was undergoing the torments of hell'.[50] Obviously the binding quality of the crossroads was ineffective in this case. And in a more recent account from Kerry in Ireland, in 1941, two farmers described being out walking when they noticed 'two men approaching them from an intersection in broad daylight. On getting closer they abruptly vanish. The farmers recognize the apparitions as neighbors "dead for a number of years."'[51] Such encounters as these could in themselves prove unfortunately transformative, as Lavater recounts of the experience of his friend John Willing, 'a godly and learned man', who upon meeting 'a walking spirite in the night season, was so much altered, that at his returning home, his owne Daughters knewe him not'.[52] A victim might 'become grayheaded in one night', and often he says 'those mens faces and heads do swel, which have seen or heard spirits, or have bene blasted with them'.[53] Such crossroads experiences were evidently to be avoided.

In its own majestic and general sweeping manner, *The Anatomy of Melancholy* paints the most active picture of wandering 'aerial spirits' or devils, claiming that they cause 'many tempests, thunder, and lightnings, tear oaks, fire steeples, houses' and 'strike men and beasts'. They also 'make it rain stones . . . wool, frogs' and cause 'whirlwinds on a sudden, and tempestuous storms'; they 'corrupt the air' and cause 'plagues, sickness . . . shipwrecks' and 'inundations'.[54] The book addresses the sceptical mode also in noting that contemporary 'meteorologists' generally refer these occurrences to 'natural causes' but still asserts that such phenomena are more often caused by 'aerial devils' in the same manner as 'when a desperate man makes away with himself'.[55] It then conflates these suicide-causing spirits with the ancient gods, who it says once 'held all the world in awe, and had several names, idols, sacrifices, in Rome, Greece, Egypt', and these to the day of writing 'tyrannise over, and deceive those Ethnics and Indians, being adored and worshipped for gods', for as Burton argues, 'the Gentiles' gods were devils (as Trismegistus confesseth in his *Asclepius*)' and these are now 'respected by our papists . . . under the name of saints'.[56] As a man very much of his time, Burton adds to this entertaining collation in pointing out that these are the type of spirits who 'desire so much carnal copulation with witches (Incubi and Succubi), transform bodies, and are so very cold, if they be touched; and that serve magicians'.[57] The 'spirits' he describes have a certain physicality; they can be touched and might desire copulation, and themselves have powers both manipulative and transformative. James I also believed in the materiality of spirits, and that it was the Devil that tempted people to suicide, 'by a voyce, or in likenesse of a man' and, as a wanderer himself, picked on those who were also already wandering, 'vpon their walking solitarie in the fieldes . . . without the company of any other'.[58] With all of these associations, the act of wandering itself comes to take on a sinister aspect, and this was enough for one woman accused of witchcraft early in the seventeenth century to have made herself a target according to her neighbours, by being suspiciously 'given to wandering up and down the countryside'.[59] A woman who wanders alone is of course automatically suspected of being at least 'loose' and here the associations had settled upon a wanderer in the most unfortunate if predictable way.[60]

The classification of wandering of ghosts, devils or the spirits of the dead was not only the territory of folk-belief or local custom but was also very pertinent to post-Reformation church debates on the precise mechanisms of the afterlife. In this case, people's ghost beliefs were active on the side of the Catholics as manifest proof of the doctrine of purgatory, and equally for many Protestants of the evidence of the apparition of demons in human form.[61] The ghost of old Hamlet, for instance, is quite the equivocator in this, and he displays the characteristics of both sides, reeking of purgatorial fire while simultaneously carrying the suspicion of being satanic in origin, rather than human. As intimated, a belief in the walking of unquiet spirits was not universal, however. Harsnett's *Declaration* tends towards ridicule of this widespread conviction as part of his critique of the credulity of the Denham exorcists' audience and victims. He illustrates the lack of credibility of these tales by telling the classical story of Creüsa, Aeneas' wife, who, after simply becoming lost, returns as a spirit to announce rather grandly that she had become 'one of the walking night-ghosts'.[62] But even in excoriating this belief, Harsnett of course records its very currency, and the idea persists in his choice of metaphor as he discusses other such walking ghosts, including the spectral appearance of Caesar to Brutus. 'Out of this, and such like Heathenish dreames', he exclaims, 'what a world of hel-work, deuil-work, and Elue-work, had we walking amongst vs heere in England.'[63] In this he primarily laments the childish spiritual credulity that resulted in the 'exorcisms', and subsequent conversions achieved by the egregious priest Dibdale and his renegade Catholics. But it is nevertheless interesting that even Harsnett, like Macbeth, feels that the metaphor best suited to communicate this relates to another kind of walking ghost.

In his extended discussion on the nature of devils, Burton describes some of the early modern controversies about the nature and substance of wandering spirits. Drawing on classical sources, he describes how Tertullian and the philosopher Porphyrius maintain that both devils and angels are 'nought but souls of men departed, which either through love and pity of their friends yet living, help and assist them, or else persecute their enemies, whom they hated', just as, Burton adds, Dido threatened to persecute Aeneas after death, saying 'My angry ghost arising from the deep, / Shall haunt thee waking, and disturb thy sleep; / ... my shade thy punishment shall know'.[64] Burton, however, is of a more materialist mind in this, describing the idea as an 'absurd tenet', and quoting David Crusius, who 'by several arguments proves angels and spirits to be corporeal'. For him, this was proven by one Facius Cardan who, on 13 August 1491, 'after the accustomed solemnities ... conjured up seven devils, in Greek apparel, about forty years of age, some ruddy of complexion, and some pale', adding that we can 'no more apprehend their natures and functions, than a horse a man's'.[65] Some of this Burton is sceptical of, especially concerning the devils' ability to 'tell the secrets of a man's heart', but he concedes that these corporeal spirits also sometimes visited men to 'reward and cherish, and sometimes, again, terrify and punish, to keep them in awe, as they thought fit'.[66] Whether corporeal or not, and whether or not they are manifestations of the related dead, their function seems to be to wander back to reward or punish the living. The currency of this trope may be seen in direct metaphorical references to paths and haunting in popular texts like Shakespeare's *Henry V* where Henry is described by the French king as being 'bred out of that bloody strain / That haunted us in our familiar paths', adding, 'let us fear / The native mightiness and fate of him' (II, iv, 52, 64–5). In this example, Englishness itself is somehow bound up with this very idea of the bothersome revenant. To a large extent then, any wanderer is potentially associated with the qualities of the road which tend towards the demonic and echo with residual spiritual beliefs lurking at the crossroads, like those outlined where Harsnett's imagination of these spiritual issues is most excited in his complaint of the 'three-way leet', which he laments 'children, old women and maides' are still afraid to cross.[67]

A not insignificant element of this story is, as Beier notes, the process of the 'de-sanctification of the poor' which took place from 1300 onwards.[68] As part of this alteration of attitudes towards the indigent, John D. Cox describes the gradual post-Reformation shift in popular drama, from 'associating the devil primarily with the upper classes to associating him with commoners'; having once been sanctified by poverty, 'the poor gradually became the objects of suspicion and rejection'.[69] For the desperate it was tempting to claim any occupation that might earn money, including the divinatory kind. One statute against wanderers of 1531 included those 'feigning themselves to have knowledge in . . . physiognomy, palmistry, or other crafty sciences . . . to the great deceit of the King's subjects'.[70] The humanist scholar Juan-Luis Vives in 1526 accused vagrants of being guilty of many crimes, including 'pandering and sorcery'.[71] Moreover, like fairies, vagrants by reputation stole children and Beier notes, among other examples, two itinerant women committed to Bridewell in 1624 'suspected to have combined together to buy and sell children'.[72] With this background it is no wonder that wanderers 'were thought to harm people with devilish practices and were compared to Robin Goodfellow', which is a polite euphemism for the Devil himself.[73] Having been desanctified, the wandering poor were demonised.

It is apparent then that, among many other social ills attributed to them, wanderers were typically likely to be associated with satanic entities. The Bible is clear in its own attribution of wandering to the Christian Devil: 'And the LORD said unto Satan, From whence comest thou? And Satan answered the LORD, and said, From going to and fro in the earth, and from walking up and down in it' (Job 2: 2). On the peripatetic nature of devils in general, Burton quotes Bodine saying that they may 'pass many miles in an instant . . . and with admirable celerity remove them from place to place'.[74] Wandering is also part of the curses of Genesis 4: 12, which applies to all: 'When thou tillest the ground, it shall not henceforth yield unto thee her strength; a fugitive and a vagabond [or 'restless wanderer'] shalt thou be in the earth'; and of Hosea 9: 17: 'My God will cast them away, because they did not hearken unto him: and they shall be wanderers among the nations', a curse which applies to all those who disobey God.[75] The imputation sticks: the vagrant, wrote William Harrison in 1577, like the Devil himself, 'runneth up and down from place to place . . . to and fro all over the realm'.[76]

On the level of the human, Burton's *Anatomy* describes how some of the causes of wandering interact and exacerbate each other. He acknowledges one of its main root causes as poverty, and specifically the kind of poverty that causes a melancholy metamorphosis, with its potential end being suicide. If one is poor, he writes, 'though he be honest, wise, learned, well-deserving, noble by birth, and of excellent good parts; yet in that he is poor, unlikely to rise, come to honour, office, or good means, he is contemned, neglected'; and when we are poor, 'we are metamorphosed in an instant, base slaves, villains, and vile drudges'; to be poor then is to be 'a servile generation, that dare refuse no task . . . be it fair or foul, he shall run fifty miles afoot tomorrow, to carry me a letter to my mistress'. Travellers in one way or another then, they are thus 'footstools for rich men to tread on, blocks for them to get on horseback, or as "walls for them to piss on"'.[77] The poor are transformed into rootless wanderers whose very extremity causes them to be mistrusted as 'like rogues and vagabonds, they go barefooted and barelegged, the soles of their feet being as hard as horse-hoofs . . . chimney-sweepers, jakes-farmers, dirt daubers, vagrant rogues, they labour hard some, and yet cannot get clothes to put on, or bread to eat'.[78] Such poverty causes people also to 'turn parasite, jester, fool' but ultimately 'it enforceth them through anguish and wearisomeness of their lives, to make away themselves; they had rather be hanged, drowned, &c., than to live witho means'.[79] Burton describes how in Lithuania people 'sell themselves, their wives and children to rich men, to avoid hunger and beggary' and asserts that 'many make away themselves in this extremity' telling of 'two brothers of Louvain that, being destitute of means, became both melancholy, and in a discontented humour massacred themselves'.[80] In these ways, not only is the poor wanderer of roads driven to suicide but the spirit of the suicide is condemned to continue the tragic journey. As we now know, that road leads to the crossroads.

Mirroring his approach to transformation, in Shakespeare's work the idea of wandering is in almost all respects depicted as negative, as inherently suspect, and this is displayed in the very fabric of the universe, from the heavens themselves downwards. In *Troilus and Cressida*, Ulysses' elegy to hierarchy, or 'degree' is an astrological rant which seems so ironically overblown that it almost speaks its opposite as it worries deeply about the wandering of planets which might affect circumstances on the ground. Stating at the outset that 'the heavens themselves, the planets, and this centre, / Observe degree, priority, and place' (I, iii, 84–5), he insists that,

> when the planets
> In evil mixture to disorder wander,
> What plagues and what portents, what mutiny,
> What raging of the sea, shaking of earth,
> Commotion in the winds! Frights, changes, horrors,
> Divert and crack, rend and deracinate,
> The unity and married calm of states
> Quite from their fixture! (I, iii, 93–100)

These wandering stars potentially destabilise every aspect of peaceful and stable society, including:

> Degrees in schools, and brotherhoods in cities,
> Peaceful commerce from dividable shores,
> The primogenity and due of birth,
> Prerogative of age, crowns, sceptres, laurels. (I, iii, 104–7)

This destabilising process then culminates in force being equated with right, justice losing its name, and consequently, he muses,

> everything includes itself in power,
> Power into will, will into appetite;
> And appetite, an universal wolf,
> So doubly seconded with will and power,
> Must make perforce an universal prey,
> And last eat up himself. (I, iii, 118–23)

This anxiety is not uncommon and the wandering bodies of the heavens of course are widely thought to have material power on earth in early modern times, providing convenient metaphors for influence of all kinds, as Queen Margaret laments in *Henry VI, Part II* of a 'lovely face' that has 'Ruled, like a wandering planet, over me' (IV, iv, 14–15). But even these heavenly movers are stunned into inactivity at the grave of the suicide Ophelia, where Hamlet sees Laertes and asks who this is whose grief 'Bears such an emphasis? whose phrase of sorrow / Conjures the wand'ring stars, and makes them stand / Like wonder-wounded hearers?'

(V, i, 244–6). Wandering is also negative when understood as a mental dysfunction when *A Comedy of Errors*'s Antipholus of Syracuse cries 'here we wander in illusions: / Some blessed power deliver us from hence!' (IV, iii, 36–7). It works negatively also as an imposition of disturbing ambiguity for the love-lorn speaker in Shakespeare's *Passionate Pilgrim*, whose lover has smiled at him only to make him uncertain of her intentions:

> 'T may be, she joy'd to jest at my exile,
> 'T may be, again to make me wander thither:
> 'Wander', a word for shadows like myself,
> As take the pain, but cannot pluck the pelf. (XII, 9–12)

In 'The Rape of Lucrece', wandering functions as a mode of helpless innocence where the speaker apostrophises 'opportunity' saying 'thy guilt is great! / . . . And in thy shady cell, where none may spy him, / Sits Sin, to seize the souls that wander by him' (II, 876, 881–2). In *King Lear*, the Earl of Kent's description of the storm uses similar ideas surrounding the wanderer to express shades of darkness and connotations of confinement and hanging, in the beautiful lines:

> Things that love night
> Love not such nights as these. The wrathful skies
> Gallow the very wanderers of the dark
> And make them keep their caves. (III, ii, 43–6)

Here also, Poor Tom describes Gloucester as 'the foul fiend Flibbertigibbet' who in his witch-like wandering 'begins at curfew, and walks till the first cock. He gives the web and the pin, squints the eye, and makes the harelip; mildews the white wheat, and hurts the poor creature of earth' (III, iv, 105–9). Jonathan Bate identifies Cordelia's reference to 'idle weeds' hanging about the mad king (IV, iv, 2) as 'beggars, vagabonds, masterless men – people on the margins who don't sustain the state'.[81] Wandering is used to express evil intent in *Romeo and Juliet*, when Paris asks 'What cursed foot wanders this way to-night, / To cross my obsequies and true love's rite?' (V, iii, 13–14). *A Midsummer Night's Dream*'s Oberon is also a fast mover like the proverbial lunar wanderer, claiming of himself and Titania, 'We the globe can compass soon, / Swifter than the wandering moon' (IV, i, 82–3); though not directly negative, this would be most obviously connected by contemporaries with the fantasies of witch-trials. *A Midsummer Night's Dream*'s Fairy also makes this connection with supernatural wandering:

> Over hill, over dale,
> Thorough bush, thorough brier,
> Over park, over pale,
> Thorough flood, thorough fire,
> I do wander everywhere,
> Swifter than the moon's sphere. (II, i, 2–7)

Further, the idea of wandering typically carries the threat of poverty, as Shakespeare references in *Richard II*, where Bolingbroke asks,

> Will you permit that I shall stand condemn'd
> A wandering vagabond; my rights and royalties
> Pluck'd from my arms perforce and given away
> To upstart unthrifts? (II, iii, 120–3)

And although it is enough that wandering is in the very nature of *Macbeth*'s witches as 'posters' or speedy travellers, their 'posting' also forms part of a menacing spell:

> The weird sisters, hand in hand,
> Posters of the sea and land,
> Thus do go about, about:
> Thrice to thine and thrice to mine
> And thrice again, to make up nine. (I, iii, 131–5)

Much contemporary wandering was caused by the enclosure of common and other land, and *The Tempest*'s masque may be an oblique reference to the hunger this caused, but Prospero ends it abruptly when he thinks of insurrectionists, as Johnathan Bate points out.[82] This was perhaps informed by the fact that Shakespeare was himself 'a part-timer dealer in, and notorious hoarder of, grain'.[83] As a particularly disturbing form of resistance to boundaries, enclosure riots were common between 1590 and 1610 as this legalised theft was shamelessly expanded.[84] This, helped by what Marx called the 'bloody legislation against vagabondage', made a displaced peasantry easy prey for the unscrupulous factory owners of later industrial times.[85] E. P. Thompson is not alone in asserting that 'enclosure (when all the sophistications are allowed for) was a plain enough case of class robbery'.[86] Thomas More's, *Utopia* (1516) finds this responsible for many social troubles in his own time including the 'necessity of stealing', caused by the increase of pastoral land 'by which your sheep, which are naturally mild, and easily kept in order, may be said now to devour men and unpeople, not only villages, but towns'.[87] The enclosure commissions of 1517–19 and 1607 produced only unreliable evidence of the amount of persons displaced in the vicious deracinating process.[88] By 1832, however, it can be argued that the enclosure movement had largely resulted in the destruction of the medieval peasantry.[89]

Such loss of agricultural land and labour also hurt tradespeople like millers whose livelihood relied on agricultural produce. Fynes Moryson reported on these problems in his 1617 *An Itinerary*, showing that 'plenty of corn decreaseth, by reason that private men, finding greater commodity in feeding of sheep and cattle than in the plow ... can by no law be restrained from turning cornfields into enclosed pastures, especially since great men are the first to break these laws'.[90] As enclosures increased during the early modern period this resulted in the devastating loss of common grazing rights and the annihilation of whole communities, many of whom ended up on the nation's roads.[91] What Thomas calls 'peregrinations from door to door' were one of early modern communities' ways of sustaining their own poor, but where this was refused and sickness or misfortune followed, the wanderer was often vulnerable to accusations of witchcraft.[92] Regarding Tudor and Stuart village life, Thomas notes the significant 'tyranny of local opinion and the lack of tolerance displayed towards nonconformity or social deviation'.[93] Such extreme parochial thinking is bound to reflect very harshly on anyone perceived as 'other' than the settled norm, especially since parishes were essentially self-policed.

To some extent, these structures of thought around wandering have depended upon a perceived opposition between that which is 'civilised'– stable, established and legitimate – and that which is understood as not exhibiting these qualities and thus counts as 'wildness', or inhabiting 'wilderness'. As we have seen, in cultural and linguistic terms the wanderer outside the settled communities has carried a sense of spiritual 'otherness', of the kind that is required to produce a haunting. In his cultural critique, Hayden White develops an idea of otherness which touches on these ideas of wildness, wilderness and wandering which is relevant to conceptions of sacred or cursed liminality surrounding the crossroads. Echoing aspects of de Certeau's understanding of place, White describes the idea of 'wildness' in the Hebrew culture which has been so influential on the West throughout its history as being not only a 'peculiarly moral condition . . . a cause and . . . consequence of being under God's curse' but also '*a place . . .* it is not only the *what* of a sin, but the *where* as well'.[94] Insofar as medieval and early modern Europe was informed by biblical ideas, in Western culture wildernesses were understood contrastingly as both moral proving grounds and inherently immoral or amoral spaces. This may explain why they might facilitate convocations of witches, wandering spirits or fairies upon the wild heaths and the untamed highways, and at the promiscuous space of the crossroads. With cultural reciprocity, such a place also takes on something of the sinfulness of the acts performed there. The example White gives is of the Hebrew word *sh'mamah* or 'wilderness', used in the sense of the 'desolation' of the violated Tamar (2 Sam. 13: 20), and also used of the desert site of the curse.[95] As recently as the eighteenth century, White notes, the term 'wilderness' referred to 'barren, treeless wastes, and civilisation was almost synonymous with the subjugation of nature'.[96] The wilderness then was 'a fearsome and terrible place' and so regarded as 'the appropriate location for the temptations of Christ'.[97] Put in the most basic terms, 'wild was bad; tamed and useful were good'.[98] Translating words such as 'wild' or 'wilderness', White discovers, the Bible finds it difficult to distinguish between 'a moral condition, a relationship, a place, and a thing'.[99] In terms of the Bible narrative, the wilderness is 'the chaos lying at the heart of darkness, a void into which the soul is sent in its degradation, a barren place from which few if any return'; but equally the wilderness can appear 'in the very heart of a human being, as insanity, sin, evil – any condition that reflects a falling away of man from God'.[100] In this picture, just as the blessed may prosper and find stability in life, the accursed rebels against the Lord can only expect to 'wither and wander aimlessly on the earth' as nomads, 'like Cain, Ham, and Ishmael', as 'angels . . . hurled down from heaven', or as 'wild men . . . hunters, sowers of confusion' and the damned.[101] In the character of the iniquitous biblical itinerant we might perceive many of the traits we have so far encountered and one is forcefully reminded in this of Harsnett's metaphor of Catholic evil, the 'hel-work, deuil-work, and Elue-work' menacing the roads of England from its cursed paths to its many haunted crossroads.[102]

From the early sixteenth century, England may have been to a certain extent a nation 'capable of management by a mature central government whose decisions would be understood, respected, easily delivered and acted upon in all parts of the realm' as Mark Brayshay suggests, but at the edges of the era's mechanisms of control were areas of fuzzy compliance, where the typical discourses of power did not quite compute.[103] Here the echoes of wildness persisted. Although travel writers of the era offer sometimes appealing narratives of journeying on the roads at this time, and fear of the highway was not so great that the volume of people travelling was affected, some popular writers felt justified in depicting the nation's roads as a dystopia of 'malevolent beggars and vagrants lying in wait and intent upon trickery and the cheating and harming of honest travellers'.[104] Also, it is the case that the roads themselves were generally in a state of disrepair, meaning that successive Acts in 1555 and 1563 had been necessary for 'amending of highways, being now both very noisome and tedious to travel in and dangerous to all passengers and carriages'.[105]

The dominant figure of the early modern period, linking many of these discourses in their own person, the cause of deep concern and punitive legislation, is the aforementioned vagrant. It was the very mobility of such so-called 'masterless men', Cresswell argues, that 'made them illegible' and therefore dangerous.[106] Such figures both reflect and are perceived to embody the threatening imposition of living unfixed by location with all its perilous concomitant freedoms from structures of authority and legitimacy. It seems to hold true, as R. H. Tawney puts it, that 'the sixteenth century lives in terror of the tramp' and this is as accurate also for the seventeenth century.[107] Although the spread of disease was one legitimate part of the fear factor, the evident widespread distress over this issue seems out of all proportion to the scale of the problem.[108] Elizabethan estimates of vagrant numbers 'varied wildly from 10,000 to 200,000', but in the period 1569–96, for instance, there may have been only 13,000–20,000 vagrants in the country at any one time.[109] If these figures are accurate, as Beier points out, the numbers involved were 'remarkably low, for all the fear and hatred they provoked among articulate Elizabethans'.[110] During the seventeenth century and after, vagrants accounted for at most 2 per cent of the population under James I and around 0.5 per cent under William and Mary.[111] Nevertheless, wandering, as we have seen a problem bordering on demonic in seriousness, was now perceived as socially endemic and out of control.[112] As Virginia A. LaMar points out, early modern governments feared wanderers not only because they 'sought to maintain themselves by begging, theft, cony-catching' but also because they 'might promote riot and rebellion'.[113]

To be placeless was in a real sense already to be a criminal and various laws were enacted to deal with the perceived issue on that level alone.[114] The Statute of Artificers (1563) specified imprisonment as the punishment for apprentices absconding from their masters' parishes and wandering abroad without a licence.[115] The Act against Vagabonds (1572), which was updated in 1597 and 1604, prescribed harsh penalties for wanderers, with the law seeing little difference between labour mobility and simple vagabondage.[116] Such people, the act determined, should be 'stripped naked from the middle upwardes and . . . openly whipped untill his or her body be bloudye, and shalbe forthwith sent from Parish to Parish by the Officers of every the same the nexte streighte way to the Parish where he was borne'.[117] As Beier says, 'governments poured out proclamations and statutes against vagrants; preachers pilloried them in the pulpits; hack writers churned out popular pamphlets about them'.[118] In 1600, the Middlesex magistrates Thomas Fowler and Richard Skevington, were 'authorised . . . to use instruments of torture when examining "Egyptians and wanderers"'.[119] The penalties for wandering also included 'refusal of alms, whipping, stocking, imprisonment, branding, ear-boring, forced labour in the galleys, slavery, deportation and hanging'.[120] To be branded like cattle, in a sense, was to be made visible.[121] The Vagrancy Act of 1576 provided for houses of correction, since it was thought that otherwise the young would 'stuff prisons and garnish gallows trees' at crossroads.[122] Beier also notes that even if nothing at all could be proven against them, the wanderer might still be 'whipped as a vagrant, or stocked and sent away', noting that authorities 'were obviously not greatly worried about the niceties of civil liberties when it came to dealing with itinerants'.[123] The new powers of examination much extended in the mid-sixteenth century, increasingly provoked an new perspective on criminality, 'of a good society *versus* a wicked one; of Christians against covens of witches; of rightful rulers against treasonous plotters; of law-abiding citizens against anti-societies of rogues'.[124] Persistent wanderers were subject to the stocks, which were often placed at a market cross or in a crossroads, or some other wayside location. In Thomas Harman's 1566 text, *A Caveat for Common Cursitors Vulgarly called Vagabonds*, he writes 'A stock's to stay sure, and safely detain / Lazy lewd loiterers, that laws do offend / Impudent persons, thus punished with pain'. Stocking seems to be an attempt at 'fixing the problem of the mobile poor by literally fixing them in place', as McRae says.[125] If this binding at the crossroads is also meant to be transformative of their behaviour, despite his championing the practice Harman is nevertheless sceptical, lamenting that 'hardly for all this, do [they] mean to amend'.[126]

The weight of the problem as it bears upon popular thinking might be seen from the descriptions of those perceived to wander. The 1597 Acte for Punyshment of Rogues, Vagabondes and Sturdy Beggars was aimed, among others, at

> Schollers going about begging ... idle persons ... using any subtile Crafte or unlawfull Games and Playes ... Juglers Tynkers Peddlers and Petty Chapmen wandring abroade ... and pretending themselves to be Egipcyans, or wandering in the Habbite Forme or Attyre of counterfayte Egipcians.[127]

These supposed 'counterfayte Egipcyans' were primarily people pretending to be gypsies, but also tended to be conflated with the 'Abram man' the counterfeit madmen of whom Thomas Dekker laments, 'These, walking up and down the country, are more terrible to women and children, than the name of Raw-head and Bloody-bones, Robin Goodfellow, or any other hobgoblin.'[128] Like *Lear*'s Poor Tom, these were persons thought to be feigning mental illness and travelling as a means to gain charity and avoid work. Dressing in what was perceived to be outlandish and foreign attire was apparently part of their schtick. The legislative concern over these figures combines paranoia over the possibility that parishes might be taken in by their feigned madness with fear animated by racism against actual Roma gypsies. Romany presence in Britain is recorded from the early sixteenth century onwards, and paranoia over their movement and activities was expressed in the 1530 Egyptians Act (22 Henry VIII, c. 10), passed by Parliament in 1531 to deal with the 'outlandish people calling themselves Egyptians'.[129] The word 'outlandish' is revealingly xenophobic, and simple fear of foreignness was also operating as an animus against wanderers especially since they were often associated with Irishness. Wandering in England was taken as a potential sign of Irish barbarism, and this was in turn amplified by the supposition that Irish people were descended from the fierce Siberian nomadic tribe the Scythians.[130] Of course to be Egyptian, Roma or Irish is not technically to be without place, so much as it is simply to be 'without' one's place; the paradox of lack in this is echoed to some extent in the term 'outlander', and its contradictory duality is mirrored in the nature of the crossroads. Hyde writes of trickster gods indulging in aimless wandering and expressing just such a 'context of no context'.[131] Tricksters like Hermes and Odysseus are described as 'polytropic', a term meaning 'much-traveled' but which may also be translated as 'turning many ways'.[132] Part of their mystery comes from this ambiguous duality, as does their sense of danger.

The statutes of 1576 and 1597 also characterised vagrants as avoiders of honest work, and identified them as 'Fencers, Bearewardes, Common Players in Enterludes, Mynstrels, Juglers, Pedlers, Tynkers and Petye Chapmen'.[133] As McRae notes, pedlars, chapmen and chapwomen were regularly figured in literature and popular discourse as 'unnervingly mysterious'.[134] Shakespeare's Autolycus is an example of this.[135] Around 1.5 per cent of those rounded up as vagrants registered their chief profession as 'minstrel'.[136] Beier cites one contemporary describing wanderers as the 'thriftless sort' who 'lick the sweat from the true labourers' brows', and self-defeatingly 'do what they can to continue their misery . . . to stray and wander about, as creatures abhorring all labour and every honest exercise'; Beier notes that 'few right-thinking Elizabethans would have dissented' from this view, since by this time 'idleness was considered a voluntary act and a form of disobedience, rebellion and sin to be punished'.[137] For other contemporaries the vagrant was a card-sharper, an extortioner or simply a thief.[138] Harman suggests that such itinerants wander 'wilily' and 'after their wicked manner'.[139] In his opinion, significantly, these people typically lurk around in 'bylanes' and 'lie and linger in highways' to waylay travellers, and in this he evokes the perceived dangers of the edges of ditches and of the junctions of roads.[140]

These perceptions and their ensuing legislation weighed heaviest of course upon the poor, who were 'forbidden to depart the realms of manor, lord and master except for occasional harvest work', as Beier notes, with a distinction being enforced between 'the impotent poor' who were eligible for relief if they stayed where they were, and 'the able poor' who were not, but who also, 'if they left the parish, were subject to punishment'.[141] Since just over half of vagrants were single males, official records refer to them as 'whole', 'sturdy' and 'lusty' rogues and hence comes their common association with rebellion and sedition. Indeed, during the 1536 Pilgrimage of Grace, the news of the northern risings was spread abroad by wanderers in both the north and the south of the country.[142] To the dominant classes such vagabonds then seemed to threaten the established order.[143] But it was not just in the discourses of authority that they were cursed; the popular literature of roguery also portrayed what Beier describes as 'a netherworld of vagabonds poised to overthrow society'.[144]

Such a wide perceived category could draw into it citizens of many origins. Sanders describes how early modern Londoners 'regularly moved between the city and its more rural hinterlands'.[145]

She mentions 'craftspeople, herbalists . . . household servants, and not least, women' as being accustomed to 'semi-detached modes of living'.[146] Theatre audiences could be described in much the same way. Dillon cites the Blackfriars residents' objection to the establishment of the Blackfriars Theatre on the grounds that it would lead to 'the great resort and gathering together of all manner of vagrant and lewd persons that, under colour of resorting to the plays, will come thither and work all manner of mischief'.[147] Manley describes the City authorities' view of theatre audiences as 'a shadowy variety of unenfranchised strangers, aliens, and nonconformists . . . Disturbingly heteroglot . . . a newly variegated and mobile population', consisting not only of 'fashionable gentry', but also of 'provincial strangers, foreigners and underworld denizens'.[148] The underlying narrative here is of fear of displacement – of the mobile, the stranger, the vagrant provincial. Players have also classically been associated with these same things, although Barbara D. Palmer's research suggests there is a more nuanced picture that we may draw of their particular peregrinations.[149]

All of this seems to be almost unremittingly negative, and even the positive view of vagrants, as most notably found in Richard Brome's *A Jovial Crew* (c. 1641) – 'Beggars! They are the only people can boast the benefit of a free state in the full enjoyment of liberty, mirth, and ease' – is largely animated in comedic opposition to this overwhelmingly dismal widespread assessment.[150] Although some of the contemporary causes of wandering, like the imposition of enclosures for instance, created a certain amount of sympathy over the plight of the wanderer, the extent of the social anxiety generated by these figures overwhelms this. The whole complex suggests that something larger than the immediate economic problem is in play, and as we have seen, this may be for various deep-seated reasons. The very condition of wandering in itself is seen as inherently suspect. Besides the supernatural and economic associations of this figure, however, wanderers also accreted other noteworthy negative connotations. Again, in his *Declaration*, Harsnett warns of the wanderer now not in the person of the elven stranger but in that of the dangerously subversive Catholic priest, or 'Limitor':

> For there as wont to walken was an Elfe,
> There walketh now the Limitor himselfe:
> In euery bush and under euery tree
> There nis none other Sucubus but hee.[151]

Not only is this terrorist priest 'wont to walken' on the highways like the Devil, but is pictured lurking around the vicinity of the road, at its margins, in bushes and under trees, like the dodgy inveigling vagrant. By necessity, contemporary Catholic priests often went incognito 'disguised as merchants, gentlemen and students', thus adding to their general sense of deceptiveness.[152] In the aftermath of the dissolution of the monasteries there was considerable Protestant opposition to mendicant clerics, and this only grew with suspicion of Catholic political intentions.[153] Philip Stubbes wrote of them in 1583 as 'drone bees, that live upon the spoil of the poor bees' and 'recommended that they be imprisoned and, if still incorrigible, hanged'.[154] One such itinerant who was arrested in Leicester in 1599 was classified as a 'vagrant, recusant priest', and a 'dangerous wandering popish recusant', the vagrancy and the wandering as notable as the recusancy.[155] Another, we may recall, was chased to his death in 1614 and then buried at the crossroads as a suicide.[156]

Another factor in the mistrust of travellers is purely practical. It is possible that the lack of any commonly available guidance around directions of travel, cheap maps or decent signage (lacking even at many crossroads) meant that any casual passenger might find themselves lacking the road and place knowledge that the hardened wanderer enjoys. As McRae puts it, the road user 'who knows his or her way all too well' not only undermines 'dominant models of social surveillance and control' but also puts ordinary people at a worrying disadvantage.[157] Dekker's *Lantern and Candle-light* (1608) imagines a mendacious wanderer of this kind who 'holds in his Hand a Map' of 'a number of Shires in England' in which he has 'with small pricks beaten out a path' with which he may take the advantage of vulnerable travellers.[158] In various pamphlets, this situation is imagined playing out against the background of a network of criminality involving safe houses, as Dekker envisages no more than twelve miles one from the next, offering haven to what he calls these 'night spirits' in their wanderings 'after they have done their deeds of darkness'.[159] Dekker persists also in his demonising description of the wanderers at 'Durrest Fair', where it seems to him 'as if Hell were broke loose'.[160]

Conflated in these ways with evil entities of one kind or another, for various reasons, wanderers and vagrants were considered not only a physical danger but also a philosophical threat, perhaps as William Carroll says, 'because their very nature was to cross boundaries, to transgress categories of all kinds'.[161] In Carroll's understanding, their 'wandering over the rural roads and urban streets of the kingdom is the external figure of their equally radical slippage between other conceptual and political categories'.[162] This conceptual slippage is in accord with Harsnett's contemporary account of one of the era's most controversial religious-philosophical controversies as he employs the compelling metaphor of the malevolent and slippery wanderer to describe the Catholic doctrine of the transubstantiation of the consecrated host. The concept, he says, adheres to an idea of 'indeterminate, vagrant, vnbounded being'; it is a 'lecture of flying formes, and vagrant substances . . . a wandering Hobgoblin, that hath no similitude of nature with the Lord of life'.[163] Again, in reaching for this metaphor in a text meant for a popular readership he attests to the currency of the vehicle as a means of conceptualising transience, unreliability, instability and falsehood.

Those characters who are perceived to wander the highways menacingly throughout the early modern period also partake of this sense of wild unboundedness – the masterless, the poor, the displaced, the itinerant criminal, the able-bodied beggar, players, musicians, Gypsies, Irish, Jews, colporteurs, soldiers and sailors,[164] the mad or melancholy, the spiritually restless, the devil Puck with his speedy boast to 'put a girdle round about the earth in forty minutes' (*MND*, II, i, 160), Ariel with his similar promise of swift travel to 'drink the air before me, and return / Or ere your pulse twice beat' (*Tempest*, V, i, 101–2), trickster archetypes like Autolycus, Mercury or Apollo (as Jonson calls Shakespeare), the witches associated with astonishing feats of travel, Faustus on his pan-European bender – all of these partake of something of this distillation of wildness that is somehow 'always present' but also 'just out of sight, over the horizon, in the nearby forest, desert, mountains, or hills'.[165] All are to some extent feared as the very image of what White calls those 'released from social control . . . in whom the libidinal impulses have gained full ascendancy'.[166] The reason wandering itself is punishable may be because it seems to exhibit and exemplify an excess of freedom which is equally attractive and repulsive in nature. Somewhere in the mix of all of this is a deep paradoxical duality which the figure of the wanderer shares with the crossroads of both binding and transformation, the true nature of the cleaving of roads. One such wandering figure which emerges to express these complexities and contradictions is Milton's Satan, who is either a political deceiver, against whose influence people needed to rediscover what Saron Achinsein calls the 'individual freedoms that had slipped through the revolutionary leaders' fingers', or he is a champion of individual liberty.¹⁶⁷ The Romantic poet Percy Shelley sees Milton's Satan as a moral being who is 'as far superior to his God, as one who perseveres in some purpose which he has conceived to be excellent in spite of adversity and torture is to one who in the cold security of undoubted triumph inflicts the most horrible revenge'.¹⁶⁸ This, far more than the personality of George Gordon Lord Byron himself, is at the root of the Byronic idea. The poet as wanderer, and as thus susceptible to demonic influence, is certainly present in eighteenth-century Romanticism, and in the preceding two centuries also an intrusive and ubiquitous Satan, as a potential inspirer of artists, figures some of the perils endemic to the business of the poet.¹⁶⁹ For the later Romantics there is disagreement on this score. Despite William Blake's positive assertion that Milton was of the Devil's party, Coleridge speaks of his Satan lending 'a dark and savage grandeur' to satanic politicians whom he calls the 'masters of mischief, the liberticides, and mighty hunters of mankind, from Nimrod to Bonaparte ... the Molochs of human nature, who are indebted for the larger portion of their meteoric success to their total want of principle'. These, Coleridge suggests, are characterised like other wanderers by their 'whirling activity' and 'outward restlessness'.¹⁷⁰

To take one example of this duality from the popular imagination of more recent times, Stephen E. Henderson explains how the theme of wandering in early twentieth-century blues music expresses a 'historical matrix of ... wanderlust and leaving' including 'the migration of Blacks after the Civil War ... and the movement from rural to urban areas' and is 'concomitant with the notion of the blues as a poetry/music of confrontation'.¹⁷¹ Ben Sidran, meanwhile, describes that after Emancipation, 'freedom was equated with mobility' and so the travelling musician, 'who had taken on the role of truth-teller from the black Preacher' and the role of trickster 'from the Devil, became the ultimate symbol of freedom'.¹⁷² The blues artist Robert Johnson's music seems more than most to embody his life experiences, and the restless wandering described in his 'Hellhound on My Trail' is taken by Karlos K. Hill not to be an expression of the joy of freedom, but rather his way of avoiding mortal danger: 'The hellhound is the song's primary evocation of lynching, ... a veiled reference to bloodhounds that would have been used to identify the scent of a fugitive.'¹⁷³ Adam Gussow sees the blues in this sense as, 'a way of symbolizing what unconsciously oppresses the black blues subject – the ever-pressuring white gaze, periodic eruptions of ritualized mob violence, the blackened knuckles and pickled fingers strewn across the lynching South'.[174] Johnson's lyrics, then, invoke the world of the black man cursed to wander and negotiate the deeply divided territory of the racist post-emancipation US, evoking shades of the biblical Cain, hinting darkly at dealings with hoodoo magic and the fear of the lynch-mob, the hellhound that stalks his wanderings.[175] It is possible to see this, however, within the broader itinerant tradition we have explored here which exploits for its own ends the suspicion of the settled for the wayfarer, those at rest for the restless, surrounding these travellers with an aura of ambitious rootlessness and thus desirable danger. This expression of the perilous nature of the wanderer has been exploited by many who would want to foster a romantic connection with the idea of the demonic, the rumours of the soul-selling Faustian pact tracing a lineage weaving back through Lil Nas X, Billie Eilish, Kanye West, Amy Winehouse, Kurt Cobain, Sid Vicious, Mick Jagger, Jerry Lee Lewis, Robert Johnson, Niccolò Paganini and the more literary *Byronic* heroes: Dorian Grey, Heathcliff, Rochester, Mr Darcy, Byron himself the source of the eponym, Milton's Satan, to Marlowe's restless Dr Faustus, and beyond into the provocative and illustrative Vice figures of medieval theatre.[176] All of these tend towards expressing the untold story of one vagrant angel cursed to wander the earth and often finding its way, like the stranger, to the eternal predicament of the crossroads.

Chapter 9

Monsters: 'Spirits of another sort'

> Just at the mirk and midnight hour
> The fairy folk will ride,
> And they that wad their true-love win,
> At Miles Cross they maun bide.
> Anon. Medieval Scottish ballad, 'Tam Lin'[1]

In his influential *Declaration*, Harsnett cautions against what he judges to be Catholic superstitions still haunting the nation. These are based upon his critique of the notoriously egregious exorcisms carried out in the 1580s by Catholic priests in Denham, Buckinghamshire. At one point, Harsnett emphasises his scepticism over the reality of things such as demons and the walking dead by contrasting this with the way that, he says, 'our children, old women and maides [are] afraid to crosse . . . a three-way leet'.[2] A 'three-way leet' is a Y-shaped crossroads, of the kind that has been particularly associated with 'triple' Hecate. Harsnett equates the fear to cross this space (especially if, for instance, one's church tithes were unpaid) with the necessity to 'ware where you walke' for fear of a menagerie of monsters which he helpfully lists as:

> bull-beggers, spirits, witches, urchins, Elves, hags, fairies, Satyrs, Pans, Faunes, Syluans, Kit with the candlesticke, Tritons, Centaurs, Dwarffs, Giants, impes, Calcars, coniurers, Nymphs, changlings, scritchowles, Incubus the spurne, the mare, the man in the oake, helwayne, the fire-drake, the puckle, Tom thumbe, hobgoblin, Tom-tumbler, Boneles, and the rest.[3]

The joyful linguistic expression of this passage merely adds to the weight of Harsnett's intended mockery but at the same time it serves to emphasise the cultural reality and breadth of the fear he describes. Its hyperbolic nature may suggest to the reader the obvious vacuum of any actual evidence of such spiritual monsters, but also this vacuum may attract a confluence of narratives around the pagan divine, monstrous nature, the demonic, the restless dead and the world of faerie which seem very much to flourish in the early modern period. A Swedish tradition alludes to the same danger when it dictates that on his marriage day a bridegroom might experience a great fear of trolls and sprites and should therefore sew pungent herbs into his clothes and avoid crossroads at all costs.[4] In a similar vein, the medieval Scottish ballad 'Tam Lin' of the epigraph above describes a young man stolen by the fairies who is rescued from their wandering company by Janet, his pregnant paramour, as they gallop over the Miles Cross crossroads near Selkirk in Scotland.[5] Besides gods and spirits then, the crossroads is an established meeting place also for other dangerous and disturbing creatures one might find wandering at night, or in the liminal places of the world.

Such meetings seem to suspend the norms of everyday life and to some extent sit outside of the everyday discourses of religion and spiritual life-after-death. For some people, of course, such an implied suspension of the natural order is exactly what they are looking for and this desire may be manifested as a belief in supernatural beings of other kinds, historically often in fairies. The connection between faeries and crossroads begins perhaps simply with the former's reputation as wanderers, often typically presiding over their own secret liminal places and unfrequented roads. Such reputations may be enhanced by their association with transformative magic, including the ability to change their own appearances and to substitute children for changelings. These disturbing characteristics may have led to these folkloric figures being commonly Christianised as demons and devils or conflated with pagan gods, and especially with the divine wanderers of the Wild Hunt, so leaning towards the liminal spaces.

It was possibly the anthropologist Van Gennep who popularised the now broadly used term 'liminal' to refer to the transition phase in rites of passage 'from one magico-religious or secular group to another'.[6] Victor Turner defined liminal individuals or entities as being 'neither here nor there; they are betwixt and between the positions assigned and arrayed by law, custom, convention, and ceremonial'.[7] As Piotr Spyra points out, 'to say that fairies are liminal amounts to stating the obvious'.[8] As such, fairies were natural frequenters of the multiliminal crossroads. In the folk tale 'Cherry of Zennor' the protagonist meets her fairy master at the crossroads and works for him until she disobeys him, whereupon she is banished from the house and can never again find the path which leads there.[9] Also, although fairies might be met there, the crossroads may also function as a place where their power is annulled – this may seem to be a contradiction, or rather may be an indication of the thinness of the place as a node of raw power to be accessed for one purpose or another. One Irish belief was that fairy-taken people could be recovered at crossroads at Halloween or the Gaelic Samain with the use of a special eye ointment and the throwing of dust or milk at the passing fairy procession.[10] Liminal beings are also often uncannily connected with the familiar, whence comes the homely nature of the Puck character. Briggs gives the example of such a familiar yet liminal place as the hearth, which was 'at the heart of the household yet connecting with the outside, with the hearthstone serving as the door to the fairy house located just underneath'.[11] In the folk tale 'The Smith and the Fairies', the changeling uses the hearth to escape up the chimney.[12] This is also reminiscent of the dual nature of a crossroads as simultaneously the most commonplace and the most exceptional of spaces.

Besides the common highways, where they might be encountered, fairies were also thought to have their own secret roads.[13] Briggs explains that, as with spirit roads, when fairies 'move in procession from hill to hill . . . it is reputed to be very unlucky to build across their regular paths or set any obstacle across them'.[14] If any house is 'built in a fairy track, the doors on the front and back, or the windows if they are in the line of the track, cannot be kept closed at night, for the fairies must march through'.[15] The only remedy for this is the 'proper placement of doors, and keeping them open', a practice that may 'appease the fairies and mitigate the bad luck that building a house in a fairy track brings to its occupants'.[16] Such secretive wanderings along mysterious paths that sometimes coincide with or cross the roads of reality gives them the suggestion of not merely magic status, but almost divine. They are literally unearthly.

Among other conflations of divinity and faerie, in 1597 James I writes about the 'kinde of spirites, which by the Gentiles was called Diana, and her wandring Court, and amongst vs was called the Phairie'.[17] At around the same time of writing, *A Midsummer Night's Dream*'s own fairy queen, Titania, is the inheritor of the rites of Diana, as Briggs says, and Diana's underworld phase is as Hecate of the crossroads.[18] Briggs sees the origin of fairy legends in the agricultural deities of a peasant economy, through their power over crops and tithes.[19] This may have provided a powerful counternarrative to the Christian idea of providence. Another connection may be found in the extreme fantasies of movement they share with those manifest in many witchcraft depositions and folk traditions. Briggs records the dramatically imaginative phenomenon of the wild galloping procession of fairies on horseback, or the 'fairy rade', as 'witnessed' by an old woman of Nithsdale in Scotland, and recounted in the 1820s.[20] These fantasies mirror the ancient religious legends of hunting gods who would ride through the night either above the clouds, the 'ghost riders' in the sky and the 'riders on the storm' of popular mythology, and more recently popular song, or spectrally on the roads in liminal places. In some traditions, if a traveller happened to see them, they might be either carried along with the hunters or become the quarry and be chased to their deaths. In German and Celtic mythologies, the Wild Hunt was 'a band of ghosts or spirits ... usually led by a divine or semi-divine figure' as Jonathan Durrant and Michael D. Bailey record.[21] Sometime during the medieval period, the leader of the Wild Hunt became conflated with the goddess Diana and the perception developed that groups of women, rather than wandering spirits, rode with her – a belief that may have informed later thinking on witches' partialities for night flight.[22] At the 1586 trial of a cunning man, Chonrad Stoeckhlin, one of the women he in turn identified as a witch accused him of riding so with 'Wuetten's army'.[23] Carlo Ginzburg identifies the Wild Hunt at this time as 'a night ride of prematurely dead humans led by a fertility goddess', while Claude Lecouteux links it with 'ancestor worship, the cult of the dead, [and] the go-betweens between men and things'.[24] Lecouteux describes the three kinds of phantom hunter as 'a demon, chasing sinners; a sinful human huntsman, condemned to roam without rest as a penance; and a wild man, who chases otherworldly prey and sometimes human livestock'.[25] All of these characteristics lead ineluctably to the crossroads as a site of potential encounter.

According to Ronald Hutton it was in the twelfth century that the related concept of 'a procession of the dead, doomed to wander the earth ... until they had atoned for their sins in life' was established 'both as a literary trope and (apparently) as a popular tradition as well'.[26] In medieval Wales there were sightings of 'Hecla's Hell-wain', the cart which carried the souls of the dead and a harbinger of doom.[27] In 1508, the Strasbourg preacher Johann Geiler von Kaisersberg, summarised the people's view of the Wild Hunt, or 'furious army', as being populated by 'those who had suffered violent deaths and were doomed to wander until judgement, each with the dress of their rank during life and the marks of how they died'; he gave the most auspicious time for this as 'the four sets of Ember Days each year, known across much of Europe as times when spirits were abroad'.[28] Martin Crusius, an annalist of south-western Germany, complained of 'unscrupulous priests' who had taught local peasants that the Wild Hunt/furious army embraced 'all who died in battle, all unbaptized children, and all whose souls wandered from their bodies in the night and could not return' and asserted that it was mostly 'visible in the Christmas season, the time of greatest darkness, and during the Ember Days' as Karl Meisen recounts.[29] For some medieval witnesses it was comprised of the ghosts of heroes (particularly King Arthur).[30] One Hans Sachs (presumably he of Meistersinger fame) claimed to have met the Hunt in a forest near Osnabrück, and found that it was populated by hanged men, with the nooses still dangling from around their necks, including one who had been freshly hanged that morning.[31]

In traditional narratives in the folklore of the British Isles, fairies were most often portrayed as merely morally ambiguous, that is they were often willing to help people but still were thought capricious in the extreme and so best left alone.[32] Despite this more equivocal history, from the perspective of biblically based Reformed doctrine fairies could only be demons. Piotr Spyra describes the progressive demonisation of fairy belief in the early modern period as an area of significant agreement between popular and elite cultures in which the authorities tended increasingly to position fairies towards the evil end of the moral spectrum.[33] It has been argued that the Reformation played a major role in this process because its emphasis on the absolute sovereignty of God left no room for other 'autonomous or semi-autonomous spiritual beings to exercise agency in the world', as Peter Marshall submits.[34] Since they must be admitted to be real, and couldn't be angels, fairies must ultimately be 'subservient to Satan, and bent on the spiritual destruction of mankind'.[35] Assimilated thus into contemporary religious orthodoxies, Herrick follows the implications of Harsnett's text to write that the religion of fairies was 'part pagan, part papistical'.[36] Burton's 1621 *Anatomy* also has much to say on this subject, citing various authorities on the subject. He summarises the Jesuit Thyraeus who tends towards the view that fairies and pucks must be 'devils or the souls of damned men that seek revenge, or else souls out of purgatory that seek ease' and this again leads us to the crossroads as the site of binding for such unquiet spirits. For Thyraeus, fairies are devils that appear to men, and 'affright them out of their wits, sometimes walking at noonday, sometimes at nights, counterfeiting dead men's ghosts', listing the places that might accommodate such wanderings as 'monasteries . . . churchyards . . . marshes, great buildings, solitary places, or . . . the scene of some murder'; the crossroads is the most obvious site missing from this list, but may be encompassed within the last two examples.[37] When Giffard's *Dialogue Concerning Witches* (1593) curses cunning men and women as agents of the Devil, he argues that they use the Bible, 'which you know is to be trusted', to convince people they 'bee haunted with fayries'.[38] Regina Buccola has also described various depositions of witchcraft in which stories of fairies 'blurred and shaded into narratives of demonic rituals'.[39] Further, as Thomas tells us, the name Oberon / Oberion was that of a demon 'frequently conjured by fifteenth- and sixteenth-century wizards long before the title became associated with the King of the Fairies'.[40] Although for some in the late sixteenth and seventeenth centuries fairies could still be either good or evil spirits, the second option was now far more probable.[41] This shift in reputation no doubt inflected the meaning of crossroads to the extent of its association with beings of this character.

The pre-eminent fairy of the Tudor and Stuart eras was Puck, who was also known as Robin Goodfellow. Indeed, he was so outstanding that his name itself became a synonym for 'fairy'. In her *The Anatomy of Puck*, Briggs identifies the name Puck as coming from the same root as 'Pixy, Phooka, Tom Poker, Bogles, Bugs and Boggarts'.[42] The *OED* places this with *pixie* and finds it cognate with the Old Icelandic and Faroese *púki* – a mischievous demon or the Devil, the Norwegian and Old Swedish *puke* – a devil, evil spirit, mischievous person, or goblin, and the Old Danish *puge*, meaning evil spirit. Charles Worthy suggests that the derivation of the word indicates deception 'by false appearances . . . to counterfeit, to delude, or to impose upon'.[43] In medieval English folklore, Puck was mainly perceived as a capricious household spirit who either annoys housewives with practical jokes or assists around the place with household duties, cleaning, sewing or churning. The gentle critique of Scot notes that such 'Virunculi terrei' as Robin Good-fellow 'would supply the office of Servants, specially of Maids; as to make a fire in the morning, sweep the house, grind Mustard and Malt, draw Water . . . rumble in houses . . . draw latches, go up and down stairs'.[44] Nothing too terrifying there then. Shakespeare's Puck admits to such trickery,

> That frights the maidens of the villagery,
> Skim milk, and sometimes labour in the quern
> And bootless make the breathless housewife churn,
> And sometime make the drink to bear no barm. (*MND*, II, i, 18–21)

When Puck designates his 'ghosts, wandering here and there', trooping home to their churchyards, floods and crossways as 'Damnèd spirits all' (III, ii, 374–5), Oberon's objection, 'But we are spirits of another sort', is given in terms of his access to the daytime and his mobility:

> I with the morning's love have oft made sport,
> And like a forester the groves may tread
> Even till the eastern gate . . .
> Turns into yellow gold his salt green streams. (III, ii, 381–4, 386)

He is not tied to a crossroads or a flood-plain and is unbound by the night's ministrations. Puck then also asserts his freedom of movement as a 'spirit of another sort':

> Up and down, up and down,
> I will lead them up and down.
> I am feared in field and town.
> Goblin, lead them up and down. (III, ii, 389–92)

Between them, they ascertain for the audience their own nature as wandering spirits and gods who are unbound by adherence to the accepted forms of Christian culture and unsubsumed by its categorical imperatives. They are therefore both free and to the same extent dangerous: the practical embodiment of mobility that Cresswell describes.[45] Puck the restless, metamorphic wanderer, as 'Robin Goodfellow', is to be taken as a euphemism for the Devil, and the Devil is himself a wanderer 'going to and fro in the earth, and . . . walking up and down in it' (Job 2: 2).[46] This deceptive, possibly evil Puck/Robin is also responsible for misleading 'nightwanderers, laughing at their harm' (*MND*, II, i, 25). It was a common belief, as Thomas says, 'that wandering fairies specialized in misleading poor travellers'.[47] Thomas Heywood's *Hierarchie of The Blessed Angells*, speaks of the *ignis fatui* that 'walke / Sometimes before vs, and then after stalke /. . . leading Trauellers out of their way, / Else causing them mongst theeues or pit-falls stray'.[48] Nashe describes the history of the 'Robin Goodfellows, elves, fairies, hobgoblins of our latter age, which idolatrous former days and the fantastical world of Greece ycleped fawns, satyrs, dryads & hamadryads', and says that it was they that 'ground they malt and had hempen shirts for their labours, danced in rounds in green meadows, pinched maids in their sleep that swept not their houses clean, and led poor travellers out of their way notoriously'.[49] As Jennifer Allport Reid argues, these were sometimes recruited into the dominant narrative to be regarded as 'ghosts which had lost their way from Purgatory and now wandered the earth troubling the living in their desperation for intercessory prayers' and were in turn presented as 'an abstract illustration of the misleading darkness of popery'.[50] Harsnett's critique of the credulity of his day laments that 'these are the times, wherein we are sicke, and mad of *Robin good fellow*, and the devil, to walke againe amongst vs'.[51] He blamed monks and priests for giving credence to a 'frightful crue' of supernatural beings and thus making the 'high-waies, old graues, pittes, and woods ends to be haunted with lights, owles, and poakers'. In the ballad 'Being the Pastimes and other Slights, Of Will-with-a-wispe, and other mad Sprights' (1648), this reputation persists when '*Robin-good-fellowes* crew . . . / *Ignis Fatuus*', sings of misleading the traveller:

> Full many a joviall sparke,
> I put beside his marke,
> As he walkes home ith' darke,
> Through Forrest Grove, or Parke
> . . .
> A small deluding light,
> Presents it selfe in sight,
> And leads him with delight,
> Through uncouth paths all night,

This figure is found not only on the road but also at the gallows: 'And Théeves upon the Gallowes sée, / What cunning merry mad blades we be.'[52]

Fairies are also generally associated with the transformative principle, as may be seen in their metamorphic propensities. So the road-spirit is transformative, as 'In sundry shapes he'l let you see, / What cuning merry mad blades we be'.[53] Fairies may sometimes appear 'in the likeness of hares, crows, black dogs'.[54] Robert Kirk in 1691 reports that their 'Bodies of congealled Air are some tymes caried aloft, other whiles grovell in different Schapes.'[55] Puck of course transforms Bottom's head into that of an ass, administers Oberon's magic flower potion and causes the transformations of all of the young lovers' fortunes, ultimately as a result of their descent into the liminal space of the woods. In another connection, from the late medieval period it was believed that 'alchemy is an elvish calling and the alchemist's expertise is elvish' as Richard Firth Green notes.[56] Alchemists, like fairies, were liminal figures 'both geographically and culturally, hovering around the edges of established communities and established beliefs'.[57] Both also shared a 'concern with secrecy' and promised rewards of an 'elusive nature' such as 'unlimited wealth and prolongation of life', fairy favour and fairy gold being, according to Green, analogues of the philosopher's stone, and fairy magic, like alchemy, encompassing rites of transformation.[58]

Quite comprehensively, Burton accuses them of being both spirits that 'necromancers ... raise and lay ... at their pleasures', and those that 'walk about midnight on great heaths and desert places, which (saith Lavater) "draw men out of the way, and lead them all night a byway, or quite bar them of their way".'[59] Taliesin Williams's poem, *Doom of Colyn Dolphyn*, records these connections in the early nineteenth century, when it describes a 'man of legends',

> Whose mind the tales of magic spell,
> And cross-road ghosts, had treasur'd well
> Of fairies' dance, when found array'd
> By midnight moon, in gloomy glade,
> And of their rings and music wild,
> Well stored his memory, from a child:
> Of phantoms grim, with eyes of wrath,
> Haunting belated traveller's path.[60]

Two hundred years previously, such spiritual entities were not quite so clearly differentiated, and 'fairies' might suffice as the popular designation.

Sometimes, Burton informs us, these road-haunters 'sit by the highway side, to give men falls, and make their horses stumble and start as they ride'.[61] At the end of the seventeenth century, Kirk pities those who might have these sorts of 'very terrifying Encounters with them, even on High Ways'.[62] In one such supposed encounter, he conflates the idea of the fairy with the wandering spirit of a dead person as he reports a sceptical minister who chanced to be travelling in a narrow lane with 'a Seer', who perceived 'a Wight of a known Visage furioslie to encounter them', and so, 'desired the Minister to turn out of the Way'. Scorning this advice, and 'holding him selfe in the Path ... when the Seer was going hastily out of the Way, they were both violently cast a side to a good Distance, and the Fall made them lame for all their Lyfe'.[63] The story continues that 'after the Minister was carried Home, one came to tol the Bell for the Death of the Man whose Representation met them in the narrow Path some Halfe ane Hour before'.[64] Conflated in this way with any mysterious happening, fairies could be thought likely to offer danger to travellers in general, but this was especially so at certain times of the year, for instance on quarter days, when it was said that they 'remove to other Lodgings ... so traversing till Doomsday ... and finding some Ease by so [journeying] and changing Habitations'.[65] Hence on these days the local people would 'usually shune to travell abroad' and attempt to 'hallow themselves, their corne and cattell, from the shots and stealth of these wandring Tribes'.[66] It would clearly be worth avoiding crossroads at such a time.

Burton perceives only harmful encounters with the terrestrial spirits he calls 'Lares, genii, fauns, satyrs, wood-nymphs, foliots, fairies, Robin Goodfellows, trulli, &c', which, since they are the spirits who are 'most conversant with men, so they do them most harm'.[67] Burton's study ranges across a network of early modern beliefs that incline towards the physical crossroads. He firstly attests to the physical reality of fairies and cites Paracelsus describing places in Germany where 'they do usually walk in little coats, some two feet long', noting that the larger kind are called 'hobgoblins, and Robin Goodfellows'.[68] Favouring their reality over that of divine forms, Burton notes the association of such fairies with pagan gods, saying that 'some think it was they alone that kept the heathen people in awe of old, and had so many idols and temples erected to them ... some put our fairies into this rank, which have been in former times adored with much superstition'.[69] In Worthy's, *Devonshire Parishes* (1887), the writer documents a local rock formation in the Parish of Sheepstor that gained fame in the English Civil War, not long after Burton was writing, as a hiding place for the lord of the manor and that had been in older times reputed to be the dwelling of pixies.[70] The belief in such invisible beings, he says, is 'deduced by some from the Lares and Larvae of the Romans', who are the 'offspring of Mercury and of the Naiad Laranda'.[71] As we have seen, these tend towards the crossroads. Worthy also sees a connection between these spirits and other gods associated with the spirits of the family departed who may historically have been buried in the house, noting the Devonshire tradition in which pixies were identified with 'the spirits of infants who had died before baptism'.[72] Such pixies then would be unquiet spirits of another kind, and ones sadly far more prevalent than those convicted of treason, murder, or *felo de se*. As an example from the town of Moneycusker in Ireland shows, some such unfortunate infants were also buried at crossroads.[73]

Fairies were regarded as likely to be encountered on the roads then, and at significant places like crossroads. The negative associations of wandering are by now familiar to us. As such a spiritual wanderer, Shakespeare's Puck is assumed to be familiar with the supernatural conventions of the movement of spirits. This is apparent when he declares that every grave,

> ... lets forth his sprite,
> In the church-way paths to glide:
> And we fairies ... do run
> By the triple Hecate's team,
> From the presence of the sun. (V, i, 373–7)

The presence of 'triple Hecate' on Puck's imagined road locates both the gliding of sprites and the fairies' run in the vicinity of the crossroads, which is her chosen place of manifestation. This association with Hecate hints both at Puck's personal evocation of Satan and at the witchcraft with which Hecate was popularly linked. Briggs sees clear connections between fairy-lore and depictions of witchcraft from early times and notes *Hamlet*'s apparent equation of witches and fairies where Marcellus declares that at Christmas 'no fairy takes, nor witch hath power to charm' (I, i, 162).[74] *Macbeth* makes the same connection between witchcraft and fairydom: 'And now about the cauldron sing, / Like elves and fairies in a ring' (IV, i, 41–2).[75]

The isomorphic interconnectedness of all these tropes of fear – of misleading fairies, disturbing transformations, the rampant pagan divine and the dead in procession on the roads – might be apparent from their obvious structural similarities. For those who shared these beliefs in some or all of these intersecting concepts, not only the spirits of hanged men but those of unbaptised children and all whose souls were doomed to wander might also have good reason to pause, or to be otherwise detained, at the binding place of the physical crossroads. Besides being a place with the ability to trap the spirits who are 'condemned to roam' in its geographic mesh, in one influential German tradition the crossroads also arrests the progress of the Wild Hunt itself in its divine form as it tried to chase unwary travellers to the death.[76] If one is being pursued by the gods in this way, one only need get to the parting of the ways for safety, whereupon the Hunt may be bound in confusion and the traveller can pass on in the road of their choosing. If, besides being a site of significant encounter, even the gods are subject to its binding qualities then the crossroads seems to offer a huge potential for alleviating the very common human feeling of powerlessness at the hands of capricious and ineluctable forces. There one might find, or leave behind, an identity or a destiny.

Chapter 10

Protection: The X in the Landscape

Hang up hooks and shears to scare
Hence the hag that rides the mare . . .
This observ'd, the manes shall be
Of your horses all knot-free.
Robert Herrick, 'Another Charm For Stables' (1648)[1]

As we have observed, the crossroads is where the corpses of the worst criminals were consigned to lie by those who firmly believed that this would have the desired arresting effect on their unquiet spirits. Crossroads-confined spirits, it might be said, are literally staked into a narrative which is both temporal and geographical. They are simultaneously bound into an eternal present, denying them belonging to a past or future narrative community, and paradoxically imprisoned in a place of permanent transit and transition. Their binding (psychological or theological), their staking into place (geographical, temporal and often literal) and their reduction to a single fixed mode of legislative or popular classification (suicide, murderer, traitor and so on), are the precise functional opposites of the transformational structures that the crossroads almost universally also embodies. Considering the concept and practice of spiritual binding, this chapter suggests that the crossroads is not only a historical site of access to binding power but has also in itself performed an apotropaic function in the geography of the landscape. This is in accordance with other signs that were perceived to manifest in geographical features. For medieval mapmakers, the 'T' shape formed by the Mediterranean Sea and the Don and the Nile rivers on their *mappaemundi* was perceived to represent a crucifix, a phenomenon which served to integrate the Christian salvation narrative into the very topography of the globe.[2] This demonstrates a commitment to the idea of such natural sympathies that might write a religious purpose into the very fabric of the earth. In the same way, the crossroads works as a device written into the landscape, whose shape accords with the symbolism of intersecting lines often used for the binding or banning of evil. As such a geosymbol, it 'gives meaning to landscape and . . . expresses and nurtures the identity of populations'.[3]

Binding rituals performed at crossroads are simply intended to keep the souls that dwell there firmly in place. In the fifth century BCE, Aeschylus alludes to a custom similar to the binding of suicides at crossroads, where 'the extremities of a murdered man were cut off and hung about the body . . . to disable the spirit of the dead from taking vengeance on the murderer'.[4] This was a binding process known in the ancient world as 'armpitting' and as Elizabeth O'Brien shows, the practice takes place in burials from the Iron Age to the nineteenth century.[5] When in the first century CE Pliny advises the burying of frogs at crossroads as a precaution against fever, it may be as an apotropaic charm to keep disease-carrying spirits immobilised at the crossroads.[6] In ancient Athens the crossroads offerings known as 'Hekate's suppers', in which pious Athenians took out food monthly for the goddess, may be interpreted either as a way of buying her protection against dangers inherent to crossroads or as a means of pinning this 'dangerous goddess' herself at the crossroads with 'prophylactic offerings'.[7] This might have been practised for both reasons, but in line with other known functions of the crossroads I would suggest that the latter is more likely. In Vodun belief, the crossroads is a gate which may also be a hindrance to spirits, and, besides dwelling there himself, the god Legbe is in some ways its doorkeeper, 'the loa who guards the crossroads', and as such he must be asked to remove the barriers there before other loas can pass across its interlacing lines.[8]

The crossroads thus also have the power to bind not only the spirits that are incarcerated there but also spiritual passers-by. There is a Belgian tradition that speaks of errant souls who have been chased back to earth by demons and are able to find a safe haven only at a crossroads, where the demons chasing them may not pass.[9] This is in accordance with folklore traditions such as those mentioned previously in which the crossroads possesses the facility to arrest the progress of the Wild Hunt of the gods. This sky-travelling party once sighted might pursue the unwary traveller to their doom but passing over a crossroads would trap the divinities like any other spirits while their quarry might hurry quickly onwards.[10] Since the Hunt is most often associated with Odin, this suggests the crossroads possesses an almost divine supernatural weight. The ability to bind a god must imply that the means of binding is more powerful than the gods themselves. Shakespeare offers an oblique reference to this tradition in *The Merry Wives of Windsor* where Falstaff is made to impersonate Herne the Hunter, the malevolent wandering spirit who roams Windsor Forest in winter with his ghostly hounds.[11] Although the concept is consonant with the legends of the Wild Hunt, as Harriet Phillips says, Herne is 'widely assumed to have been invented by Shakespeare'.[12] Mistress Page says that this supernatural character

> Doth all the winter-time, at still midnight,
> Walk round about an oak, with great ragg'd horns;
> And there he blasts the tree and takes the cattle
> And makes milch-kine yield blood (IV, iv, 30–3)

As Page points out, there are many 'that do fear / In deep of night to walk by this Herne's oak' (IV, iv, 38–9). Making milk-yielding cows bleed, as the last line states, was a bovine malady particularly associated with such wandering spirits, and one well-known ritual remedy for this was enacted at crossroads by means of transference of the evil through milk spilt at the place.[13] Besides the sky-riding of the gods, this binding function may apparently also apply to other forms of mobility. Thompson Drewal records a small but significant moment in 1978 when a Yoruba priestess was asked to decide whether to be driven to a certain ritual in a car. This resulted in an involved discussion with her religious peers after which it was decided that she should be driven only as far as the crossroads and thereafter she must go on foot.[14]

The belief in the possibility of ritually binding an entity to a geographical locality relates not only to spirits, but is also resolutely physical. The anonymously-authored *A booke of Experiments* (1622), for instance, boasts 'A spell to bind any beaste', a formula which aims to make certain 'yᵗ he may have no power to goe from yᵉ place wherin he nowe is'.[15] Binding in the physical realm may also be of an action. Ogden records a fourth-century BCE tablet curse against prostitutes and pimps which reads 'I bind Theon, himself and his girls and his trade' begging that 'Underworld Hermes, perform this act of restraint'.[16] Its supplication to Hermes suggests this binding spell is to be performed at a crossroads herm. It may be of interest in this respect that when Robert Johnson, that pre-eminent subject of twentieth-century crossroads legend, portrays an experience at the crossroads, the primary motif is also one of arrested movement:

'Standin' at the crossroad, tried to flag a ride /... Didn't nobody seem to know me, babe, everybody pass me by / Standin' at the crossroad, baby, risin' sun goin' down /... I believe to my soul, now, poor Bob is sinkin' down.'[17]

The principle of charms or rituals of spiritual binding is one which is surprisingly persistent in western Europe and the papal bull of 1326 condemning those who make 'images, rings, mirrors, phials and similar objects intended as magic bonds' was clearly of little or no general effect.[18] In the early sixteenth century, Agrippa's *Of Occult Philosophy* (1509–10) describes the popular early modern idea of ocular fascination as 'a binding' that comes from 'the spirit of the Witch, through the eyes of the bewitched, entering to his heart'.[19] He records the many natural things which were generally thought to be bound by sorceries and enchantments, by means of the 'hanging up of things' in the form of 'charmes ... images, and characters'.[20] Although later in that century Lewis Lavater wants to dispute such binding and banning magic, in that process he of course records its common currency.[21] Given his own deep gullibility in these matters, James I oddly critiques magic which uses 'the vertue of worde, herbe, & stone', which includes the 'vnlawful charmes ... practicques, freites, or other like extraordinarie actiones', which 'commonlie dafte wiues vses ... for preseruing them from euill'.[22] He does, however, condemn those who make binding magic to stop married couples having sex by 'knitting so manie knottes vpon a poynt at the time of their mariage'.[23] John Weemse acknowledges the same concept from the other side when he writes in 1636 of the popularity of so-called 'loosing witches', those who 'do no hurt at all, but remove only that hurt which the binding witch lays on the sick person'.[24]

The ritual binding or banning of a threat either to or from a particular place was indeed a popular form of protection from evil, and one which could employ many different objects each with their own logic in terms of sympathetic magic. Joseph Ford reports the apotropaic ritual of 'burying the abortive calf' under the cow barn threshold as traditional in the Yorkshire Dales (and possibly continuing even after 1918), a prophylactic practice supposed to protect against further abortions in the byre.[25] Timothy Easton also records the protective burial of animals and many instances of other objects, including 'broken and unbroken glass vessels above doorways; the insertion of broken knife blades or wooden skewers into wall cavities beside the frame; and the nailing or suspension of objects such as the ubiquitous horseshoe above the entry'.[26] Iron was often used in an apotropaic function, guarding thresholds or windows against spiritual intruders. In 1646, John Gaule gives examples of such witch-repellent techniques, the 'heating of the horseshoe ... sticking of knives acrosse ... putting of such and such things under the Threshold, and in the Bedstraw'.[27] We may be reminded of Peele's lost travellers warned not to stumble at the threshold of the smithy. Herrick's epigraph to this chapter 'Another Charm For Stables' (1648) similarly recommends that we 'Hang up hooks and shears to scare / Hence the hag that rides the mare', while another early modern document lists a surely perilous remedy from a Parson Bond of the Bermudas in which 'when a witch comes into the howse' one must 'heate an Iron red-hott' and this will make the witch 'extremely enraged'.[28] In a safer northern Indian tradition 'to make excessive rain cease', an iron harrow was 'placed in a perpendicular position at a crossroads'.[29]

Apotropaic mechanisms employed to bind or ban evil at thresholds and liminal places have sometimes lasted until relatively modern times, and take some surprising forms. Seymour, writing in 1913, after recounting the tale of Dame Alice Kyteler's crossroads witchcraft, asks 'what better embodies the spirit of the young twentieth century than a powerful motorcar [that] travels at forty-five miles an hour without an effort' whose owner doesn't believe in witchcraft but nevertheless 'fastens on the radiator a "Teddy Bear" ... by way of a mascot'.[30] Slavoj Žižck tells a story that when a visitor asked the physicist Niels Bohr if such an eminent sceptic could really believe the horseshoe he had placed above his door might bring him luck, Bohr replied that he was informed the horseshoe worked even if one did not believe in it.[31] However, even in the sceptical West, superstitious belief in the efficacy of these traditions dies hard. Ian Evans's 2010 study into hidden apotropaic objects in Australian buildings reported that after his inspection of artefacts some owners 'prefer to replace concealed objects just as they were found' and one 'was reluctant to bring them out for photography and hastened to put them back immediately the shoot was completed'.[32] Such deeply somatic latter-day credulity is hard to account for without some form of historical continuity in folk belief or blind superstition amongst a community.

Others, however, have not come so far. C. P. Hale reports a 1934 case of a contemporary Dorset man living in an environment still credulous of 'black fairies' and 'the transformation of humans into animals' and who is apparently noted by doctors to be dying from what he believed to be a witch's curse.[33] To the reporter the man expressed surprise to have been 'passed by' in such a fatal manner, saying 'I don't know why I was chosen for I have kept my witches ball in my window all these years and my bottle always full of water in the chimney place', the existence of both such artefacts the reporter attested to. Other houses in the area seemed also to have the glass 'witches balls' in the windows.[34] Meanwhile a local woman was seen 'chasing a white hare down a culvert' and informed the reporter 'there may be an evil spirit in that one . . . we cannot tell'.[35]

The Dorset man's prophylactic 'witch balls' are fairly common in the archaeological record but also feature in literary references from the early modern period onwards, when they seem to have been popularised. The charms of this kind that survive give us an insight into the workings of the apotropaic principle, and they also have connections with crossroads rituals. In Lodovico Ariosto's *Orlando Furioso* (1516), when the magical Atlantes digs up and destroys just such protective containers from under the threshold of an enchanted castle, he causes it to disappear entirely:

> Atlantes from the threshold, graved by skill,
> With characters and wondrous signs, upturned
> A virtuous stone, where, underneath the sill,
> Pots, with perpetual fire and secret, burned.
> The enchanter breaks them; and at once the hill
> To an inhospitable rock is turned.
> Nor wall nor tower on any side is seen,
> As if no castle there had ever been.[36]

In 1681 Glanvill describes a travelling cunning man who tells a woman troubled by a 'dead Spright' to bottle up her urine and 'Pins and Needles and Nails' and to bury the bottle to cure her ills.[37] Joseph Blagrave's 1671 *Astrological Practice of Physick* recommends the same, 'with a little white Salt', which concoction 'will endanger the witches life'.[38] Cotton Mather's *Late Memorable Providences* (1691) also describes just such a practice – what he calls a 'Urinary Experiment' – of which he does not approve and in which he supposes that 'the Urine must be bottled with Nails, Pins, and such Instruments in it as carry a shew of Torture with them, if it attain its End'. He concludes that 'the bare Bottling of Urine with Filings of Steel in it . . . has been found insignificant'.[39] These artefacts pose an interesting connection, however, with the burial and staking of dangerous persons at crossroads. Around 10 per cent of these bottles are found to contain heart-shaped pieces of fabric which have often been pierced by pins. In Middleton's *The Witch* (1606), Hecate mentions such a ritual, asking 'Is the heart of wax / Stuck full of magic needles?' (I, ii, 46–7). One example of this was found at the Plough Inn, King's Lynn, Norfolk dating from c. 1620s.[40] The pierced material heart of the witch-bottle mirrors the staking of the heart in a crossroads suicide burial and accords with the occurrences of knives being found at thresholds which Gordon sees also 'as an iteration of "staking"' and another form of binding or banning practice.[41]

These protective charms were not exclusive to thresholds but have also been found interred with bodies, as in the case of the grave of a young adult uncovered at the church of All Saints, Loughton, Buckinghamshire, where a seventeenth- or eighteenth-century glass steeple bottle was found 'lying between the left humerous and upper chest', that contained 'several copper pins'. A number more pins had been stuck into the bottle's cork in a practice which the archaeologist admits 'may have occurred more frequently than excavations have so far revealed'.[42] We can only guess whether the artefact was placed to protect the corpse from spiritual interference, or to protect the living from a dangerous corpse. The operation of apotropaic charms may also be conflated with a more general kind of grave magic associated with the crossroads and with outcast burial. Robert Hunt reports that a vicar of Bodmin, Cornwall found 'a bottle full of pins laid in a newly-made grave' and lists this as a 'cure for warts' in which 'each wart was touched with a new pin, and the pin then dropped into the bottle' asserting that 'burying it in the earth, and especially at a "four cross-roads" was quite sufficient'.[43] In Henry Chettle's *Tragedy of Hoffman* (1631) one character asks of his son, who has been 'rob'd of Funerall Rites' and buried outside the 'hallowed earth' of the graveyard, 'Where is the apparrell that I bad him weare / Against the force of witches and their spells', and is told, 'We buried it with him.'[44] Chettle then seems also to associate these aspects of prophylactic protection in the outcast burial and the apotropaic device.

Bethencourt notes that the characteristics of the early modern European witch include not only 'pacts with the devil, night flights, participation in collective assemblies' (often supposed to be located at crossroads), but also the 'ability to metamorphose, and . . . produce malefice against persons and property'.[45] Like crossroads, other liminal places were subject to the narratives of protection, if not acting as a guard or obstruction themselves then in need of guarding or obstructing. In this respect the household has many vulnerabilities. In his *Daemonologie* (1597), James I alerts us to the danger that if an evil spirit lodges itself, zombie-like, in a dead body, even then 'they can easely inough open without dinne anie Doore or Window, and enter in thereat'; on the other hand 'if they enter as a spirite onelie, anie place where the aire may come in at, is large inough an entrie for them: For . . . a spirite can occupie no quantitie.'[46] James was not alone in his paranoia in this respect; as James Sharpe says, most of Europe's royal houses, including the papacy, had imagined themselves 'threatened by magic' at some point during the period.[47] Though James himself may alter tack on such things in later decades, he nevertheless captures here a popular mood: of the early modern household under siege by the minions of an encroaching darkness.

These protective functions are seen generally in many traditions especially around the guarding of domestic space from the passage of evil and this also, perhaps unsurprisingly, may lead us back to the crossroads. The Yoruba god Eshu-Elegba unites liminal places conceptually as a wandering spirit who inhabits both the crossroads and thresholds of houses.[48] His mud pillar symbol is placed wherever trouble might be expected; it tends to be sited 'at doorways, where it serves not only as a protection but also to remind men of boundaries'.[49] While around 10 percent of witch bottles were found under thresholds, archaeologists estimate that around half of those discovered so far were found beneath a hearth.[50] Though less obvious perhaps than the threshold, the hearth was also a liminal space and thus a 'point of vulnerability for those who believed that dangerous creatures, including witches, were abroad at night', as Brian Hoggard says.[51] The Dorset man dying of his witch-curse was clearly nonplussed that his chimney device had failed him. Since the chimney of an open fire is always itself open, one would assume that here both ingress and egress are potential problems with respect to spiritual protection. Glanville's *Sadducismus Triumphatus* describes a spectre singing as it came down the chimney of the house of one Edward Mompesson in 1662.[52] These examples sit within the general tradition in the history of myth and folklore of the association of the hearth with the supernatural. There is an English folk tale in which the eponymous 'King of the Cats' is exposed as such in a lodge where two hunters are staying, rushes up the chimney and is 'seen no more'.[53] The same happens to the changeling in the Scottish tale 'The Smith and the Fairies'.[54] The fireplace is also the escape route for the wax dummy of a threatened child in the northern English folk tale 'The Danger Averted'.[55] An example of both hearth and saltire cross-sign being used for strange ritual purposes is in the case of Mary Hodges of Hereford, accused of witchcraft in 1662, who was seen to 'take the andirons out of the chimney, and put them cross one on other and then she falls down upon her knees and useth some prayers of witchcraft' before pissing in a dish and throwing it upon the said andirons.[56] Whatever is going on here, the magical association of the hearth and the X cross is notable. As Paul Drechsler notes, in Silesia, at certain susceptible times, it was common practice for people to take all utensils away from their (presumably unprotected) fireplaces, believing that otherwise witches passing through 'would ride on them when going with the devil to the crossroads or gallows-hill'.[57] In this last case we begin to see the connection between the threshold and hearth as liminal places requiring the protection of apotropaic devices and the crossroads as a space conceptually linked. Early modern narratives suggest that the witches who threaten the threshold and hearth will also dance freely with the Devil at the crossroads.

Although the early modern household clearly requires protection from illegitimate ingress, dabbling in such charms of apotropaic magic, as James himself points out, may also work against the dabbler as 'the deuilles rudiments . . . baites, casten out by him, for trapping such as God will permit to fall in his hands', and thus potentially backfire.[58] Of the devils, James describes how, 'falling from the grace of God wherein they were created, they continued still thereafter, and shal do while the latter daie, in wandring through the worlde'. They are, he says, 'Gods hang-men, to execute such turnes as he employes them in'.[59] In an interesting psychic twist, in James's world, God and the itinerant devils are in league to use charms as traps for unsuspecting or incautious people – just as people would themselves use charms to trap or arrest such wandering evil spirits. The apotropaic charm then becomes a nexus of binding between worlds; a cipher for the reciprocal binarism of religious bondage.

Crossroads interment persisted not simply through long custom but rather as part of what Gordon describes as a general rhetoric of apotropaic response, in this case to the problem of some or other unforgiveable sin. Fixing them at crossroads was intended to confuse spirits restricted to unidirectional wandering by utilising the inherent binding properties of the crossing of lines, in this case written large into the landscape.[60] Any crossroads partakes of the crossing of lines requisite for binding but in its most common X form it replicates the saltire, the X-shaped cross which is the most evident and dominant symbol of apotropaic power. The X sigil is iterated in many ways in the simple banning imagery of crossed polearms, swords, arms, legs, bones or keys; in both the stop sign and the no stopping sign, and in many cases in the no entry sign. The use of the apotropaic X resounds with the idea that certain signs and figures enable contact with the divine, or otherwise effect interaction with spiritual realms.

In common with other proponents of sympathetic magic of the time, Agrippa speaks of certain signs 'breathing out a harmony of some Divinity' and for many experimental and mystical thinkers of the age, the X was just such a sign, and crucial to their systems of belief.[61]

In Christian contexts the meaning of the X is varied. Its binding nature may be linked to the heraldic papal symbol of the cross-keys, which were a direct reminder of the Pope's authority over spiritual binding and loosing supposedly given to Peter by Christ: 'And I will give unto thee the keys of the kingdom of heaven: and whatsoever thou shalt bind on earth shall be bound in heaven: and whatsoever thou shalt loose on earth shall be loosed in heaven' (Matthew 16: 19).[62] This priestly function replicates ritual practice which pre-dates Christianity by many centuries as we have seen, and the Pope's crossed keys may be a holy mirror of the image of 'crossbones' in the wise man's study.[63] In the influential Neoplatonist numerology of his *Monas Hieroglyphica* (1564) John Dee acknowledges the power of the X sign as a mathematical and magically efficacious element.[64] Dee muses on the spiritual significance of the X as expressing two fives along the horizontal axis of symmetry, linking Roman numerals with his 'theories of the Cross'.[65] In Thomas Browne's Neopythagorean *Garden of Cyrus* (1658) he describes the letter X as the 'Emphaticall decussation, or fundamentall figure' linking art and nature. He also relates it to the number five, and the 'quincunx' pattern, the five dots arranged in an X like the number five on dice which have been associated with the symbolism of the five wounds of Christ, although they appear to be of pre-Christian derivation.[66] Browne sees this as 'one of the Numbers that makes up the mysticall Name of God', which express 'the intelligible Sphere, which is the Nature of God'.[67] Christian occultism had long recognised the power of the five, which Agrippa describes as 'the seale of the Holy Ghost, and a bond that binds all things, and the number of the cross, yea eminent with the principall wounds of *Christ*'; moreover, for him its use is clear, it has 'great power in expiations: For in holy things it drives away Divels.'[68] It is worth noting also that the number five has long been believed in itself to have the power both to bind and to repel. The anonymous 1622 spellbook, *A booke of Experiments* includes charms invoking the five wounds.[69] In an example of its apotropaic power, in 1566 the cunning woman Elizabeth Mortlock began her charm to protect children who were troubled by fairies with 'five Paternosters in the worship of the five Wounds of our Lord'.[70] It is possible, moreover, that a deeper connection here may predate the Catholic Church itself: Agrippa not only describes the significance of the number five as above, but also identifies it firmly within the pre-Christian world, asserting that 'the Heathen *Philosophers* did dedicate it as sacred to Mercury'.⁷¹ The fact that such an authoritative occult writer ties this figure in with one of the chief gods of the crossroads might be incidental, or merely coincidental, to the present narrative, were it not the case that so many connections occur to suggest the congruence of such ideas and beliefs around the manipulation of spiritual powers of various kinds wherever certain lines or roads meet.

The X also resonates with occult semiotic connections. In Saxony it was the tradition when passing over a crossroads to take off one's hat and chalk a cross-mark inside to protect the traveller from any evil forces connected to the place.⁷² An old charm in north-west Durham and south Northumberland to protect against frostbite involved 'wetting one's forefinger and making a cross on the toe of one's boot'.⁷³ It is perhaps a small but noteworthy example of the survival of Catholic ritualism in more Protestant times that early modern housewives and bakers still 'commonly cut the sign of the cross on the top of the dough as a means of protection against evil influences', as Thomas records.⁷⁴ In early modern folklore, even a flat-bread bannock, if carelessly unmarked with the X cross, could become a dancing-stage which might attract unwelcome attention from fairies.⁷⁵ The hot cross buns of Easter are a modern survival of this apotropaic imperative. There are also instances of crossing of limbs, as in the 'casting of the Witch into the water with thumbes & toes tyed across', presumably as a way of binding her or his power.⁷⁶ Agrippa also tells us that 'to sit cross legged, is Sorcery, therefore it was forbiden to be done in the Counsels of Princes, and Rulers, as a thing which hindred all acts'.⁷⁷ Sharpe describes an account of a witch riding a victim like a horse 'cross-legged' to an imagined sabbath.⁷⁸ It is also noteworthy that in the Hanged Man card of the Tarot the figure is suspended from his right foot with his left leg crossed behind, forming an X.⁷⁹ The X clearly has an historical apotropaic function in these varied examples, and although Clark notes other Catholic protections against witchcraft: 'the name of Christ, the sign of the cross, saints' relics, reciting the Creed, fasting and prayer, the eucharist, holy water, and the word of God', it is curious to note that, in such Christian eras, the upright Christian cross does not seem to have been the primary symbol for repelling evil.⁸⁰ The saltire X seems to have enjoyed far more potency in these matters.⁸¹

One case study of the power of the X to repel evil throws up some interesting connections with the other related themes of this book. In certain sixteenth- and seventeenth-century farmhouses in the North Yorkshire village of Glaisdale in the UK, there remain carved posts of some antiquity which since at least the nineteenth century have been known locally as 'witch posts'.[82] The carving on these posts is typically fairly simple: towards the top front, one or more 'X' symbols, some more stylised than others, sit above a series of grooves which have the appearance of books in a stack or on a shelf. One good example is typical in most respects except for its inclusion of a date which is also carved there: 1664. In the case of this post, the X symbol includes an example of the quincunx, as mentioned above (see Figure 10.1).[83] These 'witch posts' are situated on the end of the 'inglenook', a wooden partition separating the door of ingress to the room from the fireplace adjacent to it, and projecting five or six feet into the room (see Figure 10.2). Practically speaking, this partition offered warmth against any time when the door might be opened on a cold day (here by no means confined to the season of winter). But, significantly positioned thus at the end of the inglenook, tradition has it that these carved artefacts arrested the progress of a witch's spirit, or other evil spirit of some kind (those of goblins, boggles and fairies not at all excluded, according to local legend) in passing from the threshold, through the room, and up the chimney via the fireplace.[84] This understanding of the 'witch posts' with their X symbology as examples of early modern apotropaia is recommended by many accounts of the perceived necessity for such protection against the evil influence of malign intent against the householder, some of which we have already seen.[85] In the case of this house, the fact that other apotropaic signs were also found makes this even more plausible.[86]

Besides the devices of iron and glass we have considered, Easton also describes apotropaic symbols often found 'scribed, painted or carved around doorways' and surveys Suffolk houses in which infrequently used doorways and stairs to attics were often given apotropaic marks or secreted objects.[87] Specific examples of the X mark used as an apotropaic symbol are to be found in many other places also. C. J. Binding and L. J. Wilson note their incidence alongside Marian apotropaic marks in the Wookey Hole cave system, and cite their presence in sixteenth- and seventeenth-century timbered buildings, and elsewhere.[88]

Ford attests to folk belief in rituals of negation against the power of witches in the Yorkshire Dales surviving later than 1753, so there is ample cause for such marks to be required and retained into modern times.[89] But the issues at stake here also resound far more broadly. There are apotropaic functions within the semiotics of all the major

Figure 10.1 1664 witch post *in situ*, Postgate Farm, Glaisdale, North Yorkshire. (Photo: © Bill Angus, 2016)

religions of the world and in traditional cultures worldwide there are further inheritances of magical practice: in African traditional magic, Haitian Vodun and Brazilian Candomblé, for instance, which actively use apotropaic symbologies. Gale Jackson describes a Bakongo ceremony in D. R. Congo in which a binding ritual oath is enacted upon

Figure 10.2 Witch post from Stang End Farm, Danby, North Yorkshire; now in Ryedale Folk Museum. <http://www.hidden-teesside.co.uk/2014/08/06/witch-post-hutton-le-hole/> (last accessed 12 August 2021)

a 'cross drawn into the earth' upon which the petitioner stands. Perhaps unsurprisingly this represents a 'symbolic crossroads [which] creates the power of god, and brings it ... to the point where we stand'; it also recalls for the believer 'the relationship between the living and the dead, individual and community, communion and continuity'.⁹⁰ In this way the crossroads X of the Bakongo symbolises and facilitates a holistic binding of the oath to the whole history of the people and their relationship with the divine, sealed at this 'point of intersection between this, the world of the living, and the other, that of the ancestors before and beyond'.⁹¹ This is far from being an isolated example of the connection of banning and binding with the significance of the physical crossroads. The Silesian witches carrying fire irons away up the unguarded chimney to their crossroads meeting with the Devil speaks of its supernatural utility and hints at its ubiquity. It is a place of symbolic power over which spirits, and sometimes the gods themselves, cannot pass because they cannot negotiate its binding qualities. Somehow, arrested here, their spiritual or divine natures seep into the character of the place and help to form a vertical axis to add to the horizontal, helping to make it a 'thin' place between the worlds of celestial possibility and the concerns of the commonplace. Just as apotropaic charms may unwittingly trap the weaver or inscriber of the mark, tangling them in the arcane purposes of God and the lesser gods, the crossroads is a nexus for discourses of both magical binding and transition which are not contradictory; Johnston speaks of both crossroads gods Hecate and Hermes holding these in tension, 'apotropaically guarding what was inside a boundary from that which was without, as well as protecting the individual during passage through the dissociated boundary'.⁹² Here the ground of the symbol that facilitates these functions is the land itself.

The apotropaic marks discussed have the attribute of restricting or arresting the power of external evils, despite the dangers of employing such resources. In the traditional scheme of things, and in many cultures, the physical crossroads was merely the most efficacious place to exercise this power of binding or of transformation. It was a place where the power to be gained, or drained, by various ritual practices was amplified: the power to move, or to move others, to change or to wander, to banish from sanctity and deny access to honourable afterlives, to free yourself from another's influence or to bind another to your will. Moreover, the physical crossroads is in itself an apotropaic mark written into the geography of the land. Like a chronotope, it stands as a monument to the community itself, a force 'operating to shape its members' images of themselves'; it is a feature of the landscape which works as a symbol of 'the enduring moral character of its people'.⁹³ To many early modern minds, the intersection of both roads and lines carries a common meaning which pertains to the crossing of will and the possible binding, or divergence, of paths and potentialities. For contemporaries of these beliefs the conceptual connection is quite clear, and if it appears obscured to us it is only through our entirely rational rejection of their views of the harmonious nature of the universe, theories of ontological unity and sympathetic magic. Our need for protection against evil perhaps finds its comfort elsewhere as we pay dearly for the assurances of insurance. But such beliefs may not be as extinct as logic demands they should and their modern survivals in the artefacts of the 'wellness' industry may, as Niels Bohr says, 'work' in some sense whether we believe in them or not. This atheist writer noticed that he had inadvertently placed an old Greek icon by the window he most suspected a burglar might enter. If these old ideas die so hard then it is fair to ask ourselves what bindings or transformations may be found at the crossroads of the future.

Conclusion: The Parting – Intersections

There is no there there
Gertrude Stein, *Everybody's Autobiography* (1937)[1]

Like all human social phenomena, the functions of the crossroads are ultimately driven by economics and, which is virtually the same thing, the economics of belief. Its particular uses are determined by ideological and religious imperatives dating from pre-classical times. This crossing over of the 'topographical and conceptual' develops from paganism's relatively celebratory relationship with the physical world through Christianity's murkier suspicion and pessimism about our relation to this into the early modern era and from there into modern times.[2] In the early decades of the twenty-first century there are still some religious organisations and traditions that worship gods and expect transformational experiences at crossroads (notably in Haiti and Brazil). For the vast majority of people, however, there are now other more meaningful and considerably more accessible transformative rituals available.

The multifarious means of the transformation of the self and communication with the gods are now so widely available that escaping to a crossroads is unnecessary. Every liminal practice is now to be found in the broad cities of the planet or is otherwise findable along the endless trails of the internet. Both the megacities and the server farms are polynodal crossroads where gathering and distributing happen at ever-increasingly unprecedented speeds and scales.[3] The libraries and the cities of the ancient world of course carried some of these same functions. What was lacking perhaps was the assimilation of the liminal within the body of the place. The joyful and fearful phenomena of the peripheral crossroads were necessitated by the sometimes violent homogeneity of the centres of power they outlay. Rome is the archetype of the place to which all roads lead. But simultaneously Rome was also notable for the fact that it found its crossroads rituals inside its limits and made them integral to the functioning of its very streets. Simultaneously, then, Rome could be the ultimate location of inward transformation and the sprawling octopus of grand imperial expansion.

From a properly modern global perspective, the transit routes of the world now have their own mega-junctions and crossways that surely service some of the same impulses as the ancient crossroads. Flight paths are the new transitional routes and since their mid-air crossings are separated by 1,000 vertical feet, airports must be their true nodal crossroads. Perhaps now the transformation that one undergoes comes through the ease of the travel itself, where the destination context transposes the self into a new subjectivity, telling us stories that not only 'serve us as means of mass transportation', as de Certeau has it, but also provide an explanation of that exact phenomenon.[4] The beginning of this narrative shift in the transposition of the self might be located in the transition from the old highways to the new railways.[5] In the British Isles, these brought great freedoms to the urban populations, and access to transformative environments like the curative spa towns and the health-giving seaside resorts of Victorian England. Their stations were the great crossroads of their era, the iron and glass cathedrals of industrial and urban growth, sanctified by their necessity to the big idea of progress. Some of these new infrastructural forms overlaid the crossroads of earlier times, as did the massive construction of Paddington Station, and some underpassed them in the interlacing lines of the London Underground. Following the ancient routes as these great projects often have, construction and maintenance of their lines still turn up the outcast road burials of the past. As the Channel Tunnel bodies show, highway technology churns the ground and finds it full of earlier versions of itself.

After the iron rails had spread across the world, emanating from the great iron and steel works of the north of England, taking with them the trade and culture of the Western nations, the shift was to the faceless efficiency of the motorways. These far more neutral road systems re-established an anonymity to the process of travel and their reinforced concrete junctions again established the crossings of roads as the ultimate in non-places, or 'placeless spaces'.[6] In this version of thrusting modernity, the multiple crossings of a Spaghetti Junction, at the time of its building Europe's largest multi-level motorway intersection, were not only a geographical marvel, but a masterpiece. Such an ambitious creation is an art form in celebration of movement across surfaces, its aesthetic allowing humans to skim ephemerally across the superficiae of the landscape.[7] When the Junction opened in 1972, the architectural theorist Reyner Banham put together 'an itinerary for "kinaesthetes" wishing to tour "the inner complexities of this agreeable little suburban megastructure" by car'.[8] The very speed that the motorway junction enforces, however, works as a function of its non-perception as a space and in this way the liminality of the place is reinforced by its own techne. As a social phenomenon, it remains dehumanised and essentially unperceived. Suggesting flight for their space-age designers, the soaring curves of the flyover were the nearest thing they could conjure to the silver flight lines of Zarkov's rocket ship in *Flash Gordon* and the flying cars of the Jetsons. Despite their celestial ambitions, flyovers also generate another no-place in their own concrete underworld, what Peter Merriman describes as the 'solitary desolate spaces beyond the edge of the tarmac'. Merriman invokes J. G. Ballard's *Concrete Island*, in which a motorist gets marooned in this underworld as on a desert island – a triangular wasteland in which he wanders like a lost soul buried by mistake, an accidental outcast.[9] The notorious burials of Kray twins' gangster victims in the concrete posts and foundations of the under-construction motorways of the 1960s were perhaps the unmentionable outcast burials of their time. There was to be no remembrance for them beyond the vague boastings of the gangster memoire; no memorialisation in the landscape like the farmworker Tucker who hanged himself in a barn in Faulkland, Bath in 1747 and was buried at the nearby crossroads which bears his name, or in the well-tended, almost hallowed grave of Kitty Jay on its otherwise unremarkable Dartmoor fork.

This sense of rootlessness and disconnection is exacerbated by the inorganic nature of the development of the new forms of mobility and the facilitations of movement. Since they cut across or impose themselves on the landscape rather than evolving with it, railways, motorways, and airports may be seen as 'features of placelessness in their own right', as Edward Relph says.[10] And by encouraging the mass movement of human beings on an unprecedented scale, they have perhaps encouraged the spread of placelessness beyond. In this field, service stations must be the inns of such modern crossroads, brooding on or near the junctions of the motorways and major roads. These are the common-places and the in-betweens of the modern traveller, the purgatories of our new journeys. And perhaps they also retain something of the sense of revulsion that attaches to the anonymous and the unsignified, the menace of the insignificant.

What nameless horror would it imply if one were condemned to be buried under the drive-in service road of a McDonalds? As well as his crossroads and a punk song by The Stranglers, the unfortunate Tucker has a local pub named after him.[11] What folk memory does our new speedy transience allow? What of the personal, or of the person, attached to the land so swiftly passed through? Perhaps we see this only in the death-markers of garage flowers cable-tied to lampposts where the experience has come to a lethal end, and these are also pathetically etiolated and transitory.

To return to the very human imperatives of the ancient rites of crossroads we might ask, are the new depersonalised crossroads of motorway junctions, airports and cities an index of our abandonment of searching after depth or aspiring to great heights, or even of the numinous of magic?[12] This is not the case for some determined believers, as the urban shaman Chris Penczak suggests in his speculations about how cities 'connect and combine energies, elements of nature (earth, air, water, fire) and spirits', and skyscrapers 'connect worlds, from deep in the earth, to high in the sky'.[13] Without descending into mere superstition, however, we can be brave and suggest that the technologies of modernity have exceeded mere magic in lengthening life and in creating and developing opportunities for people to shape their own destinies without recourse to the ancient boundaries of understanding to find or extend their freedoms.

Looking at the boundaries we may discern further movement in the characteristics of the crossroads story. The narrative that once established firm conceptual boundaries is now increasingly fractured and fragmented, as de Certeau has it, because of the heterogeneity of authorising powers and 'the excommunication of territorial "divinities"'.[14] The long dead idea of parochial Christendom and the moribund concept of the lands of the Umma, 'narrations that organized frontiers and appropriations', are increasingly found in the tiny hands of the like-minded enthusiast, the historico-religious fanatic and the terrorist. In this respect, de Certeau identifies a resulting 'deconsecration of places haunted by the story-spirit, and the extension of neutral areas deprived of legitimacy'.[15] So we are in any case compelled to find our transformative or apotropaic liminalities internally or in conclave with others of a similar temperament in the gathering places of social media.

Meanwhile, outside the cities the wilderness has also taken another shape. As human population has tipped over into being predominantly urban (as of 2018, 4.2 billion urban and 3.4 billion rural) what was once a place of satanic temptation has now latterly been transformed into a sacred temple.[16] As Charles Warren puts it, in terms of pure economics, the land, whose 'highest calling' was once its productive use-value, is now held to be of greatest value when it is 'selected for *non*-use', in the forms of nature reserves, national parks and designated wildernesses designed to preserve the very wildness that in the past defined its fundamentally treacherous character.[17] As geographical areas were increasingly mapped and exploited (while Blake wandered 'each charter'd street, / Near where the charter'd Thames does flow') the numinous aspect of the natural world changed its shape.[18] In a similar manner, as new surveying methods took hold, 'church towers became not spires reaching to heaven but fixed points . . . for the purpose of gauging distance', as Lisa Hopkins shows.[19] Somewhere in this definitive process, the crossroads also lost its vertical axis and became again a mere metaphor for choice of life-path or moral direction. The numinous more properly abandoned its ancient post and diffused itself into the landscape. Such a shift in vertical vision, in what it was that energised the compelling allure of the crossroads, is in no way a negative matter. A thing is sometimes easier to see when it has gone.

As the climate catastrophe takes an ever more prominent role in the drama of mankind, nature itself demands that we operate more as 'visitors just passing through' as Warren puts it. This restraint should force us finally to treat nature more as a commonly nurtured space rather than acting as ruthless and acquisitive exploiters of its every geographical angle, making it the ground of all our transformative alchemical rituals.[20] It may once have been possible to state the case that wild things 'had little human value until mechanisation assured us of a good breakfast' as Aldo Leopold once said, but now it is precisely our good breakfasts that are under threat as mechanisation-driven climate change increasingly pressures harvests and the world heads towards potential food shortages on a disastrous scale.[21] Whether satanic or holy, wilderness places may be our only hope of salvation and the wanderers on those paths have maps the rest of us need. Hayden White has explored how the unveiling of such culture-defining myths as the Wild Man 'has not always been followed by the banishment of their component concepts, but rather by their interiorization'.[22] He identifies how scientific knowledge dissipates 'the ignorance which led earlier men to locate their imagined wild men in specific times and places' but argues that this does not in any way soften the ossified layers of 'psychic anxiety' where these dominant concepts originate.[23] The wild wanderers, however, are not the only crossroads denizens once best encountered at the outskirts and now manifest in the bosom of our ultra-modern cultures. Once the very gods could be located, or at least contacted, at that divine exchange. Now, to follow de Certeau's line of thinking, the gods of the classical world 'live on in our streets and in our apartments'; they were perhaps, he muses, only ever 'the agile representatives of narrativity'.[24] We might begin to ask ourselves then, to what extent we may have interiorised very many aspects of the crossroads, as this book sets them out. And we might wonder further about which of its manifestations was always an exteriorisation of an interior conceptual landscape.

The storms of the past two days in Auckland, New Zealand have taken down power lines and have driven crowds into New Lynn's library in search of battery life. Laptops and phones and the now-essential instant communication of the internet having been denied to us, the library is not only a refuge, it is a meeting place, a common-place, and again a chief marketplace of words. The dazed, the crazed, parents with small children, all those bereft of juice come in, and electronic messages and organisational structures go out along with the books. It is a place of simultaneous gathering and distribution. The internet, once popularised as the 'information super-highway', is a wide channel for news, commerce, begging and meeting. It is also our common-place. As an as-yet uncontrolled space, it is a force for mutual support and for horrific trolling, for legitimate stories of transformation and for the desperate, shady underworld transactions of the dark net. Its essential anonymity is continually under threat by the next or coming shift in economic forces; a government driven by billionaires wishing to exert executive control over the most powerful motive force of their world. It is here that we might find the closest approximation to a twenty-first-century tri-via. The www is our triple Hecate with her underworld of binding and what must stay buried, the overworld of transformational possibility and the middle ground of the real, where the rubber hits the road and, as yet, where each must be brought to the world of human experience. If a coming together is always at the same time a parting, then a new kind of transformation and of binding may be required. It may not be up to us but to those digital natives growing up with their small smart fingers already coaxing touchscreens to determine what restless spirits must be bound. And to them it lies to decide with whom we should commune in order to bring about our best metamorphoses.

Perhaps the true nature of the crossroads is to be elusive. Its dual nature might in fact cancel it out as a meaningful cultural space. It makes ambiguous the Lefebvrian distinction between everyday 'trivialised spaces' and those 'made special by symbolic means as desirable or undesirable, benevolent or malevolent, sanctioned or forbidden'.[25] The fact that it simultaneously gathers and disperses whatever comes to it means that as a concept it can only ever be useful in a metaphorical sense to modern sensibility. It may no longer be of any use for the binding of ideas and entities that societies find disturbing and it may not either be useful as a stage for the contemplation or enactment of meaningful metamorphoses. Its best use, then, might be as a historical phenomenon that serves to explain some of the imperatives and desires which energised the ideologies of religion and spirituality and which have in turn been present at the heart of great cultural movements and moments that shaped the modern world as we know it.

People will always say they are 'at a crossroads' (a friend said it to me this morning) but a crossroads is a dynamic medium, 'always in movement, always in making'.[26] Like the Roman rituals practised when crossing borders ahead of military expeditions, our stories process ahead of our social practices and open a field in which they can operate.[27] But however these linear journey narratives have served us so far, there needs to be a new story that transcends the simple choice of variations in horizontal movement that the crossroads offers, acknowledging a new vertical axis so that we might begin thinking of our potential trajectories in at least three dimensions. As mankind looks ever further outward beyond the International Space Station it is possible that the next most significant crossroads will perhaps be NASA's planned base on the Moon, Artemis Base Camp, the next small step in the long project to visit the solar system's most outlying places. Artemis, the Greek version of Diana, has often been taken as one element in the Hecate triad, whose faces look ever outward from the crossroads. These new crossing places and spaces will no doubt in time generate their own rituals of meaning and practices and rites of passage. If as a species we have lost sight of the significance of the crossroads in its physical form, its metaphorical dominance is a strong as ever. It would be very surprising, then, if it were not at some point in the future to become reified again into a physical manifestation of the hopes and dreams of human beings.

Notes

Introduction: The Ways – Transformation, Binding and Presence

1. Federico Garcia Lorca, 'Floating Bridges', <http://www.poemsofgarcialorca.com/poetry.php> (last accessed 5 July 2021).
2. Robert Frost, 'The Road not Taken', *Mountain Interval* (New York: Henry Holt, 1916), p. 1.
3. Desiderius Erasmus, *Adages, The Collected Works of Erasmus*, trans. Margaret Mann Philips (Toronto: University of Toronto Press, 1982), p. 190.
4. He gives as an instance of this the poet Theognis' path of deliberation in Euripides' *Hecuba*; Erasmus, p. 190.
5. Xenophon, *Memorabilia*, in E. C. Marchant (ed.), *Xenophon in Seven Volumes*, vol. 4 (Cambridge, MA: Harvard University Press, 1923) (II.i.29).
6. *New International Version, New Living Translation* and *The Good News Bible*. Jeremiah's account continues to record the customary response of the rebellious people of the Lord to this exhortation: 'But they said, We will not walk therein', which expresses the nature of the metaphor of the road of life in negative terms. Robert Young, *Analytical Concordance to the Bible* (McLean, VA: MacDonald, 1985), p. 1038.
7. See Peter L. Rudnytsky, *Freud and Oedipus* (New York: Columbia University Press, 1987).
8. Martin Puhvel gives special mention to Petronius, Heine, Twain, Synge, Ibsen and Galsworthy: Martin Puhvel, *The Crossroads in Folklore and Myth* (New York: Lang, 1989), p. xii.
9. Please note that any 'binding', 'transforming' or other 'spiritual' activities I refer to throughout are of course purely physical and/or psychological phenomena experienced or manifested in rituals

whose potency depends in full upon a social group's perception of the intrinsic qualities of the crossroads.
10. Francisco Bethencourt, 'Portugal: A Scrupulous Inquisition', in Bengt Ankarloo and Gustav Henningsen (eds), *Early Modern Witchcraft: Centres and Peripheries* (Oxford: Clarendon, 1990), p. 419.
11. See *OED*, 'trivia'.
12. It is a happy coincidence for this present argument that the *trivium* are also the first three of the seven essential liberal arts: grammar, logic and rhetoric.
13. Despite being perceived to be continually moving societies, hunter-gatherers have often been deeply concerned to preserve their sacred sites: see Vicki Cummings, Peter Jordan, Marek Zvelebil (eds), *The Oxford Handbook of the Archaeology and Anthropology of Hunter-Gatherers* (Oxford: Oxford University Press, 2014), p. 1237 ff. As probable animists, the very 'path to the clearing' itself might be regarded as sacred – an 'animated being' in its own right: see Yuval Noah Harari, *Sapiens: A Brief History of Humankind* (London: Vintage 2011), p. 61.
14. Heinrich Kramer and James Sprenger, *Malleus Maleficarum* (1487), trans. Montague Summers (London: John Rodker, 1928), p. 304, note 'Cross-Roads'.
15. William Francis Ryan, *The Bathhouse at Midnight: An Historical Survey of Magic and Divination in Russia* (Stroud: Sutton, 1999), p. 54.
16. Edward Balfour, *Cyclopædia of India and of Eastern and Southern Asia*, Second Edition (Madras: Scottish & Adelphi Presses, 1885), p. 534.
17. Samuel Harsnett, *A Declaration of Egregious Popish Impostures* (London: Iames Roberts, 1603), p. 135.
18. Bethencourt, 'Portugal: A Scrupulous Inquisition', p. 419.
19. Ankarloo and Henningsen, *Early Modern Witchcraft*, p. 417.
20. Puhvel, *The Crossroads*, p. 110.
21. Puhvel, *The Crossroads*, p. 110.
22. Puhvel, *The Crossroads*, p. 29. Please note that the 'Devil' is conventionally capitalised throughout to indicate the personal construction of that character in Christian doctrine. Earlier references to this figure in quotation may not adhere to his convention. Lesser devils are merely lower case.
23. William Borlase, *Observations on the antiquities historical and monumental, of the county of Cornwall* (London: W. Bowyer and J. Nichols, 1754), pp. 117–18.
24. Horace Marryat, *One Year in Sweden; including a visit to the Isle of Götland* (London: John Murray, 1862), p. 111.
25. Ryan, *The Bathhouse at Midnight*, p. 54.

26. Christopher Cobbe-Webbe, *Haverfordwest and its Story; with Old Pembrokeshire Parishes, their traditions, histories and memories* (Haverfordwest: Llewellyn Brigstocke, 1882), p. 49.
27. Puhvel, *The Crossroads*, p. 94.
28. Myrtle Hill, 'Emancipation, Famine & Religion: Ireland under the Union, 1815–1870', UCC Multitext Project in Irish History, <http://multitext.ucc.ie/d/Ireland_culture_amp_religion_1815ndash1870> (last accessed 22 June 2021). Eamon De Valera (the Irish Taoiseach 1932–48, 1951–4, 1957–9) is often misquoted as desiring an Ireland with maidens 'dancing at the crossroads', but whether he said it or not the idea has been used and misused since in Ireland as a symbol of tradition and safety.
29. Joël Bonnemaison, *Culture and Space: Conceiving a New Cultural Geography*, Chantal Blanc-Pamard, Maud Lasseur, Christel Thibault (eds), trans. Josée Pénot-Demetry (London: I. B. Tauris, 2005), p. 65.
30. Puhvel, *The Crossroads*, p. 118.
31. Puhvel, *The Crossroads*, p. 8.
32. Puhvel, *The Crossroads*, p. 1.
33. S. I. Johnston, 'Crossroads', *Zeitschrift für Papyrologie und Epigraphik*, Bd. 88 (1991), pp. 217–24, p. 220.
34. Johnston, 'Crossroads', p. 218. Hecate's title as limenoskópos designates one who watches / surveys / protects the harbour, and protects / inhabits crossroads; the harbour is also a liminal / transitional place. The epithet applies also to Zeus and Artemis. Thanks to Gina Salapata of Massey University for this translation.
35. Peter Ackroyd, *London: The Biography* (London: Vintage, 2000), p. 41.
36. Marianthi Kaplanoglou, 'The folk cult of St Phanourios in Greece and Cyprus, and its relationship with the International Tale Type 804', *Folklore*, 117.1 (2006), pp. 54–74.
37. 'Circles in Polish Mythology', *World Heritage Encyclopedia*, <http://self.gutenberg.org/articles/Circles_in_Polish_mythology> (last accessed 28 June 2021).
38. In the first six centuries of Christianity, ancient pagan stories managed to 'maintain a real currency in the world of Catholic letters' since Christian writers of the time saw this as unearthing godly 'wisdom of the ancients', if one forged in pagan half-light. However, when the materials resurface around the twelfth century, they have been subject to 'transformations of rhetoric' and forced into Christian allegorical modes; see Leonard Barkan, *The Gods Made Flesh: Metamorphosis and the Pursuit of Paganism* (New Haven and London: Yale University Press, 1986), pp. 103–4.
39. Alan Charles Kors and Edward Peters, *Witchcraft in Europe, 400–1700: A Documentary History* (Philadelphia: University

of Pennsylvania Press, 2001), pp. 63–4. Perhaps in ignorance of its historical significance, modern evangelical churches have not been so shy at appropriating an ersatz version of the symbolism of the crossroads in the choices of their names, thereby associating themselves, unwittingly one might suppose, with the forces of opposition.

40. Puhvel, *The Crossroads*, p. 37.
41. 'Hecate was worshiped by [the Athenians] in triviis': Francis Rous, *Archaelogiae Atticae libri septem: Seaven books of the Attick antiquities* (1654), <http://gateway.proquest.com/openurl?ctx_ver=Z39.88-2003&res_id=xri:eebo&rft_id=xri:eebo:citation:13530852> (last accessed 25 April 2021).
42. Robert Stapylton, *Virgil, Dido and Aeneas the fourth booke of Virgils Aeneis now Englished by Robert Stapylton Esqr* (1634), n.p., <http://gateway.proquest.com/openurl?ctx_ver=Z39.88-2003&res_id=xri:eebo&rft_id=xri:eebo:citation:99854581> (last accessed 28 April 2021).
43. Johnston, 'Crossroads', p. 217.
44. See Kitty Scoular Datta, 'Hecate' in Albert Charles Hamilton (ed.), *The Spenser Encyclopedia* (Toronto: University of Toronto Press, 1990) p. 351.
45. Although she is interchangeable with her sister gods; see 'Proserpine', Anon., *A Dictionary of Polite Literature, Or, Fabulous History of the Heathen Gods and Illustrious Heroes* (London: Scatcherd and Letterman, 1804).
46. What might lie both above and beneath crossroads is a subject of further discussion in Chapter 1, Axes: Ecstatic Heights and Nightmare Depths.
47. Johnston, 'Crossroads', pp. 217, 218.
48. Puhvel, *The Crossroads*, p. 118.
49. 'Circles in Polish Mythology', *World Heritage Encyclopedia*, <http://self.gutenberg.org/articles/Circles_in_Polish_mythology> (last accessed 28 June 2021).
50. Puhvel, *The Crossroads*, p. 30.
51. James Waylen, *The history, military and municipal, of the town of Marlborough, and more generally of the entire Hundred of Selkley* (London: J. R. Smith, 1854), p. 448.
52. Alice Morse Earle, *Colonial Days in Old New York* (London: D. Nutt, 1896), p. 258.
53. Morse Earle, *Colonial Days*, p. 258.
54. Llewellyn Lloyd, *Peasant Life in Sweden* (London: J. Childs, 1870), p. 265.
55. Charles Herbert Octavius Curtis, *Bright's Illustrated Guide to Bournemouth* (London: Simpkin, Marshall, Hamilton, Kent, 1891), p. 197.

56. Isabella Lucy Bird, *Korea and her Neighbours. A narrative of travel, with an account of the recent vicissitudes and present position of the country* (London: John Murray, 1898), p. 231.
57. Dorothy M. Owen, *Church and Society in Medieval Lincolnshire*, Volume V, in Joan Thirsk (ed.), *History of Lincolnshire* (Lincoln: History of Lincolnshire Committee, 1971), pp. 126–7.
58. Puhvel, *The Crossroads*, p. 100.
59. Johnston, 'Crossroads', p. 218.
60. Johnston, 'Crossroads', p. 218.
61. 'Lares', <http://www.classics.upenn.edu/myth/php/tools/dictionary.php?regexp=LARES&method=standard> (last accessed 22 March 2021).
62. Richard Jenkyns, *God, Space, and City in the Roman Imagination* (Oxford: Oxford University Press, 2013), p. 114.
63. Johnston, 'Crossroads', p. 217.
64. Michel de Certeau, *The Practice of Everyday Life*, trans. Steven F. Rendall (Berkeley and Los Angeles: University of California Press, 1984), p. 127.
65. De Certeau, *The Practice of Everyday Life*, p. 127.
66. Jenkyns, *God, Space, and City*, p. 114.
67. Johnston, 'Crossroads', pp. 217–18.
68. See Reuben Percy, *The Mirror of Literature, Amusement, and Instruction*, Volume 23 (London: Limbird, 1834), p. 292; Ovid, *Fasti*, trans. A. J. Boyle and R. D. Woodard (London: Penguin Classics, 2000), IV.911ff.
69. Keith Thomas, *Religion and the Decline of Magic* (London: Penguin, 1991), pp. 71–2, 74.
70. See Percy, *The Mirror of Literature*, p. 292.
71. Owen, *Church and Society*, p. 108.
72. Owen, *Church and Society*, p. 108; somewhat weirdly, such demonstrations could often be an occasion for 'horseplay and roughness', see p. 109.
73. See Thomas, *Religion*, p. 74; Gerald Lewis Bray (ed.), *Documents of the English Reformation 1526–1701* (Cambridge: James Clarke, 2004), p. 340.
74. See Nicholas Vincent, *A Brief History of Britain 1066–1485* (London: Constable & Robinson, 2011), p. 52; P. J. P. Goldberg (ed.), *Women in England: c.1275–1525* (Manchester: Manchester University Press) p. 53.
75. Augustine, *De Civitate Dei (The City of God)*, trans. John Healey (1610) (Edinburgh: John Grant, 1909), p. 174.
76. Augustine, *De Civitate Dei*, p. 174.
77. Phil Witmer, 'Five Years Later, "Yeezus" Feels Like Kanye West Made a Deal with the Devil', *Vice.com*, 19 June 2018, <https://

noisey.vice.com/en_ca/article/bj3adz/yeezus-fifth-anniversary-essay> (last accessed 6 December 2021).
78. See Puhvel, *The Crossroads*, pp. 94–6.
79. Andrew Reynolds, *Anglo Saxon Deviant Burial Customs* (Oxford: Oxford University Press, 2009), pp. 209, 212–13 ff.
80. Reynolds, *Anglo Saxon Deviant*, p. 250.
81. Johnston, 'Crossroads', p. 217.
82. Ryan, *The Bathhouse*, p. 54.
83. Paul Devereux, 'Talking and Walking with Spirits: Fresh Perspectives on a Medieval Necromantic System', in Patrick Curry (ed.), *Divination: Perspectives for a New Millennium* (London: Routledge, 2010), p. 245.
84. Carol R. Ember and Melvin Ember, *Cross-Cultural Research Methods* (Lanham, MD: AltaMira, 2009), p. 6.
85. Janette Dillon, *Theatre, Court and City, 1595–1610: Drama and Social Space in London* (Cambridge: Cambridge University Press, 2000), p. 6.
86. Henri Lefebvre, 'Reflections on the Politics of Space', *Antipode*, 8 (1976), p. 31.
87. Henri Lefebvre, *Production of Space* (London: Wiley, 1992), p. 288.
88. Peter Merriman, *Driving Spaces: A Cultural-Historical Geography of England's M1 Motorway* (London: Blackwell, 2007), pp. 1, 5. See John Urry, *Sociology Beyond Societies* (London: Routledge, 2000) and Tim Cresswell, *On the Move: Mobility in the Modern Western World* (London: Routledge, 2006).
89. Cresswell, *On the Move*, p. 2.
90. Cresswell, *On the Move*, p. 3.
91. Maurice Merleau-Ponty, *The Phenomenology of Perception* (London: Routledge and Kegan Paul, 1962), p. 102.
92. Cresswell, *On the Move*, p. 3; Merriman, *Driving Spaces*, p. 3; see also Tim Cresswell, 'Landscape and the obliteration of practice' in Kay Anderson, Mona Domosh, Steve Pile and Nigel Thrift (eds), *Handbook of Cultural Geography* (London: Sage, 2003), pp. 269–81; Barbara Bender, 'Introduction', in Barbara Bender and Margot Winer (eds), *Contested Landscapes: Movement, Exile and Place* (Oxford: Berg, 2001), pp. 1–18, p. 3.
93. Mikhail M. Bakhtin, *The Dialogic Imagination: Four Essays by M. M. Bakhtin*, trans. Caryl Emerson and Michael Holquist (Houston: University of Texas Press, 1981), p. 84.
94. Bakhtin, *The Dialogic Imagination*, p. 7.
95. Bakhtin, *The Dialogic Imagination*, p. 7.
96. Keith Basso, 'Stalking with Stories: Names, Places, and Moral Narratives among the Western Apache', in Edward Bruner (ed.), *Text, Play and Story. Proceedings of the American Ethnological Society, 1984* (Prospect Heights, Ill.: Waveland Press, 1988), pp. 44–5.

97. Bonnemaison, *Culture and Space*, p. 81
98. Bakhtin, *The Dialogic Imagination*, p. 7.
99. Bonnemaison, *Culture and Space*, p. 81.
100. Bonnemaison, *Culture and Space*, p. 81.
101. De Certeau, *The Practice of Everyday Life*, p. 115.
102. De Certeau, *The Practice of Everyday Life*, p. 115.
103. De Certeau, *The Practice of Everyday Life*, p. 117.
104. De Certeau, *The Practice of Everyday Life*, p. 117.
105. De Certeau, *The Practice of Everyday Life*, p. 117.
106. De Certeau, *The Practice of Everyday Life*, p. 126.
107. De Certeau, *The Practice of Everyday Life*, p. 117.
108. Hayden White, *Tropics of Discourse: Essays in Cultural Criticism* (Baltimore and London: Johns Hopkins University Press, 1978), p. 153.

Chapter 1. Axes: Ecstatic Heights and Nightmare Depths

1. Virgil, *Aeneid*, trans. John Dryden (New York: P. F. Collier and Son, 1909), Book VI. pp. 242–3.
2. George Eaton Simpson, 'Four Vodun Ceremonies', *The Journal of American Folklore*, 59.32 (April/June 1946), pp. 154–67, p. 166.
3. She was known as 'the Triple Goddess, or Trivia, in her three forms as Diana, Proserpina, and Hecate'; see <http://www.columbia.edu/dlc/garland/deweever/D/diane.htm> (last accessed 12 July 2021), 'quam triplicem potestatem triformem eam triplemque finxerunt, cuius in triviis templa ideo struxerunt': Because of this triple power her temples were built at the meeting of three roads; Maurus Servius Honoratus, *Commentary on the Aeneid of Vergil*, ed. Georgius Thilo (Leipzig: B. G. Teubner, 1881), 4.511. The three forms were subject to shifts in personae, sometimes including Luna of the Moon and shifting Diana to Earth.
4. Mikhail Bakhtin, *The Dialogic Imagination: Four Essays by M. M. Bakhtin*, trans. Caryl Emerson and Michael Holquist (Houston: University of Texas Press, 1981), p. 84; De Certeau, *The Practice of Everyday Life*, p. 117.
5. Thanks to Amy Hoete for drawing my attention to this interesting place.
6. P. T. Houldcroft, *A Medieval Mystery at the Crossroads* (Royston: Royston and District Local History Society, 2008), p. 5.
7. Joseph Beldam, 'X. – Royston Court House and its Appurtenances', *Archaeologia*, 40 (1866), pp. 119–37, p. 119.
8. Beldam, 'X. – Royston Court House', p. 121.
9. Houldcroft, *A Medieval Mystery*, p. 10.

10. A Reverend Ditchfield, writing in the late nineteenth century, offers the prevalence of hot cross bun eating in the area to this possibility, attributing Diana with their festal origins. Houldcroft also suggests the subterranean Mithras as a possible alternative; see Houldcroft, *A Medieval Mystery*, pp. 8–9.
11. Tobit Curteis and Naomi Luxford, 'Royston Cave: an holistic approach to conservation', *Journal of Architectural Conservation*, 20.3 (2014), pp. 170–83, p. 170.
12. Houldcroft, *A Medieval Mystery*, p. 105.
13. See L.V. Grinsell, *The Ancient Burial-Mounds of England* (London: Methuen, 1936), p. 14.
14. James allegedly became a Freemason in 1601; see Houldcroft, *A Medieval Mystery*, p. 82; Hopkins associates James with knowledge related to Freemasonry in her reading of *Antony and Cleopatra*; see Lisa Hopkins, 'Scota, Cleopatra, and Roman Law', in Sara Deats (ed.), *Antony and Cleopatra: New Critical Essays* (London: Routledge, 2004), pp. 231–42.
15. Houldcroft, *A Medieval Mystery*, pp. 9–10.
16. Houldcroft, *A Medieval Mystery*, pp. 20, 22–6. See for plan of cave at the crossroads: Beldam, 'X. – Royston Court House', p. 136.
17. Houldcroft, *A Medieval Mystery*, p. 82.
18. Houldcroft, *A Medieval Mystery*, p. 58.
19. Houldcroft, *A Medieval Mystery*, pp. 66, 76.
20. Houldcroft, *A Medieval Mystery*, pp. 12, 77.
21. Hesiod, *Theogony*, in *The Homeric Hymns and Homerica*, trans. Hugh G. Evelyn-White (Cambridge, MA: Harvard University Press, 1914), line 452.
22. Ovid, *Metamorphoses* (London: Sir Samuel Garth, 1826). Book VI, 379–87.
23. Béla Gunda, 'Gypsy Medical Folklore in Hungary', The Journal of American Folklore, 75.296 (April/June, 1962), pp. 131–46, p. 137, <http://www.jstor.org/stable/538174> (last accessed 4 August 2020).
24. Bird, *Korea and her Neighbours*, p. 231.
25. Bodleian Library, Oxford, MS Ballard 66, p. 43; Johnston, 'Crossroads', p. 224; Puhvel, *The Crossroads*, pp. 21–2.
26. Bodleian Library, Oxford, MS Ballard 66, p. 43.
27. Johnston, 'Crossroads', p. 224.
28. Heinrich Cornelius Agrippa, *Of Occult Philosophy* [1509–10], trans. J. F. (London: R. W. for Gregory Moule, 1651 [1650]), p. 95, <http://gateway.proquest.com/openurl?ctx_ver=Z39.88-2003&res_id=xri:eebo&rft_id=xri:eebo:citation:99858916> (last accessed 30 June 2021).
29. Johnston, 'Crossroads', p. 224.

30. Balfour, *Cyclopædia*, p. 29.
31. Ankarloo and Henningsen, *Early Modern Witchcraft*, p. 20.
32. John Covel, *Some Account of the Present Greek Church* (Cambridge: Cornelius Crownfield, 1722) p. 389.
33. Harsnett, *A Declaration*, p. 134.
34. Jeffrey Rusten, 'Oedipus and Triviality', *Classical Philology*, 91.2 (April 1996), pp. 97–112, pp. 108–9; see Bernd Seidensticker, 'Beziehungen zwischen den beiden Oidipusdramen des Sophokles', *Hermes* 100 (1972), p. 274; Rudnytsky, *Freud and Oedipus*, p. 324.
35. Brigitte Scheer-Schäzler, 'Heracles and Bunyan's Pilgrim', *Comparative Literature*, 23.3 (Summer 1971), pp. 240–54, p. 242.
36. Covel, *Some Account*, p. 389.
37. Pythagoras' father is supposed to have discovered him 'beneath a white poplar tree feeding himself on its fruit', a tree that was also considered to be sacred to Heracles after his defeat of the giant Cacus; see Scheer-Schäzler, 'Heracles and Bunyan's Pilgrim', p. 242.
38. A notable if slightly obscure exception to this is the fact that, in several of his sermons, Jean-Bertrand Aristide, the former priest who became Haiti's first democratically elected president, attempted a belated kind of syncretism that mixed the Vodun concept of the crossroads, 'the gateway opened by *papa Legba*' (italics in original), with the Christian concept of the cross in order to consolidate his power base in both communities; see Patrick Taylor, 'Anthropology and Theology in Pursuit of Justice', Callaloo, 15.3, *Haitian Literature and Culture*, Part 2 (Summer 1992), pp. 811–23, p. 821.
39. St John Chrysostom, 'Exorcism', <https://orthodoxwiki.org/Exorcism#Prayer_by_St._John_Chrysostom> (last accessed 23 July 2020).
40. Puhvel, *The Crossroads*, pp. 6–7.
41. Scheer-Schäzler, 'Heracles and Bunyan's Pilgrim', p. 242, n. 9.
42. Reynolds, *Anglo Saxon Deviant*, p. 216.
43. Kors and Peters, *Witchcraft in Europe*, pp. 63–4.
44. Thomas, *Religion*, p. 292.
45. Kaplanoglou, 'The folk cult of St Phanourios', p. 54.
46. Kaplanoglou, 'The folk cult of St Phanourios', p. 54.
47. Kaplanoglou, 'The folk cult of St Phanourios', p. 74.
48. Kaplanoglou, 'The folk cult of St Phanourios', p. 74.
49. Joseph L. Henderson, 'Ancient myths and modern man', in Carl G. Jung, *Man and his Symbols* (New York: Anchor, 1964), p. 156.
50. Ackroyd, *London*, p. 370.
51. Joseph L. Henderson, 'Ancient myths', p. 156.
52. Joseph L. Henderson, 'Ancient myths', p. 156.
53. Jan Chatland, 'Descriptions of Various Loa of Voodoo', Spring 1990, n.p., <http://faculty.webster.edu/corbetre/haiti/voodoo/biglist.htm> (last accessed 12 August 2020).

54. Michael Ashkenazi, *Handbook of Japanese Mythology* (New York: Oxford University Press, 2008), pp. 128–9.
55. Ashkenazi, *Handbook*, pp. 139–40.
56. Sten Konow and Poul Tuxen, *The Religions of India* (Copenhagen: Gad, 1949), p. 183.
57. John Kleiner, *Mismapping the Underworld: Daring and Error in Dante's Comedy* (Stanford, CA: Stanford University Press, 1994), p. 92. It is tempting to wonder, however, at the level of literacy of a creator who signs his work with an X.
58. Plato, *Timaeus* (36 BCE), 36b-d, cited in Guy P. Raffa, *Divine Dialectic: Dante's Incarnational Poetry* (Toronto: University of Toronto Press, 2000), p. 136.
59. Manilius, *Astronomica*, trans. G. P. Goold (Cambridge, MA: Harvard University Press, 1977), pp. 57–9.
60. George Beke Latura, 'Plato's Cosmic X: Heavenly Gates at the Celestial Crossroads', <https://www.academia.edu/1536305/Platos_Cosmic_X_Heavenly_Gates_at_the_Celestial_Crossroads> (last accessed 1 August 2020); George Beke Latura, 'Constantine's True Vision: From Plato's Chi (X) to the Christian Chi Rho', <https://www.academia.edu/2110290/Constantines_True_Vision_From_Platos_Chi_X_to_the_Christian_Chi_Rho> (last accessed 1 August 2020).
61. Latura, 'Plato's Cosmic X; Latura, 'Constantine's True Vision'.
62. Latura, 'Celestial Symbols on Roman Standards', *The Celator* (June 2011) <http://www.academia.edu/1536265/Celestial_Symbols_on_Roman_Standards> (last accessed 1 August 2020).
63. John Block Friedman, *Orpheus in the Middle Ages* (New York: Syracuse University Press, 2000), pp. 69–71; Latura, 'Celestial Symbols'. In his *Ten Books on Architecture*, Vitruvius also describes the planets' orbits as 'different points in a flight of steps', and in his *Commentary on the Dream of Scipio* (c. 400 CE), Macrobius lists the attributes a soul acquires in the various spheres; see Macrobius, *Commentary on the Dream of Scipi*, trans. William Harris Stahl (New York: Columbia University Press, 1990).
64. Friedman, *Orpheus*, pp. 69–71; Latura, 'Celestial Symbols.
65. To stretch this theme just a little, there is a kind of X hardwired inside the human brain in what is known as 'motor decussation', which describes how fibres that pass from the brain to the medulla oblongata and medulla spinalis cross over in an X 'in the anterior median fissure of the medulla oblongata'; see Thomas Lathrop Stedman, *A Practical Medical Dictionary* (New York: W. Wood, 1920), 'Decussation of pyramids'. This topography of the brain, however, suggests no evidence that the perception of the self might be configured in a similarly crosswise fashion.
66. Ruth Majercik, *The Chaldean Oracles* (Leiden, New York: E. J. Brill, 1989), p. 177.

67. Lefebvre, 'Reflections on the Politics of Space', p. 31.
68. The perceived problems with a Y-shaped cross are noted above.
69. See Francis Dvornik, *The Idea of Apostolicity in Byzantium and the Legend of the Apostle Andrew*, Dumbarton Oaks Studies, IV (Cambridge, MA: Harvard University Press, 1958).
70. Justin Martyr, *Apology on Behalf of Christians* (1.60.1) cited in Latura, 'Constantine's True Vision'.
71. See David T. Runia, *Philo of Alexandria and the* Timaeus *of Plato* (Leiden: E. J. Brill, 1986), p. 206; Latura, 'Constantine's True Vision'.
72. Kleiner, *Mismapping the Underworld*, pp. 94–5.
73. See Chapter 3, Music: Going Down to the Crossroads.
74. Samuel N. C. Lieu and Dominic Monserrat, *From Constantine to Julian: Pagan and Byzantine Views, A Source History* (London: Routledge, 1996), p. 73.
75. Lieu and Monserrat, *From Constantine to Julian*, p. 73.
76. George Beke Latura, 'Plato's X & Hekate's Crossroads – Astronomical Links', *Mediterranean Archaeology & Archaeometry*, 14.3 (2014), pp. 37–44, p. 42.
77. Latura, 'Plato's X', p. 40; Barbette Stanley Spaeth, *The Roman Goddess Ceres* (Austin: University of Texas Press, 1996), p. 107.
78. Latura, 'Plato's X', p. 40.
79. Johnston, 'Crossroads', p. 150
80. Bakhtin, *The Dialogic Imagination*, p. 7.
81. Johnston and other modern authors also note the link between Hecate and Plato's Cosmic Soul that was made around 160 CE by the authors of the Chaldean Oracles; see Johnston, 'Crossroads', p. 13; Hans Lewy, *Chaldean Oracles and Theurgy* (Cairo: l'Institut Français d'Archéologie Orientale, 1956), p. 6 ff.; Majercik, *The Chaldean Oracles*, pp. 4, 7.
82. Stuart Clark, *Thinking with Demons: The Idea of Witchcraft in Early Modern Europe* (Oxford: Oxford University Press, 1997), p. 35.
83. Clark, *Demons*, p. 35.

Chapter 2. Magic: Transformation and Self-determination

1. Anon., Bodleian Library, Oxford, MS e. MUS 173, p. 23.
2. Thomas, *Religion*, p. 206; Cresswell, *On the Move*, p. 2.
3. Thomas, *Religion*, p. 291.
4. William Vaughan, *The Golden-Grove* (1600), sig. 8v., cited in Thomas, p. 269.

5. Thomas, *Religion*, p. 294.
6. Thomas, *Religion*, p. 539.
7. Puhvel, *The Crossroads*, p. 20. The relationship of wandering devils to crossroads is explored in Chapter 9 herein.
8. Robert Muchembled, 'Satanic Myths and Cultural Reality', in Ankarloo and Henningsen, *Early Modern Witchcraft*, p. 148; James Sharpe, *Instruments of Darkness* (Philadelphia: University of Pennsylvania Press, 1996), p. 15.
9. Sharpe, *Instruments of Darkness*, pp. 14–15.
10. Thomas, *Religion*, p. 521.
11. John D. Cox, *The Devil and the Sacred in English Drama, 1350–1642* (Cambridge: Cambridge University Press, 2000), p. 180.
12. Thomas, *Religion*, pp. 528–9.
13. Bodleian Library, Michael MS 276; see also *The Key of Solomon the King (Clavicula Salomonis)*, trans. and ed. S. L. M. Mathers (London: G. Redway, 1888), p. 94.
14. Bonnemaison, *Culture and Space*, p. 81
15. E. E. Evans-Pritchard, *Witchcraft, Oracles and Magic among the Azande* (Oxford: Clarendon Press, 1937), p. 21, cited in Sharpe, *Instruments of Darkness*, p. 13.
16. Christopher A. Faraone, 'An Accusation of Magic in Classical Athens', *Transactions of the American Philological Association* (1974), 119 (1989), pp. 149–60, p. 159.
17. Theophrastus, *The Characters*, trans. R. C. Jebb (1870), XVI <http://www.eudaemonist.com/biblion/characters/> (last accessed 8 April 2021).
18. Theophrastus, XVI.
19. *Elegies*, 1.1.11 cited in Puhvel, *The Crossroads*, p. 5; see for more revered stones, *Pausanias's Description Of Greece*, trans. J. G. Frazer (London: Macmillan, 1898), p. 378.
20. Borlase, Observations, p. 118.
21. Puhvel, *The Crossroads*, p. 10.
22. Newbell Puckett, *Folk Beliefs of the Southern Negro* (Chapel Hill: University of North Carolina Press, 1926; Montclair, NJ: Patterson Smith, 1968), p. 424.
23. E. M. Fogel, *Beliefs and Superstitions of the Pennsylvania Germans* (Ithaca: Cornell University Press, [1915] 2009), p. 364.
24. Kehinde Adeola Ayeni, 'Crossroads' <http://www.kehindeayeni.com/2011> (last accessed 18 June 2021).
25. David J. Hess, 'Umbanda and Quimbanda Magic in Brazil: Rethinking Aspects of Bastide's Work', *Archives de Sciences Sociales des Religions*, 79 (July–September 1992), pp. 135–53, p. 141.
26. Puhvel, *The Crossroads*, pp. 49–50.

27. Johnston, 'Crossroads', p. 224, n. 29.
28. Puhvel, *The Crossroads*, pp. 50–2.
29. Puhvel, *The Crossroads*, p. 11.
30. Ryan, *The Bathhouse*, p. 54.
31. Kramer and Sprenger, *Malleus Maleficarum*, p. 409. The *Malleus Maleficarum* was employed in a significant way mainly by late Elizabethan Protestants, which is an irony given its resolutely Catholic provenance and relation to the Inquisition; see Thomas, *Religion*, p. 523.
32. Kramer and Sprenger, *Malleus Maleficarum*, p. 409.
33. Thomas, *Religion*, p. 214.
34. Christina Larner, *Witchcraft and Religion: The Politics of Popular Belief* (Oxford: Basil Blackwell, 1984), p. 57.
35. Thomas, *Religion*, p. 273.
36. Johnston, 'Crossroads', p. 223.
37. Bill Griffiths, *Aspects of Anglo-Saxon Magic* (Hockwold-cum-Wilton: Anglo Saxon Books, 1996), p. 35.
38. Agrippa, *Of Occult Philosophy*, p. 490.
39. Anon., *A booke of Experiments taken out of dyvers augthors* (1622), Bodleian Library, Oxford, MS. E. Mus 243, pp. 47–8.
40. Anon., Bodleian Library, Oxford, MS e. MUS 173, p. 23.
41. 'Ascariel' seems to appear only here, while 'Agla' is a kabbalistic notarikon for 'You, O Lord, are mighty forever'; see 'Notarikon' in Sol Steinmetz, *The Dictionary of Jewish Usage: A Guide to the Use of Jewish Terms* (Lanham, NC: Rowman & Littlefield, 2005). Katharine M. Briggs notes various examples of 'church magic', the combination of witchcraft spells with Christian forms, from examples of contemporary manuscripts in the British Museum. One such example is:

> *A method of bringing a disobedient spirit into subjection*
> Make a fire of drye cowturds brimstone and such like stincking stuffe, & write the spirits name in virgine parchment, then burne it, saying the curse following . . . O most mighty God, and most gracious father and mercifull Lord which by thy just judgement avengedst the serpent in Paradise for alluring man to disobey thy commaundements, vouchsafe I bessech thee to condemne and curse this disobedient N: which doth contemne and disobey thy holy and blessed name. Amen.

See Katharine M. Briggs, *The Anatomy of Puck* (London: Routledge and Kegan Paul, 1959), p. 253.
42. Thomas Middleton, *The Witch*, ed. Elizabeth Schafer (London: A&C Black, 1994).

43. Thomas Nashe, *The Terrors of the Night* (1594), p. 12 <http://www.oxford-shakespeare.com/Nashe/Terrors_Night.pdf> (last accessed 29 July 2021).
44. Nashe, *Terrors*, p. 12.
45. Bodleian Library, Oxford, MS e. MUS 238, p. 3.
46. Anon. *A booke of Experiments*, pp. 47–8.
47. Bodleian Library, Oxford, MS e. MUS 238, p. 3.
48. Nashe, *Terrors*, pp. 4–5.
49. Bodleian Library, Oxford, MS e. MUS 173, p. 35.
50. Bodleian Library, Oxford, MS e. MUS 238, p. 3.
51. Thomas Middleton's *The Witch* (c. 1606) is possibly the best early modern example of this, while *Macbeth* offers a more cartoonish rendering. Middleton's Hecate, however, is a mortal who locates rituals in her cave and in a forest clearing, while Macbeth's witches do seem to be at a crossroads by the implication of their meeting with Macbeth on a route across the heath, and by Banquo's request for directions. Their Hecate is divine meanwhile, again implying a crossroads in the vicinity, though this is not explicit. See Chapter 4 herein, p. 101.
52. Larner, *Witchcraft and Religion*, p. 3.
53. Kramer and Sprenger, *Malleus Maleficarum*, p. 304, note 'Cross-Roads'.
54. William Marion Miller, 'How to Become a Witch', *The Journal of American Folklore*, 57.226 (October–December 1944), p. 280.
55. Christine D. Worobec, 'Witchcraft Beliefs and Practices in Pre-revolutionary Russian and Ukrainian Villages', Russian Review, 54.2 (April 1995), pp. 165–87, p. 172, <http://www.jstor.org/stable/130913> (last accessed 28 May 2021).
56. Worobec, 'Witchcraft', p. 172.
57. Johnston, 'Crossroads', p. 223.
58. Daniel Ogden, *Magic, Witchcraft, and Ghosts in the Greek and Roman Worlds* (Oxford: Oxford University Press, 2002), p. 234.
59. Ogden, *Magic*, p. 234.
60. Puhvel, *The Crossroads*, p. 21.
61. Puhvel, *The Crossroads*, p. 21.
62. St. John D. Seymour, *Irish Witchcraft and Demonology* (London: Portman, 1913), p. 27.
63. Seymour, *Irish Witchcraft*, p. 27.
64. Richard Ledrede, *The Sorcery Trial of Alice Kyteler: A Contemporary Account* (Asheville, NC: Pegasus Press, 2004), p. 63.
65. Seymour, *Irish Witchcraft*, p. 27.
66. Puhvel, *The Crossroads*, pp. 21–2.
67. Michael D. Bailey, 'From Sorcery to Witchcraft: Clerical Conceptions of Magic in the Later Middle Ages', *Speculum*, 76.4 (October

2001), pp. 960–90, p. 982. The story is also told in Kramer and Sprenger's *Malleus*, p. 304.
68. George L. Burr (ed.), *The Witch Persecutions in Translations and Reprints from the Original Sources of European History*, vol. 3, no. 4 (Philadelphia: University of Pennsylvania, 1898–1912), pp. 23–8, p. 25.
69. Describing this typically vicious occurrence, Burr describes a very human touch added to this story by a letter, 'in quivering hand', secretly passed by Junius to his daughter at his trial, explaining that 'whoever comes into the witch prison must become a witch or be tortured until he invents something out of his head and – God pity him – bethinks him of something'; see Burr, *Witch Persecutions*, p. 27.
70. Puhvel, *The Crossroads*, pp. 29–30.
71. Waylen, *The history*, p. 448.
72. Marryat, *One Year in Sweden*, p. 111.
73. Marryat, *One Year in Sweden*, p. 111.
74. Walter Keating Kelly, *Curiosities of Indo-European Tradition and Folk-Lore* (London: Chapman & Hall, 1863), p. 124.
75. Lloyd, *Peasant Life in Sweden*, p. 265; John Stow, *A Survey of London* (1598), ed. William J. Thoms (London: Whittaker, 1842), p. 39.
76. Lloyd, *Peasant Life in Sweden*, p. 265.
77. Lloyd, *Peasant Life in Sweden*, p. 265.
78. Puhvel, *The Crossroads*, p. 45.
79. Cobbe-Webbe, *Haverfordwest*, p. 49.
80. Cobbe-Webbe, *Haverfordwest*, p. 49.
81. Curtis, Guide to Bournemouth, p. 197.
82. D. G. Brinton, 'Reminiscences of Pennsylvania Folk-Lore', *The Journal of American Folklore*, 5.18 (July–September 1892), pp. 177–85, p. 182.
83. Eveline Camilla Gurdon, *County FolkLore: Suffolk* (London: D. Nutt, 1893), p. 14.
84. Irish Folklore Commission Manuscripts, vol. 191, p. 330, cited in Puhvel, *The Crossroads*, p. 34.
85. Harry Middleton Hyatt, *Hoodoo – Conjuration – Witchcraft – Rootwork* [1935–9] (Washington DC: Western Publishing Company, 1970), p. 98.
86. Hyatt, *Hoodoo*, p. 103 (quotation updated).
87. Hyatt, *Hoodoo*, p. 105 (quotation updated).
88. James M. Campbell (ed.), *Gazetteer of the Bombay Presidency* (Bombay: Municipal Printing Press, 1946), p. 120.
89. George Eaton Simpson, 'Magical Practices in Northern Haiti', *The Journal of American Folklore*, 67.266 (October–December 1954), pp. 395–403, p. 397.

90. Simpson, 'Magical Practices', p. 397.
91. Hess, 'Umbanda and Quimbanda Magic in Brazil', p. 141.
92. Hess, 'Umbanda and Quimbanda Magic in Brazil', p. 140.
93. Gunda, 'Gypsy Medical Folklore in Hungary', p. 137.
94. Gunda, 'Gypsy Medical Folklore in Hungary', p. 137.
95. Since Hungary abolished hanging as a death penalty in 1988, this seems possible. Specific evidence for this is lacking however.
96. See Ryan, *The Bathhouse*, p. 54.
97. De Certeau, *The Practice of Everyday Life*, p. 117.
98. See Thomas, *Religion*, pp. 527, 540.
99. Larner, *Witchcraft and Religion*, p. 83.

Chapter 3. Music: Going Down to the Crossroads

1. Robert Johnson, 'Cross Road Blues', <https://www.azlyrics.com/lyrics/robertjohnson/crossroadblues.html> (last accessed 24 June 2021).
2. For a summarised version, see Gayle Dean Wardlow, *Chasin' That Devil Music: Searching for the Blues* (San Francisco: Miller Freeman Books, 1998), pp. 91–4.
3. Maiko Kawabata, 'Virtuosity, the Violin, the Devil: What Really Made Paganini "Demonic"?', <https://journals.cdrs.columbia.edu/wp-content/uploads/sites/13/2015/03/current.musicology.83.kawabata.85-108.pdf> (last accessed 15 May 2021).
4. Betsy Schwarm, 'The Devil's Trill Sonata by Tartini' <https://www.britannica.com/topic/The-Devils-Trill> (last accessed 15 June 2021).
5. In the Scottish Highlands it was said that the fairies could teach one to play the pipes; see J. F. Campbell, *Tales of the West Highlands*, vol. 12 (Edinburgh: Edmonston and Douglas, 1862), p. 311.
6. Darci Sprengel, '"More powerful than politics": Affective magic in the DIY musical activism after Egypt's 2011 Revolution', *Popular Music*, 38.1 (2019), pp. 54–72.
7. There was also a case of an archer in the reign of Mary Tudor who was arrested as a witch because he was just too good; see Thomas, *Religion*, p. 644.
8. In fact, the blues singer who did claim to have done this was Johnson's friend, Tommy Johnson (no relation); see Adam Gussow, *Beyond the Crossroads: The Devil and the Blues Tradition* (Chapel Hill: University of North Carolina Press, 2017), pp. 202–3.
9. Nick Morgan, 'Amy Winehouse, Shepherd's Bush Empire, London ~~February 2nd, March 9th~~, May 29th 2007', <http://www.whisky-fun.com/Gigs/Amy-Winehouse.html> (last accessed 24 June 2021).

10. Marybeth Hamilton, 'Sexuality, Authenticity and the Making of the Blues Tradition', *Past & Present*, 169 (November 2000), pp. 132–60, p. 160, <http://www.jstor.org/stable/651266> (last accessed 12 June 2021).
11. Marybeth Hamilton, 'Sexuality', p. 160.
12. Andrew Buncombe, 'The Grandfather of Rock 'n' Roll: The Devil's Instrument', *The Independent*, 26 July 2006.
13. Marybeth Hamilton, 'Sexuality', p. 160.
14. George Lipsitz, *The Possessive Investment in Whiteness: How White People Profit from Identity Politics* (Philadelphia: Temple University Press, 2006), pp. 119–20.
15. Lipsitz, *Possessive Investment*, pp. 119–20.
16. Luc Sante, 'The Genius of Blues', *New York Review of Books*, 11 August 1994, p. 52; Marybeth Hamilton, 'Sexuality', p. 160.
17. Sofie Balliu, 'The Paradoxical Position of the White Rapper in HipHop Music: A Genre Fixated on Authenticity', pp. 55–9, <https://lib.ugent.be/fulltxt/RUG01/002/212/912/RUG01-002212912_2015_0001_AC.pdf> (last accessed 24 May 2021).
18. For more details on these forms of authenticity, see James O. Young, *Cultural Appropriation and the Arts* (Chichester: John Wiley & Sons, 2010), p. 34ff.
19. Theodore Gracyk, *I Wanna Be Me: Rock Music and the Politics of Identity* (Philadelphia: Temple University Press, 2001), p. 109.
20. Lipsitz, *Possessive Investment*, pp. 119–20.
21. Lipsitz, *Possessive Investment*, pp. 119–20.
22. Margaret Thompson Drewal, *Yoruba Ritual* (Indianapolis: Indiana University Press, 1992), p. 26.
23. Lipsitz, *Possessive Investment*, pp. 119–20. Robert Farris Thompson suggests that Yoruba art itself surrounds material places and objects with 'intuitions of the power to make good things come to pass'. See Robert Farris Thompson, *The Flash of the Spirit* (New York: Oxford University Press, 1984), p. 19.
24. Thompson Drewal, *Yoruba Ritual*, pp. xiii, xv.
25. Thompson Drewal, *Yoruba Ritual*, p. xix.
26. Thompson Drewal, *Yoruba Ritual*, p. 26.
27. Thomas, *Religion*, p. 564.
28. Sara Graça da Silva and Jamshid J. Tehrani, 'Comparative phylogenetic analyses uncover the ancient roots of Indo-European folktales', *Royal Society Open Science*, 3.1 (20 January 2016), <https://royalsocietypublishing.org/doi/10.1098/rsos.150645> (last accessed 18 July 2021).
29. S. Baring-Gould, *The Lives of the Saints*, Volume 2 (London: John C. Nimmo, 1897), n.p. <http://www.gutenberg.org/files/45604/45604-8.txt> (last accessed 4 July 2021).

30. Baring-Gould, *Lives*.
31. *The History of Doctor Johan Faustus*, trans. H. G. Haile (Urbana: University of Illinois, 1965), p. 24 (my italics).
32. Although Macbeth and Banquo must presumably have been following some sort of path, rather than simply breaking out across the treacherous heather.
33. Agrippa, *Of Occult Philosophy*, p. 255.
34. Nanette de Jong and Barbara Lebrun, 'Introduction: the notion of magic in popular music discourse', *Popular Music*, 38.1 (2019), pp. 1–7.
35. Agrippa, *Of Occult Philosophy*, p. 255.
36. Agrippa, *Of Occult Philosophy*, p. 256. Zachary Loeffler and Owen Coggins have studied those who claim similar effects for music to the present day: see Zachary Loeffler, 'The only real magic': enchantment and disenchantment in music's modernist ordinary', *Popular Music*, 38.1 (2019), pp. 8–32; Owen Coggins, 'Dirty, soothing, secret magic: individualism and spirituality in New Age and extreme metal music cultures', *Popular Music*, 38.1 (2019), pp. 105–20, p. 109ff.
37. Gustav Henningsen, 'The Ladies from Outside', in Ankarloo and Henningsen, *Early Modern Witchcraft*, pp. 196, 198.
38. Lawrence Southerne, *Fearefvll Newes from Coventry or A true Relation and Lamentable Story of one Thomas Holt of Coventrey a Musitian: Who through Covetousnesse and Immoderate love of money, sold himselfe to the Devill, with whom he had made a contract for certaine yeares. And also of his most Lamentable end and death, on the 16. Day of February. 1641. To the terror and Amazement of the Inhabitants thereabouts* (London: Iohn Thomas, 1642), p. 3.
39. Southerne, *Fearefvll Newes*, p. 3.
40. Southerne, *Fearefvll Newes*, p. 4.
41. Thomas, *Religion*, p. 568.
42. Puhvel, *The Crossroads*, p. 116.
43. A. W. Whitney and C. C. Bullock, *Folk-Lore from Maryland; Memoirs of the American Folk-Lore Society*, 18 (1925), p. 78.
44. Gussow, *Beyond the Crossroads*, p. 203.
45. C. Lee, *Some Negro Lore from Baltimore* (J.A.F.L, 1892), p. 110, cited in Puckett, *Folk Beliefs*, p. 553.
46. Hyatt, *Hoodoo*, p. 104.
47. Hyatt, *Hoodoo*, p. 104.
48. Hyatt, *Hoodoo*, p. 108 (reported speech amended from the original which transcribed for accent).
49. Hyatt, *Hoodoo*, p. 100 (reported speech amended from the original which transcribed for accent).
50. Puhvel, *The Crossroads*, p. 17.

51. Puckett, *Folk Beliefs*, p. 554.
52. Lewis Hyde, *Trickster Makes This World* (New York: North Point Press, 1999), p. 76.
53. Brian Brazeal, 'The Music of the Bahian Caboclos', *Anthropological Quarterly*, 76.4 (Autumn 2003), pp. 639–69, p. 640.
54. 'Music' in David W. Bercot, *A Dictionary of Early Christian Beliefs* (Peabody, MA: Hendrickson, 1998).
55. Hyde, *Trickster*, p. 32.
56. *The Gods of Roman Britain: A Diverse Dictionary of Deities* <http://roman-britain.co.uk/romano-british-gods.htm> (last accessed 23 July 2021).
57. Hyde, *Trickster*, p. 219.
58. Horace, *The Odes, Epodes, and Carmen Seculare of Horace* (London: J. Oswald, 1712), p. 42.
59. Barbara C. Bowen, 'Mercury at the Crossroads in Renaissance Emblems', *Journal of the Warburg and Courtauld Institutes*, 48 (1985), pp. 222–9, p. 227.
60. Joe E. Tarry, 'Music in the Educational Philosophy of Martin Luther Author', *Journal of Research in Music Education*, 21.4 (Winter 1973), pp. 355–65; Frank Burch Brown, 'Religious Music and Secular Music: A Calvinist Perspective, Re-formed', *Theology Today*, 60 (2006), pp. 11–21, p. 14.
61. Samuel Rowley, *When You See Me You Know Me* [1605] (London: Williams and Nokgate, 1874), p. 52.
62. James Charles Cobb, *Redefining Southern Culture: Mind and Identity in the Modern South* (Athens: University of Georgia Press, 1999), pp. 107–8.
63. Donald K. Sharpes, *Lords of the Scrolls: Literary Traditions in the Bible and Gospels* (New York: Peter Lang, 2005), p. 300; Willis Barnstone and Marvin W. Meye (eds), *The Gnostic Bible* (Boston: New Seeds, 2003), p. 797.
64. A. L. Beier, *Masterless Men* (London: Methuen, 1985), p. 97.
65. Beier, *Masterless Men*, p. 97.
66. Beier, *Masterless Men*, p. 96.
67. Beier, *Masterless Men*, p. 97.
68. Beier, *Masterless Men*, pp. 96–7.
69. Beier, *Masterless Men*, p. 96.
70. Mark Brayshay, *Land Travel and Communications in Tudor and Stuart England* (Liverpool: Liverpool University Press, 2014), p. 175.
71. Beier, *Masterless Men*, p. 97.
72. Robert Burton, *The Anatomy of Melancholy* (London: Henry Cripps, [1621] 1623), l. 2297–9.
73. Beier, *Masterless Men*, p. 98.

74. Beier, *Masterless Men*, p. 98.
75. Beier, *Masterless Men*, p. 97.
76. Bodleian Library, Oxford, MS. Wood D. 19/4, n.p.
77. Bodleian Library, Oxford, MS. Wood D. 19/4, n.p.
78. Hugh Benham, *John Taverner: His Life and Music* (Aldershot: Ashgate, 2003), p. 11.
79. John Milton, '*Comus*, A Mask Presented at Ludlow Castle (1634)', The John Milton Reading Room, <https://www.dartmouth.edu/~milton/reading_room/comus/text.shtml> (last accessed 20 June 2021).
80. Thomas, *Religion*, p. 627.
81. Thomas, *Religion*, pp. 615–16.
82. Thomas, *Religion*, p. 616.
83. Thomas, *Religion*, pp. 86, 266.
84. Kramer and Sprenger, *Malleus*, pp. 74–5.
85. Barkan, *The Gods Made Flesh*, p. 56.
86. Roger Bacon, *Frier Bacon his discovery of the miracles of art, nature, and magick*, trans. T. M. (London: Simon Miller at the Starre in St Pauls Church-yard, 1659), p. 12, <http://gateway.proquest.com/openurl?ctx_ver=Z39.88-2003&res_id=xri:eebo&rft_id=xri:eebo:citation:99858887> (last accessed 10 July 2021).
87. Bonnemaison, *Culture and Space*, p. 81.
88. See Catherine A. Henze, *Robert Armin and Shakespeare's Performed Songs* (Abingdon: Routledge, 2017), pp. 155–72; William Shakespeare, *The Tempest*, ed. Virginia Mason Vaughan and Alden T. Vaughan (London: Arden, 2011), pp. 18–20; 'Johnson, Robert (c. 1583–1633)', *Oxford Dictionary of National Biography* (Oxford: Oxford University Press, 2004).
89. Henze, *Robert Armin*, p. 155.
90. John P. Cutts, 'An Unpublished Contemporary Setting of a Shakespeare Song', *Shakespeare Survey*, 9 (1956), pp. 86–9, p. 86.
91. Henze, *Robert Armin*, p. 156.
92. Daniel Albright, *Musicking Shakespeare: A Conflict of Theatres* (Rochester, NY and Woodbridge: University of Rochester Press, 2007) pp. 21ff., p. 17.
93. Albright, *Musicking Shakespeare*, p. 17.
94. Vaughan and Vaughan also describe the potential connections between *The Tempest*'s Ariel and John Dee's familiar spirit Uriel; see Shakespeare, *The Tempest*, Vaughan and Vaughan (eds), pp. 27–30. Here they also discuss biblical usages of the term 'Ariel' in relation to the altar and the voracious consumption of offerings.
95. See Henze, *Robert Armin*, p. 155; Shakespeare, *The Tempest*, Vaughan and Vaughan (eds), pp. 18–20.

96. See Shakespeare, *The Tempest*, ed. Vaughan and Vaughan, p. 59.
97. See Shakespeare, *The Tempest*, ed. Vaughan and Vaughan, p. 63.
98. See Peggy Muñoz Simonds, '"My charms crack not": The Alchemical Structure of *The Tempest*', *Comparative Drama*, 31.4 (Winter 1997–8), pp. 538–70.
99. John S. Mebane, *Renaissance Magic and the Return of the Golden Age: The Occult Tradition of Marlowe, Jonson, and Shakespeare* (Lincoln, NE and London: University of Nebraska Press, 1989), p. 85.
100. Albright, *Musicking Shakespeare*, p. 143.
101. 2 Corinthians 11: 14; Hebrews 13: 2; Genesis 3: 1.
102. Bacon, *Frier Bacon*, p. 35. T. M. says in translating this he 'followed Dr Dees edition, printed at Hamburg, 1618', see p. 51.
103. Barkan, *The Gods Made Flesh*, pp. 19, 37.
104. Kramer and Sprenger, *Malleus*, p. 245.
105. John Cotta, *The Infallible True And Assured Witch* (London: Richard Higginbotham, 1624), p. 35.
106. Cotta, *Infallible*, p. 35.
107. Kramer and Sprenger, *Malleus*, p. 1.
108. Kramer and Sprenger, *Malleus*, p. 1.
109. Kramer and Sprenger, *Malleus*, p. 133.
110. Kramer and Sprenger, *Malleus*, p. 133.
111. Nashe, *Terrors*, p. 5.
112. Nashe, *Terrors*, p. 5.
113. Nashe, *Terrors*, p. 6.
114. Joseph Glanvill, *Some philosophical considerations touching the being of witches and witchcraft written in a letter to the much honour'd Robert Hunt, Esq.* (London: E. C., 1667), pp. 11–12.
115. When he appears to concede that 'perhaps sometimes the confederate Spirit puts tricks upon the senses of the spectators, and those shapes are onely illusions', this is just for the sake of his argument and he is in fact still making the opposite case; Glanvill, *Some philosophical considerations*, p. 16.
116. Sharpe, *Instruments of Darkness*, p. 136.
117. Seymour, *Irish Witchcraft*, p. 27.
118. Ledrede, *Sorcery Trial*, p. 63.
119. Burr, *Witch Persecutions*, p. 24.
120. George Giffard, *A Dialogue Concerning Witches and Witchcraftes* (London: John Windet, 1593), p. 6; Bodleian Library, Oxford, 8465 MSS Ashmole 547. In Britain, and more widely in Europe, witches were believed to be able to turn themselves, among other things, into hares: see Puhvel, *The Crossroads*, p. 33.
121. Giffard, *A Dialogue*, p. 6; Bodleian Library, Oxford, 8465 MSS Ashmole 547.
122. Giffard, *A Dialogue*, p. 26; Bodleian Library, Oxford, 8465 MSS Ashmole 547.

123. Giffard, *A Dialogue*, p. 85; Bodleian Library, Oxford, 8465 MSS Ashmole 547.
124. Giffard, *A Dialogue*, p. 24; Bodleian Library, Oxford, 8465 MSS Ashmole 547.
125. Barkan, *The Gods Made Flesh*, p. 292.
126. Mebane, *Renaissance Magic*, pp. 144–5.
127. Mebane, *Renaissance Magic*, pp. 144–5.
128. Katharine Eisaman Maus, *Ben Jonson and the Roman Frame of Mind* (Princeton: Princeton University Press, 1984), p. 90.
129. Mebane, *Renaissance Magic*, p. 116.
130. Lewis Lavater, 'Of Ghosts and Spirites, Walking by Night' (1572), trans. R. H. (London: Thomas Creede, 1596), p. 12.
131. Lavater, 'Of Ghosts and Spirits', p. 168.
132. Bacon, *Frier Bacon*, p. 12.
133. Anon., *The mad pranks and merry jests of Robin Goodfellow* (London: F. Grove, 1828), p. 11.
134. Joseph Glanvill, *Saducismus Triumphatus, or, Full and plain evidence concerning witches and apparitions in two parts: the first treating of their possibility, the second of their real existence*, <http://quod.lib.umich.edu/e/eebo/A42824.0001.001/1:19.4?rgn=div2;view=fulltext> (last accessed 19 June 2021).
135. Incidentally, the contemporary musician Robert Johnson is not known to have had a hand in this since its writing at 1595–6 predates his involvement with the company.
136. Barkan, *The Gods Made Flesh*, pp. 91–3.
137. Burton, *Anatomy of Melancholy*, l. 875–6.
138. Glanvill, *Saducismus Triumphatus*, p. 81.
139. Hyde, *Trickster*, p. 17 ff. In the indigenous American Raven myth, the hungry transformative trickster even goes so far as to eat itself; see Hyde, *Trickster*, p. 27.
140. Hyde, *Trickster*, p. 27.

Chapter 4. Gods: Appointments with the Divine

1. Bowen, 'Mercury at the Crossroads', p. 222.
2. Hyde, *Trickster*, p. 46.
3. Konow and Tuxen, *Religions of India*, p. 183.
4. Ashkenazi, *Handbook*, pp. 139–40.
5. Puhvel, *The Crossroads*, p. 7.
6. Puhvel, *The Crossroads*, p. 15.
7. Puhvel, *The Crossroads*, p. 15.
8. Puhvel, *The Crossroads*, pp. 8–9.
9. P. J. L. Frankl, 'The Word for "God" in Swahili', *Journal of Religion in Africa*, 20, Fasc. 3 (October 1990), pp. 269–75.

10. Puhvel, *The Crossroads*, p. 10.
11. Puhvel, *The Crossroads*, p. 2.
12. F. Max Müller (ed.), *Satapatha-Brahmana, The Sacred Books of the East*, vol. 12 (Oxford: 1882), p. 438.
13. Thomas Stevens, *Around the World on a Bicycle . . .: From Teheran to Yokohama* (London: Sampson Low, 1888), p. 455.
14. See John Eric Sidney Thompson, *Maya History and Religion* (Norman: University of Oklahoma Press, 1970); Allen J. Christenson, *Art and Society in a Highland Maya Community* (Austin: University of Texas Press, 2003).
15. Chatland, 'Descriptions of Various Loa of Voodoo', n.p.
16. Chatland, 'Descriptions of Various Loa of Voodoo', n.p.
17. Chatland, 'Descriptions of Various Loa of Voodoo', n.p.
18. Hess, 'Umbanda and Quimbanda Magic in Brazil', p. 141.
19. Hyde, *Trickster*, p. 119.
20. See Chapter 3 herein and Robert Palmer, *Deep Blues: A Musical and Cultural History of the Mississippi Delta* (New York: Penguin, 1981), pp. 60, 126.
21. Baba Raul Canizares, *Santeria and the Orisha of the Crossroads* (New York: Original Publications, 2000), pp. 23–4.
22. Chatland, 'Descriptions of Various Loa of Voodoo', n.p.
23. Chatland, 'Descriptions of Various Loa of Voodoo', n.p.
24. Chatland, 'Descriptions of Various Loa of Voodoo', n.p.
25. Chatland, 'Descriptions of Various Loa of Voodoo', n.p.
26. Chatland, 'Descriptions of Various Loa of Voodoo', n.p.
27. Joan Westcott, 'The Sculpture and Myths of Eshu-Elegba, the Yoruba Trickster. Definition and Interpretation in Yoruba Iconography', *Africa: Journal of the International African Institute*, 34.4 (October 1962), pp. 336–54, p. 343.
28. Melville J. Herskovitsand Frances S. Herskovits, *Dahomean Narrative: A Cross-Cultural Analysis* (Evanston: Northwestern University Press, 1958), p. 35.
29. See Ócha'ni Lele, *The Diloggún: The Orishas, Proverbs, Sacrifices, and Prohibitions of Cuban Santería* (Rochester, VT: Destiny, 2003).
30. Westcott, 'Sculpture and Myths', p. 337.
31. William Bascom, *African Art in Cultural Perspective* (New York and London: Norton, 1973); Timothy Mobolade, 'Ibeji customs in Yorubaland', *African Arts*, 4.3 (1971), pp. 14–15; Robert Farris Thompson, *Black Gods and Kings* (Bloomington/London: UCLA, Indiana University Press, 1971). Westcott, 'Sculpture and Myths', p. 350.
32. Reginald Scot, *The Discoverie of Witchcraft*, p. 522, <http://gateway.proquest.com/openurl?ctx_ver=Z39.88-2003&res_id=xri:eebo&rft_id=xri:eebo:citation:12043638> (last accessed 23 April 2021).

33. Puhvel, *The Crossroads*, p. 5.
34. John Bell, *Bell's New Pantheon; or, historical dictionary of the gods, demi-gods, heroes, and fabulous personages of antiquity* (London: J. Bell, 1790), p. 39.
35. Bell, *Pantheon*, p. 39.
36. Bell, *Pantheon*, p. 39.
37. Robert Graves, *The Greek Myths* (London: Folio Society, 2001), pp. 68–72, 93; Horace, *The Odes*, p. 42.
38. Puhvel, *The Crossroads*, p. 4.
39. Bowen, 'Mercury at the Crossroads', p. 222.
40. Bowen, 'Mercury at the Crossroads', p. 222.
41. Borlase, Observations, p. 177.
42. Borlase, Observations, p. 177.
43. Borlase, Observations, p. 125ff. There may even be a Scottish cairn dedicated to the blues guitarist Robert Johnson; see BBC *Nationwide*, 15 December 1970, <https://www.youtube.com/watch?v=7BcF10-qjGE> (last accessed 4 July 2021).
44. Teone Taare Tikao and Herries Beattie, *Tikao Talks* (Auckland: Penguin, 1990), p. 71.
45. Tikao and Beattie, *Tikao Talks*, p. 71.
46. Richard North, *Heathen Gods in Old English Literature* (Cambridge: Cambridge University Press, 1997), p. 81; John C. Pope (ed.), *Homilies of Ælfric: A Supplementary Collection* (London: Early English Text Society, 1968), p. 684.
47. Various magical incantations associate Wednesday – Woden's day – with Mercury (see p. 46 herein).
48. Christopher P. Jones, *Between Pagan and Christian* (Cambridge, MA: Harvard University Press, 2014), pp. 123–4. Something of this recasting of earlier religious practices to fit the incoming narrative may be seen in more modern times where translations of the Bible into the Yoruba language use the word 'Eshu' for 'Devil', even though Eshu is a complex deity associated with many good qualities; see Hyde, *Trickster*, p. 10.
49. Puhvel, *The Crossroads*, p. 4.
50. Bowen, 'Mercury at the Crossroads', p. 227.
51. Jean Baudion, *Recuiel d'Emblemes Divers* (Paris: Jacques Villery, 1638), p. 518, cited in Bowen, 'Mercury at the Crossroads', p. 227.
52. Bowen, 'Mercury at the Crossroads', p. 227.
53. Henry Sacheverell Homer, *An enquiry into the means of preserving and improving the publick roads of this kingdom* (London: S. Parker, 1767), p. 36.
54. Thomas Wright, *Wanderings of an antiquary: chiefly upon the traces of the Romans in Britain*, (London: J. B. Nichols, 1854), pp. 17–18.

55. R. G. Collingwood and R. P. Wright (eds), *The Roman Inscriptions of Britain* (Oxford: Oxford University Press, 1995), to Mercury: pp. 64, 79, 90, 374, 533, 645, 655, 661, 736; to Diana: pp. 43, 108, 370, 397, 652, 671. Wright, *Wanderings of an Antiquary*, p. 232.
56. Collingwood and Wright (eds), *Roman Inscriptions*, pp. 220, 432, 533.
57. Johnston, 'Crossroads', p. 220.
58. Bowen, 'Mercury at the Crossroads', p. 222.
59. Johnston, 'Crossroads', p. 220.
60. Maggie Kilgour, 'Writing on Water', *English Literary Renaissance*, 29 (1999), pp. 282–305, p. 298, n. 58.
61. Bowen, 'Mercury at the Crossroads', p. 225.
62. Bodleian Library, Oxford, MS Ashmole 846, p. 2.
63. As in Martianus Capella's *Marriage of Philology and Mercury*, see Bowen, 'Mercury at the Crossroads', p. 223.
64. Lyndy Abraham, *A Dictionary of Alchemical Imagery* (Cambridge: Cambridge University Press, 1998), p. 124, cited in Ian Donaldson, *Ben Jonson, A Life* (Oxford: Oxford University Press, 2011), p. 318.
65. Donaldson, *Ben Jonson*, p. 318.
66. Ben Jonson, 'To the Memory of My Beloved Master William Shakspeare, and What He Hath Left Us', <https://www.poetryfoundation.org/poems/44466/to-the-memory-of-my-beloved-the-author-mr-william-shakespeare> (last accessed 23 June 2021).
67. Joseph Maurone, 'The Trickster Icon and Objectivism', *The Journal of Ayn Rand Studies*, 3.2 (Spring 2002), pp. 229–58, p. 229.
68. Robert Farris Thompson, *Black Gods and Kings*, pp. 119–20.
69. Thomas, *Religion*, p. 564.
70. Thomas, *Religion*, p. 564.
71. Carl Jung, *Alchemical Studies, The Collected Works*, vol.13 (Princeton NJ: Princeton University Press, 1966), p. 237.
72. Hyde, *Trickster*, pp. 10, 104.
73. Hyde, *Trickster*, p. 10.
74. Hyde, *Trickster*, p. 181.
75. Hyde, *Trickster*, pp. 76, 45.
76. Hyde, *Trickster*, p. 72.
77. Vladímir Propp, *Morphology of the Folktale* (Austin: University of Texas Press, 1968), p. 39, cited in Hyde, *Trickster*, p. 220.
78. Puhvel, *The Crossroads*, p. 4.
79. 'Hecate' <http://ovid.lib.virginia.edu/trans/MetindexEFGHI.htm#Hecate> (last accessed 23 June 2021).
80. Northrop Frye, Troni Yvette Grande, Garry Sherbert (eds), *Northrop Frye's Writings on Shakespeare and the Renaissance* (Toronto: Toronto University Press, 2010), p. 496.

81. Ankarloo and Henningsen, *Early Modern Witchcraft*, p. 23.
82. Richard Linche, *The fountaine of ancient fiction Wherein is liuely depictured the images and statues of the gods of the ancients, with their proper and perticular expositions* (1599), <http://gateway.proquest.com/openurl?ctx_ver=Z39.88-2003&res_id=xri:eebo&rft_id=xri:eebo:citation:99843588> (last accessed 4 June 2021).
83. Albert Charles Hamilton, *The Spenser Encyclopedia*, p. 351.
84. Bell, *Pantheon*, p. 372.
85. Bell, *Pantheon*, p. 372.
86. Bell, *Pantheon*, p. 372.
87. Johnston, 'Crossroads', p. 219.
88. Henry George Liddell and Robert Scott, *An Intermediate Greek-English Lexicon* (Oxford: Clarendon Press, 1889), <http://www.perseus.tufts.edu/hopper/text;jsessionid=716FE9451F28A58ACD10956E97B4B3B0?doc=Perseus%3Atext%3A1999.04.0058%3Aalphabetic+letter%3D*l%3Aentry+group%3D12%3Aentry%3Dlimenosko%2Fpos> (last accessed 23 June 2021). See also 'Hecate' <http://ovid.lib.virginia.edu/trans/MetindexEFGHI.htm#Hecate> (last accessed 23 June 2021).
89. Ammianus Marcellinus, *The Roman historie containing such acts and occurrents as passed under Constantius, Iulianus, Iovianus, Valentinianus, and Valens, emperours. Rerum gestarum libri*, trans. Philemon Holland (London: Adam Islip, 1609), <http://gateway.proquest.com/openurl?ctx_ver=Z39.88-2003&res_id=xri:eebo&rft_id=xri:eebo:citation:99849494> (last accessed 23 June 2021).
90. Robert Graves, *King Jesus*, 348–9 (RosettaBooks, 2014), Kindle Version.
91. Graves, *King Jesus*, 348–9 Kindle Version.
92. John Roberts (ed.), *Oxford Dictionary of the Classical World* (Oxford: Oxford University Press, 2007), <http://www.oxfordreference.com/view/10.1093/acref/9780192801463.001.0001/acref-9780192801463-e-1005> (last accessed October 2020); Sharpe, *Instruments of Darkness*, pp. 154–5.
93. Roberts, *Oxford Dictionary of the Classical World*; Sharpe, *Instruments of Darkness*, pp. 154–5.
94. John Stow, *A Survey of London* (1603), vol. 1, ed. Charles Lethbridge Kingsford (Oxford: Clarendon Press, 1971), p. 266.
95. Respectively, Norman Nathan 'Two Notes on Shakespeare: Fontibell and Fountains', *Names*, 39.1 (1991), pp. 39–41; Richard Wilson, 'To great St Jaques bound: All's Well That Ends Well in Shakespeare's Europe', *Actes des congrès de la Société française Shakespeare*, 22 (2005), pp. 273–90, p. 279.
96. Bell, *Pantheon*, p. 372.

97. Puhvel, *The Crossroads*, p. 3. Johnston is careful to say that the polluted remains left at crossroads in Greek culture were not part of Hecate's suppers, although it may be the case that she was nevertheless expected to deal with them in some way; see Johnston, 'Crossroads', p. 221.
98. 'Hecate' <http://ovid.lib.virginia.edu/trans/MetindexEFGHI.htm#Hecate> (last accessed 23 June 2021)
99. Bruno Snell (ed.), *Tragicorum Graecorum Fragmenta*, vol. 1. (Göttingen: Vandenhoek and Ruprecht, 1986), p. 115. Ronald Hutton, 'The Wild Hunt and the Witches' Sabbath', *Folklore*, 125.2 (2014), pp. 161–78.
100. Bell, *Pantheon*, p. 372.
101. Linche, *The fountaine*.
102. 'Hecate' <http://ovid.lib.virginia.edu/trans/MetindexEFGHI.htm#Hecate> (last accessed 23 June 2021)
103. Bell, *Pantheon*, p. 372.
104. Johnston, 'Crossroads', p. 218.
105. Linche, *The fountaine*.
106. L. R. Farnell, 'Hekate in Art' in *The Goddess Hekate: Studies in Ancient Pagan and Christian Religion and Philosophy*, vol. 1, ed. Stephen Ronan (Hastings: Chthonios, 1992), pp. 36–54.
107. Apostolos N. Athanassakis and Benjamin M. Wolkow (eds), *The Orphic Hymns* (Baltimore: Johns Hopkins University Press, 2013), line 13.
108. Eusebius of Caesarea: *Praeparatio Evangelica*, (c. 313 CE), trans. E. H. Gifford (1903), Book V, Chapter VIII, p. 139.
109. Eusebius of Caesarea: *Praeparatio Evangelica*, p. 139.
110. Eusebius of Caesarea, *Praeparatio Evangelica*, p. 203.
111. Eusebius of Caesarea: *Praeparatio Evangelica*, p. 203.
112. Ankarloo and Henningsen, *Early Modern Witchcraft*, p. 23.
113. Gary K. Waite, *Heresy, Magic and Witchcraft in Early Modern Europe* (Houndmills: Palgrave Macmillan, 2003), p. 32.
114. Kramer and Sprenger, *Malleus*, p. 5, note 'Diana or Herodias'.
115. Alan Bernstein, 'The Ghostly Troop and the Battle Over Death: William of Auverne (d. 1249) Connects Christian, Old Norse and Irish Views', in Muzhou Pu (ed.), *Rethinking Ghosts in World Religions* (Leiden and Boston: Brill, 2009), pp. 115–62, p. 141.
116. Kramer and Sprenger, *Malleus*, p. 5 note 'Diana or Herodias.'
117. Scot, *The Discoverie of Witchcraft*, p. 522.
118. 1 Cor. 10: 20.
119. 'Hecate' <http://ovid.lib.virginia.edu/trans/MetindexEFGHI.htm#Hecate> (last accessed 23 June 2021); Johnston, 'Crossroads', p. 217.
120. Laura Annawyn Shamas, *'We Three': The Mythology of Shakespeare's Weird Sisters* (New York: Peter Lang, 2007), p. 81.
121. Francis Rous, *Archaelogiae Atticae libri septem Seaven books of the Attick antiquities: containing the description of the cities glory,*

government, division of the people, and townes within the Athenian territories, their religion, superstition, sacrifices, account of the yeare, a full relation of their judicatories (1654), <http://gateway.proquest.com/openurl?ctx_ver=Z39.88-2003&res_id=xri:eebo&rft_id=xri:eebo:citation:13530852> (last accessed 14 June 2021).
122. Bell, *Pantheon*, p. 372.
123. Johnston, 'Crossroads', p. 219.
124. Bell, *Pantheon*, p. 372.
125. Bell, *Pantheon*, p. 372.
126. Bell, *Pantheon*, p. 372. Ovid (fragment) Bodleian Library, Oxford, MS Rawl. Poet 133. p. 160.
127. Graves, *King Jesus*, 348–9 Kindle Version.
128. Ovid, *Metamorphoses*, trans. Brookes More (Boston: Cornhill, 1922), lines 159–237, <http://www.perseus.tufts.edu/hopper/text?doc=urn:cts:latinLit:phi0959.phi006.perseus-eng1:7.159> (last accessed 5 December 2019).
129. See Chapter 2 herein: 'Burye this plate in a crosse waye', p. 44.
130. Albert Charles Hamilton, *The Spenser Encyclopedia*, p. 351.
131. Albert Charles Hamilton, *The Spenser Encyclopedia*, p. 351.
132. Albert Charles Hamilton, *The Spenser Encyclopedia*, p. 351.
133. Hesiod, *Theogony*, lines 411–52.
134. Lisa Hopkins, 'The Low Road and the High Road: *Macbeth* and the Way to Scotland', in Lisa Hopkins and Bill Angus (eds), *Reading the Road, from Shakespeare's Crossways to Bunyan's Highways* (Edinburgh: Edinburgh University Press, 2021), p. 24.
135. Shamas, 'We Three', p. 54.
136. Northrop Frye et al. (eds), *Northrop Frye's Writings*, p. 496.
137. See Lynn S. Meskill, *Ben Jonson and Envy* (Cambridge: Cambridge University Press, 2009), pp. 172–7.
138. John D. Cox, *The Devil*, p. 196.
139. Molly Hand, '"You take no labour": Women Workers of Magic in Early Modern England', in Michelle M. Dowd and Natasha Korda (eds), *Working Subjects in Early Modern English Drama* (London: Routledge, 2016), p. 170.
140. Stapylton, *Virgil, Dido and Aeneas*.
141. John Gay, 'Trivia', in *Court Poems*, Book III (London: J. Roberts, 1716), pp. 4–7.
142. Hyde, *Trickster*, p. 9.
143. Hyde, *Trickster*, pp. 75, 299.
144. Hyde, *Trickster*, pp. 299–300.
145. Hyde, *Trickster*, p. 260.
146. Hyde, *Trickster*, p. 264.
147. Hyde, *Trickster*, pp. 125–6.
148. Hyde, *Trickster*, p. 247.

Chapter 5. Terminus: The Night, the Crossroads and the Stake

1. Bob Dylan, 'Murder Most Foul', *Rough and Rowdy Ways* (Columbia, 2020).
2. Christopher Gerrard and Alejandra Gutierrez (eds), *The Oxford Handbook of Later Medieval Archaeology in Britain* (Oxford: Oxford University Press, 2018), p. 861.
3. Robert Halliday, 'Criminal graves and rural crossroads', *British Archaeology*, 25 (June 1997), <http://archive.is/FTicE> (last accessed 12 July 2021); in Wiltshire there was found the 'gallows of the Prior of Bradenstoke at Wypeshull' which is 'at cross-roads E. of Wilcot Green'; see 'Royal forests: Appendices' in Elizabeth Crittall (ed.), *A History of the County of Wiltshire*: vol. 4 (1959), pp. 433–57, <http://www.british-history.ac.uk/report.aspx?compid=102826&strquery=crossroads gallows> (last accessed 25 October 2020).
4. Plato, *The Laws of Plato*, trans. Thomas L. Pangle (Chicago: University of Chicago Press, 1980), cited in Puhvel, *The Crossroads*, p. 84.
5. Plato, *The Laws of Plato*, p. 268.
6. Reynolds, *Anglo Saxon Deviant*, p. 213.
7. Tania Dickinson, *Cuddesdon and Dorchester-on Thames* (Oxford: British Archaeological Reports, 1, 1974), p. 23. 'Hundreds' were the official subdivisions English counties from the late Saxon period onwards.
8. Reynolds, *Anglo Saxon Deviant*, pp. 53, 233.
9. Johnston, 'Crossroads', p. 220.
10. Johnston, 'Crossroads', p. 220, n.17.
11. Thomas Rogers Forbes, *Chronicle from Aldgate: Life and Death in Shakespeare's London* (New Haven and London: Yale University Press, 1971), p. 168.
12. Excommunicates could also be buried 'in the limits and meres of the parish', though this could be bought off at a price; see Clare Gittings, *Death, Burial and the Individual in Early Modern England* (London: Croom Helm, 1984), pp. 76–7.
13. Reynolds, *Anglo Saxon Deviant*, p. 216.
14. Cited in Forbes, *Aldgate*, p. 166. This is the Statute of 4 Geo. IV 1823; writing of this, T. S. Hughes quotes 'On the twenty-seventh, [May 1823] Mr. Lennard obtained leave to bring in a bill, abolishing the old and barbarous law, which sentenced the corpse of one guilty of felo-de-se to be buried at two cross-roads, with a stake driven through it; leaving the burial to be performed in private, without the ceremonies of our church'; see T. S. Hughes, *History of England, from the accession of George III to the accession of Queen Victoria*

(London: Bell and Daldy, 1846), p. 21). Certain restrictions were also placed on the burials of recusants, which might also lack a burial service and be interred at night; see Forbes, *Aldgate*, pp. 30–1.
15. Michael MacDonald and Terence R. Murphy, *Sleepless Souls, Suicide in Early Modern England* (Oxford: Clarendon, 1990), p. 349.
16. John Charles Cox, *The Parish Registers of England* (London: Methuen, 1910), p. 114, cited in Jeremy Harte, 'Maimed Rites: Suicide Burials in the English Landscape', *Time and Mind: The Journal of Archaeology, Consciousness and Culture*, 4.3 (November 2011), pp. 263–82, p. 268; see also MacDonald and Murphy, *Sleepless Souls*, p. 223.
17. Forbes, *Aldgate*, p. 169.
18. Robert Halliday, 'The Roadside Burial of Suicides: An East Anglian Study', *Folklore*, 121 (April 2010), pp. 81–93, p. 83.
19. Alfred Kingston, *Fragments of Two Centuries. Glimpses of country life when George III was king* (Royston: Warren Bros, 1893), p. 98.
20. Kingston, *Fragments*, p. 98.
21. R. A. Houston, *Punishing the Dead? Suicide, Lordship, and Community in Britain, 1500–1830* (Oxford: Oxford University Press, 2010), pp. 4–5.
22. Houston, *Punishing the Dead?*, p. 209.
23. Houston, *Punishing the Dead?*, p. 196; John Parker (ed.), *The Parish Register of Thirsk in the County of York, North Riding* (Leeds: Yorkshire Parish Register Society, 1911), p. 55.
24. For the siting of ancient gallows at boundaries see Reynolds, *Anglo Saxon Deviant*, pp. 272–3, 126, 135. For boundary burial see Houston, *Punishing the Dead?*, p. 195; Andrew Reynolds, 'Burials, boundaries and charters in Anglo-Saxon England: a reassessment', in Sam Lucy and Andrew Reynolds (eds), *Burial in Early Medieval England and Wales* (London: Routledge, 2002), pp. 181–3; Sam Lucy, *The Anglo-Saxon way of death: Burial rites in early England* (Stroud: Sutton, 2000), pp. 148–9.
25. John D. Cox, *The Devil*, p. 167.
26. Johnston, 'Crossroads', p. 217.
27. Reynolds, *Anglo Saxon Deviant*, pp. 208–9.
28. Reynolds, *Anglo Saxon Deviant*, p. 210; Roberta Gilchrist and Barney Sloane, *Requiem: The Medieval Monastic Cemetery in Britain* (London: The Museum of London, 2005), p. 72.
29. Reynolds, *Anglo Saxon Deviant*, p. 212.
30. Reynolds, *Anglo Saxon Deviant*, p. 216.
31. Cited in Reynolds, *Anglo Saxon Deviant*, p. 217.
32. Charles Harper, *Notes and Queries*, 165.26 (30 December 1933), p. 466.

33. Halliday, 'Roadside Burial', p. 83.
34. Balfour, *Cyclopædia*, p. 534.
35. As R. A. Houston and C. Phythian-Adams have documented; see Houston, *Punishing the Dead?*, p. 218; Charles Phythian-Adams, 'Ritual constructions of society', in Rosemary Horrox and W. Mark Ormrod (eds), *A Social History of England 1200–1500* (Cambridge and New York: Cambridge University Press, 2006), p. 375.
36. Reynolds, *Anglo Saxon Deviant*, p. 209–10.
37. See tarot example on pp. 151–2, 215.
38. Houston, *Punishing the Dead?*, p. 217; General Register Office OPR 684/6.
39. Houston, *Punishing the Dead?*, p. 217; General Register Office OPR 684/6.
40. Halliday, 'Criminal graves'.
41. Halliday, 'Criminal graves'.
42. Gilchrist and Sloane, *Requiem*, p. 72
43. C. Wanklyn, *Notes and Queries*, 164.25 (24 June 1933), p. 443.
44. Walter Oswald Wait, *Rugby: past and present, with an historical account of neighbouring parishes* (Rugby: Albert Frost & Sons, 1893), p. 125.
45. As of 1893 the stocks still existed 'at the cross-roads in the adjoining hamlet of Thornton. They are of iron, but the top bar is lost. On the authority of the late Marquess de Rothwell a man was seen confined there as recently as 1863'; see William Douglas Caröe, *Sefton. A descriptive and historical account* (London: Longmans, 1893), p. 122. 'Pillory was antiently a Post erected in Cross-Roads, by the Lord as a Mark of his Seigneory, with his Arms on it, and sometimes a Collar to tye Criminals', John Harris, *A supplement to Dr. Harris's Dictionary of Arts and Sciences* (M. Cooper, J. Clarke, T. Comyns, C. Bathurst; T. Gardner, 1744), p. 145. A 'brickbuilt parish cage stood on a triangle of waste on the crossroads near the White Hart in 1857. It was demolished about 1870'; see 'West Bergholt: Local government', *A History of the County of Essex: Volume 10: Lexden Hundred (Part) including Dedham, Earls Colne and Wivenhoe* (2001), pp. 34–5, <http://www.british-history.ac.uk/report.aspx?compid=15140&strquery=crossroads gallows> (last accessed 25 October 2020).
46. Not all those hanged were buried under gallows – buried in Christ Church Greyfriars, Farringdon is one 'Alice La. Hungerford, hanged at Tiborne for murdering her husband, 1523'; see Stow, *A Survey of London*, p. 322. For further examples of burial under gallows see Reynolds, *Anglo Saxon Deviant*, pp. 122, 126, 133, 135.
47. See Halliday, 'Criminal graves'.

48. John Strype, *Ecclesiastical Memorials Relating Chiefly to Religion and the Reformation of it and the Emergencies of the Church of England* (Oxford: Clarendon Press, 1822), p. 342.
49. Richard Challoner, *Memoirs of Missionary Priests: And Other Catholics of Both Sexes, that Have Suffered Death in England on Religious Accounts, from the Year 1577 to 1684* (Philadelphia: John T. Green, 1839), respectively, pp. 12, 64, 125. The remains of one Fr. Philip Powell, executed at Tyburn in 1646, were allowed to be buried in a cemetery, but only by express permission of Parliament; see Challoner, *Memoirs of Missionary Priests*, p. 167.
50. Gittings, *Death*, p. 71.
51. J. E. B. Gover, Allen Mawer and F. M. Stenton (eds), *The Place-Names of Middlesex* (Nottingham: The English Place-Name Society, 1942), p. 6.
52. Reynolds, *Anglo Saxon Deviant*, p. 246.
53. Alongside oak, elm was the traditional coffin wood. For siting of places of execution including gallows at pagan sites by Christianised monarchs see Reynolds, *Anglo Saxon Deviant*, pp. 237–8.
54. V. A. C. Gatrell, *The Hanging Tree* (Oxford: Oxford University Press, 1994), p. 7.
55. Gatrell, *The Hanging Tree*, p. 7.
56. Gatrell, *The Hanging Tree*, p. 30.
57. Gatrell, *The Hanging Tree*, p. 7.
58. Gatrell, *The Hanging Tree*, p. 8.
59. Although London reaches out towards its suburb and eventually envelops it, Tyburn is always essentially connected to the life of the city. In 1236 and again in 1432 projects were put in place for Tyburn to give its water to medieval London, pumped in to central conduits like the Standard on Cheapside. So even in its liminality, Tyburn is from early medieval times an essential part of the fundament of the city: not only taking life, but also providing it in the most elemental way to the growing metropolis. See Stow, *A Survey of London*, pp. 18, 82, 109.
60. Ackroyd, *London*, p. 526.
61. 'Camden Town and Kentish Town', *Old and New London: Volume 5* (1878), pp. 309–24, <http://www.british-history.ac.uk/report.aspx?compid=45239&strquery=cross roads witch> (last accessed 12 June 2021).
62. Joseph Ford, *Some Reminiscences and Folk Lore of Danby Parish and District* (Whitby: Horne and Son, 1953), pp. 153–5.
63. Raymond H. Hayes, *Old Roads and Pannierways in North East Yorkshire* (North York Moors National Park, 1988), p. 15.
64. Another similar situation is found in the parish of Hampnett in Gloucester, where a 'Hangman's Stone, recorded from 1759,

possibly marked the site of gallows at the ancient crossroads midway along the parish's southern boundary'; see Carold Davidson Cragoe, A. R. J. Jurica and Elizabeth Williamson, *A History of the County of Gloucester: Volume 9: Bradley Hundred. The Northleach area of the Cotswolds* (London: Victoria County History, 2001), pp. 81–91, <http://www.british-history.ac.uk/report.aspx?compid=66464&strquery=crossroads gallows> (last accessed: 25 October 2020).
65. Graham Platts, *Land and People in Medieval Lincolnshire*, vol. 4, ed. Maurice Barley, *History of Lincolnshire* (Lincoln: History of Lincolnshire Committee, 1985), p. 55. For siting of gallows at highways see Reynolds, *Anglo Saxon Deviant*, pp. 116, 126, 242, 246.
66. Gatrell, *The Hanging Tree*, p. 29.
67. Jeffrey R. Watt, *Choosing Death: Suicide and Calvinism in Early Modern Geneva* (Kirksville, MO: Truman State University, 2001), p. 86.
68. MacDonald and Murphy, *Sleepless Souls*, p. 19.
69. Janet Clare, '"Buried in the Open Fields": Early Modern Suicide and the Case of Ofelia', *Journal of Early Modern Studies*, 2 (2013), pp. 241–52, p. 242.
70. Houston, *Punishing the Dead?*, p. 196; Gerald Bray, *Tudor Church Reform: The Henrician Canons of 1535 and the Reformatio Legum Ecclesiasticarum* (Woodbridge: Boydell Press, 2000), canon 10.12, p. 35. For examples of removals, see Margaret Aston, 'Death', in Rosemary Horrox (ed.), *Fifteenth-Century Attitudes: Perceptions of Society in Late Medieval England* (Cambridge: Cambridge University Press, 1994), p. 217, and N. J. G. Pounds, *A History of the English Parish: The Culture of Religion from Augustine to Victoria* (Cambridge: Cambridge University Press, 2000), p. 428.
71. Reynolds, *Anglo Saxon Deviant*, p. 250.
72. MacDonald and Murphy, *Sleepless Souls*, p. 20.
73. MacDonald and Murphy, *Sleepless Souls*, p. 20.
74. MacDonald and Murphy, *Sleepless Souls*, p. 31.
75. MacDonald and Murphy, *Sleepless Souls*, pp. 29, 31.
76. MacDonald and Murphy, *Sleepless Souls*, p. 34.
77. Hugh Latimer, *The Works of Hugh Latimer*, ed. G.E. Corrie (Cambridge: Parker Society, 1844–5), p. 435.
78. See Richard Gilpin, *Daemonologia Sacra; or, a Treatise on Satan's Temptations* (London: J. D., 1677), pp. 108–16.
79. MacDonald and Murphy, *Sleepless Souls*, p. 75.
80. Michael Dalton, *The Countrey Justice*, 3rd edn (London: 1626), p. 234.
81. Michael MacDonald, 'The Secularization of Suicide in England 1660–1800', *Past & Present*, 111 (May 1986), pp. 50–100, p. 53.

82. MacDonald and Murphy, *Sleepless Souls*, p. 53ff.
83. MacDonald and Murphy, *Sleepless Souls*, pp. 34, 36–41.
84. MacDonald and Murphy, *Sleepless Souls*, p. 17.
85. MacDonald and Murphy, *Sleepless Souls*, p. 18.
86. MacDonald and Murphy, *Sleepless Souls*, p. 18.
87. Harte, 'Maimed Rites', p. 277.
88. MacDonald and Murphy, *Sleepless Souls*, p. 15.
89. 'The diarey of Robert Birrel, burgess of Edinburgh', in John Graham Dalyell, *Fragments of Scottish History* (Edinburgh: Constable, 1798), p. 45.
90. 'Staking was unusual in the north of England and unknown in Scotland'; see Houston, *Punishing the Dead?*, p. 6.
91. Ogden, *Magic*, p. 164.
92. John Thomas McNeill and Helena Margaret Gamer, *Medieval handbooks of penance: a translation of the principal 'libri poenitentiales' and selections from related documents* (New York: Octagon, 1965), p. 339, cited in Stephen Gordon, 'Disease, Sin and the Walking Dead in Medieval England', in Effie Gemi-Iordanou, Stephen Gordon, Robert Matthew, Ellen McInnes and Rhiannon Pettitt (eds), *Medicine, Healing and Performance* (Oxford: Oxbow, 2015), p. 57.
93. Bruno O'Donoghue, 'Parish Histories and Placenames of West Cork', <http://www.kilmichael.org/hisodon.htm> (last accessed 13 June 2021). One Devonshire tradition maintained that the souls of infants who died before baptism came back as pixies; see Charles Worthy, *Devonshire Parishes* (London: George Redway, 1887), p. 26.
94. Christopher Daniell, *Death and Burial in Medieval England, 1066–1550* (London: Psychology Press, 1997), p. 106
95. Harte, 'Maimed Rites', p. 278.
96. Robert Pashley, *Travels in Crete* (Cambridge: John Murray, 1837), p. 231.
97. Harte, 'Maimed Rites', p. 279.
98. John Weever, *Ancient Funerall Monuments* (London: Thomas Harper, 1631), p. 22.
99. César de Saussure, *A Foreign View of England in the Reigns of George I. & George II: The Letters of Monsieur César de Saussure to His Family*, trans. and ed. M. Van Muyden (London: John Murray, 1902), p. 201.
100. Houston, *Punishing the Dead?*, p. 201.
101. Houston, *Punishing the Dead?*, p. 201.
102. Houston, *Punishing the Dead?*, p. 201. An early nineteenth-century South Shields source also mentions a protruding stake: see William Brockie, *Legends and Superstitions of the County of Durham* (Sunderland, 1886), pp. 151–2. An instance from London in 1590 may be seen in Forbes, *Aldgate*, p. 136.
103. William Dimond, 'Fragment in Blank Verse', *Petrarchal Sonnets, and Miscellaneous Poems* (London: R. Cruttwell, 1800), p. 122.

104. Gittings, *Death*, p. 73. There is one European example of a crossroads burial with a noose around the neck which was to protrude above ground; see Reynolds, *Anglo Saxon Deviant*, p. 216.
105. W. Fulbecke, *A parallele or conference of the civill law, the canon law, and the common law of this realme of England: Wherein the agreement and disagreement of these three lawes, and the causes and reasons of the said agreement and disagreement, are opened and discussed* (London: 1601), f. 90.
106. Houston, *Punishing the Dead?*, p. 191; Dalton, *The Countrey Justice*, pp. 234–5.
107. MacDonald and Murphy, *Sleepless Souls*, p. 139. Mapping this onto the 1817 map of the area, the best guess for this slightly ambiguous location is the now very innocuous junction of B126 Cable Street and B108 Cannon St Road, just outside the now closed Crown and Dolphin pub. Apparently, gas-pipe installers accidently revealed Williams's remains here in 1886, and when the body was subsequently exhumed the landlord of the pub kept the skull on display; see 'Ratcliff Highway Murders', <http://knowledgeoflondon.com/murders.html> (last accessed 1 May 2021).
108. 'Interment of John Williams, the murderer', *Edinburgh Annual Register*, 2 January 1812, pp. 4–6.
109. 'Interment of John Williams, the murderer', *Edinburgh Annual Register*, 2 January 1812, p. 6.
110. Florike Egmond, 'Execution, dissection, pain and infamy – a morphological investigation', in Florike Egmond and Robert Zwijnenberg (eds), *Bodily Extremities: Preoccupations with the Human Body in Early Modern European Culture* (Aldershot: Ashgate, 2003), pp. 92–128, p. 104.
111. Gatrell, *The Hanging Tree*, p. 84.
112. Thomas, *Religion*, p. 242.
113. Gittings, *Death*, pp. 67–8.
114. Agrippa, *Of Occult Philosophy*, p. 103.
115. Gittings, *Death*, p. 68.
116. When he was taken for a witch, Johannes Junius, the Burgomaster of Bamberg in Germany, confessed that 'on the day after an execution was held, he was at a witch-dance at the Black Cross, where Beelzebub had shown himself'; see Burr, *Witch Persecutions*, p. 25. Though the agonised fantasy of a torture victim, this shows something of the demonic associations expected of such a place as the crossroads. After all, the Devil is 'God's hang-man', as King James himself asserts: James I, *Daemonologie* (1597), pp. xiii–xiv, <http://www.sacred-texts.com/pag/kjd/index.htm> (last accessed 20 May 2021).
117. Gittings, *Death*, p. 31.
118. Gittings, *Death*, pp. 108–9.
119. Gittings, *Death*, p. 12.

120. Thomas Sparke, *A brotherly perswasion to unitie* (London: 1607), p. 37.
121. Gittings, *Death*, p. 31.
122. Gatrell, *The Hanging Tree*, p. 87.
123. Gittings, *Death*, p. 116.
124. Gittings, *Death*, p. 139.
125. This was also a Welsh practice; see Puhvel, *The Crossroads*, p. 100.
126. Houston, *Punishing the Dead?*, p. 222
127. Gatrell, *The Hanging Tree*, pp. 123–4.
128. *Gentleman's Magazine*, v (1735), pp. 557–8, cited in MacDonald and Murphy, *Sleepless Souls*, pp. 129–30.
129. Terence R. Murphy, '"Woful Childe of Parents Rage": Suicide of Children and Adolescents in Early Modern England, 1507–1710', *The Sixteenth Century Journal*, 17.3 (Autumn, 1986), pp. 259–70, p. 269.
130. John Constable, *The Southwark Mysteries* (London: Oberon Books, 1999), pp. 9, 264–5, 291, 304–5, 338–9.
131. Stow, *A Survey of London*, p. 449.
132. Megan B. Brickley, Adrian Miles and Hilary Stainer, *The Cross Bones Burial Ground, Redcross Way, Southwark, London* (London: Museum of London, 1999), pp. vii, 4, 29; John Walsh, 'Tales of the City: At the Cross Bones graveyard you can almost hear', *The Independent*, 14 March 2006.
133. Lord Brabazon, Letter to the Editor, *The Times*, 10 November 1883, cited in John Constable, 'Cross Bones graveyard' <http://crossbones.org.uk/history/> (last accessed 19 January 2021).
134. Houston, *Punishing the Dead?*, pp. 4–5.
135. Richard Bellamy (ed.), *Beccaria: On Crimes and Punishments and other Writings* (Cambridge: Cambridge University Press, 1995), p. 830.
136. Houston, *Punishing the Dead?*, pp. 4–5.
137. Houston, *Punishing the Dead?*, p. 362.
138. Houston, *Punishing the Dead?*, p. 14; see also Andrew Wood, 'Fear, Hatred and the Hidden Injuries of Class in Early Modern England', *Journal of Social History*, 39 (2006), pp. 815–16.
138. MacDonald and Murphy, *Sleepless Souls*, p. 351.
139. Gittings, *Death*, p. 73.
140. *The Cumberland Pacquet; or, Ware's Whitehaven Advertiser*, 818 (16 June 1790); 882 (6 September 1791); 883 (13 September 1791); Houston, *Punishing the Dead?*, p. 202.
141. Houston, *Punishing the Dead?*, p. 362; Watt, *Choosing Death*, p. 88.
142. John Donne, *Biathanatos* (London: John Dawson, 1644), p. 74.
143. Donne, *Biathanatos*, p. 87.
144. Donne, *Biathanatos*, pp. 88–9.
145. Realino Marra and Marco Orrù, 'Social Images of Suicide', *The British Journal of Sociology*, 42.2 (June 1991), pp. 273–88, p. 278.
146. Harte, 'Maimed Rites', p. 272.

147. John Thrupp, *Anglo-Saxon Home: A History of the Domestic Institutions and Customs of England, from the Fifth to the Eleventh Century* (London: Longman, 1862), p. 87, n. 2.
148. Puhvel, *The Crossroads*, pp. 81–2.
149. John George Wood, *Natural History of Man* (London: George Routledge & Sons, 1880), p. 471.
150. Ewa Felińska, *Revelations of Siberia. By a Banished Lady*, ed. Colonel Lach Szyrma (London: Colburn & Co.,1852), p. 28.
151. Puhvel, *The Crossroads*, p. 11.
152. Borlase, *Observations*, p. 362.
153. Philip Alexander Prince, *Parallel Universal History: Being an Outline of the History and Biography of the World, Divided Into Periods* (London: Whittaker, 1838), p. 387.
154. E. S. Chalk, *Notes and Queries*, 166.7 (17 February 1934), p. 122.
155. V., *Notes and Queries*, 167.2 (18 August 1934), p. 122.
156. J. P. Bacon Philips, *Notes and Queries*, 167.9 (1 September1934), p. 158.
157. C. Wanklyn, *Notes and Queries*, 164.25 (24 June 1933), p. 443.
158. H. Askew, *Notes and Queries*, 165.24 (16 December 1933), p. 429.
159. H. Askew, *Notes and Queries*, 166.3 (20 January 1934), p. 49.
160. Joseph E. Morris, *Notes and Queries*, 166.9 (3 March 1934), p. 156.
161. W. Bradbrooke, *Notes and Queries*, 166.2 (13 January 1934), p. 33.
162. Charles Harper, *Notes and Queries*, 165.26 (30 December 1933), p. 466.
163. Joseph E. Morris, *Notes and Queries*, 166.4 (27 January 1934), p. 69; Joseph E. Morris, *Notes and Queries*, 166.12 (24 March 1934), p. 211.
164. See <https://www.legendarydartmoor.co.uk/kitty_jay.htm> (last accessed 30 June 2021).

Chapter 6. Literature: Liminal Ground in Early Modern Drama

1. Earl Daniels, 'Crossroads Burial', *Prairie Schooner*, 11.1 (Spring 1937), p. 37.
2. Dora Mary Shorter, *Ballads and Poems* (London: J. Bowden, 1899), p. 46.
3. Taliesin Williams, *Doom of Colyn Dolphyn. A poem; with notes* (London: Longman & Co., 1837), pp. 147–8.
4. Thomas Hood, 'Faithless Nelly Gray' <http://www.bartleby.com/380/poem/522.html> (last accessed 12 May 2021).
5. Dimond, 'Fragment in Blank Verse', p. 122.
6. Mary Meeke, *The Sicilian* (Minerva Press, for William Lane, 1798), p. 13.

7. James Samuel Stone, *The Heart of Merrie England* (Philadelphia: Porter & Coates, 1887), p. 68.
8. For siting of gallows at highways see Reynolds, *Anglo Saxon Deviant*, pp. 116, 126, 242, 246.
9. Platts, *Land and People*, p. 55.
10. Daniel Defoe, *Essay Upon Projects* (London: Printed by R. R. for Tho. Cockerill, 1697), p. 84.
11. Andrew McRae, *Literature and Domestic Travel in Early Modern England* (Cambridge: Cambridge University Press, 2009), p. 90; Defoe, *Essay Upon Projects*, p. 101.
12. M. G. Lay and James E. Vance, *Ways of the World: A History of the World's Roads and of the Vehicles that Used Them* (New Brunswick, NJ: Rutgers University Press, 1992), p. 189.
13. Hyde, *Trickster*, p. 224.
14. Thomas Nashe, *Martin's Month's Mind* (1589), cited in Gittings, *Death*, p. 49.
15. Gittings, *Death*, p. 67.
16. Gittings, *Death*, p. 67. Pat Rogers, 'The Waltham Blacks and the Black Act', *The Historical Journal*, 17 (1974), pp. 465–86.
17. See E. A. J. Honigmann, *Shakespeare: The 'Lost Years'* (Manchester: Manchester University Press, 1985), p. 5.
18. Frank Walsh Brownlow, *Shakespeare, Harsnett, and the Devils of Denham* (London and Toronto: Associated University Presses, 1993), p. 109. The earlier date of October 1583 has been suggested, though sources seem to agree on the December date; see Robert Harrison, 'Edward Arden', *Dictionary of National Biography* (London: Smith, Elder and Co., 1885–1900), vol. 2, p. 74.
19. Frank Walsh Brownlow, *Shakespeare, Harsnett*, p. 109.
20. See, respectively, Peter Ackroyd, *Shakespeare: The Biography* (London: Vintage, 2006) p. 94, and John Cooper, *The Queen's Agent: Francis Walsingham at the Court of Elizabeth I* (London: Faber and Faber, 2011), p. 255.
21. Ackroyd, *Shakespeare*, p. 95; William Shakespeare, *King Henry VI, Part 3*, ed. John D. Cox and Eric Rasmussen (London: Arden, 2001), p. 110.
22. She was also the aunt of the gunpowder conspirator Robert Catesby.
23. Charlotte Carmichael Stopes, *Shakespeare's Warwickshire Contemporaries* (Stratford-upon-Avon: Shakespeare Head Press, 1907), p. 160.
24. Frank Walsh Brownlow, *Shakespeare, Harsnett*, p. 108.
25. Edgar Fripp, *Shakespeare's Haunts Near Stratford* (Oxford: Oxford University Press, 1929), pp. 30–1.
26. Various scholars have also suggested further connections of this kind between Shakespeare and the Catholic missionaries Edmund

Campion, executed on 1 December 1581, and Robert Southwell, another distant relation, who was put to death on 21 February 1595. Both of these were also despatched at Tyburn: respectively, Richard Wilson, *Secret Shakespeare: Studies in Theatre, Religion and Resistance* (Manchester: Manchester University Press, 2004) p. 127; Gerard Kilroy, *Edmund Campion: A Scholarly Life* (London: Ashgate, 2015), pp. 355–6. Jonson admired Southwell and talked about him with William Drummond: see Donaldson, *Ben Jonson*, pp. 175–6. Southwell found secret lodging with Lord Vaux and later the Countess of Arundel and Surrey's house in the Strand; Donaldson notes connections between this kind of Catholic persecution and Jonson's *Epicene* of 1609–10 and John Donne's *Pseudo Martyr*; see Donaldson, *Ben Jonson*, pp. 184, 259–61.
27. See Kenneth Muir, 'Samuel Harsnett and King Lear', *The Review of English Studies*, 2.5 (January 1951), pp. 11–21; Frank Walsh Brownlow, *Shakespeare, Harsnett*, p. 107. Jonathan Bate notes personal connections between Shakespeare and Dibdale, see Jonathan Bate, *Soul of the Age: The Life, Mind, And World of William Shakespeare* (London: Penguin, 2009), p. 154.
28. Wilson, *Secret Shakespeare*, p. 116.
29. Tracey Hill, *Anthony Munday and Civic Culture* (Manchester: Manchester University Press, 2004), p. 2.
30. John Klause, *Shakespeare, the Earl, and the Jesuit* (Madison, NJ: Fairleigh Dickinson University Press, 2008), p. 290, n. 41.
31. William Shakespeare, *All's Well That Ends Well*, ed. Russell Fraser (Cambridge: Cambridge University Press, 1985).
32. In *AYLI, CYM, LLL, MM, 1HIV* (3), *HVIII, HV, MV* (2), *2HIV* (2), *2HVI* (2), *TEMP* (2), *HAM* (4).
33. William Shakespeare, *Love's Labours Lost*, ed. Richard David (London: Methuen, 1968).
34. Cited in Darryll Grantley, *London in Early Modern Drama: Representing the Built Environment* (London: Palgrave Macmillan, 2008), p. 44.
35. Grantley, *London in Early Modern Drama*, p. 31. Grantley notes that Tyburn is also mentioned in William Wager's *Enough Is as Good as a Feast* (1559–70), see p. 33. This and other gallows locations are mentioned in many other cases: see pp. 43–4, 52, 102–3, 131.
36. Brian Vickers has argued convincingly that Peele wrote Act I and the first two scenes in Act II of *Titus Andronicus*; see Brian Vickers, *Shakespeare, Co-Author* (Oxford: Oxford University Press, 2004) p. 154.
37. Marjorie Garber, *Shakespeare After All* (New York: Pantheon, 2004), p. 78.
38. Claire Hansen, *Shakespeare and Complexity Theory* (New York: Routledge, 2017) pp. 75–103.

39. Gittings, *Death*, p. 69, Margita Eddy, 'Mapping Shakespeare's London', 2015, <https://web.archive.org/web/20170926164623/http:/map.shakespeare.kcl.ac.uk:80/> (last accessed 4 August 2021).
40. Gittings, *Death*, p. 140.
41. Gittings records one church in which, between 1580 and 1640, 118 people were buried inside the church itself; see Gittings, *Death*, pp. 140–1.
42. Gittings, *Death*, p. 72. Hales vs Petit had sectarian overtones, Hales being a Protestant ruined under Mary Tudor, his suicide was therefore held as anti-Protestant propaganda; see MacDonald and Murphy, *Sleepless Souls*, pp. 61–3.
43. See Arnold Van Gennep, *The Rites of Passage*, trans. M. B. Vizedom and G. L. Caffee (Chicago: University of Chicago Press, 1960), esp. Chapter 8.
44. MacDonald and Murphy, *Sleepless Souls*, p. 46.
45. Victor Turner, *The Ritual Process* (New York: Aldine De Gruyter, 1969), p. 97.
46. Michael MacDonald, 'Ophelia's Maimèd Rites', *Shakespeare Quarterly*, 37.3 (Autumn 1986), pp. 309–17, p. 314. See Charles Moore, *A Full Inquiry into the Subject of Suicide*, 2 vols (London: Printed for J. F. and C. Rivington, 1790), vol. 1, pp. 310–11; Thomas, *Religion*, pp. 594–5.
47. 'Prior to about 1660, the *non compos mentis* verdict was very seldom used. Among the coroners' inquisitions filed in the central courts between 1487 and 1660, only 1.6 per cent of suicides were returned *non compos mentis*. Almost all the rest were declared *felo de se*': MacDonald, 'Ophelia's Maimèd Rites', p. 310, citing Public Record Office, London, KB 9, 10, 11; PL 26; HCA 1/83. Although a *non compos mentis* verdict was by far the best outcome for the families involved, it lost the government the chance of appropriating the victim's goods. Hence, 'suicide verdicts climbed remorselessly through the sixteenth century; their highest incidence was in the 1570s, that decade in which parish registers begin to record highway burial'; see Harte, 'Maimed Rites', p. 279.
48. Public Record Office, London, KB 9, 10, 11; PL 26; HCA 1/83.
49. MacDonald, 'Ophelia's Maimèd Rites', p. 312. Barbara Smith sees connections with the contemporary Hales v. Petit case; see Barbara Smith, 'Neither Accident nor Intent: Contextualizing the Suicide of Ophelia', *South Atlantic Review*, 73.2 (Spring 2008), pp. 96–112, p. 105. Janet Clare argues that the gentry and nobility were more likely to be 'given the benefit of the doubt by juries or protected by bogus verdicts'; see Clare, 'Buried in the Open Fields', p. 243. According to MacDonald and Murphy, 67 per cent of aristocrats were convicted, compared with 93 per cent of commoners: see MacDonald and Murphy, *Sleepless Souls*, p. 127.

50. MacDonald, 'Ophelia's Maimèd Rites', pp. 309–17, 314; Gordon, 'Disease, Sin and the Walking Dead', p. 57.
51. Smith, 'Neither Accident nor Intent', pp. 101–3, see n. 5.
52. Thomas Rogers Forbes, 'London Coroners Inquests for 1590', *Journal of the History of Medicine and Allied Sciences* (1973) XXVIII (4), pp. 376–86, p. 378; see also Forbes, *Aldgate*, pp. 165–9, n. 7.
53. Peter Marshall, 'Confessionalisation and Community in the Burial of English Catholics, c. 1570–1700', in Nadine Lewycky and Adam David Morton (eds), *Getting Along?: Religious Identities and Confessional Relations in Early Modern England* (Farnham: Ashgate, 2012), p. 68.
54. Anon., *The Whole business of Sindercome, from first to last, it being a perfect narrative of his carriage, during the time of his imprisonment in the Tower of London* (1657), <http://gateway.proquest.com/openurl?ctx_ver=Z39.88-2003&res_id=xri:eebo&rft_id=xri:eebo:citation:99863809> (last accessed 14 June 2021).
55. Weever, *Ancient Funerall Monuments*, p. 22.
56. Clare notes that Q3's 'She should in ground unsanctified have lodged' replaces [Q1's] 'buried in the open fields': a more distant, less poignant evocation of popular rites of desecration'; see Clare, 'Buried in the Open Fields', p. 250.
57. R. S. Guernsey suggests that where the stake was visible, passers-by would 'cast a stone at it'; see R. S. Guernsey, 'Ecclesiastical Law in *Hamlet*: The Burial of Ophelia' (New York: The Shakespeare Society of New York, 1885), p. 27.
58. See F. W. Moorman, 'Shakespeare's Ghosts', *The Modern Language Review*, 1.3 (April 1906), pp. 192–201, pp. 193, 197. In some cultures, the very act of separation from the body was suspect, as the Māori rangatira Teone Taare Tikao related: 'When the *wairua* [spirit] left the human body and wandered about it became a devil or a ghost'; see Tikao and Beattie, *Tikao Talks*, p. 76.
59. Gittings, *Death*, pp. 111–12.
60. Gittings, *Death*, pp. 111–12.
61. Robert Herrick, *Works of Robert Herrick*, vol. 1, ed. Alfred Pollard (London: Lawrence & Bullen, 1891), p. 8.
62. John Aubrey, *Remaines of Gentilisme and Judaisme*, [1686–7], ed. James Brittan (London: W. Satchell, Peyton, & Co., 1881), p. 35.
63. William Shakespeare, *Macbeth*, ed. Nicholas Brooke (Oxford: Oxford University Press, 1994).
64. Moorman, 'Shakespeare's Ghosts', pp. 193, 197.
65. Gittings, *Death*, p. 60.
66. Balfour, *Cyclopædia*, p. 186.
67. See Van Gennep, *Rites of Passage*, Chapter 8.

68. William Shakespeare, *A Midsummer Night's Dream*, ed. Harold F. Brooks (London: Arden, 2002).
69. Gittings, *Death*, p. 73.
70. Paul Devereux, *Spirit Roads* (London: Collins and Brown, 2003), pp. 28, 45–7.
71. Harsnett, *A Declaration*, p. 134.
72. Johnston, 'Crossroads', p. 218.
73. De Certeau, *The Practice of Everyday Life*, p. 118.
74. De Certeau, *The Practice of Everyday Life*, pp. 116, 122–3.
75. De Certeau, *The Practice of Everyday Life*, p. 123.
76. De Certeau, *The Practice of Everyday Life*, p. 123.
77. De Certeau, *The Practice of Everyday Life*, p. 127.
78. William Kemp, *Kemps nine daies vvonder*, 1600, p. 32, <http://gateway.proquest.com/openurl?ctx_ver=Z39.88-2003&res_id=xri:eebo&rft_id=xri:eebo:citation:99854667> (last accessed 30 January 2021).
79. George Peele, *The Old Wives Tale*, ed. Patricia Binney (Manchester: Manchester University Press, 1980).
80. da Silva and Tehrani, <https://royalsocietypublishing.org/doi/10.1098/rsos.150645>.
81. See Bill Angus, *Intelligence and Metadrama in the Early Modern Theatre* (Edinburgh: Edinburgh University Press, 2018); Bill Angus, *Metadrama and the Informer in Shakespeare and Jonson* (Edinburgh: Edinburgh University Press, 2016).
82. See Lisa Hopkins, 'Marlowe's Reception and Influence' in Patrick Cheney (ed.) *The Cambridge Companion to Christopher Marlowe* (Cambridge: Cambridge University Press, 2004), pp. 282–96.
83. George Peele, 'The honour of the garter Displaied in a poeme gratulatorie: entitled to the worthie and renowned Earle of Northumberland. Created Knight of that order, and installd at Windsore. Anno Regni Elizabethæ. 35. die Iunij. 26' (1593), University of Oxford Text Archive, <http://ota.ox.ac.uk/tcp/headers/A09/A09227.html> (last accessed 7 March 2021).
84. Peele, 'The honour of the garter'.
85. A. W. Bullen, 'Introduction' (1888), in A. W. Bullen (ed.), *The Works of George Peele* (Port Washington, NY: Kenniket Press, 1966), pp. xxiv–xxv.
86. William Bradley Otis and Morriss H. Needleman, *An Outline-history of English Literature: To Dryden* (New York: Barnes & Noble, 1962), p. 176.
87. Francis Meres, *Palladis Tamia* or *Wits Treasury* (1598), fol. 282; Bullen, 'Introduction', p. xxii.
88. David H. Horne (ed.), *The Life and Minor Works of George Peele* (New Haven: Yale University Press, 1952), p. 128.

89. Horne, *The Life and Minor Works of George Peele*, p. 131.
90. Terence G. Schoone-Jongen, *Shakespeare's Companies* (London: Ashgate, 2008), p. 28.
91. Duncan Salkeld, *Shakespeare Among the Courtesans: Prostitution, Literature, and Drama, 1500–1650* (London: Routledge, 2016), pp. 98, 144–5, 161. See also Katherine Duncan-Jones, *Shakespeare, Upstart Crow to Sweet Swan, 1592-1623* (London: A&C Black, 2011), pp. 107–8.
92. See Vickers, *Shakespeare, Co-Author*, pp. 148–243, 154, improving on earlier assessments such as those set out by Eugene M. Waith in William Shakespeare, *Titus Andronicus*, ed. Eugene M. Waith (Oxford: Oxford University Press, 1994), pp. 11–20, where he considers whether Shakespeare revised Peele or Peele revised Shakespeare and concludes it is wholly by Shakespeare.
93. Or 'senex as juventus' as Jackson I. Cope has it; see Jackson I. Cope, 'Peele's *Old Wives Tale*: Folk Stuff Into Ritual Form', *ELH*, 49.2 (Summer 1982), pp. 326–38, p. 329.
94. Apuleius, *The Golden Ass*, trans. W. Aldington [1566] (Cambridge, MA: Harvard University Press, 1915), p. 3.
95. Peele, *The Old Wives Tale*, p. 20.
96. Madge is a barn-owl in a popular ballad, see Ben Jonson, *Bartholmew Fair*, ed. G. R. Hibbard (London: A&C Black, 2007) (1.4.69, n. 69); see also Mary Ellen Lamb, 'Old Wives' Tales, George Peele and Narrative Abjection', *Critical Survey*, 14.1 (2002), pp. 28–43, p. 35.
97. Raven Grimassi, *Encyclopedia of Wicca & Witchcraft* (St. Paul, MN: Llewellyn, 2002) p. 207.
98. Bethencourt, 'Portugal: A Scrupulous Inquisition', p. 419.
99. Puhvel, *The Crossroads*, pp. 88–90.
100. Peele, *The Old Wives Tale*, n. 351.2.
101. Unless Erestes' full name is supposed to be 'Old Man at the cross', which I concede to be plausible. However, as I maintain, the whole action of the play is in the vicinity of the crossroads in any case.
102. In Faustus's case, the study is a mere substitute for the crossroads in any case, as previously stated.
103. Peele, *The Old Wives Tale*, n. 221–2.
104. Peele, *The Old Wives Tale*, n. 221–2.
105. Dante, *Inferno, Canto XXXI*.
106. See A. R. Braunmuller, *George Peele* (Boston: Twayne, 1983), p. 58.
107. Lamb, 'Old Wives' Tales', p. 36.
108. For another literary example of this see the church stile scene in Chapter 12 of Charlotte Bronte's *Jane Eyre*.
109. Lamb, 'Old Wives' Tales', p. 36.
110. An eleventh-century homily *De Falsis Deis*: 'There was also a man called Mercury, he was very crafty and deceitful in deed and trickeries, though his speech was fully plausible. The heathens made him a renowned god

for themselves; at crossroads they offered sacrifices to him frequently and they often erringly brought praise-offerings to hilltops, all through the devil's teaching. This false god was honored among the heathens in that day, and he is also called by the name Odin in the Danish manner'; Richard Marsden (ed.), *The Cambridge Old English Reader* (Cambridge: Cambridge University Press, 2004), pp. 205–8.
111. Cope, 'Peele's *Old Wives Tale*', p. 332.
112. Cope, 'Peele's *Old Wives Tale*', p. 332.
113. For extensive discussion of early modern metadrama and authority see Angus, *Intelligence and Metadrama* and *Metadrama and the Informer*.
114. De Certeau, *The Practice of Everyday Life*, p. 118.
115. Here the food seems to perform the same function as *kai* (food) often does in Māori ceremonies, serving to break the *tapu* of the ritual with its everyday *noa* quality.

Chapter 7. Hallowed Roads: Routes to the Crossroads

1. George Beattie, 'The Dream' (1824), <http://www.scotstext.org/roughs/george_beattie/john_o_arnha.asp> (accessed 28 April 2021).
2. Cresswell, *On the Move*, p. 2.
3. Julie Sanders, *The Cultural Geography of Early Modern Drama, 1620–1650* (Cambridge: Cambridge University Press, 2011), pp. 167–8.
4. John Ogilby, *Britannia, Or, the Kingdom of England and Dominion of Wales Actually Survey'd with a Geographical and Historical Description of the Principal Roads, Explain'd by One Hundred Maps on Copper-Plates : With the Ichnography, Or Drought of the several Cities, Chief Towns, &c., and a View of the Churches, Houses, and Places of Pote on the Road : Also an Account of the most Remarkable Passages of Antiquity Relating to them, and of their Present State / by John Ogilby* (London: Abel Swall and Robert Morden, 1698), ProQuest, <https://search-proquest-com.ezproxy.massey.ac.nz/books/britannia-kingdom-england-dominion-wales-actually/docview/2248517686/se-2?accountid=14574> (last accessed 17 May 2021).
5. Owen, *Church and Society*, pp. 2–3.
6. Owen, *Church and Society*, p. 16.
7. Penny Drayton, 'Landmark and Sacred Trees of Leicestershire and Rutland', *Mercian Mysteries*, 9 (November 1991), n.p.
8. Anon. 'The burial of the dead', *Whitby Gazette and Herald*, 18 August 2005, <http://www.gazetteherald.co.uk/news/6669440.The_burial_of_the_dead/> (last accessed 27 June 2021).
9. Thomas Gray, 'Elegy Written in a Country Churchyard' (1751), <https://www.poetryfoundation.org/poems/44299/elegy-written-in-a-country-churchyard> (last accessed 18 May 2021).

10. Anon., 'The Muse debauched by Superstitious fancy' in Isaac Kimber and Edward Kimber (eds), *The London Magazine, or, Gentleman's Monthly Intelligencer*, vol. 28 (London: R. Baldwin, 1759), pp. 45–6.
11. William Mason, 'Elegy VI. Written in a Church-Yard in South Wales, 1787', *The Works of William Mason*, vol. 1 (London: T. Cadell and W. Davies, 1811), pp. 114, 116.
12. George Beattie, 'The Dream' (1824), <http://www.scotstext.org/roughs/george_beattie/john_o_arnha.asp> (last accessed 28 April 2021).
13. 'An "ancient" church-way from Little Clanfield to Pound Lane, mostly suppressed at inclosure in 1839, was presumably the churchway which crossed West field in the 13th century': 'Clanfield: Introduction', *A History of the County of Oxford*: vol. 15: Bampton Hundred (Part Three) (2006), pp. 112–22, <http://www.british-history.ac.uk/report.aspx?compid=117012&strquery=church-way> (last accessed 25 April 2021). 'A "church way" from Buckhurst Hill to the parish church at Chigwell existed in 1586': 'Chigwell: Introduction', *A History of the County of Essex*: vol. 4: Ongar Hundred (1956), pp. 18–22, <http://www.british-history.ac.uk/report.aspx?compid=15534&strquery="church-way"> (last accessed 25 April 2021). 'A piece of land ... in the Isle of Thanet between ... the church way of St. Nicholas on the east and the common footpath called "a Mylleway" on the west': *A Descriptive Catalogue of Ancient Deeds*: vol. 6 (1915), pp. 204–17, 'Deeds: C.5301 – C.5400', <http://www.british-history.ac.uk/report.aspx?compid=64483&strquery=church-way> (last accessed 25 April 2021). 'The Church Way which had been damaged by the horses of Thomas Webb, the tenant of Churchend Mill, in 1449': 'Eastington: Introduction', *A History of the County of Gloucester*: vol. 10: *Westbury and Whitstone Hundreds* (1972), pp. 123–7, <http://www.british-history.ac.uk/report.aspx?compid=15782&strquery=church+way> (last accessed 25 April 2021). 'The "church way" across the common (Orford Road)': 'Walthamstow: Introduction and domestic buildings', *A History of the County of Essex*: vol. 6 (1973), pp. 240–50, <http://www.british-history.ac.uk/report.aspx?compid=42775&strquery=church+way> (last accessed 25 April 2021). 'In 1630 there was a case in the church court about Church Way from Noke to Islip ... along which Noke parishioners had carried their dead for burial in Islip. Witnesses stated that it had been used up to about 50 years before, but had become a cow pasture and was impassable': 'Parishes: Noke', *A History of the County of Oxford*: vol. 6 (1959), pp. 268–76, <http://www.british-history.

ac.uk/report.aspx?compid=63746&strquery=church+way> (last accessed 25 April 2021). Before 'the 16th and the end of the 18th centuries ... the road pattern of the parish ... elements were the east-west route along the scarp where the village lay, traceable north-east through Merriott to Ham Hill, and the medieval highway or "old church way" from the village south-west through Craft to the Windwhistle ridge': 'Parishes: Hinton St. George', *A History of the County of Somerset*: vol. 4 (1978), pp. 38–52, <http://www.british-history.ac.uk/report.aspx?compid=117080&strquery=church+way> (last accessed 25 April 2021). 'Direct road to Melbourne runs southwards from the church at Thornton; it was called "Melbourne church way" in 1577': 'Thornton', *A History of the County of York East Riding*: vol. 3: *Ouse and Derwent Wapentake, and part of Harthill Wapentake* (1976), pp. 179–90, <http://www.british-history.ac.uk/report.aspx?compid=23024&strquery=church+way> (last accessed 25 April 2021). 'In 1715 there was a "church way" from Wigwig to Much Wenlock': 'Much Wenlock', *A History of the County of Shropshire*: vol. 10: *Munslow Hundred (part), The Liberty and Borough of Wenlock* (1998), pp. 399–447, <http://www.british-history.ac.uk/report.aspx?compid=22888&strquery=church+way> (last accessed 25 April 2021).
14. 'Parishes: Manningford Abbots', in Elizabeth Crittall (ed.), *A History of the County of Wiltshire*: vol. 10 (London: Victoria County History, 1975), pp. 106–12, <http://www.british-history.ac.uk/vch/wilts/vol10/pp106-112> (last accessed 25 April 2021).
15. Owen, *Church and Society*, p. 16.
16. 'Parishes: Headington', in Mary D. Lobel (ed.), *A History of the County of Oxford*: vol. 5 (London: Victoria County History, 1957), pp. 157–68, <https://www.british-history.ac.uk/vch/oxon/vol5/pp157-168#anchorn232> (last accessed 25 April 2021).
17. Devereux, 'Talking', p. 247.
18. Devereux, 'Talking', p. 247.
19. Bible, New International Version (1984).
20. Devereux, 'Talking', p. 246.
21. Tikao and Beattie, *Tikao Talks*, p. 66.
22. Devereux, 'Talking', p. 246
23. Devereux, 'Talking', p. 245.
24. Devereux, 'Talking', p. 246.
25. Devereux, 'Talking', p. 245.
26. Devereux, 'Talking', p. 245.
27. David McOmish, 'Cursus: solving a 6,000-year-old puzzle', *British Archeology*, 69 (March 2003), n.p. <http://www.britarch.ac.uk/ba/ba69/feat1.shtml> (last accessed 2 March 2021).

28. Mike Addelman, '"Cursus" is older than Stonehenge', 10 June 2008, <http://www.manchester.ac.uk/discover/news/article/?id=3719> (accessed 12 January 2018).
29. Addelman, 'Cursus'.
30. Addelman, 'Cursus'.
31. McOmish, 'Cursus'. See also <http://www.sheffield.ac.uk/archaeology/research/2.4329/index> (accessed 17 June 2018).
32. McOmish, 'Cursus'.
33. McOmish, 'Cursus'.
34. McOmish, 'Cursus'.
35. Cited in Nicolas Bergier, *The General History of the Highways, In all Parts of the World, More Particularly in Great Britain* (London: D. Brown, 1712), p. 160.
36. John Lelend, *The Itinerary of John Leland in or about the years 1535–1543*, vol. 2 (Carbondale: Southern Illinois University Press, 1964), p. 36.
37. Kramer and Sprenger, *Malleus*, p. 317.
38. Cited in Wallace Notestein, *A History Of Witchcraft In England From 1558 To 1718* (Washington DC: The American Historical Association, 1911) p. 18.
39. Notestein, *A History of Witchcraft*, p. 18.
40. James Fitzjames Stephen, *A History of the Criminal Law of England* (Cambridge: Cambridge University Press, 2014), p. 431.
41. Ackroyd, *London*, pp. 131–2.
42. Thomas, *Religion*, p. 74.
43. De Certeau, *The Practice of Everyday Life*, p. 117.
44. Thomas, *Religion*, pp. 71–2.
45. Alan Bernstein, 'The Ghostly Troop and the Battle Over Death: William of Auverne (d. 1249) Connects Christian, Old Norse and Irish Views', in Muzhou Pu (ed.), *Rethinking Ghosts in World Religions* (Leiden and Boston: Brill, 2009), pp. 115–62, p. 141.
46. Thomas, *Religion*, p. 73.
47. Tracey Hill, *Anthony Munday*, p. 11.
48. Tracey Hill, *Anthony Munday*, p. 12.
49. Tracey Hill, *Anthony Munday*, pp. 15, 163; Laurence Manley, 'Of Sites and Rites', in David L. Smith, Richard Strier and David Bevington (eds), *The Theatrical City: Culture, Theatre and Politics in London 1576–1649* (Cambridge: Cambridge University Press, 1995), pp. 35–54, p. 46.
50. Tracey Hill, *Anthony Munday*, p. 14.
51. Stow, *A Survey of London*, p. 251; Tracey Hill, *Anthony Munday*, p. 13.
52. William Andrews, *Old Church Lore* (Wakefield: E. P. Publishing, 1975), p. 142.

53. Marina Devine, 'Cheapside Cross (Eleanor Cross)', *The Map of Early Modern London*, ed. Janelle Jenstad, University of Victoria, 20 June 2018, <mapoflondon.uvic.ca/ELEA1.htm> (last accessed 25 June 2021).
54. Jean-Louis Backès, 'Artemis', in Pierre Bunuel (ed.), *Companion to Literary Myths, Heroes and Archetypes* (London and New York: 1992), pp. 128–34, p. 131.
55. Stow, *A Survey of London*, p. 266.
56. George Abbott, 'Cheap-side crosse censured and condemned' (1600), <http://gateway.proquest.com.ezproxy.massey.ac.nz/openurl?ctx_ver=Z39.88-2003&res_id=xri:eebo&rft_id=xri:eebo:image:137637> (last accessed 23 June 2021).
57. Abbott, 'Cheap-side crosse', p. 7.
58. Abbott, 'Cheap-side crosse', p. 5.
59. Abbott, 'Cheap-side crosse', p. 3.
60. 'The Dolefull lamentation of Cheap-side crosse' (London: 1641), p. 7, <http://gateway.proquest.com.ezproxy.massey.ac.nz/openurl?ctx_ver=Z39.88-2003&res_id=xri:eebo&rft_id=xri:eebo:image:63013:4> (last accessed 30 June 2021).
61. Anon., *The Popes proclamation: together with the lawes and ordinances established by him and his shavelings, concerning his adherents and rights which hee claimeth in England. Whereunto is added six articles exhibited against Cheapside Crosse, whereby it stands guilty of high treason, and ought to be beheaded* (London: s.n., 1641), p. 5, <http://gateway.proquest.com.ezproxy.massey.ac.nz/openurl?ctx_ver=Z39.88-2003&res_id=xri:eebo&rft_id=xri:eebo:image:156958:4> (last accessed 12 July 2021).
62. Forbes, *Aldgate*, p. 165.
63. Forbes, *Aldgate*, p. 168.
64. Forbes, *Aldgate*, p. 165.
65. Manley, 'Of Sites and Rites', p. 44.
66. Manley, 'Of Sites and Rites', p. 51.
67. Manley, 'Of Sites and Rites', p. 45.
68. Stow, *A Survey of London*, p. 196.
69. Cited in Tracey Hill, *Anthony Munday*, p. 128.
70. Tracey Hill, *Anthony Munday*, pp. 128–9.
71. Tracey Hill, *Anthony Munday*, p. 181.
72. Lisa Hopkins, *Shakespeare on the Edge: Border-crossing in the Tragedies and the Henriad* (London: Ashgate, 2013), p. 137.
73. See William Amos Abrams (ed.), *The Merry Devil of Edmonton* (Durham, NC: Duke University Press, 1942) (I, i, 55, 59; I, iii, 28,124,135; III, i, 55; III, ii, 146; IV, ii, 61; V, i, 88, 93, 246, 260).
74. For these locations cf. Abrams, *The Merry Devil*, p. 184.
75. Sanders, *Cultural Geography*, p. 155.

Chapter 8. Wanderers: The Predicament of a Stranger

1. Cited in Burton, *Anatomy of Melancholy*, l. 2384.
2. Robert Johnson, 'Hellhound on my trail', cited in Marybeth Hamilton, 'Sexuality', p. 160.
3. Ayeni, 'Crossroads'.
4. The various cognates of the word 'wanderer' include wind (rhyming with 'sinned') and wind (rhyming with 'kind') linking it to being erratic, to vagueness and to vagabondage. <https://www.etymonline.com>, 'wander', 'wanderer', 'wandering' (last accessed 2 July 2021)
5. De Certeau, *The Practice of Everyday Life*, p. 115.
6. Zygmunt Bauman, *Legislators and Interpreters* (Oxford: Polity Press, 1987), p. 40; Cresswell, *On the Move*, p. 11.
7. Lewis Mumford, *The City in History* (New York: Harcourt, Brace and World, 1961), p. 269.
8. Cresswell, *On the Move*, pp. 11–12.
9. Cresswell, *On the Move*, p. 12.
10. Zygmunt Bauman, *Life in Fragments: Essays in Postmodern Morality* (Oxford: Blackwell, 1995), p. 94; Cresswell, *On the Move*, p. 12.
11. De Certeau, *The Practice of Everyday Life*, p. 117
12. De Certeau, *The Practice of Everyday Life*, p. 103.
13. De Certeau, *The Practice of Everyday Life*, p. 103.
14. Hyde, *Trickster*, p. 13.
15. Maurice Merleau-Ponty, *The Phenomenology of Perception* (London: Routledge and Kegan Paul, 1962), p. 102
16. *Tarleton's Newes out of Purgatorie* (London: c. 1590), n.p., cited in Briggs, p. 124.
17. *Tarleton's Newes*, cited in Briggs, *Anatomy of Puck*, p. 125.
18. Nancy Rosenfeld, *The Human Satan in Seventeenth-Century Literature: from Milton to Rochester* (Aldershot: Ashgate, 2008), p. 40.
19. Thomas Nashe, *The Unfortunate Traveller or The Life of Jack Wilton* (London: T. Scarlet for C. Burby, 1594), p. 52.
20. James I, *Daemonologie*, p. 20, <http://www.sacred-texts.com/pag/kjd/index.htm> (last accessed 6 May 2021).
21. Thomas, *Religion*, p. 711.
22. Thomas, *Religion*, pp. 717–18.
23. Ogden, *Magic*, p. 149.
24. Ogden, *Magic*, p. 149.
25. Ogden, *Magic*, p. 149. Tertullian, *De Anima*, ed. S. Thelwall and D. Holmes (Edinburgh: Clark, 1870), Ch. 56.
25. Moorman, 'Shakespeare's Ghosts', pp. 198–9.

26. Burton, *Anatomy of Melancholy*, l. 1007.
27. Thomas, *Religion*, p. 701.
28. Lavater, 'Of Ghosts and Spirits', pp. 1, 71, 97.
29. Scot, *The Discoverie of Witchcraft*, p. 521.
30. Thomas, *Religion*, p. 286.
31. Briggs, *Anatomy of Puck*, p. 133.
32. Stephen Gordon, 'Domestic Magic and the Walking Dead in Medieval England: A Diachronic Approach', in *The Materiality of Magic*, ed. Ceri Houlbrook and Natalie Armitage (Oxford: Oxbow Books, 2015), pp. 65–84, p. 66; see also C. S. Watkins, *History and the Supernatural in Medieval England* (Cambridge: Cambridge University Press, 2007), pp. 185–93.
33. Frederick Andrew Inderwick, *Interregnum, A.D. 1648–1660. Studies of the Commonwealth, legislative, social and legal* (London: Sampson Low, 1891), p. 136.
34. Moorman, 'Shakespeare's Ghosts', pp. 193, 197.
35. Agrippa, *Of Occult Philosophy*, p. 451.
36. *Mists's Weekly Journal*, 81 (5 November 1726), cited in MacDonald and Murphy, *Sleepless Souls*, p. 212.
37. Lavater, 'Of Ghosts and Spirits', p. 80.
38. Lavater, 'Of Ghosts and Spirits', p. 80.
39. Lavater, 'Of Ghosts and Spirits', pp. 90–1.
40. Lavater, 'Of Ghosts and Spirits', pp. 90–1.
41. Puhvel, *The Crossroads*, p. 123.
42. Lavater, 'Of Ghosts and Spirits', p. 212.
43. Puhvel, *The Crossroads*, p. 123.
44. John Bell, *Bell's Edition of Shakespeare* (London and York: John Bell, 1788), p. 71.
45. Lavater, 'Of Ghosts and Spirits', p. 189.
46. Puhvel, *The Crossroads*, p. 94.
47. See Puhvel, *The Crossroads*, pp. 94–6.
48. Puhvel, *The Crossroads*, p. 110.
49. Jeffrey Burton Russell, *Witchcraft in the Middle Ages* (Ithaca, NY: Cornell University Press, 1972), p. 119.
50. John Fox, *A Dreadful Example for Wicked Husbands* (Edinburgh: 1807), p. 4, cited in MacDonald and Murphy, *Sleepless Souls*, p. 212.
51. Puhvel, *The Crossroads*, p. 94.
52. Lavater, 'Of Ghosts and Spirits', p. 96.
53. Lavater, 'Of Ghosts and Spirits', p. 96.
54. Burton, *Anatomy of Melancholy*, l. 1182.
55. Burton, *Anatomy of Melancholy*, l. 1182.
56. Burton, *Anatomy of Melancholy*, l. 1187.
57. Burton, *Anatomy of Melancholy*, l. 1187.

58. James I, *Daemonologie*, pp. 32–3.
59. Sharpe, *Instruments of Darkness*, p. 63.
60. Bate, *Soul of the Age*, p. 182.
61. Moorman, 'Shakespeare's Ghosts', pp. 198–9.
62. Harsnett, *A Declaration*, p. 133.
63. Harsnett, *A Declaration*, p. 134.
64. Burton, *Anatomy of Melancholy*, l. 1123.
65. Burton, *Anatomy of Melancholy*, l. 1138–41.
66. Burton, *Anatomy of Melancholy*, l. 1141.
67. Harsnett, *A Declaration*, p. 134.
68. Beier, *Masterless Men*, pp. 4–5.
69. John D. Cox, *The Devil*, pp. 201–2.
70. Beier, *Masterless Men*, p. 103.
71. Beier, *Masterless Men*, p. 6.
72. William Shakespeare, *Henry V*, 'some night tripping fairy had exchanged / . . . our children where they lay' (I, i, 86–7). Beier, *Masterless Men*, p. 67.
73. Beier, *Masterless Men*, p. 8.
74. Burton, *Anatomy of Melancholy*, l. 1129–31.
75. Bible, King James Version, 1611.
76. Beier, *Masterless Men*, p. 69.
77. Burton, *Anatomy of Melancholy*, l. 2251–2.
78. Burton, *Anatomy of Melancholy*, l. 2257–8.
79. Burton, *Anatomy of Melancholy*, l. 2277–85.
80. Burton, *Anatomy of Melancholy*, l. 2291–2.
81. Bate, *Soul of the Age*, p. 56.
82. Bate, *Soul of the Age*, see p. 137.
83. Bate, *Soul of the Age*, p. 56.
84. Dillon, *Theatre, Court and City*, p. 105.
85. Randy Hodson and Teresa A. Sullivan, *The Social Organization of Work* (Belmont, CA: Wadsworth, 1995), p. 21.
86. E. P. Thompson, *The Making of the English Working Class* (London: Penguin, 1991), p. 237.
87. Thomas More, *Utopia* (1516) <https://www.gutenberg.org/files/2130/2130-h/2130-h.htm> (last accessed 15 June 2021).
88. Joan Thirsk and H. P. R. Finberg, *The Agrarian History of England and Wales: Volume 4, 1500 1640* (Cambridge: Cambridge University Press, 1967).
89. Barrington Moore, *Social Origins of Dictatorship and Democracy: Lord and Peasant in the Making of the Modern World* (Boston: Beacon Press,1966), pp. 25–9.
90. David R. Holeton, 'Fynes Moryson's Itinerary: A Sixteenth Century English Traveller's Observations on Bohemia, its Reformation, and

its Liturgy', *The Bohemian Reformation and Religious Practice*, 5.2 (Prague: Academy of Sciences of the Czech Republic, 2005), pp. 379–410.
91. Maurice Beresford, *The Lost Villages of England* (Stroud: Sutton, 1998), p. 28.
92. Thomas, *Religion*, p. 662.
93. Thomas, *Religion*, p. 629.
94. White, *Tropics of Discourse*, p. 159.
95. White, *Tropics of Discourse*, p. 159.
96. White, *Tropics of Discourse*, p. 159.
97. White, *Tropics of Discourse*, p. 159.
98. Charles Warren, 'Wilderness' in Stephan Harrison, Steve Pile and Nigel Thrift (eds), *Patterned Ground: Elements of Nature and Culture* (London: Reaktion, 2004), pp. 139–41, p. 139.
99. White, *Tropics of Discourse*, p. 159.
100. White, *Tropics of Discourse*, p. 160.
101. White, *Tropics of Discourse*, p. 160.
102. Harsnett, *A Declaration*, p. 134.
103. Brayshay, *Land Travel*, p. 10.
104. Brayshay, *Land Travel*, pp. 117, 116.
105. Joseph Robson Tanner (ed.), *Tudor constitutional documents, A.D. 1485–1603* (Cambridge: Cambridge University Press, 1922), pp. 498–9. Jennifer Allport Reid also notes the roads' frequent impassibility; see Jennifer Allport Reid, '"Fallen Am I in Dark Uneven Way": Wandering from the Road in Early Modern Folklore and Drama' in Lisa Hopkins and Bill Angus (eds), *Reading the Road, from Shakespeare's Crossways to Bunyan's Highways* (Edinburgh: Edinburgh University Press, 2019), pp. 146–65, p. 147. Considering this and the above conceptual background to travelling in itself it is perhaps unsurprising that when she was abroad on the nation's roads, Elizabeth I would typically travel with 600 carts and around 1,000 people in retinue; see Brayshay, *Land Travel*, p. 228.
106. Cresswell, *On the Move*, p. 13.
107. R. H. Tawney, *The Agrarian Problem in the Sixteenth Century* (New York: Harper & Row, 1967), p. 275.
108. Brayshay, *Land Travel*, pp. 177–9.
109. Beier, *Masterless Men*, p. xix; A. L. Beier, 'Vagrants and the Social Order in Elizabethan England', *Past & Present*, 64 (August 1974), pp. 3–29, p. 5.
110. A. L. Beier, 'Vagrants', p. 6.
111. A. L. Beier, 'Vagrants', p. 6.
112. McRae, *Literature and Domestic Travel*, p. 91. See pp. 94–5 for further description of social anxieties around wandering.
113. Virginia A. LaMar, *Travel and Roads in England* (Washington DC: Folger Library, 1960), p. 2.

114. McRae, *Literature and Domestic Travel*, p. 95.
115. Dillon, *Theatre, Court and City*, p. 104.
116. Dillon, *Theatre, Court and City*, p. 104.
117. 39 Elizabeth, c. 4, reprinted in *Tudor Economic Documents: Being Select Documents Illustrating the Economic and Social History of Tudor England*, vol. 2, ed. R. H. Tawney and Eileen Power (London: Longmans, 1924), pp. 354–62.
118. Beier, *Masterless Men*, p. xx.
119. Donaldson, *Ben Jonson*, p. 114.
120. Beier, 'Vagrants', p. 15.
121. Cresswell, *On the Move*, p. 13.
122. Beier, *Masterless Men*, p. 56.
123. Beier, 'Vagrants', p. 16.
124. Beier, *Masterless Men*, p. 12.
125. Thomas Harman, *A Caveat for Common Cursitors Vulgarly called Vagabonds* (London: William Griffith, 1566), p. 153. McRae, *Literature and Domestic Travel*, p. 98.
126. Harman, *Caveat*, p. 153
127. 39 Elizabeth, c. 4, pp. 355–6.
128. Thomas Dekker, *O Per Se O* (1612) in A. V. Judges (ed.), *The Elizabethan Underworld* (London: Routledge and Kegan Paul, 1965), pp. 371–2.
129. Thomas Edlyne Tomlins and John Raithby, *The Statutes at Large, of England and of Great Britain: from Magna Carta to the Union of the Kingdoms of Great Britain and Ireland* (London: G. Eyre and A. Strahan, 1811), p. 89.
130. Lisa Hopkins and Matthew Steggle, *Renaissance Literature and Culture* (London: Continuum, 2006), pp. 105–6.
131. Hyde, *Trickster*, pp. 39–40.
132. Hyde, *Trickster*, p. 52.
133. Beier, 'Vagrants', p. 11.
134. McRae, *Literature and Domestic Travel*, p. 103.
135. Tawney and Power, *Tudor Economic Documents*, p. 355.
136. Beier, 'Vagrants', p. 12.
137. Beier, 'Vagrants', p. 10.
138. Beier references Harrison's *The Description of Britain*, ed. Edelen, p. 183, to this statement, cited in 'Vagrants', p. 11.
139. Harman, *Caveat*, pp. 109, 116.
140. Harman, *Caveat*, p. 117.
141. Beier, 'Vagrants', p. 28.
142. Beier, *Masterless Men*, p. 141.
143. Beier, *Masterless Men*, p. xix.
144. Beier, *Masterless Men*, p. 7.
145. Sanders, *Cultural Geography*, p. 163.
146. Sanders, *Cultural Geography*, p. 163.

147. Dillon, *Theatre, Court and City*, p. 98.
148. Manley, 'Of Sites and Rites', p. 50.
149. Barbara D. Palmer, 'Early Modern Mobility: Players, Payments, and Patrons', *Shakespeare Quarterly*, 56. 3 (Fall 2005), pp. 259–305.
150. Richard Brome, *A Jovial Crew* (c. 1641), ed. Helen Ostovich, Modern Text, 2010, <https://www.dhi.ac.uk/brome/viewOriginal.jsp?play=JC&type=TEXT> (last accessed 25 June 2021).
151. Harsnett, *A Declaration*, p. 138.
152. Beier, *Masterless Men*, p. 140.
153. John D. Cox, *The Devil*, pp. 201–2.
154. Beier, *Masterless Men*, p. 6.
155. Beier, *Masterless Men*, pp. 102–3.
156. Peter Marshall, 'Confessionalisation and Community in the Burial of English Catholics, c. 1570–1700', in Lewycky and Morton (eds), *Getting Along?*, p. 68.
157. McRae, *Literature and Domestic Travel*, p. 91.
158. Thomas Dekker, *Lantern and Candle-light* (1608) in *Rogues, Vagabonds and Sturdy Beggars: New Gallery of Tudor and Early Stuart Rogue Literature*, ed. Arthur F. Kinney (Amherst: University of Massachusetts Press, 1990), p. 256.
159. Dekker, *O Per Se O*, p. 379, cited in McRae, *Literature and Domestic Travel*, p. 97.
160. Dekker, *O Per Se O*, pp. 368–9.
161. William Carroll, *Fat King, Lean Beggar: Representations of Poverty in the Age of Shakespeare* (Ithaca, NY and London: Cornell University Press, 1996), p. 6.
162. Carroll, *Fat King, Lean Beggar*, p. 6.
163. Harsnett, *A Declaration*, pp. 159–60.
164. Beier, *Masterless Men*, pp. 92–4.
165. White, *Tropics of Discourse*, p. 166.
166. White, *Tropics of Discourse*, p. 166.
167. Sharon Achinstein, *Milton and the Revolutionary Reader* (Princeton: Princeton University Press, 1994) p. 202.
168. Percy Bysshe Shelley, *A Defense of Poetry* (1821), p. 290, <https://www.gutenberg.org/files/5428/5428-h/5428-h.htm> (last accessed 28 April 2021).
169. Rosenfeld, *Human Satan*, p. 46.
170. Samuel Taylor Coleridge, *On the Constitution of the Church and State* (London: Hurst, Chance & Company, 1830), p. 263.
171. Stephen E. Henderson, 'The Heavy Blues of Sterling Brown: A Study of Craft and Tradition', *Black American Literature Forum*, 14.1 (Spring 1980), pp. 32–44, p. 35.
172. Ben Sidran, *Back Talk* (New York: De Capo, 1981), p. 24.
173. The restlessness is caused not only by the hellhound spectre of the lynch mob, but also from apotropaic hoodoo magic keeping him from

returning home. Hot foot powder is a mixture of acerbic and irritant minerals, herbs and spices, such as chilli powder, salt and pepper with added ingredients, such as powdered wasp's nests or graveyard dirt:

> You sprinkled hot foot powder, mmm,
> Around my door, all around my door.
> You sprinkled hot foot powder, mmm,
> All around your daddy's door, hmm hmm hmm.
> It keep me with ramblin' mind, rider,
> Every old place I go, every old place I go

Robert Johnson, 'Hellhound on My Trail', cited in Karlos K. Hill, 'The Lynching Blues: Robert Johnson's, Hellhound on My Trail as a Lynching Ballad' (2015) <http://southernstudies.olemiss.edu/study-the-south/the-lynching-blues/#fn:13> (last accessed 17 June 2021).

174. Adam Gussow, *Seems Like Murder Here: Southern Violence and the Blues Tradition* (Chicago: University of Chicago Press, 2002), p. 27.
175. More than 4,300 lynchings occurred in the US between 1877 and 1950: Ed Pilkington, 'The sadism of white men: Why America must atone for its lynchings', <https://www.theguardian.com/world/2018/apr/26/lynchings-sadism-white-men-why-america-must-atone> (last accessed 27 May 2021).
176. The 'Byronic hero' is a haunted, moody character and usually fictional. The term is coined in honour of the Romantic poet Lord Byron: 'characteristic of, or after the manner of Byron or his poetry' (*OED*). It is worth mentioning that in many ways the contemporary understanding of early modern literature was shaped by the early critical interpretations of such Romantic poets.

Chapter 9. Monsters: 'Spirits of another sort'

1. James Johnson, *The Scottish Musical Museum; Consisting of Upwards of Six Hundred Songs, with Proper Bases for the Pianoforte*, Vol. V (Edinburgh: James Johnson & Co., 1787), pp. 423–5, p. 424.
2. Harsnett, *A Declaration*, p. 134.
3. Harsnett, *A Declaration*, p. 135.
4. R. Chambers (ed.), *The Book of Days* (London and Edinburgh: W. & R. Chambers, 1863) entry for 1 June <http://www.thebookofdays.com/months/june/index.htm> (last accessed 23 March 2021).
5. James Johnson, *The Scottish Musical Museum*, p. 424. The ballad is in fact quite murky about whether or not Janet has been raped by Tam Lin, making the whole narrative even more disturbing. It is most likely of medieval provenance and is first mentioned in Robert Wedderburn's *The Complaynt of Scotland* (1549). Many thanks to James Bragg for suggesting this connection.

6. Van Gennep, *Rites of Passage*, p. 11.
7. Victor Turner, *The Forest of Symbols: Aspects of Ndembu Ritual* (Ithaca: Cornell University Press, 1967), p. 95.
8. Piotr Spyra, 'Ben Jonson's The Alchemist: The Essential Guide to Early Modern Fairy Belief', *Folklore*, 128.3 (2017), pp. 292–313, p. 297.
9. Robert Hunt, *Popular Romances of the West of England* (London: Chatto & Windus, 1930), pp. 102–6, cited in Briggs, *Anatomy of Puck*, pp. 223–4.
10. Puhvel, *The Crossroads*, pp. 42–3.
11. Briggs, *Anatomy of Puck*, p. 118.
12. J. F. Campbell, *Tales of the West Highlands*, pp. 57–60, cited in Briggs, *Anatomy of Puck*, p. 216. The same thing happens when the eponymous 'King of the Cats' is exposed as such in a lodge where two hunters are staying, and is 'seen no more'; see Hartland, *English Fairy and Folk Tales*, cited in Briggs, *Anatomy of Puck*, p. 213. The same happens to the wax dummy of the threatened child in 'The Danger Averted'; see W. Henderson, *Folk-Lore of the Northern Counties of England and the Borders* (London: The Folk-Lore Society, 1879), pp. 14–15, cited in Briggs, *Anatomy of Puck*, p. 220.
13. Robert Kirk, *The Secret Commonwealth of Elves, Fauns & Fairies A Study in Folk-Lore & Psychical Research* (1691), ed. Andrew Lang (London: David Nutt, 1893), p. 11.
14. Briggs, *Anatomy of Puck*, p. 23.
15. Walter Yeeling Evans-Wentz, *The Fairy-Faith in Celtic Countries* (London: Oxford University Press, 1911), p. 38.
16. Evans-Wentz, *The Fairy-Faith*, p. 38.
17. James I, *Daemonologie*, p. 73.
18. Briggs, *Anatomy of Puck*, p. 44; and that Oberon derives through *Huon of Bordeaux* from Alberich, the magical German dwarf.
19. Briggs, *Anatomy of Puck*, pp. 42–3.
20. Briggs, *Anatomy of Puck*, pp. 245–6. For the Wild Hunt in the folk tradition of the time, see Edward Bever, *The Reality of Witchcraft* (Basingstoke: Palgrave, 2008), pp. 96, 240.
21. Jonathan Durrant and Michael D. Bailey (eds), *Historical Dictionary of Witchcraft* (Lanham, MC: Scarecrow, 2003), p. 204.
22. Durrant and Bailey, *Historical Dictionary of Witchcraft*, p. 204.
23. Wolfgang Behringer, *The Shaman of Oberstdorf*, trans. H. C. Erik Midelfort (Charlottesville: Virginia University Press, 1998), pp. 22–67.
24. Carlo Ginzburg, *The Night Battles: Witchcraft and Agrarian Cults in the Sixteenth and Seventeenth Centuries*, trans. John and Anne Tedeschi (London: Routledge, 1983), pp. 40–8, cited in Hutton, 'The Wild Hunt', p. 161; Claude Lecouteux, *Phantom Armies of the Night: The Wild Hunt and the Ghostly Processions of the Undead* (Rochester, VT: Inner Traditions Bear and Company, 2011), p. 199.

25. Lecouteux, *Phantom Armies*, pp. 56–84.
26. Hutton, 'The Wild Hunt', pp. 167–8.
27. Briggs, *Anatomy of Puck*, p. 21.
28. Karl Meisen, *Die Sagen vom Wütenden Heer und Wilden Jäger* (Münster: Aschendorffsche, 1935), pp. 96–7.
29. Meisen, *Die Sagen*, p. 121.
30. Jean-Claude Schmitt, *Ghosts in the Middle Ages* (Chicago: Chicago University Press, 1994), pp. 118–19.
31. Meisen, *Die Sagen*, pp. 101–3.
32. See Linda-May Ballard, 'Fairies and the Supernatural on Reachrai', in Peter Narváez (ed.) *The Good People: New Fairylore Essays* (Lexington: University Press of Kentucky, 1997), pp. 47–93, p. 48.
33. Spyra, 'Ben Jonson's *The Alchemist*', p. 296.
34. Peter Marshall, 'Protestants and Fairies in Early-Modern England', in *Living with Religious Diversity in Early Modern Europe*, ed. C. Scott Dixon, Dagmar Freist and Mark Greengrass (Farnham: Ashgate, 2009), pp. 139–60, p. 140.
35. Marshall, 'Protestants', p. 140.
36. Thomas, *Religion*, p. 729.
37. Burton, *Anatomy of Melancholy*, I. 1207.
38. Giffard, *A Dialogue*, p. 21; Bodleian Library, Oxford, 8465 MSS Ashmole 547.
39. Regina Buccola, *Fairies, Fractious Women and the Old Faith: Fairy Lore in Early Modern British Drama and Culture* (Selinsgrove: Susquehanna University Press, 2006), p. 126.
40. Thomas, *Religion*, p. 728.
41. See Thomas, *Religion*, p. 729.
42. Briggs, *Anatomy of Puck*, p. 21.
43. Worthy, *Devonshire Parishes*, p. 27.
44. Scot, *The Discoverie of Witchcraft*, p. 521.
45. Cresswell, *On the Move*, p. 3.
46. Robert Weimann, *Shakespeare and the Popular Tradition in the Theater*, ed. Robert Schwarz (Baltimore, MD: Johns Hopkins University Press, 1987), p. 193; and see here for Robin as folk-hero. Here we see again Coleridge's perceived restlessness: Samuel Taylor Coleridge, *The Statesman's Manual* (London: Gale and Fenner, 1816), pp. 34–5. In early modern minds a ubiquitously wandering Satan is also an inspirer of artists, as Rosenfeld suggests: Rosenfeld, *Human Satan*, p. 46.
47. Thomas, *Religion*, p. 732.
48. See Reid, 'Fallen Am I'; Thomas Heywood, *The hierarchie of the blessed angells Their names, orders and offices the fall of Lucifer with his angells* (London: 1635), sig. 2V1^r.
49. Nashe, *Terrors*, p. 5.

50. Reid, 'Fallen Am I', pp. 148–9; see also C. P., *The Sheepherd's New Kalender* (London: 1700), sig. E1ʳ.
51. Harsnett, *A Declaration*, p. 166.
52. Anon., 'Being the Pastimes and other Slights, Of Will-with-a-wispe, and other mad Sprights', 1648, University of Oxford Text Archive, <http://tei.it.ox.ac.uk/tcp/Texts-HTML/free/B03/B03398.html> (last accessed 12 April 2021).
53. Anon., 'Being the Pastimes'.
54. Burton, *Anatomy of Melancholy*, I. 1202.
55. Kirk, *The Secret Commonwealth*, p. 25.
56. Richard Firth Green, 'Changing Chaucer', in Geoffrey Chaucer, *The Canterbury Tales*, ed. Harold Bloom (New York: Infobase, 2008), pp. 179–202, pp. 180, 194.
57. Firth Green, 'Changing Chaucer', p. 184.
58. Firth Green, 'Changing Chaucer', pp. 186–90.
59. Burton, *Anatomy of Melancholy*, I. 1192–1213.
60. Taliesin Williams, *Doom of Colyn Dolphyn*, pp. 16–17.
61. Burton, *Anatomy of Melancholy*, l. 1214.
62. Kirk, *The Secret Commonwealth*, p. 25.
63. Kirk, *The Secret Commonwealth*, p. 34.
64. Kirk, *The Secret Commonwealth*, pp. 34–5.
65. Kirk, *The Secret Commonwealth*, p. 25.
66. Robert Kirk, 'The Secret Commonwealth of Elves, Fauns and Fairies', in Michael Hunter (ed.) *The Occult Laboratory: Magic, Science and Second Sight in Late Seventeenth-Century Scotland* (Woodbridge: Boydell, 2001), pp. 77–106, pp. 79–80.
67. Burton, *Anatomy of Melancholy*, l. 1192.
68. Burton, *Anatomy of Melancholy*, l. 1197.
69. Burton, *Anatomy of Melancholy*, l. 1193–4.
70. Worthy, *Devonshire Parishes*, p. 25.
71. Worthy, *Devonshire Parishes*, p. 26.
72. Worthy, *Devonshire Parishes*, p. 26.
73. O'Donoghue, 'Parish Histories', n.p.
74. Briggs, *Anatomy of Puck*, pp. 99, 51.
75. Briggs, *Anatomy of Puck*, pp. 99, 51.
76. Puhvel, *The Crossroads*, pp. 98–9, 106.

Chapter 10. Protection: The X in the Landscape

1. Robert Herrick, 'Another Charm For Stables' (1648), <https://www.public-domain-poetry.com/robert-herrick/another-charm-for-stables-19152> (last accessed 7 June 2021).

2. Ingrid Baumgärtner, 'Winds and Continents: Concepts for Structuring the World and its Parts', in Ingrid Baumgärtner, Nirit Ben-Aryeh Debby and Katrin Kogman-Appel (eds), *Maps and Travel in the Middle Ages and the Early Modern Period* (Berlin: De Gruyter, 2019), p. 111.
3. Bonnemaison, *Culture and Space*, p. 81.
4. Elizabeth O'Brien, *Post Roman Britain to Anglo-Saxon England: Burial Practices Reviewed* (Oxford: Hadrian, 1999), p. 54.
5. See Ogden, *Magic*, pp. 68, 121–2.
6. Johnston, 'Crossroads', p. 224.
7. Johnston, 'Crossroads', p. 219, see n.12.
8. Simpson, 'Four Vodun Ceremonies', p. 159.
9. Puhvel, *The Crossroads*, p. 109.
10. Puhvel, *The Crossroads*, pp. 98–9, 106.
11. Puhvel, *The Crossroads*, p. 113, n.2.
12. Harriet Phillips, 'Late Falstaff, the Merry World, and The Merry Wives of Windsor', *Shakespeare*, 10.2 (2014), pp. 111–37, p. 125. Some debate remained around this in the early twentieth century; see E. J. Forsdyke, 'A Stag-Horn Head from Crete', *Journal of Hellenic Studies*, 40.2 (1920), pp. 174–9, p. 178, n.14.
13. Similar annulling ceremonies at crossroads were practised in Germany, Syria, Denmark, India and among the Jews of eastern Poland; see Puhvel, *The Crossroads*, pp. 34–6.
14. Thompson Drewal, *Yoruba Ritual*, p. 8.
15. Anon. *A booke of Experiments*, p. 43.
16. Ogden, *Magic*, p. 215.
17. Robert Johnson, 'Cross Road Blues', <https://www.azlyrics.com/lyrics/robertjohnson/crossroadblues.html> (last accessed 24 June 2021).
18. John XXII, *Super illius specula* (1326), cited in Julio Caro Baroja, 'Witchcraft and Catholic Theology', in Ankarloo and Henningsen, *Early Modern Witchcraft*, p. 29.
19. Agrippa, *Of Occult Philosophy*, p. 101.
20. Agrippa, *Of Occult Philosophy*, p. 79.
21. Lavater, 'Of Ghosts and Spirits', p. 214.
22. James I, *Daemonologie*, p. 11.
23. James I, *Daemonologie*, p. 12.
24. Thomas, *Religion*, p. 654.
25. Ford, *Some Reminiscences*, pp. 105–6.
26. Timothy Easton, 'The use of conjoined Vs to protect a dwelling', appendix to C. J. Binding, T. Easton and L. J. Wilson, 'Ritual protection Marks in Goatchurch Cavern, Burrington Combe, North Somerset', *UBSS Proceedings*, 23.2 (2005), pp. 119–33, p. 127.
27. John Gaule, *Select cases of conscience touching vvitches and vvitchcrafts* (London: W. Wilson for Richard Clutterbuck, 1646), p. 76,

<http://gateway.proquest.com/openurl?ctx_ver=Z39.88-2003&res_id=xri:eebo&rft_id=xri:eebo:citation:99862519> (last accessed 23 April 2021). The burial of threshold blessings is a practice banned as witchcraft in Bernhard Albrecht's *Magia* of 1628; see Stuart Clark 'Protestant Demonology' in Ankarloo and Henningsen, *Early Modern Witchcraft*, p. 69.

28. Also, taking the urine of the person who has lost goods and putting it 'into a new earthen pott, & putt therin something resembling the goods lost', adding in nails and other pieces of iron and heating it will bring home the goods; see Bodleian Library, Oxford, 6544 (56) MS Aubrey 24, p. 85. Of the use of iron in magic, various other sources are useful: Lewis Lavater talks of a certain kind of spirit which is 'especially haunting in pittes, where metall moste aboundeth' and describes mine spirits who are 'cruell and terrible to behold' to the 'labourers digging for mettall'; see Lavater, 'Of Ghosts and Spirits', p. 74. Roger Bacon speaks of ancient wisdom where people would 'make certain prayers over Iron red hot' as a means of discerning the innocent from the guilty see Roger Bachon, *The Mirror of Alchemy*, ed. Stanton J. Linden (New York and London: Garland, 1992), p. 51. Dame Kyteler's demonic black man would be typically accompanied by two others, one or all of whom one carried rods of iron; see Seymour, *Irish Witchcraft*, p. 27, Ledrede, *Sorcery Trial*, p. 63. One Suffolk cure for the ague involved driving 'a large nail into the ground up to the head'; see Gurdon, *County FolkLore*, p. 14.
29. William Crooke, *The Popular Religion and Folklore of Northern India*, Volume I (London: 1896), p. 77.
30. Seymour, *Irish Witchcraft*, p. 249.
31. See also Abraham Pais, *Inward Bound: Of Matter and Forces in the Physical World* (Oxford: Clarendon, 1986), p. 210.
32. Ian Joseph Evans, PhD Thesis, 'Touching Magic: Deliberately Concealed Objects in Old Australian Houses and Buildings', University of Newcastle, NSW, Australia, 2010, p. 28.
33. C. P. Hale, 'Witchcraft in Dorset', *Notes and Queries*, 166.7 (17 February 1934), p. 115.
34. Hale, *Notes and Queries*, p. 115.
35. Hale, *Notes and Queries*, p. 115.
36. Lodovico Ariosto, *Orlando Furioso* (1516) trans. William Stewart Rose, 1996, Canto 4, XXXVIII, <http://www.gutenberg.org/cache/epub/615/pg615.html> (last accessed 19 April 2021).
37. Glanvill, *Saducismus Triumphatus*, pp. 205–8.
38. Joseph Blagrave, *Astrological Practice of Physick*, 1671, pp. 154–5, cited in Ralph Merrifield, *The Archeology of Ritual and Magic* (London: Batsford, 1987), p. 170.

39. Cotton Mather, *Late memorable providences relating to witchcrafts and possessions clearly manifesting, not only that there are witches, but that good men (as well as others) may possibly have their lives shortned by such evil instruments of Satan* (London: Tho. Parkhurst, 1691), p. 59, <http://gateway.proquest.com/openurl?ctx_ver=Z39.88-2003&res_id=xri:eebo&rft_id=xri:eebo:image:95922:42> (last accessed 14 March 2021). It seems also that the dwellings of ex-slaves might typically be protected by 'ceramic jars on both sides of front doors'; see also Lipsitz, *Possessive Investment*, p. 131.
40. Brian Hoggard, 'The Archaeology of Counter-witchcraft and Popular Magic' in Owen Davies and Willem de Blecourt (eds), *Beyond the Witch Trials: Witchcraft and Magic in Enlightenment Europe* (Manchester: Manchester University Press, 2004), p. 172. Gordon, 'Domestic Magic', pp. 76–7.
41. Gordon, 'Domestic magic', p. 78.
42. Hoggard, 'The Archaeology', p. 174.
43. Robert Hunt, *Popular Romances of the West of England or, The Drolls, Traditions, and Superstitions of Old Cornwall* (Canton, OH: Pinnacle Press, 2019), p. 59.
44. Henry Chettle, *Tragedy of Hoffman* (1631), pp. 59, 71 <http://gateway.proquest.com/openurl?ctx_ver=Z39.88-2003&res_id=xri:eebo&rft_id=xri:eebo:image:8232:5> (last accessed 24 April 2021).
45. Bethencourt, 'Portugal: A Scrupulous Inquisition', p. 403.
46. James I, *Daemonologie*, p. 59. Agrippa insists that devils have bodies 'although it be a spirituall body, yet it is most sensible, and being touched, suffers'; others, he says, are 'taken with *Terrene* pleasures, and lust; of which are hobgoblins, and Incubi, and Succubi', see pp. 403–4, <http://gateway.proquest.com/openurl?ctx_ver=Z39.88-2003&res_id=xri:eebo&rft_id=xri:eebo:citation:99858916> (last accessed 30 May 2021).
47. Sharpe, *Instruments of Darkness*, p. 14.
48. Westcott, 'Sculpture and Myths', p. 337.
49. Westcott, 'Sculpture and Myths', p. 345.
50. Hoggard, 'The Archaeology', p. 173.
51. Hoggard, 'The Archaeology', p. 173.
52. Glanville, *Saducismus Triumphatus*, p. 98.
53. Edwin Sidney Hartland, *English Fairy and Folk Tales*, cited in Briggs, *Anatomy of Puck*, p. 213.
54. J. F. Campbell, *Tales of the West Highlands*, p. 216.
55. W. Henderson, *Folk-Lore*, p. 220.
56. Thomas, *Religion*, pp. 613–14.

57. Paul Drechsler, *Brauch und Volksglaube in Schlesien* (Breslau: B. G. Teubner, 1903), p. 108, cited in Puhvel, *The Crossroads*, p. 32.
58. James I, *Daemonologie*, p. 15.
59. James I, *Daemonologie*, p. 20.
60. Stephen Gordon, 'Disease, Sin and the Walking Dead', p. 56.
61. Constantine's *chi-rho*, for instance, see Agrippa, *Of Occult Philosophy*, p. 445.
62. Philippe Levillain, *The Papacy* (London: Routledge, 2002), p. 689.
63. Ford, *Some Reminiscences*, p. 99.
64. John Dee, 'Theorum XVI', *Monas Hieroglyphica* (Antwerp: 1564), trans. J. W. Hamilton-Jones, 1947, <http://www.esotericarchives.com/dee/monad.htm#theorem1> (last accessed 17 June 2021).
65. Dee, 'Theorum XVI'.
66. Not too far from Glaisdale, by the road between Castleton and Rosedale (at NZ 6822 0199) is a large squat block of stone named 'Fat Betty', a moors way-marker of at least medieval vintage topped with a rudely stylised Christian cross which also incorporates the same five circular marks. See also David Williams, *The Five Wounds of Jesus* (Leominster: Gracewing, 2004).
67. Thomas Browne, *Garden of Cyrus* (1658), <http://penelope.uchicago.edu/gardennoframes/garden5.html> (last accessed 23 April 2021).
68. Agrippa, *Of Occult Philosophy*, p. 188.
69. Anon., *A booke of Experiments*, p. 23.
70. Thomas, *Religion*, p. 217.
71. Agrippa, *Of Occult Philosophy*, p. 188.
72. Puhvel, *The Crossroads*, pp. 32–3.
73. J. W. Fawcett, 'Folklore: Crossing one's shoe', *Notes and Queries*, 166.7 (17 February 1934), pp. 121–2.
74. See Thomas, *Religion*, pp. 589–90.
75. See 'The Fashionable Fairies' and 'The Tacksman's Ox', in Thomas Keightley, *Fairy Mythology* (London: G. Bell, 1900), pp. 304–5, 390.
76. Gaule, *Select cases*, p. 76.
77. Agrippa, *Of Occult Philosophy*, p. 105.
78. Sharpe, *Instruments of Darkness*, p. 278.
79. Houldcroft, *A Medieval Mystery*, p. 58.
80. Clark, *Demons*, p. 530. Many of these, however, are very much contested throughout the period, being obviously allied to one side of the Reformation schism. Amongst early modern Protestants, many, if not all, Catholic rites were regarded as 'thinly concealed mutations of earlier pagan ceremonies'; see Thomas, *Religion*, p. 74.

81. There are also later exceptions. On 4 July 1881, a 45-year-old Russian carpenter named Gavrilo Vasil'ev became totally incapacitated by the loss of his apotropaic cross and was subsequently committed by his family to Preobrazhensky Psychiatric Hospital in Moscow: Christine D. Worobec, 'Witchcraft Beliefs and Practices in Prerevolutionary Russian and Ukrainian Villages', *Russian Review*, 54.2 (April 1995), pp. 165–87, p. 172, n.19.
82. See Bill Angus, 'The Apotropaic Witch-Posts of Early Modern Yorkshire: A Contextualisation', *Material Religion*, 13.4 (13 February 2018), pp. 55–82. Examples may also be found in the Ryedale Folk Museum in Hutton-le-Hole, UK, and the Pitt Rivers Museum, Oxford, UK.
83. Because of this, the Glaisdale carvings have been associated with imagery surrounding the Pilgrimage of Grace, the 1536 local rising against Henry VIII's rejection of Papal authority; see Nicholas Rhea, 'Blessed houses marked with an X', 'Countryman's Diary', *Darlington and Stockton Times*, 1 April 2011. At the centre of the red banner of the Pilgrimage of Grace was a bleeding heart, its blood dripping into a grail, surrounded at the corners by four pierced and disembodied hands and feet, thus making up the five wounds. So, flying the flags of this one gibbet, many of the northern Catholic gentry involved ended at another. A total of 216 were hanged at Tyburn in June and July of 1537, including 'half a dozen abbots, 38 monks, and 16 parish priests'; see Charles Wriothesley, *A Chronicle of England During the Reigns of the Tudors from A.D. 1485 to 1559*, ed. William Douglas Hamilton (London: J. B. Nichols, 1875), pp. 63–4.
84. *A Dictionary of English Folklore* notes, with a little confusion over the exact geography of the post's siting in the room, that any 'witch, in order to gain power over a dwelling house, must go through the house and past the hearth. The door and chimney were the only means of access, but she could not pass the witch post with its cross. Hence it was a defence at the hearth', see *A Dictionary of English Folklore*, ed. Jacqueline Simpson and Steve Roud (Oxford: Oxford University Press, 2003).
85. Thanks to Andrew Elliott of Glaisdale for this connection. For more on witch posts in seventeenth-century houses, see Mary Nattrass, 'Witch Posts', *Gwerin*, 3.5 (June 1962), pp. 254–67 and R. H. Hayes and J. G. Rutter, 'Cruck-Framed Buildings in Ryedale and Eskdale', *Scarborough and District Archaeological Society Research Report*, 8 (1972), pp. 87–95.
86. In the same house as the dated post at Postgate Farm there is a fireplace with a number of carvings of a circle intersected by sections of

other circles, producing a six-petalled flower-like design using interlacing lines: the 'daisy wheel'. This is another apotropaic symbol and is also to be found in many localities throughout the UK and elsewhere, especially those dating from the early modern period. In 2014 archeologists discovered an underfloor beam in a room intended for occupation by James I, dated precisely to 1606, which faced the fireplace and was covered in apotropaic designs of this kind: see James Shapiro, *1606 Shakespeare and the Year of* Lear (London: Faber and Faber, 2015), p. 222. They are often found where food or wine was stored, as is probably the case with the one carved into a beam of the cellar in the house where Shakespeare was born, see: <https://www.shakespeare.org.uk/explore-shakespeare/blogs/witch-markings-magic-old-buildings/> (last accessed 12 August 2021). There is another daisy-wheel at the sixteenth-century White Swan in Henley-in-Arden, not far from Stratford: <http://thewhiteswanhotel.com/history-of-the-white-swan/>, and one at the early fourteenth-century Bradford on Avon tithe barn: <https://www.english-heritage.org.uk/daysout/properties/bradford-on-avon-tithe-barn/history-and-research/> (both last accessed 17 June 2021). Ian Evans also records similar daisy-wheel marks carved into fireplace lintels, windows and doors in various seventeenth-century houses, and once written on a ceiling 'with smoke from a candle'; see Evans, 'Touching Magic', p. 23. My gratitude and thanks to Mark and Moya Hollingworth for kind access to their house for this research, and again to Andrew Elliott for facilitating the process.
87. Easton, 'The use of conjoined Vs', pp. 119–33, 131.
88. C. J. Binding and L. J. Wilson, 'Ritual protection marks in Wookey Hole and caves in the Cheddar Gorge, Somerset', *UBSS Proceedings*, 25.1 (2010), pp. 47–73, 58–9; Timothy Easton, 'Ritual Marks on Historic Timber', *Weald and Downland Open Air Museum Magazine*, (Spring 1999), pp. 22–30. Apotropaic marks in other places are often found to include a Marian 'double V' formation, invoking the protection of the Virgin of Virgins, a design which persists throughout the early modern period and into more modern times; see Timothy Easton, 'The use of conjoined Vs' and 'Ritual protection Marks'.
89. Ford, *Some Reminiscences*, p. 95. Sharpe attests to the advice of cunning men and women being popular into the nineteenth century; see *Instruments of Darkness*, p. 70. If we accept that astrologers and spiritualists are their inheritors, we can trace this to the present day.
90. Gale Jackson, 'The Way We do: A Preliminary Investigation of the African Roots of African American Performance', *Black American*

Literature Forum, 25.1, The Black Church and the Black Theatre (Spring, 1991), pp. 11–22, p. 18.
91. Gale Jackson, 'The Way We do', p. 18.
92. Johnston, 'Crossroads', p. 220, n. 15.
93. Bakhtin, *The Dialogic Imagination*, p. 7; Basso, pp. 44–5.

Conclusion. The Parting – Intersections

1. Gertrude Stein, *Everybody's Autobiography* (New York: Random House, 1937), p. 289.
2. Janette Dillon, *Theatre, Court and City, 1595–1610: Drama and Social Space in London* (Cambridge: Cambridge University Press, 2000), p. 6.
3. The term 'infostrada' or info-highway was coined in 1972 by Andrzej Targowski; see Andrew Targowski, *The History, Present State, and Future of Information Technology* (Santa Rosa: Western Michigan University, 2016), p. xv.
4. De Certeau, *The Practice of Everyday Life*, p. 115.
5. The UK's early canal network concerns a medium unsuited to crossways rituals.
6. Peter Merriman, *Driving Spaces: A Cultural-Historical Geography of England's M1 Motorway* (Oxford: Blackwell, 2007), p. 5.
7. On the M6 motorway at Gravelly Hill, Birmingham, UK.
8. Merriman, *Driving Spaces*, p. 2; see also Reyner Banham, *Los Angeles: The Architecture of Four Ecologies* (London: Penguin, 1972), pp. 84–5.
9. Peter Merriman, 'Freeways' in Stephan Harrison, Steve Pile and Nigel Thrift (eds), *Patterned Ground: Elements of Nature and Culture* (London: Reaktion, 2004), pp. 86–8, p. 88.
10. Edward Relph, *Place and Placelessness* (London: Pion, 1976), p. 90.
11. The Stranglers, 'Tucker's Grave', <https://www.youtube.com/watch?v=psLbkD6MpAM> (last accessed 10 May 2021).
12. Steve Pile, 'Cities' Wilderness' in Harrison et al., *Patterned Ground*, pp. 146–8, p. 146.
13. Pile, 'Cities' Wilderness', p. 148.
14. De Certeau, *The Practice of Everyday Life*, p. 125.
15. De Certeau, *The Practice of Everyday Life*, p. 125.
16. Charles Warren, 'Wilderness' in Harrison et al., *Patterned Ground*, pp. 139–41, p. 139.
17. Warren, 'Wilderness', p. 140.
18. William Blake, 'London', <https://www.poetryfoundation.org/poems/43673/london-56d222777e969> (last accessed 25 November 2021).

19. Lisa Hopkins, *Shakespeare on the Edge* (London: Ashgate, 2005), p. 137.
20. Warren, 'Wildnerness' p. 141.
21. Aldo Leopold, *A Sand County Almanac, and Sketches Here and There* (New York: Oxford University Press, 1949), p. vii.
22. Hayden White, *The Tropics of Discourse* (London: Johns Hopkins University Press, 1985), p. 153.
23. White, *Tropics of Discourse*, p. 153.
24. De Certeau, *The Practice of Everyday Life*, pp. 129–30.
25. Lefebvre, *Production of Space*, p. 288.
26. Cresswell, *On the Move*, p. 3; Merriman, 'Freeways', p. 3; see also Cresswell, 'Landscape' in Anderson et al., *Handbook of Cultural Geography*, pp. 269–81; Bender, 'Introduction', in Bender and Winer, *Contested Landscapes*, pp. 1–18, p. 3.
27. De Certeau, *The Practice of Everyday Life*, p. 125.

Index

Abbott, George, 163
Achinsein, Saron, 191
Adeola, Kehinde, 42
Ælfric (Anglo-Saxon), 43, 90
Aeschylus, 206
Agricola, Gregor, 10, 50
Agrippa, Cornelius, 29, 63, 173, 212n, 214–15
  Fourth Book of Agrippa, 43
  Of Occult Philosophy, 43–4, 121, 208
Albright, Daniel, 72, 74
Alcamenes, 95
Alciato, Andrea, 84, 88–9, 91
All Hallow's Eve, 52, 173, 196
Anatomy of Melancholy, The, 172, 175–6, 179, 198–9; *see also* Burton
Anglo-Saxon, 16, 43, 112
  burial 106–7, 110–12, 115, 155
Ankarloo, Bengt, 94
Apollo (classical god), 36, 67, 91, 94; *see also* oracle
apotropaic device, 65, 98, 111, 192n, 206, 208–19, 211
  cross, 16–18, 23, 51, 57, 110, 141, 151, 205, 213–16, 219
  see also chronotope; saltire
apparition, 6–7, 76, 151, 165, 172, 175, 176
Apuleius, 146, 172
Ariel (*The Tempest*), 72, 191; *see also* Shakespeare
Artemis *see* Diana
Ashkenazi, Michael, 33, 85
Askew, H., 126

Astrological Practice of Physick (Balgrave), 210
Aubrey, John, 140
Audoneus, Saint, 31
Augustine, Saint, 15, 75, 138

Bacchus (classical god), 91
Backès, Jean-Louis, 163
Bacon, Roger, 71, 74, 79, 209n
Bailey, Michael D., 197
Bakhtin, Mikhail, 19–20, 26, 38
Banham, Reyner, 223
Bantu (African), 86
Barkan, Leonard, 71, 74, 82
Basso, Keith, 20
Bate, Jonathan, 181, 182
Beattie, George, 154, 156
Beier, A. L., 68, 178, 185–6, 188
Beldam, Joseph, 26
Bell, John, 88, 94, 96, 98
Bernstein, Alan, 98, 162
Bertha, Dame (Germanic god), 51
Bethencourt, Francisco, 148, 211
Bhairava (Hindu god), 33, 85
Binding, C. J., 216
Bird, Isabella Lucy, 11, 28
Birrel, Robert, 117
Black Cross, 50, 121n
Blake, William, 192, 225
Bohr, Niels, 209, 220
Bonnemaison, Joël, 20, 21, 41, 71
Booke of Experiments, A, 46, 207, 214
Borlase, William, 6, 89, 125
Bowen, Barbara C., 88, 90, 92
Bradbrooke, W., 126

Brayshay, Mark, 184
Brazeal, Brian, 66
Briggs, Katherine M., 45n, 172–3, 196–7, 199, 204
Bright's Illustrated Guide to Bournemouth, 10, 52
Brown, John *see* Cobbe-Webbe
Browne, Thomas, 214
Brownlow, Frank Walsh, 133
Buccola, Regina, 199
Bullen, A. W., 145
Bunyan, 170–1
Burchard of Worms, 31, 117
burial mound, 27, 110, 111
Burton, Robert, 69, 82, 172, 176, 177–9, 198, 202–3; *see also The Anatomy of Melancholy*
Byron, Lord, 193

Calvin, John, 67, 138
Campbell, James M., 54
candomblé (Brazilian religion), 66, 217
Canizares, Baba Raul, 86
Carroll, William, 190–1
Catholicism
  and paganism, 30, 42n, 71, 86
  the Pope, 124, 133, 214
  priests, 112, 132–3, 135, 177, 189–90, 194
  and Protestantism, 13, 137n, 161–3, 176, 190, 215, 216n
  purgatory, 121, 170, 176
  Roman Catholic, 125
  and superstition, 5–6, 30, 142, 184, 191, 194
cemetery *see* graveyard
Ceres (classical god), 37, 91, 103
de Certeau, Michel, 12, 20–1, 26, 142–3, 152–3, 162, 168, 169, 183, 222, 224, 226
Chaldeans, 35
Chalk, E. S., 126
Challoner, Richard, 111–12
Chatland, Jan, 87

Cheapside Cross *see* Eleanor Cross
Chettle, Henry, 145, 211
Chimata-no-kami (Japanese God), 33, 85
chi-rho (of Constantine) 27, 34, 36
Christian cross 8, 30, 31n, 35–7, 214–15; *see also* crucifixion
Christmas Eve, 64
chronotope, 19–20, 26, 38, 219; *see also* Bakhtin
Chrysostom, Saint John, 31
church-way path, 14, 22, 102, 154–60, 204
churchyard 52, 126, 128, 132, 137, 199, 200
  burial, 110, 111, 115, 122, 123, 126, 132
  see also graveyard
Circe (witch), 75
Clare, Janet, 115, 138n
Clark, Stuart, 38, 215
Clement of Alexandria, 67
Cobbe-Webbe, Christopher, 52
Coleridge, 192
conjuror *see* sorcerer
Constantine, Emperor, 27, 34, 36
Cope, Jackson I., 152
corpse, 80, 121, 137, 142, 211
  ambulatory, 111, 122, 136, 140, 151, 153, 170–4
  desecration of, 116–17, 119, 120, 123–4, 129, 140n
  staking, 17, 108–11, 117–21, 124, 126, 129–31, 138–41, 143, 164, 210–11
  of undesirable, 16, 28, 114–15, 137, 164, 170, 205, 210
  see also church-way path; outcast dead; suicide
Covel, John, 30
Cox, John D., 178
cremation, 159
Cresswell, Tim, 19, 154, 168–9, 185, 200
Cromwell, Oliver, 68, 112, 139

Cross Bones (cemetery), 123
Crossroads (film), 58
crossroads cross, 161, 163–4
crucifix, 36, 106, 161, 205
Crusius, David, 177
Crusius, Martin, 198
cursus (Neolithic), 14, 159–60
Cynthia (classical god) 38, 102–4;
   see also Hecate

Dalton, Michael, 116, 119
Daniell, Christopher, 117
Daniels, Earl, 129
Dante, 36, 146, 150
Dee, John, 34, 73, 214
Defoe, Daniel, 131
Dekker, Thomas, 131, 187, 190
demons, 76–7, 96–7, 171–2,
   175–8, 198–9, 212n, 206, 213
  banishment of, 11
  communication with, 6, 47,
    49–50, 103
  demonic influence, 57, 116,
    138, 192
  demonic power, 10, 16, 50,
    58–9, 62–3, 67, 74–5
  see also exorcism; the Devil;
    sacrifice
Devereux, Paul, 157, 158
Devil, the (Christian), 30, 45–7,
   58, 60, 62, 64–5, 116, 176,
   178
  devil-worship, 40, 42–3, 50,
    53, 90
  deals with, 57, 58, 62–3, 65–6,
    82–3, 131, 211
  and transformation 52, 75–8
  as trickster, 93
  see also exorcism; Robin
    Goodfellow; witch
devils *see* demons
Dialogue Concerning Witches, A
   (Giffard), 77–8, 199
Diana (classical god), 27, 94, 97–8,
   103, 163, 196–7, 227

  statue of 91, 94, 95, 163
  see also Hecate
Dillon, Janette, 18–19, 165, 189
Dimond, William, 118, 129
Diomedes (classical God), 75
Dionysus *see* Bacchus
Dives and Pauper, 172
divination, 10, 29, 42–3, 85, 87
  Icelandic, 158
  and prophecy, 15
djinn *see* Jinn
Doctor Faustus see Faustus
Donne, John, 124
Dosōjin (Japanese god), 8,
   33, 85
Drechsler, Paul, 213
Durrant, Jonathan, 197
Dylan, Bob, 106

Easton, Timothy, 208, 216
Eden, Garden of, 30–1
Egmond, Floricke, 121
Eleanor Cross, 162–4
Eleusinian Mysteries, 37
Elizabeth I (Queen), 13, 34, 68,
   103, 113, 133, 185n
  Royal Injunctions, 13, 162
elves, 6, 51, 189, 204
Ember, Carol R. and Melvin, 18
Eminem, 59
Erasmus, 2
Eshu, 61, 86, 93, 105
Eshu Elegba (Yoruba god), 8, 60,
   87, 212
Eshu Elegbara, 55, 60
Eusebius of Caesarea, 96–7
Evans, Ian, 209, 216n
Evans-Pritchard, E. E., 41
exorcism, 40, 116, 137
  Catholic, 134–5, 142, 174, 176,
    177, 194
  of the Devil, 109
  Korean, 11, 28
  of spirits, 31, 162, 174
  of the unquiet dead, 16

Exu, The (Quimbanda god), 54–5, 87; *see also* Eshu Elgbara
Exus (Brazilian gods), 42, 86; *see also* Santeria
Ezekiel, 43, 157–8

Faerie Queene (Spenser), 9, 100
fairies, 63, 194–204, 209, 214
  in the British Isles, 198
  changeling, 195–6, 212
  dancing, 202, 212
  as demons, 198–9
  in England, 209
  fairy magic, 201, 202
  fairy house, 196
  fairy paths, 158, 159, 196
  fairy procession, 196–7
  in Germany, 203
  as ghosts, 202
  as gods, 203
  in Ireland, 196
  in Scotland, 58n, 110, 195, 212
  in Shakespeare, 102, 151, 159, 178n, 182, 196, 204
  stolen by, 178, 195–6
  as tricksters, 200, 203
  in Wales, 52
  and witchcraft, 204
  see also Puck; Robin Goodfellow
Farris Thompson, Robert, 61n, 93
Faustus, 9, 82–3, 191
  Doctor Faustus (Marlowe), 62, 78, 131, 193
  Faustian mythology 16, 21, 58, 66, 144, 153
fertility rite, 32, 42, 55, 71, 150, 152
Forbes, Thomas Rogers, 107, 108, 139, 164
Ford, Joseph, 208, 216
Forman, Simon, 92
Formicarius (Nider), 43, 50
Freemasonry, 26–7
Freud, Sigmund, 2–3
Fripp, Edgar, 133

Frost, Robert, 1
Frye, Northrop, 94, 103
Fulbecke, W., 118
funeral, 61, 155
  denial of, 115, 124, 141, 211
  procession, 11, 122
  pyre, 141
  rituals, 140, 122
  see also outcast dead
funeral route *see* church-way path

gallows, 55, 115, 121, 130, 135, 186
  burial, 82, 106–7, 109, 111–15, 117, 121, 132, 136
  in literature, 135, 143, 201
  sites, 107, 109n, 112–14, 130–1, 135, 161
  see also Eleanor Cross; hanging; Tyburn
Ganesha (Hindu god), 85
Garber, Marjorie, 136
Gatrell, V. A. C., 113, 122
Gaule, John, 209
Gay, John, 104
Genii, 172
Gennep, Arnold Van, 137, 195
geosymbol, 20, 41, 71, 206; *see also* Bonnemaison
Gilpin, Richard, 116
Ginzburg, Carlo, 197
Gittings, Clare, 121–2, 124, 132
Glanville, Joseph, 76, 80, 210, 212
God (Christian), 14–15, 63, 158, 178–9, 184, 198, 213
  in the Bible, 42
  and the Devil, 77–8, 93, 116
  and witchcraft, 44–6, 77
  see also Eden
Golding, Arthur, 99
Gordon, Stephen, 173, 211, 213
Gracyk, Theodore, 59
Grantley, Darryll, 135
Graves, Robert, 95, 99
graveyard 65, 123, 137, 158, 211; *see also* churchyard

Gray, Thomas, 155–6
Greece, Ancient, 5, 16, 37, 43, 87, 95–6
  crossroads burial, 16, 124
  rituals, 48–9, 55
  shrines, 32
Green, Richard Firth, 202
Greene, Robert, 68, 145, 146
Groats-Worth of Wit (Greene/Chettle), 145
Gussow, Adam, 192–3

Hades (place), 37–8, 67, 94
Hale, C. P., 209–10
Halliday, Robert, 111
Halloween *see* All Hallow's Eve
Hamilton, Marybeth, 59
Hamlet (Shakespeare), 39, 80, 102, 134, 138, 176, 180–1, 204
Hand, Molly, 103
Hanged Man (tarot-card), 151–2, 215
hanging, 55n, 106–7, 114, 161, 190, 216n
  gallows burial, 16, 111–15, 117–19, 132
  hung, drawn and quartered, 133
  and magic, 121
  spirits, 198, 204
  suicide, 108, 110, 116, 122, 127, 134–5, 139, 175, 223
  see also gallows; Tyburn
Hardy, Thomas, 118
Harman, Thomas, 186, 188
Harper, Charles, 110, 127
Harrison, William, 94, 117, 160, 179
Harsnett, Samuel, 176–7, 184, 189–91, 201
  and Shakespeare, 134, 140
  'three-way leet', 5–6, 23, 30, 142, 148, 178, 194–5
Harte, Jeremy, 116–17, 125
Hayes, Raymond, 114

Heaven (Christian), 30, 38, 184, 214
Hecate (classical god), 8, 9, 38, 91, 94–104, 107
  and Christianity, 28
  depictions, 37, 95
  Hecate's Suppers, 9, 95, 98, 206
  and magic, 41, 48–9, 219
  in Middleton, 45, 73, 210
  in Milton, 103–4
  mythology 11–12, 28
  in Shakespeare, 69, 100–2, 204
  triple Hecate, 9, 26, 94, 99, 102–4, 163, 194, 204, 226, 227
  in Virgil, 25, 103
Hegel, 23
Hell (Christian), 30, 58, 150, 170, 175
  and Hecate, 9, 28
  'Hecla's Hell-wain', 197
  and music, 67–8
hellhound, 74, 168, 192–3
Henderson, Joseph L., 33
Henderson, Stephen E., 192
Henningsen, Gustav, 94
Henry VIII, 68, 161
Heracles 2, 8, 30n, 90, 91; *see also* Xenophon
Hermes *see* Mercury
hermit, 8, 26
Herrick, Robert, 140, 198, 205, 209
Hesiod, 28, 96, 100
Hess, David J., 54
hexennacht *see* St Walpurga's Night
Heywood, Thomas
  Hierarchie of the Blessed Angells, 200
Hill, Karlos K., 192
Hindu traditions, 8, 29, 85, 141
  Brahman, 41
hobgoblin, 6, 147, 166, 191, 203, 212n
Hoggard, Brian, 212

Holland, Henry, 39
Holland, Philemon, 95
Homer, Henry Sacheverell, 90–1
Hood, Thomas, 129
hoodoo magic (America), 53, 192n, 193
Hopkins, Lisa, 101, 165, 225
Horne, David H., 145
Houldcroft, P. T., 26–7
Houston, R. A., 109, 110–11, 115, 119, 122, 123–4
Hunt, Robert, 211
Hutton, Ronald, 197
Hyde, Lewis, 66, 86, 93, 104–5, 169, 187

Infallible True and Assured Witch, The, (Cotta), 75
Interlude of Youth, 135
Iron Age, 155, 206

Jackson, Gale, 217–19
James I/VI, King, 26–7, 72, 121, 216n
  1611 Bible, 43
  Daemonologie, 171, 211
  and spirits, 171, 176, 196, 211–13
  and witchcraft, 23, 208
Johnson, Robert (16th C), 72–3
Johnson, Robert (20th C), 36, 55, 57–60, 68, 83, 168, 192–3, 207–8
Johnston, S. I., 9, 12–13, 109
  on Hecate, 8n, 9, 11–12, 91, 95n, 107, 219
  on rituals, 43, 48, 107
de Jong, Nanette, 63
Jonson, Ben, 72, 78, 81–2
  Cynthia's Revels, 102–3
  Masque of Queens, 103
  Mercury Vindicated, 92
  poetry, 92
  A Tale of a Tub, 143
Jovial Crew, A (Brome), 189

Jenkyns, Richard, 12
Jesus Christ, 36, 62, 173, 184, 214–15
  statue of, 162–3
Jinn (Arabic genies), 5, 58, 85
Jones, Christopher P., 90
Jung, Carl, 93
Jurdon Cros (statue), 11

von Kaisersberg, Johann Geiler, 198–9
Kalfu (Haitian god), 86; *see also* Vodou
Kaplanoglou, Marianthi, 32
Kelly, Walter Keating, 51
Kemp, William, 143
Key of Solomon the King, The, 41, 46
Kingston, Alfred, 108–9
Kirk, Robert, 201, 202
Kitty Jay's Grave, 127, 223
Klaus, John, 134
Kleiner, John, 36
Kunado (Japanese god), 85
Kyteler, Dame Alice, 49, 209

Lactantius, 30
Laertius, Diogenes, 42
LaMar, Virginia A., 185
Lamb, Mary Ellen, 151
Lares Compitales, 12–13, 87–8, 170, 172, 203
  shrines, 12, 88
Larner, Christina, 56
Larvae, 172
Latimer, Hugh, 116
Latura, George Beke, 34, 37
Lavater, Lewis, 78, 172, 173–5, 202, 208, 209n
Lebrun, Barbara, 63
Lecouteux, Claude, 197
Ledrede, Richard, 49
Lee, C., 65
Lefebvre, Henri, 18–19, 35–6, 226–7

Legba (African god), 25, 86–7, 93, 206; *see also* Eshu Elegba; Papa Legba; Vodou
lemures, 172
Leopold, Aldo, 225
Lévi-Strauss, Clause, 132
Leyland, John, 160
lich *see* corpse
lich-way *see* church-way path
Like Will to Like, 135
Linche, Richard, 94, 96
Lipsitz, George, 59
Lloyd, Llewellyn, 10, 52
Loki (Norse god), 93
Lorca, Federico García, 1
Lord Maam (Guatemalan god), 86
Lucifer *see* the Devil
Ludi Compitales (Roman festival), 87
Luna (classical god), 9, 94, 96, 163; *see also* Hecate
Luther, Martin, 67, 138

Macbeth (Shakespeare), 100–2, 140–1, 173
  witches, 40, 57n, 62, 69, 101, 131, 182, 204
MacDonald, Michael 116, 117, 137
McOmish, David, 159
McRae, Andre, 19, 186, 188, 190
Manilius, 34
Malleus Maleficarum (Kramer and Sprenger), 42, 47, 71, 75, 98, 160–1
Manes, 172
Manichaeism, 40–1, 68
Manley, Laurence, 164, 189
Māori (people), 89–90, 153n, 158
Marlowe, Christopher, 62, 78, 131, 145, 193; *see also* Faustus
Marra, Realino, 124–5
Marryat, Horace, 6, 51
Marshall, Peter, 198

Martyr, Justin, 36, 67
Mary (mother of Jesus) *see* Virgin Mary
Marx, Karl, 182
Masonry *see* Freemasonry
Mason, William, 156
Mather, Cotton, 210
Maurone, Joseph, 93
Maus, Katharine Eisaman, 78
May Day, 6, 53; *see also* St Walpurga's Night
de Meath, Petronilla, 49, 76
Mebane, John S., 73, 78
Medea (witch), 28, 99; *see also* Ovid
Meisen, Karl, 198
Mercury (classical god), 87, 88–94, 104–5, 152, 187–8, 203
  depictions of, 32–3, 84, 88–9, 91–2
  and Hecate, 12, 26, 38, 94, 103, 149, 219
  and music, 67
  and rituals, 46, 207, 215
  tomb of, 84, 89
Merleau-Ponty, Maurice, 19, 170
Merriman, Peter, 19, 223
Merry Devil of Edmonton, The, 165–6
Meskill, Lynn S., 103
Metamorphoses (Ovid), 28, 99–100
Middleton
  Michaelmas Term, 76
  The Witch, 45, 47n, 73–4, 210
Midsummer Night's Dream, A (Shakespeare), 16, 79–81, 102, 151, 155, 174, 181–2, 191, 196, 199–200; *see also* Oberon; Puck
Miller, William Marion, 47
Milton, John, 191–2, 193
  Comus, 70, 103–4
Mirandola, Pico della, 73
Moorman, F. W., 141

Morris, Joseph E., 126, 127
Morse Earle, Alice, 10
Moryson, Fynes, 183
Mulmutius (sorcerer), 160
Mulungu (Bantu god), 86
Mumford, Lewis, 168–9
Munday, Anthony, 134, 162, 165
Murphy, Terence, 116, 117, 123, 137

Nashe, Thomas, 75–6, 132, 200–1
  The Terrors of the Night, 45–6
  The Unfortunate Traveller, 171
necromancy, 45, 62, 78, 202
Neoplatonism, 71, 214
von Nettesheim, Heinrich Cornelius Agrippa, 29
Norse mythology, 90, 93, 152
Notary Art of Solomon, 43
Novatian, 67

Oberon, 199
  Oberon, the Fairy Prince (Johnson), 72
  in Shakespeare 16, 80, 155, 181, 200, 201
  see also A Midsummer Night's Dream
O'Brien, Elizabeth, 206
Oedipus, 2–3, 15, 30; *see also* Sophocles
Odin (Norse god), 6, 45, 46, 90, 152, 206–7; *see also* Wild Hunt
Odysseus, 187–8
Odyssey, The (Homer), 2, 88
Ogden, Daniel, 117, 207
Ogilby, John, 154
Ogum (orisha spirit), 54, 86
Old Wives Tale, The (Peele), 22, 143, 145–53
oracle
  at Delphi, 2, 103
  at Branchidae, 97
orisha (Yoruba spirits), 66, 86; *see also* Yoruba; candomblé

Orlando Furioso (Lodovico), 210
Orrù, Marco, 124–5
outcast dead, 134
  burial 16–17, 22, 43, 48, 109, 123–4, 128, 130, 137, 164, 211–3
  grave magic, 211
  souls of, 141, 143, 223
  see also corpse; suicide
Ovid, 71, 74, 96, 99
  Ovidian, 78, 79
  see also Metamorphoses
Owen, Dorothy M., 155

Paganini, Niccolo, 16, 57–8
paganism, 56, 70, 163
  and Catholicism, 30, 42n, 71, 86
  and Christianity, 8, 33, 36–8, 40, 70–1, 90, 96–7, 113, 141, 221
  and fairies, 198, 203
  and Protestantism, 116
  rituals, 46, 120
  symbols, 34
Palmer, Barbara D., 189
Papa Ghede (Haitian spirit), 86; *see also* Vodou
Papa Legba (Haitian god), 31n, 33, 87; *see also* Eshu Elegba; Legba; Vodou
Paraskeva, Saint, 55
Pashley, Robert, 117–18
Pausanias, 95
Peele, George, 22, 135–6, 143–6, 150, 153, 209
Penczak, Chris, 224
Persia, Ancient, 42
  Zend Avesta, 8
Philips, J. P. Bacon, 126
Pilgrimage of Grace, 188, 216n
Piśāchas (Hindu goblin), 85
Plato, 2, 34–6, 41, 48, 104–5, 106
  Platonic concepts, 15
Pliny, 29, 206
Plotinus, 63
poltergeist, 5

Pomba Gira (African spirits), 42, 55
Prince, Philip Alexander, 125–6
Prophetess, The (Fletcher and Massinger), 103
Propp, Vladímir, 93–4
Proserpina (classical god), 37, 45, 94, 100, 149; *see also* Hecate
Protestantism, 10, 13, 116
  and Catholicism, 13, 137n, 161–3, 176, 190, 215, 216n
  and Paganism, 116
Puck, 196, 199
  in Shakespeare, 16, 70, 79–80, 102, 110, 141, 155–6, 191, 199–201, 204
  see also A Midsummer Night's Dream; Robin Goodfellow
Puckett, Newbell, 65–6
Puhvel, Martin, 10, 11, 49, 52, 85–6, 88, 125, 174
purgatory *see* Catholicism

Quimbanda, 42, 54, 86–7

Rākshasas (Hindu goblin), 85
Reformation, the, 71, 116, 160, 164, 198, 215n
post-Reformation, 176, 178
Regino of Prum, 97
Reid, Jennifer Allport, 201
Relph, Edward, 223
restless spirit *see* unquiet dead
Reynolds, Andrew, 106–7, 109
Robert Artisson *see* Son of Art
Roberts, John, 95
Robigalia (Roman festival), 13
Robin Goodfellow, 70, 79, 170, 178, 199, 201, 203
  in Shakespeare, 199–200
  see also the Devil; *A Midsummer Night's Dream*; Puck
rogation (Christian celebrations), 13, 109, 162, 164
de Roja, Fernando, 29

Rosenfeld, Nancy, 171
Rous, Francis, 9, 98
Royal Injunctions *see* Elizabeth I
Rudra (Indian god), 86
Runia, David T., 36
Rusten, Jeffrey, 30
Ryan, William Francis, 55

Sachs, Hans, 198
Sacrapant (sorcerer), 146–52
sacrifice, 49, 97, 105
  animal, 46, 49, 50, 65, 99
  to demons, 40
  Hindu, 85
  human, 86, 88, 115
  Malawian, 86
  Persian, 8
  Roman, 91, 94, 99
  sacrificial objects, 32, 48
  for transformation, 10, 15, 44, 61, 102–3
  see also witch
St Hans's Eve (festival), 52
St John (festival), 53
Salkeld, Duncan, 145
saltire cross, 17–18, 35–6, 151, 212–18
Sambucus, 67
Sanders, Julie, 19, 154, 166, 188
Sante, Luc, 59
Santeria (religion), 86
Satan *see* the Devil
Saussure, de César, 118
Scot, 98, 199
  Discoverie of Witchcraft, 43, 87, 172
Selden, John, 91
Seymour, Saint John D., 49, 209
Shakespeare, 22, 72, 81, 82, 92–3, 131–6, 142–4, 179, 182
  All's Well that Ends Well, 95, 134–5
  As You Like It, 94
  Comedy of Errors, A, 81, 181
  Henry IV, Part 1, 39, 80, 100

Henry IV, Part 2, 80
Henry V, 135, 177
Henry VI, Part 1, 100
Henry VI, Part 2, 180
Henry VI, Part 3, 133
King Lear, 100, 134, 181, 187
Love's Labour's Lost, 135
Merchant of Venice, the, 166
Merry Wives of Windsor, the, 81, 151, 159, 207
Passionate Pilgrim, 181
and Peele, 135–6, 145, 153
"Rape of Lucrece", 181
Richard II, 135, 182
Romeo and Juliet, 181
The Tempest, 72–3, 182, 191
Timon of Athens, 80
Titus Andronicus, 135–6, 145
Troilus and Cressida, 80, 179–80
Winter's Tale, the, 188
see also Hamlet; Macbeth; *A Midsummer Night's Dream*
shaman, 11, 125, 224
Shamas, Laura Annawyn, 101
Sharpe, James, 212, 215
Shelley, Percy, 192
Shorter, Dora Mary, 129
Sidran, Ben, 192
da Silva, Sara Graça, 62
Son of Art, 49, 76; *see also* Kyteler
Sophocles, 3; *see also* Oedipus
Southerne, Lawrence, 63
Sparke, Thomas, 122
spirit hounds (Welsh), 6
spiritual binding, 23, 80, 205, 206, 208, 214
Sprengel, Darci, 58
sprite, 6, 44, 51, 100, 102, 161, 195; *see also* elves
Spyra, Piotr, 195, 198
sorcerer, 45, 47, 66, 75, 104
  France, 29, 49–50
  Portugal, 6
  see also witch

Stapylton, Robert, 103
Stein, Gertrude, 221
Stephen, James Fitzjames, 161
Stevens, Thomas, 86
Stone, James Samuel, 130
Stopes, Charlotte Carmichael, 133
Strabo, 89
Stubbes, Philip, 190
St Walpurga's Night, 6, 50, 53; *see also* May Day
Survey of London (Stow), 52, 95, 123, 162–5

Tarleton's Newes out of Purgatorie, 170
Tartini, Guiseppe, 57–8
Tate, Francis, 122
Tawney, R. H., 185
Tehrani, Jamshid J., 62
Tertullian, 88, 172, 177
Tibullus, 8, 41
Tikao, Teone Taare, 90, 140n, 158
Theodore of Cyprus, Saint, 8, 32, 55
Theophilus (archdeacon), 62
Theophrastus, 8, 41
Thomas, Julian, 159
Thomas, Keith, 39–40, 58, 93, 172, 183, 199, 200, 215
Thompson, E. P., 182
Thompson Drewal, Margaret, 61, 207
'three-way leet' *see* Harsnett
tomb, 29, 82, 135–6, 145; *see also* graveyard; Mercury
Tragedy of Hoffman (Chettle), 211
Triple Goddess *see* Hecate
Trivia *see* Hecate
trolls, 52, 195
Turner, Victor, 137, 195
Tyburn, 81, 112–14, 122, 133–5, 143, 161, 216n
Tyrteus, 168

Umbanda (religion), 42, 86
unquiet dead, 6, 43, 92, 102, 150–3, 203, 205, 226
  binding, 16, 106, 141, 198
  walking, 14, 140, 151, 173–5
  and witchcraft, 43–4
  see also corpse; church-way path; outcast dead
Urry, John, 19
ustrechnyi (Russian goblin), 5; see also Puck
Utopia (More), 124, 182–3

Vaughan, William, 39
Vickers, Brian, 145
Virgil
  Aeneid, 25, 94
  Dido and Aeneas, 9, 103, 177
Virgin Mary, 8, 45, 62
Vives, Juan-Luis, 178
Vodou (Haiti), 15, 25, 31n, 33, 54, 86–7, 206, 217

Wait, Walter Oswald, 111
walpurgisnacht see St Walpurga's Night
Wanklyn, C., 111, 126
Warren, Charles, 225
Waylen, James, 10, 51
Webster, 79
Weemse, John, 208
Weever, John, 118, 139
Westcott, Joan, 87
Wheatstraw, Peetie, 64
When You See Me You Know Me (Rowley), 67
White, Hayden, 23, 183–4, 191, 225–6

Wild Hunt, 6, 98, 195, 197–8, 204, 206–7
Williams, Taliesin, 129, 202
Wilson, L. J., 216
Wilson, Richard, 134
Winehouse, Amy, 58
witch, 40, 45, 47, 63, 70, 161, 191, 215
  -bottle, 147, 211, 212
  -curse, 209–10, 212
  dance 6, 50, 69, 73, 77, 101, 121n, 213
  and the dead, 43–4
  witch's demon, 76
  and the Devil, 42, 43, 75–8, 80, 82–3, 211, 213, 219
  -hunters, 48
  post, 18, 216–17
  repelling, 208–13, 215
  trial, 10, 29, 41, 50, 56, 182, 197
  see also Hecate; *Macbeth*; Middleton
Witch's Night see St Walpurga's Night
Woden see Odin
Worobec, Christine D., 47
Worthy, Charles, 199, 203

Xenophon, 2, 89; see also Heracles

Yachimata-hiko (Japanese god), 85
Yachimata-hime (Japanese god), 85
Yoruba (people), 8, 61, 87, 168, 207
  religion, 60
  see also Eshu-Elegba; orisha

Žižek, Slavoj, 209

EU representative:
Easy Access System Europe
Mustamäe tee 50, 10621 Tallinn, Estonia
Gpsr.requests@easproject.com

www.ingramcontent.com/pod-product-compliance
Lightning Source LLC
Chambersburg PA
CBHW052045220426
43663CB00012B/2456